AT THE CROSSROADS

Published for the

OMOHUNDRO INSTITUTE OF

EARLY AMERICAN HISTORY AND CULTURE,

Williamsburg, Virginia,

by the

UNIVERSITY OF NORTH CAROLINA PRESS,

Chapel Hill and London

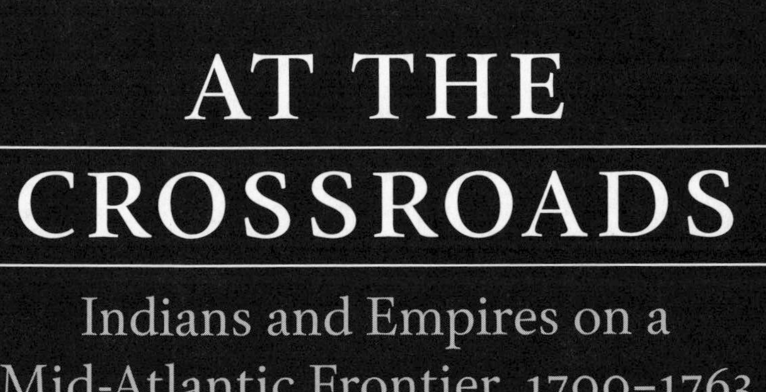
AT THE
CROSSROADS
Indians and Empires on a
Mid-Atlantic Frontier, 1700–1763
JANE T. MERRITT

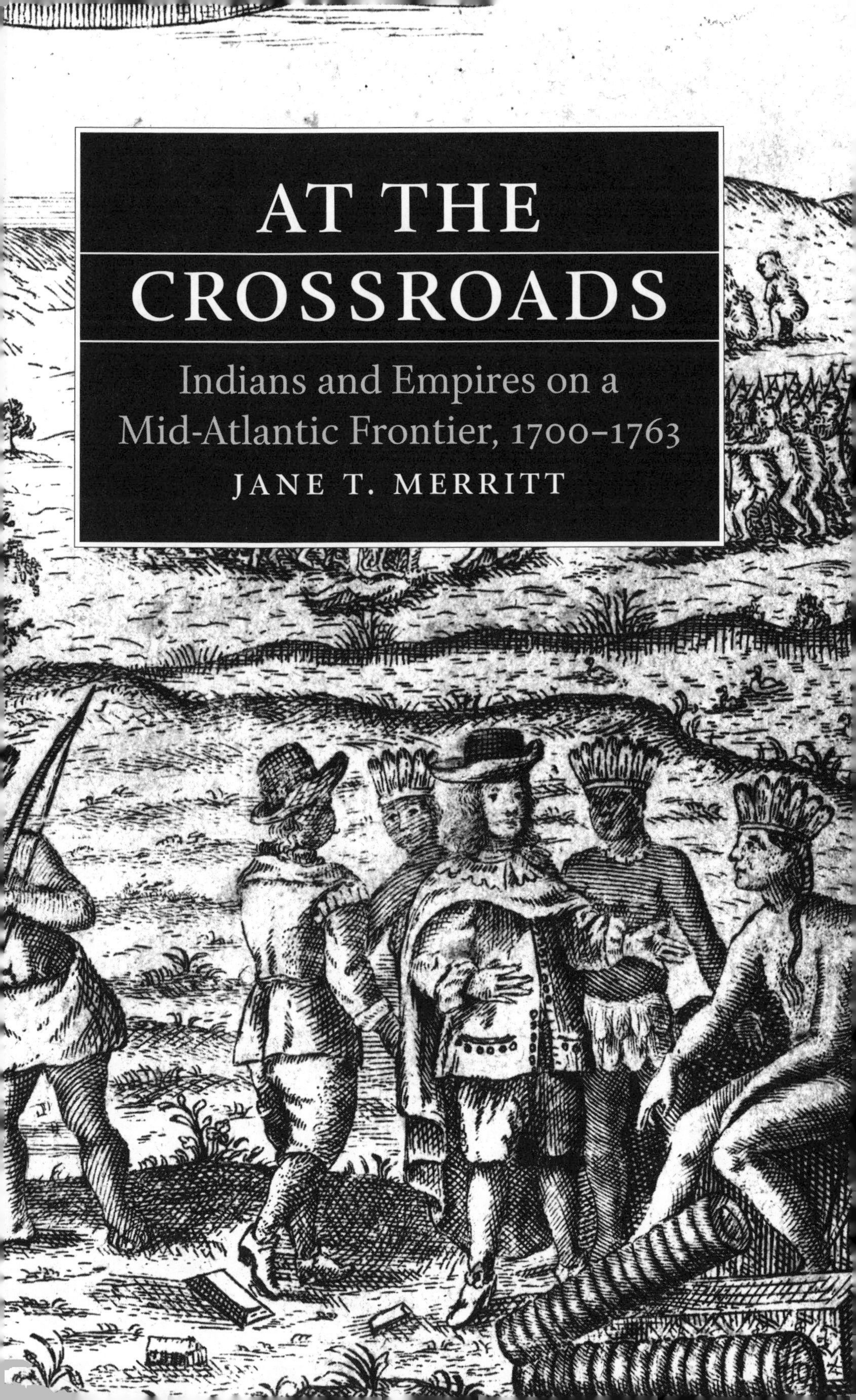

The Omohundro Institute of Early American History and Culture is sponsored jointly by the College of William and Mary and the Colonial Williamsburg Foundation. On November 15, 1996, the Institute adopted the present name in honor of a bequest from Malvern H. Omohundro, Jr.

Manufactured in the United States of America

Library of Congress Cataloging-in-Publication Data
Merritt, Jane T.
At the crossroads : Indians and empires on a mid-Atlantic frontier, 1700–1763 / Jane T. Merritt.
p. cm.
"Published for the Omohundro Institute of Early American History and Culture, Williamsburg, Virginia."
Includes bibliographical references and index.
ISBN 0-8078-2789-4 (alk. paper) — ISBN 0-8078-5462-X (pbk.: alk. paper)
1. Indians of North America—Pennsylvania—History—18th century.
2. Indians of North America—Pennsylvania—History—17th century.
3. Whites—Pennsylvania—Relations with Indians. 4. Frontier and pioneer life—Pennsylvania. 5. Pennsylvania—Race relations—History—18th century. 6. Pennsylvania—Race relations—History—17th century.
I. Omohundro Institute of Early American History & Culture. II. Title.
E78.P4M47 2003
305.897'0748'09032—dc21
2002013318

The paper in this book meets the guidelines for permanence and durability of the Committee on Production Guidelines for Book Longevity of the Council on Library Resources.

This volume received indirect support from an unrestricted book publications grant awarded to the Institute by the L. J. Skaggs and Mary C. Skaggs Foundation of Oakland, California.

cloth 07 06 05 04 03 5 4 3 2 1
paper 07 06 05 5 4 3 2

ACKNOWLEDGMENTS

Never in my wildest dreams as a child did I envision becoming an academic. At some point in the past, however, I made some random choices, perhaps opted out of one job for another, until I found myself back in graduate school and embarking on an unexpected road that led me in this direction. Now, after nearly a decade of probing society's more perplexing questions on race and identity in early America and teaching a new generation of students about the consequences of cultural encounters, I can't imagine doing anything else. Like many of life's passages, writing this book also began in a haphazard way. I stumbled across sources, compiled seemingly useless data on Indian converts, and stared long and listlessly at notecards spilling from an old file drawer. Teasing this disparate information into a coherent whole was far more than an easy or solitary journey. As the adage goes, "It takes a village." Over the past ten years, my village has been peopled with a wonderful mixture of colleagues, friends, and family, each lending assistance and advice, at times in the most surprising ways.

In graduate school, the Department of History at the University of Washington provided the basic foundation, thanks to the challenging and inspiring guidance of John Findlay, Richard Johnson, and Richard White. They demanded more from me than I thought possible and helped me hone conceptual tools that later shaped the larger arguments of this book. During that time, I received a fellowship from the McNeil Center for Early American Studies (then the Philadelphia Center) under the direction of Richard Dunn. While discovering a new world of archival materials, I also found inspiration in a like-minded academic community and received invaluable feedback from other early Americanists at informal lunches and seminars. The Center welcomed me back in subsequent years, allowing me to complete additional research at later stages of writing. The staff at numerous archives offered their assistance in finding sources. In the Philadelphia area, I spent long hours at the American Philosophical Society, the Historical Society of Pennsylvania, and the Library Company of Philadelphia. Shorter trips to the Moravian Archives in Bethlehem, the

Northampton County Archives, the Presbyterian Historical Society, the State Museum of Pennsylvania and the Pennsylvania State Archives in Harrisburg, and the William L. Clements Library in Ann Arbor, Michigan, proved valuable.

For six years, the institution where I teach, the College of Arts and Letters at Old Dominion University, has provided incidental support, including a summer research grant. And, of course, the race to tenure, like a hanging rope, has kept me focused. More important, through the generous funding of an Andrew W. Mellon Postdoctoral Research Fellowship from the Omohundro Institute of Early American History and Culture, I was able to take research leave for a year to complete major revisions to the manuscript. I benefited immensely from the close readings and responses that colloquia participants offered as well as the congenial atmosphere.

I must also thank the many friends and colleagues who have read and commented on conference papers and essays that became different portions of the book. Some assisted me through casual comments that helped coalesce the flotsam and jetsam of the mind. Those who I am indebted to for a variety of small things include, in no particular order, Rose Beiler, Jean Soderlund, Ruth Herndon, Gregory Dowd, Rhys Isaac, Kathleen Brown, Daniel Usner, Cami Townsend, Liam Riordan, Jacquelyn Miller, Ann Little, Karim Tiro, Evan Haefeli, Alice Nash, Bill Pencak, Jon Butler, and Neal Salisbury. And Friday mornings with the Sumatra Sisters (Carolyn Lawes, Sujata Moorti, and Mona Danner) simply kept me sane.

Finally, I thank my family who have done nothing more than endure the long days of work, the missed birthdays, the despondent stares, and the unreturned phone calls. My parents, Joan and Richard, have been together for more than fifty years and recognize the rewards of time and commitment. But Bob endured the final moments with love, friendship, and humor. Thank you.

CONTENTS

MAPS, ILLUSTRATIONS, & TABLES

MAPS

ILLUSTRATIONS

TABLES

ABBREVIATIONS & SHORT TITLES

APS
American Philosophical Society, Philadelphia

HSP
Historical Society of Pennsylvania, Philadelphia

Moravian Records
Records of the Moravian Mission among the Indians of North America (New Haven, Conn., [1978]), microfilm, 40 reels, from original materials at the Archives of the Moravian Church, Bethlehem, Pa.

MPCP
Minutes of the Provincial Council of Pennsylvania, from the Organization to the Termination of the Proprietary Government, 10 vols., Colonial Records of Pennsylvania (Philadelphia and Harrisburg, Pa., 1851–1852)

PA
Pennsylvania Archives, 1st Ser., 12 vols., ed. Samuel Hazard (Philadelphia and Harrisburg, Pa., 1852–1856)

AT THE CROSSROADS

INTRODUCTION
At the Crossroads

In October 1736, during a treaty council outside Philadelphia at Stenton, Pennsylvania, the Seneca chief Kanickhungo, representing the Six Nations, explained to the proprietor Thomas Penn that, soon after his father William Penn "came into this Country, he and we treated together." "He opened and cleared the Road between this Place and our Nations, which was very much to our good Liking, and it gave us great Pleasure. We now desire that this Road, for the mutual Accommodation and Conveniency of you and us, who travel therein to see each other, may be kept clear and open, free from all Stops or Incumbrances." In a few words, the Iroquois leader invoked a simple element of the landscape, "the Road," as a metaphor for communication, diplomacy, and cultural exchange between Indians and whites. Yet the road also referred to a physical space, a passage that connected national territories, communities, and people, a space used by many parties. Experience had taught Kanickhungo that shared roads often suffered from "Stops or Incumbrances"—like brambles, competition for resources and political power stood in the way of cooperation. He thus invoked the memory of the first colonial peacemaker who had advocated tolerance toward native peoples, and he gently reprimanded the son for his apparent deficiencies. Kanickhungo, like many eighteenth-century Americans, tried to articulate ways that coexistence could work. As representative of one imperial power addressing another, he drew on metaphors that implored native Americans and Euramericans to be equally responsible for keeping the route between their communities clear, to share that frontier as they negotiated a better understanding.[1]

Employing the image of the road to visualize Indian-white relations is useful, partly because the metaphor was integral to eighteenth-century cultural encounters and diplomacy. But roads can also provide an apt metaphor for historians, proffering new paths of inquiry through the tan-

1. *MPCP,* IV, 83.

gled landscape of the past. As we construct a more complete picture of native peoples in contact, we can no longer think in terms of two roads meeting, where American Indians are offered few choices: assimilate Euramerican worldviews or resist change. Modern scholarship has explored new and complex relationships within native cultures and between Indians and whites during the first two centuries of contact, discovering roads less traveled. Historians have picked apart the evolution of native American cultural practices, their reactions to the Euramerican presence in North America, and the impact of new technologies on Indian societies. Some have demonstrated the intricate political developments within Indian nations, some the adaptations to a Euramerican market economy and an increasingly white-dominated social landscape, some the various effects of religious revivalism and pan-Indian political activities during the eighteenth and nineteenth centuries, and some the social and gender reordering of native communities. Indeed, the Indian experience of a colonial New World begins to look more like a crossroads, a place where many paths converged, providing divers possibilities and directions to those who passed through.[2]

2. Arnold Krupat, *Ethnocriticism: Ethnography, History, Literature* (Berkeley, Calif., 1992), 25–26, argues that we should reject the dichotomies of resistance and assimilation and conqueror and victim and look instead at the multifaceted dynamics of cultural differences and power relations. My study strives to use a dialogic model of interrogation rather than an oppositional model. Other works using a similar interpretive model include Daniel K. Richter, *The Ordeal of the Longhouse: The Peoples of the Iroquois League in the Era of European Colonization* (Chapel Hill, N.C., 1992); Daniel H. Usner, Jr., *Indians, Settlers, and Slaves in a Frontier Exchange Economy: The Lower Mississippi Valley before 1783* (Chapel Hill, N.C., 1992); Jean M. O'Brien, *Dispossession by Degrees: Indian Land and Identity in Natick, Massachusetts, 1650–1790* (Cambridge, 1997); Gregory Evans Dowd, *A Spirited Resistance: The North American Indian Struggle for Unity, 1745–1815* (Baltimore, 1992); Kathleen M. Brown, "The Anglo-Algonquian Gender Frontier," in Nancy Shoemaker, ed., *Negotiators of Change: Historical Perspectives on Native American Women* (New York, 1995), 26–48; Kathleen Bragdon, "Gender as a Social Category in Native Southern New England," *Ethnohistory,* XLIII (1996), 573–592; Ann Marie Plane, *Colonial Intimacies: Indian Marriage in Early New England* (Ithaca, N.Y., 2000); Claudio Saunt, *A New Order of Things: Property, Power, and the Transformation of the Creek Indians, 1733–1816* (New York, 1999); James H. Merrell, *The Indians' New World: Catawbas and Their Neighbors from European Contact through the Era of Removal* (Chapel Hill, N.C., 1989). In "The Indians' New World: The Catawba Experience," *William and Mary Quarterly,* 3d Ser., XLI (1984), 537–565, Merrell postu-

This book examines the interactions at one such cultural crossroads in Pennsylvania between the late seventeenth century and the 1760s. From the first meeting of the Lenni Lenapes with William Penn, purported to have taken place under an old elm tree at Shackamaxon in October 1682, Indians in the mid-Atlantic region negotiated a common space with European settlers along a shifting frontier where roads both literally and figuratively passed through and between communities, connecting their lives and histories. Here, well-established Indian paths and newly laid colonial roads crisscrossed the landscape, often overlapping. These roads brought travelers along valley floors nestled between the ridges of what Delawares called the Kittatinny, or Endless, Mountains, which linked Iroquoia in the north with the gateway to the Chesapeake Bay. Eventually white inhabitants of New York would use these same paths to reach central Maryland and Virginia. The waterways that connected the Susquehanna and Delaware Rivers to each other and to more distant passages of the Great Lakes region snaked through narrow ravines in the mountain ridges, thus providing all who lived in the mid-Atlantic with commercial networks for trade and travel. Indian trails, with names such as the Tulpehocken Path, Nanticoke Path, Allegheny Path, and the Warriors' Path, which passed through wind and water gaps in the mountains, connected communities or provided specific people with access across the frontier. During this period, roads brought together many groups of immigrant peoples who tried, if somewhat imperfectly, to understand each other.[3]

Kanickhungo's open road and the subsequent convergence of peoples had far-reaching consequences, however, that even diplomats could not foresee. At this crossroads, Indians and whites arrived with a certain willingness to cooperate, but, in negotiating their differences, they redefined

---

lated that contact between native Americans and Europeans "was more a matter of subtle cultural processes than mere physical displacements" (538).

3. H. Frank Eshleman, *Lancaster County Indians: Annals of the Susquehannocks and Other Indian Tribes of the Susquehanna Territory from about the Year 1500 to 1763, the Date of Their Extinction . . .* (Lancaster, Pa., 1908), 125; Paul A. W. Wallace, *Indians in Pennsylvania* (1961; reprint, Harrisburg, Pa., 1975), 40–44, 54–55; Francis Jennings, *The Ambiguous Iroquois Empire: The Covenant Chain Confederation of Indian Tribes with English Colonies from Its Beginnings to the Lancaster Treaty of 1744* (New York, 1984), 74–80; Barry C. Kent, *Susquehanna's Indians,* Anthropological Series No. 6 (Harrisburg, Pa., 1984), 10–11.

themselves and each other. In the following pages, I argue that the differences among Pennsylvania immigrants—whether political, economic, social, religious, ethnic, or racial—once negotiable and often tolerated at a local level, became increasingly characterized by race ("Indianness") by the 1760s. The construction of race as a category is not a new supposition; humans have divided themselves into different groups based on cultural, social, or economic factors throughout history. Less clear, however, is why prolonged intercultural contact often produces deep and long-lasting animosities that are cast in racial terms. In eighteenth-century Pennsylvania, racial divisiveness was not a foregone conclusion, especially in light of the colony's initial policies of tolerance. Yet, by the 1760s, the hybrid nature of frontier life, the competition for resources, and the tensions of an imperial war had engendered a nationalist sentiment among both white and Indian populations. Rather than roads connecting communities, Pennsylvanians called for new territorial and political boundaries to separate and control people. In turn, race became a tool for placing individuals on one side or the other of those national boundaries. Instead of community-based strategies for negotiating alliances and coexistence, as suggested by Kanickhungo in the 1730s, native Americans and Euramerican settlers turned to once-distrusted confederations or empires for protection and support.

Many forces triggered the deterioration of personal relations between Indians and whites in the eighteenth century. Both the frontier as a point of contact and the dynamics of colonial power within that frontier zone affected how Indians and whites reacted to each other. The first part of the book looks at migration and community building in Pennsylvania during the first half of the eighteenth century and the tensions between local autonomy and colonial authority. Before 1750, the frontier was relatively open—akin to what Marvin Mikesell and later John Mack Faragher have called "frontiers of inclusion." It was a region on the fringes of empire, between but not yet dominated by the imperial influences of Great Britain and France. The Indian and white populations were nearly equal outside Philadelphia, and their relations were relatively fluid. From 1700, a variety of ethnic groups moved into the region north and west of Philadelphia between the Delaware and Susquehanna Rivers. Delawares, Germans, Mahicans, Scots-Irish, English, Tutelos, Shawnees, and Iroquois came together to form new communities, sometimes overlapping and sometimes defiantly separate but invariably connected by interdependent social, economic, and political networks that drew Indians and non-Indians together.[4]

Kinship and clan affiliations often guided the actions of these local communities. As white traders, political agents, and missionaries became more visible on the frontier, Indians attempted to incorporate them into their regional support networks. Whites, in turn, sometimes accepted the responsibilities of reciprocity entailed in these kinlike relationships and shared in the material and emotional lives of Indians. Moravian missionaries, for example, participated in Indian alliances, as did many individual fur traders or political go-betweens. Although whites sometimes vied for use of the same land and resources, they also negotiated social and economic relations that brought relative stability to the frontier. Although Indians increasingly depended on a market economy, which changed the nature of reciprocal alliances, they also used economic exchange to their own advantage, whether to gain access to needed goods and services or as a means of political leverage and to critique white society. As long as the penetration of colonial infrastructures on the frontier was minimal, Indians and whites had to rely on each other for a modicum of support. As long as Euramerican settlement on the frontier did not outpace the ability of Indians to incorporate them into their communities, roads and metaphors of the road would act as bridges between their cultures.

Imperial infrastructures might have been weak on the frontier before the Seven Years' War, but internal colonialism—that control imposed by local governing bodies over subject populations—still helped to shape the course of Indian-white relations in Pennsylvania. During the first half of the eighteenth century, Great Britain was creating an empire in North America, with varying degrees of success. In Pennsylvania, empire building entailed continual negotiations between the proprietors and the Six Nations, who competed with each other for local political power and attempted to dominate those who lived on the inclusive frontier of Pennsylvania. Although the two groups sometimes disagreed over specific issues, they cooperated more often than not to regulate the disposition of land

4. Marvin Mikesell, "Comparative Studies in Frontier History," *Annals of the Association of American Geographers*, L (1960), 64–74; John Mack Faragher, "'More Motley than Mackinaw': From Ethnic Mixing to Ethnic Cleansing on the Frontier of the Lower Missouri, 1783–1833," in Andrew R. L. Cayton and Fredrika J. Teute, eds., *Contact Points: American Frontiers from the Mohawk Valley to the Mississippi, 1750–1830* (Chapel Hill, N.C., 1998), 305.

and direct the settlement and development of frontier communities in their respective suzerainties. At times, leaders pitted Indian and white inhabitants against each other to make a larger point to their colonial rivals. For the proprietors and the Six Nations, frontier inhabitants provided a protective buffer from each other but also established broader claims to territory.[5]

Yet internal factionalism also hampered internal colonialism. Instead of a unified, omnipotent colonial authority conquering or subduing a homogeneous population, marginal and often antagonistic parties within these political structures competed over who would control the frontier. Religious groups exerted power within and outside normal political channels, for instance, but were mostly at odds with provincial leaders and the proprietors. To enhance their own position in Pennsylvania, Quakers and Moravians established separate alliances with local Indian groups, who, in turn, were disaffected with the Six Nations. Delawares and other independent Indian communities, having gained the support of Quakers and Moravians, paid metaphoric lip service to their "uncles," the Iroquois, but denounced any concrete obligations to them as a political authority. White settlers also worked outside existing political systems. Profiting from the animosities between Quaker assembly members and the proprietors, they avoided paying quitrents, squatted on western lands, and freely used available natural resources. Before the 1750s, Indian and white frontier communities as far west as the Ohio Valley were able to manipulate colonial factions or use militant resistance to render colonial authorities ineffective and maintain relative autonomy.

Within this context of negotiated power relations, individual communities struggled to position themselves in a rapidly changing world. Native Americans, in particular, confronted new cultural choices, or roads, that veered from older practices, responses, and beliefs. Yet they approached these challenges with a keen ability to adapt. Chapters 3 and 4 examine how Indians, particularly those living in and around German Moravian mission towns, adjusted to the growing presence of white settlers before

5. Eric Hinderaker, *Elusive Empires: Constructing Colonialism in the Ohio Valley, 1673–1800* (New York, 1997), xi. Warren R. Hofstra, "'The Extention of His Majesties Dominions': The Virginia Backcountry and the Reconfiguration of Imperial Frontiers," *Journal of American History*, LXXXIV (1997–1998), 1286, sees similar negotiations occurring on the Virginia frontier during the first three decades of the eighteenth century.

1755 and the effects these interactions had on the dynamics within Indian communities and their relationship to colonial authorities. Their societies in a state of flux, native Americans found that adapting to some Euramerican practices, such as Christianity, and participating in a larger market economy provided new strategies for survival. Euramerican social systems and economic practices did not replace customary native habits, however; instead, many Indians, contending with shifting circumstances, created new identities from the cultural material at hand.[6]

Adaptation to Euramerican culture also came at a price. By 1754, Christian mission communities began to unravel, even as they succeeded economically. Partially jealous of the success of the Christian Indians and their independent alliance with the Moravians, the Six Nations reasserted pressure on Christian Indians to move north into the Six Nations' sphere of influence. Adaptation also brought Christian Indians into direct economic competition with white settlers, who increasingly encroached on Indian lands. These external forces exacerbated internal conflicts, and the subsequent social fractures within the mission communities further eroded Indian autonomy in Pennsylvania. Delawares and Mahicans, for instance, although nominally united as Christians, still harbored deep-seated ethnic animosities toward each other and, by the early 1750s, began to make separate decisions accordingly. Gender and generational conflict also divided native families, prompting individual members to question

6. Pierre Bourdieu, *In Other Words: Essays towards a Reflexive Sociology,* trans. Matthew Adamson (Stanford, Calif., 1990), 60, 61, 62. Bourdieu looks at "habitus (or system of dispositions), practical sense, and strategy," including a subject's emotions, mannerisms, and perceptions, and their effects on the historical actions of humans. See also Michelle Rosaldo, "Toward an Anthropology of Self and Feeling," in Richard A. Shweder and Robert A. LeVine, eds., *Culture Theory: Essays on Mind, Self, and Emotion* (New York, 1984), 146; Anthony P. Cohen, "Culture as Identity: An Anthropologist's View," *New Literary History,* XXIV (1993), 207; Greg Dening, "Introduction: In Search of a Metaphor," and Richard White, "'Although I am dead, I am not entirely dead. I have left a second of myself': Contructing Self and Persons on the Middle Ground of Early America," both in Ronald Hoffman, Mechal Sobel, and Fredrika J. Teute, eds., *Through a Glass Darkly: Reflections on Personal Identity in Early America* (Chapel Hill, N.C., 1997), 2, 418; James Clifford, *The Predicament of Culture: Twentieth-Century Ethnography, Literature, and Art* (Cambridge, Mass., 1988), 9; William H. Sewell, Jr., "The Concept(s) of Culture," in Victoria E. Bonnell and Lynn Hunt, eds., *Beyond the Cultural Turn: New Directions in the Study of Society and Culture* (Berkeley, Calif., 1999), 52–55.

the efficacy of cultural accommodation and rethink where their loyalties lay.

In essence, by 1755, Pennsylvania Indians had reached another crossroads, where they would revisit their past, account for their present, and make choices about their future. The third part of the book deals with this transition, a period occupied with war and attempts at peace but dominated by the consolidation of colonial powers over an intensified frontier. By the late 1740s, white settlers flocked to sparsely populated frontier regions not yet ceded by Indians. The proprietors and provincial governors complained that immigrants acted illegally, yet these colonial leaders also used white settlers as a toehold for their own claims to western lands. The imperial conflict between Britain and France over North America opened the way for colonial expansion into the frontier as well. Both nations vied for domination of the lucrative fur trade in the Ohio Valley, which required the cooperation of Indians. Inadvertently, or perhaps intentionally, they invited fierce competition between local Indian and white communities for land and resources. The Seven Years' War, an outgrowth of these imperial conflicts, further undermined the negotiated interactions between Indians and whites and became a litmus test of their loyalties. As Britain and its Iroquois allies consolidated power over frontier regions, Indian and white communities were pressed to clarify their relationship with those nations and, consequently, with each other. Indians living between the Delaware and Susquehanna Rivers and in the Ohio Valley attacked white settlements along the Pennsylvania frontier during 1755 and 1756 and launched the colony into wider war. They committed very specific acts of violence on very specific people, especially those inhabiting contested land. In return, white settlers exacted a bloody revenge on Delawares, in particular, but soon indiscriminately on Indians as a whole.[7]

The savage frontier war in Pennsylvania did not necessarily come to pass because of racial divisions between Indians and whites. The violence that broke out in 1755 and 1756 was not between strangers; it was between people who had become neighbors, if not kin. Rather than a

7. Jeremy Adelman and Stephen Aron, "From Borderlands to Borders: Empires, Nation-States, and the Peoples in Between in North American History," *American Historical Review*, CIV (1999), 814–816. Although I use the term "frontier" rather than "borderland," I assume the same kinds of "accommodations between invaders and indigenes and the hybrid residuals of these encounters" that Herbert Eugene Bolton describes in the Spanish borderlands (815).

sign of essential differences between communities, the conflict, instead, was born of their familiarity, even similarity. By the 1750s, both physical and cultural boundaries between Indian and white communities on the Pennsylvania frontier had been blurred. Indians and whites grappled with common social, economic, and political concerns. Peoples across Pennsylvania experienced a noticeable revitalization of religious activity, they wrestled with shifting gender and social relations within the household, they struggled to subsist in an expanding transatlantic market economy, and they hoped to create alliances with more powerful political forces without losing the integrity of their own communities. Still, Indians and whites who had been able to share common ground felt a deep sense of betrayal by the other during the war. White settlers, driven from their farms by hostile Delawares, concluded that outward signs of a common humanity and a willingness to adapt elements of English civilization did not reflect Indians' allegiances. Indians, too, realized that the ritualized alliances that had affirmed their relationships with white neighbors had lost shared meaning.[8]

Between 1756 and 1758, a series of treaty conferences took place in Pennsylvania where frontier inhabitants addressed the deep hostilities that separated them. They tried to piece together the history of their common past and restore the roads that had connected their communities. Quakers gained political influence as engineers of Indian diplomacy and became arbitrators for the eastern Delawares who had attacked white frontier settlements. But Quakers and Delawares also had to contend with the political machinations of the Pennsylvania Assembly, the proprietors, and the Six Nations. Here, at least two different ways of recording events came into play and, sometimes, into conflict. For diplomatic purposes, native Americans drew on the oral traditions of their cultures and used wampum to record and remember key events. By contrast, Euramericans relied on written documents, such as deeds of purchase, private and public correspondence, and transcripts of legislative meetings. These two methods of commemorating and communicating events did not necessarily compete. In eighteenth-century political forums, Indians and whites recognized and

8. David Murray, *Forked Tongues: Speech, Writing, and Representation in North American Indian Texts* (Bloomington, Ind., 1991), 19, reminds us that cultural differences between people "needed to be demonstrated and defined even when, or especially when, the instability of the bases of difference was becoming more and more evident."

used each other's methods to reach agreement. Common metaphors and diplomatic rituals brought warring factions together to negotiate, but the conferences also exposed the contested memories that each had of the past and its present meaning. No one could agree completely on the relationship between Indian nations and how those alliances might affect the terms of peace with Pennsylvania. Had the Iroquois conquered the Delawares in the seventeenth century, thus claiming power over their current political actions? Did Delawares, in turn, willingly sell land to the English? Who should be blamed for the recent war and the current diplomatic impasse? As they debated exactly how events had unfolded and who had made what promises, conflicting memories of the past took shape. Indeed, political representatives began to articulate different histories that reflected the diverging national interests of native inhabitants and the increasingly imperial aspirations of Euramericans.[9]

Instead of smoothing over cross-cultural conflict, the diplomatic war of words underlined some glaring differences between communities and contributed to those differences. Part 4 looks specifically at the ways that Pennsylvanians redrew physical and metaphysical boundaries between their communities and how racial rhetoric emerged by 1763 to displace the nuanced interactions that had previously characterized relations between native Americans and white settlers in Pennsylvania. Indians and whites used their increasingly dissimilar memories of the past to justify violent retaliation during the Seven Years' War and to assert their own group solidarity. In the late 1750s, leaders of frontier communities em-

9. Joanne Rappaport, *The Politics of Memory: Native Historical Interpretation in the Columbian Andes* (Durham, N.C., 1998), 10–13, examines nineteenth-century indigenous documents for clues to twentieth-century native life and sees the nineteenth century as a time of "reinvention," where myth, memory, and tradition all collide to do service for the present. See also M. I. Finley, "Myth, Memory, and History," *History and Theory*, IV (1965), 295–296; Immanuel Wallerstein, "The Construction of Peoplehood: Racism, Nationalism, Ethnicity," in Etienne Balibar and Immanuel Wallerstein, *Race, Nation, Class: Ambiguous Identities* (New York, 1991), 78; Kerwin Lee Klein, "On the Emergence of *Memory* in Historical Discourse," *Representations*, LXIX (2000), 143–145. Although I make connections between a remembered past, the rise of nationalist sentiment, and the growing use of racialized categories to differentiate other nations, I am not suggesting that an essentialized racial memory emerged during the eighteenth century. Instead, I ground my discussion in specific ways that people recalled events, treaties, and relationships before and during the war in order to manipulate current power relations.

phasized the need for new territorial boundaries, such as a line of forts manned by colonial militias, to control trade and diplomacy and to avoid further hostilities. The desire for physical separation also reverberated in new portrayals of the people that faced each other across those boundaries. Categories of difference were not new to the eighteenth century. Indians and whites in North America had always carved their social world into various groupings of us and them, sometimes predicated on religious, linguistic, or ethnic characteristics, sometimes on differences of rank and status. English writers in the early modern period had often depicted Indians as physically akin to Europeans, but at an earlier stage of cultural development. The environment had supposedly played an important role in their so-called primitive appearance and culture, their faces merely darkened by the sun and body paint. William Penn, and later the Moravians, believed that Indians were related to the Jews, "of the stock of the Ten Tribes," because of the resemblance of their "Countenance" and rituals. Native Americans, therefore, could be encouraged to rejoin the civilized peoples of Europe, eventually to become their cultural equals. But the eighteenth century brought the Enlightenment and a range of scientific categories that attached bodily differences—such as skin color, complexion, and facial features—to the temperament, social character, and national culture of different groups of people.[10]

Consequently, by the mid-eighteenth century, "Indianness" as a racial category had changed dramatically since initial contact between English and Indians. Early admiration for Indians' physical grandeur and their

10. Albert Cook Myers, ed., *William Penn's Own Account of the Lenni Lenape or Delaware Indians*, rev. ed. (Somerset, N.J., 1970), 41–42. See also Roxann Wheeler, *The Complexion of Race: Categories of Difference in Eighteenth-Century British Culture* (Philadelphia, 2000), 6–11; Joanne Pope Melish, *Disowning Slavery: Gradual Emancipation and "Race" in New England, 1780–1860* (Ithaca, N.Y., 1998), 4–6; Karen Ordahl Kupperman, "Presentment of Civility: English Reading of American Self-Presentation in the Early Years of Colonization," and Joyce E. Chaplin, "Natural Philosophy and an Early Racial Idiom in North America: Comparing English and Indian Bodies," both in *WMQ*, 3d Ser., LIV (1997), 193–197, 229–252. Mary Louise Pratt, *Imperial Eyes: Travel Writing and Transculturation* (New York, 1992), 32, reminds us that, during the mid-eighteenth century, scientific ideas of differences also emerged, thus "naturalizing" the concept of racial categories. Carl von Linné's system of categorizing man, a seemingly benign system that simply observed the workings of humankind and natural science but that had destructive colonial implications, was published in 1758 (*Systema naturae*, 10th ed.).

adaptability often gave way to suspicions of immutable differences that became a mirror for colonial fears. Environmentalism, after all, could work both ways. If Indians did not or could not become English, the English might find themselves transformed by the same dangerous effects of the American wilderness. Puritans in New England, pressed by pious urgency, had projected their inner demons onto Indians, thus alleviating the confusion or ambivalence of their own sinful natures. In eighteenth-century Pennsylvania, a struggle with saintliness did not necessarily dictate the contours of alien others. Instead, Euramericans in the mid-Atlantic region grappled with issues of loyalty to colonial authority, ethnic and religious rivalries, economic competition, and control over land and natural resources. By the 1750s, white frontier inhabitants had experienced a brutal war, restricted access to land, and the tightening grip of colonial control. In turn, they projected their anxieties onto Indian others to regain a sense of stability and to express their own place in the British empire.[11]

Colonial leaders had their own ideas about the place of white settlers. They often viewed Indians and whites on the margins as similarly uncontrollable, a threat to social order. They even pitted these communities against each other to weaken their resistance to authority. A language of "savagism" emerged that was used to describe frontier inhabitants as a whole but that was based on essentialized qualities supposedly peculiar to Indians. Images of the ideal Indian or good Indian encompassed an impossible set of expectations that rendered natives as stoic, wise, noble, articulate, but ultimately conciliatory. After the brutal frontier fighting of the Seven Years' War, the ideal's opposite, the savage or bad Indian, became a prevalent negative measure of behavior and a means for criticizing native American allies who had turned against the English as well as white frontier inhabitants who resisted authority. On one level, then, sav-

11. John Canup, *Out of the Wilderness: The Emergence of an American Identity in Colonial New England* (Middletown, Conn., 1990), 7, 10, 79–80. See Mechal Sobel, "The Revolution in Selves: Black and White Inner Aliens," in Hoffman, Sobel, and Teute, eds., *Through a Glass Darkly,* 163–205, for a concise essay on concepts of self and other. She asserts that "othering" was an essential part of early modern self-fashioning. As a communal-minded "we-self" gave way to more modern concepts of "I-self," there was a "heightened personal concern with difference" (171). Whites projected negative personal traits onto African American and native American alien others as part of identity formation.

agery was not necessarily racially bounded. White elites used the rhetoric to describe and control whites as much as Indians. White frontier inhabitants turned the label on Indians to redefine their own relationship with colonial leaders. By the 1760s, savagery was associated with Indianness, and those native Americans who displayed particular physical traits most often suffered the violent consequences evoked by a generalized fear and hatred of savages.[12]

White frontier inhabitants, such as the Scots-Irish who had been marginalized within the empire, even lumped together with Indians as savages, used violence and the language of savagism as a way to position themselves within the English colonial world, to distinguish themselves as loyal subjects of Great Britain and worthy of its economic and political benefits by denying that Indians had those same rights. The Paxton Boys, for example, redirected their anger over British control onto Indians as enemy others when they murdered a small group of peaceful Conestogas in late 1763. They accused those Indians who had adapted to English culture and subordinated themselves to colonial authority of deceptively hiding behind a mask of civility and breaking their promises of friendship. Like similar diatribes against Pennsylvania Indian communities, the Paxtons' narrative retold past Indian relations as brutal violence (on the part of Indians) and unappreciated sacrifice (on the part of whites). Other Euramericans, who condemned the Paxtons' attack, described a different Indian past of primitive innocence to condemn the less-than-ideal present. Yet, whether depicting them as "perfidious" enemies deserving death or once-noble and now-dependent children meriting protection, white settlers manipulated representations of Indians to subvert

12. See Robert F. Berkhofer, Jr., *The White Man's Indian: Images of the American Indian from Columbus to the Present* (New York, 1978), 25–31; Nancy Shoemaker, "How Indians Got to Be Red," *AHR*, CII (1997), 625–644; Alden T. Vaughan, "From White Man to Redskin: Changing Anglo-American Perceptions of the American Indian," in Vaughan, *Roots of American Racism: Essays on the Colonial Experience* (New York, 1995), 3–33. Even though racial categories in general were most often by-products of imperial expansion or European colonialism, the ways that white Europeans described and used race in their encounters with native Americans were profoundly different from those used in encounters with Africans. African otherness seemed more indelibly related to skin color and was inextricably tied to the system of slavery. See Winthrop D. Jordan, *White over Black: American Attitudes toward the Negro, 1550–1812* (Chapel Hill, N.C., 1968); David Brion Davis, "Constructing Race: A Reflection," *WMQ*, 3d Ser., LIV (1997), 7–18.

their claims to territory and equal participation in the 1760s. As competition for resources intensified, as new memories of incompatible pasts gained credence, the once-inclusive frontier changed, and Euramerican immigrants rhetorically usurped Indian nativity and their rights to native lands.[13]

Indians, too, struggled to assert their own identities in relation to competing empires and to respond to racial epithets, which had taken on a life of their own. They had to define themselves vis-à-vis the language of savagism, even deconstruct it. Christian Indians, in particular, did not recognize themselves in the pervasive racial stereotypes, and, hoping to protect the communities and kinship networks they had carefully built, they tried to strip off savage markers and to refashion themselves as model Indians, incapable of violence. Indians also struggled to relate their own versions of the history they had shared with white Pennsylvanians, denying culpability for relations gone awry. Instead, like some Euramericans, Indians drew on images of an ideal past, pointing to William Penn's seventeenth-century policies of tolerance as evidence that his heirs had failed to uphold his legacy of peace. In essence, native Americans and Euramericans blamed each other for undermining the potential peace embedded in an idealized past. Their narratives of a golden age of peaceful coexistence not only belied the brutal violence of the late 1750s and 1760s but created unrealistic expectations that further polarized relations and punctuated the essentialized racial differences found in savagism.

Race and racial rhetoric about Indianness, which had emerged from the complex entanglements of economic competition, the struggle for political power and autonomy, ethnic and religious conflict, and rising nationalist sentiment, increasingly set the tone for Indian-white relations in the late eighteenth century and beyond. Between the 1780s and the Era of Removal, a similar process of contact and conflict repeatedly played out as American settlers moved into frontier regions west of the Ohio River. Initial contact with native Americans led to tentative cooperation based on mutual needs. As the white population increased, however, disagreements over economic resources and ownership of land grew, leading to violent confrontations with Indian communities. Frontier settlers, al-

13. *A Declaration and Remonstrance of the Distressed and Bleeding Frontier Inhabitants of the Province of Pennsylvania* . . . , Feb. 13, 1764, in John R. Dunbar, ed., *The Paxton Papers* (The Hague, 1957), 108.

though hoping to distance themselves from government interference, appealed to local or federal authorities and the military for protection. As happened in the 1750s and 1760s, nation building and internal colonialism intersected to create a dynamic tension between the United States and the Indian and white frontier inhabitants they hoped to manipulate. The United States needed the presence of its own citizens to claim territory that the British might otherwise take back in the Northwest or that the Spanish might resettle in the Southwest. From the 1790s to the War of 1812, the United States army suppressed Indian resistance with force. Still, government agents sought to protect western tribes by arresting white squatters on Indian lands, even as they contemplated plans for Indian removal. Their attempts to control frontier populations by law, persuasion, or military force further aggravated conflicts between Indian and white communities. By the early nineteenth century, even more than the eighteenth, white settlers marshaled the now-familiar tropes of good and bad Indian to justify the conquest of native Americans and to assert their own nationalist self-interests. Once wielded by angry Scots-Irish on the mid-Atlantic frontier in the midst of a brutal but intimate war, the language of savagism entered the daily parlance of white Americans to dispossess Indians of land and to excuse themselves from a role in that dispossession. Rhetorically, savage Indians eventually gave way to noble, dying Indians, but native Americans did not disappear. They might have been pushed to the margins, but they continue to draw us all back to the crossroads to reencounter ourselves.[14]

14. Laura Jane Murray, "Going Native, Becoming American: Colonialism, Identity, and American Writing, 1760–1820" (Ph.D. diss., Cornell University, 1993), 5–6, traces how "settler colonialism and colonization of indigenous people" were interconnected. Murray places the origins of American nationalist sentiment in the post-Independence years. I, however, suggest the roots of this nationalist sentiment are found in the frontier conflicts of the 1750s and 1760s and are predicated on making Indians into enemy others. See also Philip J. Deloria, *Playing Indian* (New Haven, Conn., 1998), 7; Renée L. Bergland, *The National Uncanny: Indian Ghosts and American Subjects* (Hanover, N.H., 2000), 3–4, 15–16; Jill Lepore, *The Name of War: King Philip's War and the Origins of American Identity* (New York, 1998), xiv–xx; Faragher, "'More Motley than Mackinaw,'" in Cayton and Teute, eds., *Contact Points*, 315–319.

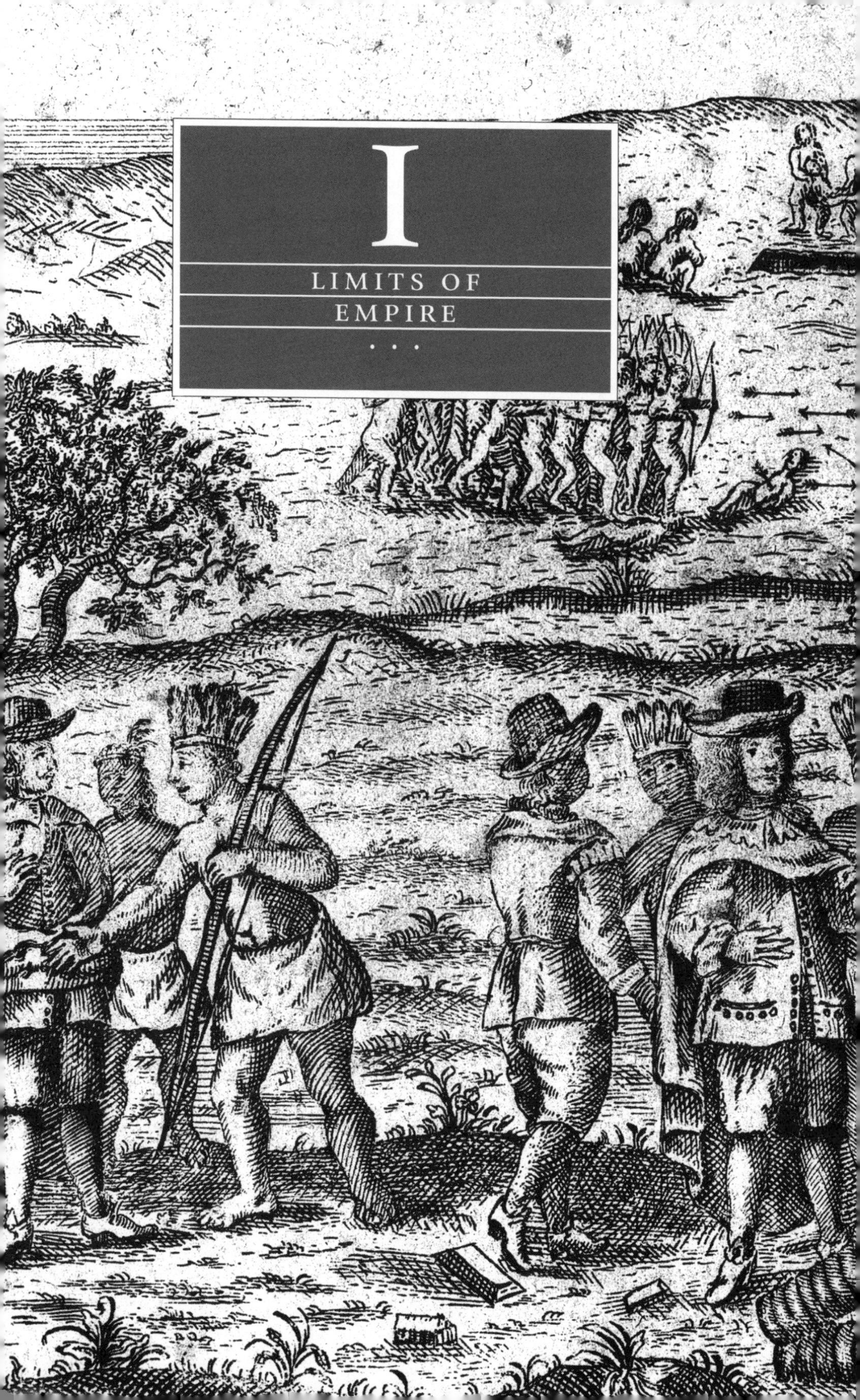

I

LIMITS OF EMPIRE

. . .

1

CULTURAL COMMUNITIES AND THE POLITICS OF LAND

• • •

In the late nineteenth century, a legend still circulated among the Scots-Irish communities of Northampton County, Pennsylvania, concerning their initial encounters with Indians in North America. "Tradition has it" that in 1728, "when the first settlers arrived, one of them asked for a drink." "Where upon an Indian squaw said: 'give me a gourd and I will fetch you some'; and at that she disappeared and returned with the gourd full of cool, sparkling water." This encounter led to the discovery of Hay's Spring and a site "for their future home," Craig's Settlement. Far from the violent confrontations between Scots-Irish and Indians emphasized by popular and academic histories of the region, this legend presents a different and more ambiguous picture of cultural interactions. In part, the story allowed nineteenth-century descendants of Scots-Irish immigrants to embrace an Indian past and become heirs of the country in which they now lived. In the minds of these descendants, native inhabitants of the early eighteenth century had given assistance to their European ancestors, led them to a source of water, and, by inference, invited them to stay, making the newcomers one of their own. Even though these Europeans might have eventually displaced their hosts, their arrival and settlement was sanctioned, their nativity established. This rhetorical transfer of American heritage also helped to separate Scots-Irish from more recent European arrivals, in particular Irish Catholics, who faced harsh criticism from a predominantly Anglo-Saxon nation. Through the magical tale of an Indian maiden's blessing, Scots-Irish could shed their immigrant status and become Americans.[1]

1. [John Cunningham Clyde], *The Scotch-Irish of Northampton County, Pennsylvania* (Easton, Pa., 1926), 18–19. Clyde's compilation of stories, genealogies, and historic

Still, nineteenth-century myth and memory are not completely without a grain of historic eighteenth-century truth. The tradition of Hay's Spring at Craig's Settlement can shed light on the complex nature of cultural encounters, the elusive meaning of those encounters, and their consequences. First, it acknowledged that native Americans already inhabited the land when European immigrants arrived in North America, a fact that eighteenth-century Indians emphasized in their own remembrances of these early encounters. By 1760, some 175,000 strangers had come to eastern Pennsylvania looking for "their future home." From Europe, along with Scots-Irish, came English, Germans, Welsh, French Huguenots, Swedes, Finns, and Dutch, hoping to recreate a piece of the Old World in their New World communities. They met various native groups, some of whom had arrived a generation earlier, also seeking a place of refuge. During the late seventeenth and early eighteenth century, Delawares, Mahicans, Tutelos, Shawnees, Nanticokes, Conoys, and Iroquois made their way west, north, and south into the eastern parts of Pennsylvania. Between 1700 and the 1760s, each ethnic group, whether Indian or white, created its own sense of place, naming the natural surroundings to reflect a recently abandoned homeland and rebuilding social structures to reflect the cultural habits of past generations. And, though each might have brought preconceptions about the other, invariably, as Scots-Irish tradition conceded, these communities, whether by choice or by circumstance, had to negotiate interdependent social, economic, and political relations for their survival.[2]

---

documents was mostly derived from local histories published in the 1870s and 1880s, at the height of Irish immigration to America as well as efforts to confine western Indians on reservations. On some level, urban ghettos and reservations served a similar purpose of controlling marginalized populations. See also M. I. Finley, "Myth, Memory, and History," *History and Theory,* IV (1965), 281–302; Werner Sollors, *Beyond Ethnicity: Consent and Descent in American Culture* (New York, 1986), 115–130; and Richard White, *Remembering Ahanagran: Storytelling in a Family's Past* (New York, 1998), a study of the complex relationship between memory, history, and identity.

2. *MPCP,* IV, 707–708, VI, 95; Thomas J. Sugrue, "The Peopling and Depeopling of Early Pennsylvania: Indians and Colonists, 1680–1720," *Pennsylvania Magazine of History and Biography,* CXVI (1992), 26–27. It is nearly impossible to estimate the total Indian population for Pennsylvania. Sugrue estimates eleven thousand as the highest Indian population in the Delaware watershed in 1600 (11). By 1779, an estimated thirty-two hundred people spoke Munsee and Unami (Delaware), mostly in the Ohio Valley. See Ives Goddard, "Delaware," in William C. Sturtevant, gen. ed.,

Such negotiated cooperation for common goals was necessarily fraught with tensions that often turned to antagonism. Land was key to Indian and white migration and subsistence. Consequently, during the early decades of the eighteenth century, land became central to the power dynamics between Indian and white communities in Pennsylvania. As long as the frontier was sparsely populated, earlier migrants could afford to welcome, if warily, white newcomers. Once neighbors, how they would divide or use that land became more complicated. Not surprisingly, colonial authorities tried to use the competition for land for their own purposes. Both the proprietor William Penn and the leaders of the Iroquois Confederacy monitored the frontier region north and west of Philadelphia, between the Delaware and Susquehanna Rivers, hoping to control the distribution of land and natural resources, thereby expanding their own political power over the region's inhabitants. Pennsylvania proprietors, strapped with personal debts, needed to sell land to European migrants to raise revenue. White settlers became "point men," a buffer from the potentially hostile French and their native allies as well as a source of income. The Six Nations also used land to enhance their authority. They dangled the promise of land purchases in front of the English in return for trade goods and political alliances. At the same time, they used the threat of land sales to demand obedience from reluctant Delawares. Attempts by colonial Pennsylvania leaders and the Iroquois to dominate the frontier often undermined potential cooperation between Indian and white inhabitants, but more dangerous to the interdependence of settler communities was the collaboration of colonial powers. By the 1730s, Pennsylvania relied on the cooperation of the Six Nations to legitimize its own expansion, drawing the province deeply and inextricably into Indian affairs. In turn, the Six Nations needed an English alliance to bolster their own powers. The most salient result of this political partnership, the Walking Purchase of 1737, dispossessed Delawares of their land in eastern Pennsylvania.

Rather than keeping them apart, the politics of land instead intertwined Indian and white interests further. With varying degrees of suc-

---

Handbook of North American Indians, XV, Bruce G. Trigger, ed., *Northeast* (Washington, D.C., 1978), 214. Francis Jennings, *Ambiguous Iroquois Empire: The Covenant Chain Confederation of Indian Tribes with English Colonies from Its Beginnings to the Lancaster Treaty of 1744* (New York, 1984), 118, estimates only thirty-two hundred to four thousand Delawares in 1641. None of these estimates includes Susquehannocks, Iroquois, Shawnees, or other smaller tribes present in Pennsylvania.

cess, Indian and white settlers avoided the force of colonial authority. For instance, white squatters, one step ahead of land agents, refused to pay quitrents, an annual tax on property use, or stole small timber from proprietary lands. Delawares and other Indian groups, in turn, refused to acknowledge the political authority of the Iroquois and would not move from land that the Iroquois sold. Since the imperial reach in each case was limited, more often these local communities had to negotiate the parameters of power directly with each other. This chapter and the next explore the initial cultural dialogues between Indians and whites as they attempted to share territory, to trade and control resources, and to understand the social practices and precepts of their neighbors.

Before the onset of large-scale colonial settlement in the late seventeenth century, the Iroquois Confederacy, wary of alliances between their traditional enemies and European nations, extended their power over native peoples in the northeast. They did so by various means. They threatened violence, they exercised diplomatic persuasion to encourage cooperation with the Iroquois nations, and they were ultimately able to absorb remnant Indian groups who had been defeated in battle, displaced by the encroachment of Europeans, or decimated by disease. By the late 1660s, non-Iroquois people made up nearly two-thirds of some Iroquois villages. Those Indians whom they did not absorb through adoption or conquest the Iroquois made subordinate allies or "props of the Longhouse," creating a buffer between their nations and the expanding colonial world. Still, the Iroquois often used the cooperation of European powers in North America to maintain authority over other Indians. By 1649, the Iroquois (then the Five Nations) had allied with the Dutch, had defeated their major competitors, the Hurons, and dominated the beaver fur trade as middlemen. When the English ousted the Dutch from New York, many Iroquois welcomed the friendlier climate of trade and confirmed the new political alliance with ceremonies of the Covenant Chain, a series of partnerships created among English colonists, colonial governors, and Indian groups in the northeast. The Mohawks, in particular, readily assisted New England to suppress Metacom's forces in 1675–1676 and used the opportunity to intimidate a long-standing enemy, the Mahicans. Defeating and absorbing their enemies or making tributaries of their neighbors, the Iroquois exerted far-reaching power beyond their homeland. Bordering their southern flank, Pennsylvania Indians always had a contentious relationship with the Iroquois.[3]

The Susquehannocks, one of these smaller, assertive native groups that struggled against Iroquois domination, had a population between twenty-four hundred and sixty-five hundred. In the early seventeenth century, they hunted, fished, and planted corn, beans, and squash for their subsistence and competed with Delaware River tribes to monopolize intercommunity trade along the Susquehanna River. After the English settled Maryland, the Susquehannocks began to trade furs and pottery with the colony's inhabitants. Late in the seventeenth century, fearing an Iroquois attack from the north, many Susquehannocks sought refuge in Maryland, whose government encouraged their migration, hoping they would become "a Bullwarke and Security of the Northerne parts of this Province." Maryland, anticipating Iroquois aggression, assumed the Susquehannocks would help to negotiate a treaty alliance with the Six Nations. Instead, during the crisis of Bacon's Rebellion in 1675 and 1676, when animosity toward Indians escalated, the Virginia and Maryland colonial militias drove the Susquehannocks back north. With the Susquehannock population diminished owing to epidemic diseases and warfare, the Iroquois League and the Delaware River Indians absorbed many of the survivors. A small band that resettled at the confluence of the Susquehanna River and Conestoga Creek in 1697, along with members of Seneca, Oneida, Cayuga, and Tuscarora bands, became known simply as the Conestoga Indians. Although Susquehannocks ceased to exist as a separate political entity and abandoned many of their seventeenth-century communities, their legacy of resilience and adaptability influenced future settlement patterns. The region between the Susquehanna and Delaware Rivers soon accommodated many migrant native groups and refugees.[4]

3. Jennings, *Ambiguous Iroquois Empire,* 95; Daniel K. Richter, *The Ordeal of the Longhouse: The Peoples of the Iroquois League in the Era of European Colonization* (Chapel Hill, N.C., 1992), 65–66, 134–142, 239. Until 1720, the Iroquois Confederacy consisted of five nations: Senecas, Cayugas, Onondagas, Oneidas, and Mohawks. Tuscaroras joined in the 1720s as the sixth nation.

4. Jennings, *Ambiguous Iroquois Empire,* 115, 127, 136–141, 147, 154; Francis Jennings, "Susquehannock," in Sturtevant, gen. ed., *Handbook of North American Indians,* XV, Trigger, ed., *Northeast,* 362, 364–365; Barry C. Kent, *Susquehanna's Indians,* Anthropological Series No. 6 (Harrisburg, Pa., 1984), 8, 22, 29, 49–56; Maryland Assembly,

The sparsely populated lands of the Delaware and Susquehanna River valleys attracted the attention of whites as well, and the Iroquois faced competition to dominate the region. In March 1681, according to European custom, Quaker William Penn took legal possession as "true and absolute" proprietor of a large region in the mid-Atlantic when he received a charter for the province of Pennsylvania from Charles II of England. He envisioned his colony as a purposeful "holy experiment," where religious tolerance and enlightened political and legal structures might assure individual liberties for anyone living there. His tolerance, however, came at a price to most settlers in Pennsylvania. Penn attempted to control all aspects of land disposition, migration, settlement, and economic exchange for both Indians and whites. He relied on quitrents as a source of income from white settlers. To assure this income, he needed to attract immigrants quickly. He reserved large tracts of land and offered a number of favorable deals to wealthy friends and patrons, who, in turn, brought over indentured servants and settler groups. Initial investors could pick up five-thousand-acre tracts for one hundred pounds, and Penn offered ten prime acres in Philadelphia for those who purchased at least five hundred acres on the frontier and "a 50-acre bounty for each servant settled, and a three-year period free from quitrents." Finally, Penn managed to reserve large tracts of land, designated "manors," for himself, especially in those regions rich in natural resources, such as timber and mineral deposits.[5]

Although beneficial to himself and other English investors, William

---

Council Minutes, May 2, 1661, in William Hand Brown, ed., *Archives of Maryland*, I (Baltimore, 1884), 406–408 (quotation on 407); H. Frank Eshleman, *Lancaster County Indians: Annals of the Susquehannocks and Other Indian Tribes of the Susquehanna Territory from about the Year 1500 to 1763, the Date of Their Extinction . . .* (Lancaster, Pa., 1908), 78–79; Paul A. W. Wallace, *Indians in Pennsylvania* (1961; reprint, Harrisburg, Pa., 1975), 11. Wallace speculates that the term *Conestoga* was derived from the Iroquois name for Susquehannock, *Gandastogues*, or "people of the blackened ridgepole."

5. Gary B. Nash, *Quakers and Politics: Pennsylvania, 1681–1726*, rev. ed. (Boston, 1993), 4, 47; Mary M. Schweitzer, *Custom and Contract: Household, Government, and the Economy in Colonial Pennsylvania* (New York, 1987), 89; James T. Lemon, *The Best Poor Man's Country: A Geographical Study of Early Southeastern Pennsylvania* (Baltimore, 1972), 101; Thomas Penn to Richard Peters, May 30, 1750, "Manuscript Papers on the Indian and Military Affairs of the Province of Pennsylvania, 1737–1775," APS. William Penn's sons continued his pattern of controlling settlement and were probably more successful at collecting quitrents.

FIGURE 1. *Penn's Treaty with the Indians.* By Benjamin West. 1771–1772. Courtesy, Pennsylvania Academy of the Fine Arts, Philadelphia. Gift of Mrs. Sarah Harrison (the Joseph Harrison, Jr., Collection). *The painting is one of the most famous and ubiquitous depictions of initial encounters between the English and Lenni Lenapes in Pennsylvania. It renders the two sides as equals for purposes of trade but possibly represents the triumph of British imperialism and industry.*

Penn's colonial policies were paradoxical with respect to Indians. Unlike administrators in other regions, Penn insisted on purchasing land from Indians to clear title for subsequent sale to white settlers. In reality, however, he often sold large tracts to potential settlers or land speculators before Indians agreed on treaty provisions. Premature white migration then forced Indians to move or sell land they would not have otherwise abandoned. The stipulations of deeds that accompanied treaties further muddied the clarity of these sales. Penn might have thought he had purchased all land and "Lakes, Rivers, Rivulets, Fountains, Streams, Trees, Woods, Underwoods, Mines, Royalties, and other Mines, Minerals, Quarries, Hawkings, Huntings, ffishings, fowlings and other Royalties, Privileges, and Powers" attached to that land. Indians, however, probably understood these deeds to extend only the use of land, not ownership, to their new white neighbors. Indians would have assumed that they could continue to live on these lands and, as the "Indian squaw" of myth had done, simply share needed resources.[6]

Penn's social and political ideals also contained good intentions toward native populations, even as they led to provisions that undermined native independence. On one hand, Penn admired Indians immensely. To Penn, they had "a deep natural sagacity," even an equal capacity of intellect. He found Indians "deliberate in council, and as designing, as I have ever observed among the politest of our Europeans." Penn's faith as a Quaker certainly guided him to encourage tolerance toward Indians, but at times his admiration of them also served to criticize his own countrymen, for whom he had little tolerance. Penn thought "the low dispensation of the poor Indian out shines the lives of those Christians, that pretend an higher." Perhaps believing that their presence would help to enlighten white Christians, Penn and his sons, who succeeded him as proprietors when he died in 1718, invited various tribes to settle in Pennsylvania, reserving land for Indian habitation. To mediate any conflict that might arise between white settlers and Indians, Penn established, or at least envisioned, equity under English law, insisting that "all differences between the planters and the Natives shall also be ended by Twelve men, that is by six Planters and Six Natives, that so we may Live friendly Together, and as much as in us Lyeth, Prevent all occasions of Heart Burnings and mischiefs."[7]

Whether from a sentiment of paternalism or economic necessity, the protections and privileges William Penn wanted to extend to Indian communities primarily furthered his own interests. According to his critics, Penn's open invitation to outside tribes came with profit in mind. Colonel Robert Quary, a justice in the vice admiralty court at Philadelphia, complained that "Mr. Penn endeavors all he can to invite foreign and French Indians, known to be villanous, and but lately come from Canada, to settle

6. Deed from Widaagh (Orytyagh) and Adnaggy-junkquagh, sachems of the Susquehannah Indians, to William Penn, Sept. 13, 1700, *PA,* 1st Ser., I, 133; William Cronon, *Changes in the Land: Indians, Colonists, and the Ecology of New England* (New York, 1983), 58–68; Francis Jennings, *The Invasion of America: Indians, Colonialism, and the Cant of Conquest* (Chapel Hill, N.C., 1975), 129.

7. William Penn to Robert Boyle, Aug. 5, 1683, and "William Penns' Conditions and Laws concerning Treatment of Indians," July 11, 1681, in Albert Cook Myers, ed., *William Penn's Own Account of the Lenni Lenape or Delaware Indians,* rev. ed. (Somerset, N.J., 1970), 44–45, 55.

FIGURE 2. William Penn and Indian Family. *Courtesy, The Historical Society of Pennsylvania, Philadelphia [Soc Print small B17 FF17].* *By the nineteenth century, textbooks, such as George Bancroft's* History of the United States of America . . . , *6 vols. (New York, 1883–1885), portrayed William Penn as a benevolent father to primitive and docile natives.*

in this country, only for the benefit of a trade with them, which he takes care wholly to engross to himself, by ordering the Indians not to permit any to trade with them but such as produce an indented license under his seal." In addition, the land he reserved for "foreign" and resident Indians served to control European immigrants as much as to protect Indians. By legally tying up land, Penn could force white settlers to rent or purchase property directly from him, instead of Indians, preventing whites from settling in some regions. Conestoga Manor, surveyed in 1717, contained only 415 acres reserved for Indian use. The remaining 16,000 acres, which he guarded jealously against white squatters, belonged to Penn personally. Ultimately, Penn did not consider Indians independent from a larger, more powerful political authority but insisted that they, like their white neighbors, owed allegiance to the proprietor and the king of England. In April 1701, Penn promised the Indians on the Susquehanna that they "shall have the full and free priviledges and Immunities of all the Said Lands" reserved for them, as long as they, like other English inhabitants, acknowledged "the Authority of the Crown of England and Government of this Province." In other words, freedom to inhabit land and subordination to colonial power went hand in hand.[8]

William Penn was not alone in attempting to control migration, settlement, and the actions and interactions of Indians and whites. Iroquois also used land to manipulate Indians and English in Pennsylvania and to enhance their own powers. Although they suffered devastating military defeats by French allied Wyandots, Ottawas, Miamis, and Illinois during the 1690s and were drawn into the imperial battles of King William's War, the Iroquois Confederacy managed to negotiate political neutrality and separate trade agreements with both the English and the French in 1701. The power to conquer and colonize their western borders thus limited, the Iroquois turned to the Pennsylvania frontier as a place to exert authority. The Six Nations knew that the English valued land above all else,

8. Col. Robert Quary, "An Abstract of Several Informations Relating to Irregular Proceedings and Other Undue Practices in Pennsylvania" (1700), in Edward Armstrong, ed., *Correspondence between William Penn and James Logan, Secretary of the Province of Pennsylvania, and Others, 1700–1750: From the Original Letters in Possession of the Logan Family,* 2 vols. (Philadelphia, 1870–1872), I, 24; Treaty agreement, Apr. 23, 1701, *PA,* 1st Ser., I, 144–145; Kent, *Susquehanna's Indians,* 62. Besides the reserve at Conestoga adjacent to Penn's private manor, Penn's sons set aside sixty-five hundred acres in 1735 at the Forks of the Delaware called the "Indian Tract Manor," separate from the larger Walking Purchase. Whether this tract was ever used by Indians is unclear. See A. D. Chidsey, Jr., *The Penn Patents in the Forks of the Delaware* (Easton, Pa., 1937), 25–26; Eric Hinderaker, *Elusive Empires: Constructing Colonialism in the Ohio Valley, 1673–1800* (New York, 1997), 103–104. Unlike other British policymakers in the eighteenth century, Penn never promoted intermarriage as a means of integrating Indians as subjects.

so they made their claims to land a cornerstone in negotiating for gifts, assistance, military alliances, or favors from British colonial governments. In July 1727, for instance, representatives from the Six Nations in Philadelphia claimed "the sole Right" to sell Susquehanna River land "by their Conquests over the old Inhabitants," despite the English insistence that Governor Thomas Dongan of New York had already relinquished those lands to William Penn. The Iroquois further insisted that Pennsylvania meet their terms before they would agree to any new purchase. As late as 1744, the Six Nations claimed rights to various portions of Pennsylvania, Maryland, and Virginia. In treaty conferences, they successfully intimidated the colonies with veiled threats of attack and managed to receive tribute for repeated capitulation of the same frontier lands.[9]

In claiming authority to sell land to the English by rights of conquest, the Iroquois also asserted political power over the Indians who migrated to Pennsylvania or who now lived there. The Susquehannocks' dispersion in the late seventeenth century left land uninhabited and a power vacuum in eastern Pennsylvania. The Indian peoples who settled along the Susquehanna River tended to establish small, decentralized communities with no military capacity. Many already acknowledged their subordination, but each community had to negotiate a working relationship with the Six Nations. From Tioga near the colonial boundary between New York and Pennsylvania to Pequea in the south, one could travel by river through Shawnee and Nanticoke settlements at M'cheuwami in the Wyoming Valley, where the Iroquois had placed their representatives and controlled the balance of power. The Nanticokes, under the leadership of their chief Robert White, became significant mediators between the many ethnic Indian groups settled on the Susquehanna River. Delawares from New Jersey, Tutelos from Virginia, and Iroquois lived south of Wyoming at Shamokin, and Conoys from Maryland settled further south at the branch of the Juniata River because "they were ill used by the white People in the Place where they had lived," and they sought new land "for the Benefit of Hunting."[10]

9. James Logan to John Penn, July 10, 1727, Penn Papers, Official Correspondence, I, HSP; *MPCP,* IV, 706, 710, 715.

10. *MPCP,* V, 22; Conrad Weiser to Peters, July 5, 1746, Conrad Weiser Papers, I, Correspondence, HSP; Kent, *Susquehanna's Indians,* 10, 74, 77; Treaty of Lancaster, July 2, 1744, Canassatego presenting Indian grievances to the Council, in Carl Van Doren and Juilan P. Boyd, eds., *Indian Treaties Printed by Benjamin Franklin, 1736–*

Only the Shawnees and the Delawares were relatively successful in maintaining their autonomy, despite political pressures from both Pennsylvania and the Iroquois. Several bands of Shawnees, for instance, weary of war in the west and reassured by the Iroquois that earlier animosities had been forgotten, migrated to Pennsylvania in the late seventeenth century from the Mississippi and Ohio Valleys. The Pennsylvania government also encouraged their settlement, and they established trade relations with the colony. By the 1690s, Shawnees had settled along the Delaware River at Pechoquealing, among Minisinks, more often called Munsees. Another sixty families applied to the provincial government to settle near Conestoga, at Paxtang. Though they were supposedly under the protection of the Six Nations, they thought themselves independent of Iroquois governance, because they treated separately with William Penn in 1701 at Conestoga. Twenty years later, the governor of Pennsylvania sent word to the Susquehanna Shawnees, requesting their continued loyalty to the memory of William Penn and to "our Great King George who is the Head of all the English and of their Brethren." As was customary, he sent gifts to confirm their alliance. Ironically, though not unusually, the gifts included "five Gallons of Rum to chear their Hearts at hearing of these his Words, and one Strowd Match Coat." Although the government, according to William Penn's wishes, repeatedly banned the sale of liquor to protect Indian societies, it also used alcohol's seductive qualities to pacify Indian allies.[11]

At the very least, their gifts sent mixed messages and ultimately worked against peaceful coexistence and the English attempt to turn Indians into subjects. The Shawnees found themselves caught in a conflict generated by too much colonial oversight and alcohol. In May 1728, two Shawnees, accused of murdering two Conestoga Indians while drunk, escaped cap-

---

1762 (Philadelphia, 1938), 67–69. For the location of Pennsylvania Indian towns, see Barry C. Kent, Janet Rice, and Kakuko Ota, "A Map of Eighteenth Century Indian Towns in Pennsylvania," *Pennsylvania Archaeologist,* LI (1981), 1–18. For native groups' migrating to the Susquehanna region, see Peter C. Mancall, *Valley of Opportunity: Economic Culture along the Upper Susquehanna, 1700–1800* (Ithaca, N.Y., 1991), esp. 33.

11. *MPCP,* II, 388, III, 219, 441–442; Jennings, *Ambiguous Iroquois Empire,* 196–200, 236–237; Kent, *Susquehanna's Indians,* 80–88; Charles Callender, "Shawnee," in Sturtevant, gen. ed., *Handbook of North American Indians,* XV, Trigger, ed., *Northeast,* 622–623; Penn's law of trade, Dec. 5, 1682, in Myers, *Penn's Own Account of the Lenni Lenape,* 59; Act of Oct. 28, 1701, in Eshleman, *Lancaster County Indians,* 157.

ture. Enraged, a band of seventeen or eighteen young Conestoga warriors, "painted for the Warr, all armd," threatened to destroy the entire Shawnee nation. The Shawnees condemned white traders, if not the English government, for introducing and selling liquor to their people (which often sparked intercommunity violence). By September, bristling at Iroquois attempts to push them into war with the English, many of the Shawnees near Conestoga returned to the Ohio Valley. For years, the Pennsylvania government and the Iroquois attempted to woo them back, fearful that the Shawnees might ally with the French against them. In the fall of 1732, Pennsylvania sent wampum belts and rum, assuring them of "a large Tract laid out for them about their Town, near Pextan, which should always be kept for them and their Children for all time to come, or so long as any of them continued to live with us." Other Shawnee communities that had found some independence on the Delaware River avoided confrontations with colonial officials by removing instead to the Wyoming Valley, to the village of Skehandowana (later called the Shawnee Flats), under the leadership of Kakowatcheky. In April 1744, Kakowatcheky and his followers joined earlier migrants at Logg's Town, west of the Allegheny Mountains, leaving only scattered but defiantly independent Shawnee communities in Pennsylvania. The most important of these surviving communities in the Wyoming Valley, under the leadership of Paxnous, successfully resisted direction from and subordination to either Iroquois or English.[12]

Like the Shawnees, Delaware Indians also sought to maintain their autonomy from the Six Nations, whom they and the Susquehannocks had fought in the mid-seventeenth century. The various cultural groups who came to be known as Delawares had long inhabited the Delaware River valley, although their myths spoke of ancestors who had migrated from a country "beyond the Father of Waters, and near the wide sea in which the sun sank." By the seventeenth century, these Delaware River natives incorporated three major language groups: the Munsees (Minisinks), the Unalachtigos (northern Unamis, or Jerseys), and the Unamis

12. John Wright to James Logan, May 2, 1728, Treaty with Thomas Penn and James Logan, Mar. 20, 1737–1738, *PA*, 1st Ser., I, 213, 551; Charles A. Hanna, *The Wilderness Trail; or, The Ventures and Adventures of the Pennsylvania Traders on the Allegheny Path* (New York, 1911), 185; *MPCP*, III, 462, IV, 234; Kent, Rice, and Ota, "A Map of Eighteenth Century Indian Towns," *Pa. Arch.*, LI (1981), 10; Wallace, *Indians in Pennsylvania*, 177; Kent, *Susquehanna's Indians*, 90–91.

(Lenni Lenapes). The Lenni Lenapes, whose name translates as "a male of our kind," or the "real people," lived on the western shores of the lower Delaware River, where Philadelphia was eventually built. The Unalachtigos inhabited the eastern bank of the Delaware in central New Jersey. The Munsees lived farther north at the Delaware Water Gap. Whatever their linguistic or self-designated clan differences, these native peoples shared similar family and community structures, living in either longhouses or domed, circular wigwams covered in bark. Their households were matrilineal, where descent passed through the women, although men held political power and status. For subsistence, they cultivated corn in semisedentary villages from which individual families left for extended periods to hunt and fish.[13]

At the turn of the eighteenth century, the forces that drew Shawnees into Pennsylvania and pushed Susquehannocks out also affected the Delawares' movements and community formation. As more Europeans migrated into the mid-Atlantic region, they pushed Indians from New Jersey and the Delaware River valley into eastern Pennsylvania. A group of Unalachtigos, for example, migrated west from New Jersey to try their luck building new communities at the Forks of the Delaware, north of

13. Alfred Mathews and Austin N. Hungerford, *History of the Counties of Lehigh and Carbon, in the Commonwealth of Pennsylvania* (Philadelphia, 1884), 1; Francis Jennings, "Pennsylvania Indians and the Iroquois," in Daniel K. Richter and James H. Merrell, eds., *Beyond the Covenant Chain: The Iroquois and Their Neighbors in Indian North America, 1600–1800* (Syracuse, N.Y., 1987), 77; "Questions Put to Heckewelder," John Heckewelder Papers, 1755–1822, box 1, folder 27, HSP; John Heckewelder, *History, Manners, and Customs of the Indian Nations, Who Once Inhabited Pennsylvania and the Neighbouring States*, rev. ed., ed. William C. Reichel (1876; facsimile reprint, Bowie, Md., 1990), 47; Goddard, "Delaware," in Sturtevant, gen. ed., *Handbook of North American Indians*, XV, Trigger, ed., *Northeast*, 214, 225. Munsees used these terms for Delaware River peoples. Eighteenth-century Englishmen sometimes distinguished the three groups as Munsees, Forks Indians, and Delawares; see Kent, *Susquehanna's Indians*, 91, 94; Frank G. Speck, *A Study of the Delaware Indian Big House Ceremony* (Harrisburg, Pa., 1931), 14; Anthony F. C. Wallace, *King of the Delawares: Teedyuscung, 1700–1763* (1949; reprint, Syracuse, N.Y., 1990), 8–9; Wallace, *Indians in Pennsylvania*, 25–27; R. Michael Stewart, Chris C. Hummer, and Jay F. Custer, "Late Woodland Cultures of the Middle and Lower Delaware River Valley and the Upper Delmarva Peninsula," Marshall J. Becker, "Cultural Diversity in the Lower Delaware River Valley, 1550–1750: An Enthnohistorical Perspective," and Herbert C. Kraft, "Late Woodland Settlement Patterns in the Upper Delaware Valley," all in Custer, ed., *Late Woodland Cultures of the Middle Atlantic Region* (Newark, N.J., 1986), 82, 94, 112.

Philadelphia. By the 1720s, these Indians lived in scattered settlements spread between the Delaware and Lehigh (Lecha) Rivers. Small Delaware towns, such as Sakhauwotung, Clistowackin, and Lechawekink along the Delaware River and Hockendauqua, Buchkabuchka (the Lehigh Water Gap) and Meniolagomekah, were all connected by Indian paths but, more important, by a network of kin relations that bound their communities together. One of the more prominent Delaware families, led by Chief Nutimus, settled at Clistowackin, whereas his nephew Teedyuscung, the head of another important Delaware family, stayed at the edges of the Kittatinny, or Endless, Mountains on land that later would be known as Nazareth and Bethlehem.[14]

Though the three factions of Delaware River Indians—Munsees, Unalachtigos, and Unamis—might have had marked distinctions between their communities, clans, families, and dialects and might have chosen different paths of migration and settlement in Pennsylvania, the colonial government treated them as one nation, the Delawares. The Six Nations also saw these tribes as one political nation and continually struggled to control them. Although the Shawnees considered them "grandfathers," or elders, by the 1710s and 1720s the Delawares had a similar tributary status as props of the Longhouse. Still, the Iroquois were not particularly successful in managing these subordinate tribes. During the early eighteenth century, the Delawares refused to assist the Iroquois in their campaigns against southern Indians, and, until the 1730s, they treated separately with Pennsylvania.[15]

With two relatively strong and autonomous tributary Indian groups settled in Pennsylvania, the Six Nations sought to establish a presence among them. By the late 1720s, Shickellamy, an Oneida appointed by the Iroquois, acted as "viceroy" or "vice-regent" or "overseer" of Indians in

14. Kent, Rice, and Ota, "A Map of Eighteenth Century Indian Towns," *Pa. Arch.*, LI (1981), 8–11 and map; Jennings, *Ambiguous Iroquois Empire*, 263; *MPCP*, VIII, 211; William C. Reichel, ed., *Memorials of the Moravian Church*, I (Philadelphia, 1870), 218–219.

15. Goddard, "Delaware," in Sturtevant, gen. ed., *Handbook of North American Indians*, XV, Trigger, ed., *Northeast*, 222. Munsees were more often distinguished as a separate nation. See Becker, "Cultural Diversity," in Custer, ed., *Late Woodland Cultures*, 195–198; Richter, *Ordeal of the Longhouse*, 239; Heckewelder, *History, Manners, and Customs*, esp. 87; Jennings, *Ambiguous Iroquois Empire*, 204–205, 245; *MPCP*, III, 100.

Pennsylvania and as a go-between for the Iroquois and English. He lived near and then at Shamokin, which was an important native trade town situated where four major Indian trails, including a "Warrior's Path," came together and three branches of the Susquehanna River intersected. Many refugees from other colonial regions gravitated to Shamokin. Indians from three linguistic groups—Algonquian, Iroquois, and Siouan—lived there. Although Shamokin was a place of refugees and a temporary home for Iroquois warriors traveling south to fight, the Six Nations laid claim to the land. Shamokin was originally a Delaware settlement founded around 1720, and its name came from the Delaware word Schachameki, "the place of eels," or Shumokenk, "where horns or antlers are plenty," both describing available resources for native subsistence. The region was also a fertile place for cultivating crops and other food sources. In July 1743, naturalist John Bartram, traveling with Conrad Weiser, found outside Shamokin "an old *Indian* field of excellent soil, where there had been a town, the principal footsteps of which are peach-trees, plums and excellent grapes." Moravian missionaries visiting Shamokin also found peach trees, a suggestion "that this was a very old Indian settlement." Whether ancient or not, the Six Nations used this native precedence to construct a history of Iroquois occupation. They often referred to Shamokin and its vicinity as a place where their ancestors' "Bones are scattered," thus a place where "there has always been a great council Fire." Like the Scots-Irish memory of their Hay's Spring home, the Iroquois tied themselves and their ancestors to the town to give their occupation legitimacy. Like the river it lay on, Shamokin was central to trade and travel as well as to the political control of the region.[16]

16. For the best look at the development of Shamokin, see James H. Merrell, "Shamokin, 'the very seat of the Prince of darkness': Unsettling the Early American Frontier," in Andrew R. L. Cayton and Fredrika J. Teute, eds., *Contact Points: American Frontiers from the Mohawk Valley to the Mississippi, 1750–1830* (Chapel Hill, N.C., 1998), 16–59. See also Merrell, "Shickellamy, 'A Person of Consequence,'" in Robert S. Grumet, ed., *Northeastern Indian Lives, 1632–1816* (Amherst, Mass., 1996), 228; John H. Carter, *Early Events in the Susquehanna Valley* . . . (Millville, Pa., 1981), 26; Maurice C. Jones, "Memorandum of the Names and Significations Which the 'Lenni Lenape,' Otherwise Called 'the Delawares,' Had Given to Rivers, Streams, Places, etc., within the States of Pennsylvania, New Jersey, Maryland, and Virginia . . . Taken from the Papers of the Rev. John Heckewelder . . . ," HSP, *Proceedings*, I (Philadelphia, 1847), 127; John Bartram, *Travels in Pensilvania and Canada* (Ann Arbor, Mich., 1966) (originally published as *Observations on the Inhabitants, Climate, Soil, Rivers, Productions, Animals,*

MAP 1. Frontier Settlements in Pennsylvania, 1700–1740. *Drawn by Gerry Krieg*

The Iroquois might have asserted some dominance over Pennsylvania Indians by placing representatives at important crossroads. William Penn might have claimed some dominance over white settlement by controlling the sale and distribution of land. But neither had much experience managing the two groups together. As the evolution of Shamokin and the Susquehanna River region suggests, during the first half of the eighteenth century the regions west and north of Philadelphia were becoming a patchwork of native ethnic enclaves where the physical boundaries between communities were not always clear. White migration and the growing population of Euramericans added another element into the mix. Pennsylvania Indians sometimes invited individuals to live and work among them. They assigned land to white traders or squatters that lived beyond the legal limits of the province and had become their friends. In June 1683, Shauk-a-num and Et-hoe sold one hundred acres of land "lying neer Cohanzey on Delaware-river" to John Nicholls for a handful of trade goods. As long as people were dispersed, individual Indians and whites could usually live together on the margins of the formal political world as neighbors, friends, even kin. In 1725, trader Edmund Cartlidge received a deed for a "plantation Lyeing In a Turn of Conestogoe Creek Called by the name of the Indian Pointt" from Wiggoneeheenah, a Delaware, "In Consideration of the Greatt Love and Resspectt as well as for Divers Large presents made unto mee by my true and Loveing friend." The deed's language, although formulaic and probably composed by Cartlidge to validate his claim to landownership, still provides intriguing evidence of the emotional as well as monetary value of these exchanges. Wiggoneeheenah would have interpreted gifts from Cartlidge as a sign of respect and, in turn, would have allowed him to share the resources available on Conestoga Creek. Thus, the tradition that produced the memory of a welcoming Indian woman might not have been so far-fetched.[17]

---

and Other Matters Worthy of Notice . . . [London, 1751]), 19; W[illia]m M. Beauchamp, ed., *Moravian Journals Relating to Central New York, 1745–66* (Syracuse, N.Y., 1916), 28; *MPCP,* VI, 116.

17. Deed from Wiggoneeheenah to Edmund Cartlidge, Apr. 8, 1725, no. 11, Logan Family Papers, 1664–1871, XI, Indian Affairs, HSP. There were many such private transactions. For instance, see Indian deed, June 25, 1683, Historical Society Collection, Miscellaneous Manuscripts, 1661–1931, Indians, HSP. Other areas of the mid-Atlantic region tended to be ethnically diverse as well, such as the New York

Inadvertently, Indians' generosity to a few also cleared the road for settlement of larger groups of ethnic whites, which, in turn, increased population density and the possibilities of conflict. Beginning in the 1720s, English, German, and Scots-Irish immigrants rapidly spread from Philadelphia west toward the Susquehanna River to what became Lancaster and York Counties and north to the Forks of the Delaware, later known as Lehigh, Carbon, and Northampton Counties. Scots-Irish, in particular, moved to the fringes of English settlement. The Presbyterian Church, established in Philadelphia in 1706, acted as a conduit for European sojourners. Some had probably been caught in a series of economic crises in Ulster, which made immigration to the American colonies an attractive alternative. As tenant farmers and small entrepreneurs, rent increases, shortened leases, and bad harvests in Ireland in the 1720s put a stranglehold on their livelihood. According to shipmaster John Stewart, they were poor people fleeing "the oppression of Landlords and Tyths." Pennsylvania provided endless possibilities for Scots-Irish. Some moved west from Philadelphia into the Susquehanna River area, settling at Pequea, which the Shawnees had abandoned a decade before, and Paxton, which the Delawares had recently occupied and which was close to the Indian community at Conestoga. Between 1728 and 1730, Scots-Irish built a loose cluster of dwellings called the Hunter Settlement along the Delaware River in Northampton County just north of Clistowackin, where Delawares still lived. Fifteen miles to the west, just as oral history had recorded, a group of sixteen Scots-Irish families founded Craig's Settlement, which lay below the Delaware town of Hockendauqua on the Lehigh River, where the Indians cultivated orchards of apple and pear trees and, at least initially, allowed these strangers to stay.[18]

---

backcountry. See Thomas E. Burke, Jr., *Mohawk Frontier: The Dutch Community of Schenectady, New York, 1661–1710* (Ithaca, N.Y., 1991), 123–141. For a discussion of squatters' rights in Pennsylvania, see Schweitzer, *Custom and Contract,* 99–100.

18. James H. Smylie, *Scotch-Irish Presence in Pennsylvania* (University Park, Pa., 1990), 5; John Stewart to proprietors, May 3, 1736, in [Clyde], *The Scotch-Irish of Northampton County,* 3; George Chambers, *A Tribute to the Principles, Virtues, Habits, and Public Usefulness of the Irish and Scotch Early Settlers of Pennsylvania,* 2d ed. (Chambersburg, Pa., 1871), 51–52; Kent, Rice, and Ota, "A Map of Eighteenth Century Indian Towns," *Pa. Arch.,* LI (1981), 10; Mathews and Hungerford, *History of Lehigh and Carbon,* 4, 6; A. D. Chidsey, Jr., *The Forks of the Delaware in Pennsylvania: An English Province in America under the Penn Proprietaries, 1681–1783,* map, Northampton County Historical and Genealogical Society, Easton, Pa., 1938.

While Indians and whites tested the waters of intercultural living, the Pennsylvania government struggled to keep its hold on the frontier. After William Penn's death in 1718, in particular, the colonial infrastructure was at its weakest, yet control of the frontier regions was crucial to the province's future. Between 1718 and 1732, Penn's sons by his second wife—John, Thomas, and Richard—attempted to consolidate their claim to their father's estate against Penn's eldest Anglican son, William, Jr. As they fought in the courts of England, Pennsylvania was left without direct proprietary supervision. James Logan, William Penn's secretary and land agent, tried to carry out the policies that the late proprietor had put in place. He also took the opportunity to strengthen his own position among the Philadelphia elite and to seize sole power over land distribution and sales.[19]

Logan, however, found little support among native denizens of the frontier. First, he struggled to maintain the goodwill of Indians, even as he asked for more land concessions. During the 1720s, Logan thought there was "an absolute necessity that further Purchases from the Indians should be made without delay." He begged the new proprietors to visit Pennsylvania to deal directly with native groups because "of the Regard that has industriously been kept up in these People to your father's memory in all our Treaties and Communications with them." Logan cultivated this memory, even myth, of William Penn as the Indian's advocate and friend and tried to convince Indians that Penn's sons had also inherited their father's benevolent spirit and, therefore, should be granted the same privilege to purchase land. The power of association sometimes worked to convince Indians to sell individual tracts. In 1730, for example, Hockanootamen, an Indian living near the Schuylkill River (in Berks County) granted Logan, as his "brother and ffriend," the land he occupied on Sakung (Sacony) Creek and, certainly with Logan's approval, condemned "the Dutch folks and other People settled on it without his Leave or my Leave." According to the deed, Hockanootamen's friendship and subsequent land grant had been possible only because "Old William Penn was my Brother, I have seen him often, and his Children are as my Children." Yet not all Indians trusted Logan. Some remembered a different blueprint for settlement, and they, too, called upon the memory of William Penn to preserve their own rights

19. Jennings, *Ambiguous Iroquois Empire*, 276–277; Nash, *Quakers and Politics*, 318–335.

to land. In the fall of 1725, several chiefs of the Brandywine Indians, a group of Unami Delawares, protested attempts to survey and sell their lands. They brandished a twenty-year-old document that was a "Grant from the Govern." for lands along the Brandywine Creek. Even though "it was so defaced that he could not read any more of it than a word here and there," it still bore the provincial seal, and through it the Indians claimed their right to remain.[20]

White immigrants also proved stubborn and unwilling to accept direction from the Pennsylvania government. James Logan and the proprietors encouraged settlement and hoped that Euramericans on the frontier would act as a buffer between the English to the east and potential Indian aggression to the west. Instead, many of these inhabitants proved "troublesome settlers to the government and hard neighbors to the Indians." Samuel Blunston complained to Thomas Penn in 1738 that many people "put up Cabbins" on land "Beyond the Indian purchase," which took them from the government's reach and into direct competition with Indian communities. More often, it seemed, white settlers fought with each other over land. Some forcibly evicted others from contested plantations. One group burned the cabins of German immigrants and moved onto their homesteads. White settlers took each other to court over boundaries and sued surveyors as accomplices to land fraud. They were, as James Steel, the surveyor general of Pennsylvania, surmised, "Litigeous and troublesome one to another, that they are perpetually falling out about that wch do's not properly belong to either of them." In actuality, the proprietors and provincial agents allowed only "Subjects of England" to secure property licenses or deeds. Although Governor William Keith in the 1720s had promoted the immediate naturalization of newcomers, many of the frontier dwellers were not English and could not purchase their homesteads outright. Germans, especially, complained bitterly about this policy, which kept many from full ownership of the land that they might have inhabited for a lifetime. Foreigners, such as Jan Strieper,

20. James Logan, Richard Hill, Isaac Norris, and Samuel Preston (trustees) to John, Thomas, and Richard Penn, undated, Simon Gratz Collection, case 2, box 12, "Supreme Court of Pennsylvania, H-R," HSP; Deposition of Thomas Chandler, Aug. 16, 1725, no. 12, Hockanootamen deed, July 7, 1730, no. 15, Logan Family Papers, 1664–1871, XI, Indian Affairs, HSP. In September 1706, Logan spoke of "a very troublesome claim of the Indians" at Brandywine; see Logan to William Penn, Sept. 15, 1706, in Armstrong, ed., *Correspondence between Penn and Logan,* II, 167.

sometimes held land patents, but, if they did not become British subjects before their death, they forfeited rights to the land. After Strieper's death in 1727, his children lost possession of nearly forty-five hundred acres in Durham township because he had not been naturalized.[21]

Still, the proprietors encouraged migration and settlement of English and non-English alike, even as provincial agents had only partial success in enforcing Penn's land policies. Large grants to the Pennsylvania elite had stimulated an influx of laborers and immigrant groups, whom they could not always control. James Logan and his assistants often felt overwhelmed by the numbers, vocalizing their frustrations through ethnic slurs about "idle," "worthless," or "indigent" Scots-Irish and Germans "perpetually crowding in upon us." Although there were a few of what Logan referred to as "good sober Irish," most often he maligned immigrant character and habits. In September 1728, Logan lamented: the "Palatines crowd in upon us and the Irish yet faster of wch no less than 6 ships are arrived at New castle and this place within these ten dayes and many more are daily expected. As the numbers of these People encrease upon us, so will the Difficulties of settling them." As immigrants pushed west into frontier regions, they became a problem to be surmounted rather than a sign of provincial growth to be celebrated. They often ignored colonial authority and acted on their own impulses. Many refused to pay quitrents, as the proprietors' rent collectors soon found. By the late 1730s, in Lancaster County alone, some fifty thousand pounds of quitrents were past due, and the collector felt that "nothing less than a miracle can Enable these poor people to

21. "Abstract of Letter from T. Story," Oct. 9, 1718, Logan to John Penn, Oct. 18, 1728, Penn Papers, Official Correspondence, I, 65, II, 33, HSP; Samuel Blunston to Thomas Penn, Jan. 27, Oct. 19, 1737, Mar. 25, 1738, Lancaster County Papers, 1724–1816, HSP; James Steel to J. Mitchel, Oct. 8, 1725, Logan Family Papers, James Steel's Letter Book, 1715–1732, XXXVIII, HSP; Steel to Thomas Reid, Sept. 28, 1731, Logan Family Papers, Miscellaneous Volumes, Steel's Letter Book, 1730–1741, XXXIX, HSP; Reuben Gold Thwaites, ed., *Early Western Travels, 1748–1846*, I (Cleveland, Ohio, 1904), 238nn; John R. Dunbar, ed., *The Paxton Papers* (The Hague, 1957), 5; *Report of the Commission to Locate the Site of the Frontier Forts of Pennsylvania*, I (Harrisburg, Pa., 1896), 528; Nash, *Quakers and Politics*, 318–335; Jennings, *Ambiguous Iroquois Empire*, 276–277; Petition from James Logan, May 15, 1727, German petition to the governor, Jan. 16, 1734, Strieper Papers, 1632–1773, Bucks County (Pa.) Papers, 1682–1850, I, 139–149, 199–229, HSP. Logan repossessed Strieper's property for his personal use but then petitioned the proprietors to trade it for better land, since the Indians still laid claim to it.

become masters of this Cash in an honest way very speedily." If settlers were cash poor, however, many felt entitled to use the wealth of natural resources at their fingertips. Although many immigrants lived on land "without any Grants, licence or Method," they often took advantage of frontier isolation to make money on land speculation. In the spring of 1738, Samuel Blunston complained to Thomas Penn that many white inhabitants were "going about and Marking unsetled places and then keeping Em for a market and selling them to Newcomers or strangers." Others cut timber on the proprietors' private lands, such as the manor near Conestoga, or secretly mined mineral deposits of lead and ore. The prohibition of non-English immigrant landownership in the 1720s and 1730s and the legal measures taken to extract rents and compliance from these settlers came back to haunt the Pennsylvania government several decades later when angry frontier inhabitants violently protested what they saw as exclusion from the privileges of empire.[22]

Such were the dynamics and inherent tensions of early migration within the context of colonialism. Indians and whites, maneuvering between two powerful political entities, tended to be less concerned about each others' activities, if not friendly. Instead, they sought ways to limit the effects of colonial authority. The proprietors and the Six Nations, to some extent, had labored separately for the submission and loyalty of frontier peoples. By the late 1720s, however, these colonial powers would try a new strategy of cooperation. Although their joint efforts forced Delawares to cede land in eastern Pennsylvania, the end results were politically disastrous. Delawares would be alienated from the Pennsylvania government and the Six Nations for decades. Cooperation between these two powers also revealed ultimately competing agendas that left the Iroquois wary of their Euramerican neighbors to the south.

In the initial phase of colonial cooperation, James Logan, desperate to maintain his influence over frontier expansion, first tried to manipulate native politics with the quiet coercive help of the Six Nations. Unamis

22. Blunston to Thomas Penn, Mar. 3, 1737/8, Lancaster County Papers, 1724–1816, HSP; Logan to John Penn, Sept. 11, 1728, Logan to John, Thomas, and Richard Penn, Apr. 24, 1729, Logan to Steel, Nov. 18, 1729, Logan to Thomas Penn, Oct. 19, 1730, Steel to proprietors, Aug. 2, 1731, all in Penn Papers, Official Correspondence, II, 21, 53, 101, 145, 179, HSP; Steel to John Watson, Mar. 15, 1721/2, Logan Family Papers, Steel's Letter Book, 1715–1732, XXXVIII, 51, HSP.

(Lenni Lenapes) had moved west to the Schuylkill River sometime before 1709 and established the Delaware town Tulpewihácki, meaning "land abounding with Turtles." By the early 1720s, a group of Palatinate Germans migrated from the Schoharie Valley in New York and settled "among the Indians." In 1723, fifteen of these German families petitioned the Pennsylvania governor for land in what they now called the Tulpehocken Valley, which the "Schuylkill Indians" occupied. Only after fifty more families joined the Germans in 1728 did the Delawares begin to complain to the governor. As long as the settlers were few, Delawares could coexist, but as the number of white settlers increased Indians protested that "they had been much abused by having their Corn (wch they never use to fence) destroy'd by the Cattle of these new-comers whom they knew not." Tulpewihácki's leader Sassoonan (also known as Allumapees) met with Logan in June 1728 but returned dissatisfied. He had reminded the proprietors' agent and the provincial governor that he had never sold land to these people, nor had he been compensated for the land that whites now occupied. He was most worried "that his Children may wonder to see all their Fathers Lands gone from them, without his receiving any thing for them, that the Christians now make their Settlements very near them, and they shall have no place of their own left to live on." Sassoonan struggled to keep Tulpehocken from the hands of white settlers, but he also tried to fend off interfering Iroquois, who reprimanded the Delawares to do no more than "plant Corn and mind their own private Business." Shickellamy, the Iroquois representative from Shamokin, had carefully watched the treaty process between Sassoonan and Logan. Logan, in turn, used the silent threat of Iroquois authority to urge the Delawares' compliance. After several years of pressure from both Germans and the provincial government, Delawares officially sold their Tulpehocken land. On August 11, 1731, Sassoonan released the claim of the Schuylkill Indians to land along the upper branches of that river. The Pennsylvania government had persuaded Sassoonan to transfer to the German settlers five hundred acres "in consideration of the Love and Goodwill that I bear to my friend James Logan."[23]

23. Jones, "Memorandum of the Names and Significations," HSP, *Proc.*, I (1847), 125; Bartram, *Travels in Pensilvania,* 10. The region might have been home to actual turtles, but the name could also imply that Delawares of the turtle clan or phratry

But James Logan was no friend to the Delawares. Rather, he wanted to manipulate the Delawares' political succession to ensure that he could purchase more land from a tractable ally. The Iroquois also wanted to work with English colonial powers to further subordinate Delawares in Pennsylvania. Logan began by cultivating the allegiance of Sassoonan's two nephews, Opekasset and Shakataulin, who were set to succeed him. By 1731, however, Opekasset had died of smallpox, and Sassoonan had stabbed Shakataulin, possibly because Sassoonan begrudged his position as Logan's protégé. Sassoonan exercised his remaining political power to make a successor of his third nephew, Pisquetomen, whom Logan could not manipulate, let alone influence. At conferences in 1728 and 1731, Pisquetomen objected to the cession of Tulpehocken land and the small price that Pennsylvania had paid. Consequently, Logan strove to "have that fellow [Pisquetomen] laid aside and a better substituted in his place." He marshaled the assistance of Shickellamy, the representative of the Six Nations, and a new friend of the Iroquois, German immigrant Conrad Weiser, to prevent Sassoonan and Pisquetomen from acting independently. The Six Nations forced Sassoonan to live out his days under their thumb in Shamokin, but the next generation of Unami Delawares, under the leadership of Pisquetomen and his brothers Shingas and Tamaqua, left their birthplace and moved to the Ohio Valley to establish independent communities in the west, trying to avoid the costly concessions made by their elders.[24]

---

lived there. See also Isaac Norris et al. to John, Thomas, and Richard Penn, Nov. 13, 1731, Penn Papers, Indian Affairs, I, 1687–1753, HSP; *MPCP,* III, 319, 337, 338; I. Daniel Rupp, *History of the Counties of Berks and Lebanon* (1844; reprint, Spartanburg, S.C., 1984), 131; Carter, *Early Events in the Susquehanna Valley,* 186–188; Logan to John Penn, Aug. 2, 1731, Penn Papers, Official Correspondence, II, 181, HSP; Jennings, *Ambiguous Iroquois Empire,* 305; [Charles Thomson], *Causes of the Alienation of the Delaware and Shawanese Indians from the British Interest* (Philadelphia, 1867) (originally published as *An Enquiry into the Causes of the Alienation of the Delaware and Shawanese Indians from the British Interest . . .* [London, 1759]), 20–21; Sassoonan deed, Aug. 11, 1731, no. 16, Logan Family Papers, 1664–1871, XI, Indian Affairs, HSP.

24. Isaac Norris, Samuel Preston, and Logan to John, Thomas, and Richard Penn, Nov. 13, 1731, Penn Papers, Indian Affairs, I, 1687–1753, HSP; Logan to John, Thomas, and Richard Penn, Aug. 26, 1731, Penn Papers, Official Correspondence, II, 191, HSP; Logan to Conrad Weiser, Sept. 30, 1747, Richard Peters Papers, 1697–1845, II, pt. 2, HSP; Jennings, *Ambiguous Iroquois Empire,* 263, 311, 342–346; [Thomson], *Alienation of*

Although control over local Indian politics eluded James Logan, he soon learned that alliances with larger native political entities worked just as well for his purposes. Throughout the late 1720s, Logan nurtured diplomatic relations with the Six Nations in New York. Their cooperation reached fruition in the following decade. In the early 1730s, Penn's sons Thomas, Richard, and John, now proprietors, became interested in land north of Philadelphia at the Forks of the Delaware. Although Logan admitted that there "never was any pretence of a purchase made on [William Penn's] account within thirty miles of the Nearest of those Indian settlements," the new proprietors claimed rights to the Forks land by the authority of treaties negotiated by their father. They first tried to gain the confidence of Delaware leaders. In 1734, Nutimus and Tishcohan (also known as Tishecunk or Captain John by the English) met with Thomas and John at Durham simply to clarify past treaties and "the bounds of previous purchases made with their ancestors [which] were uncertain and needed to be settled again." The official provincial record indicates that the Delaware chiefs, though they did not recall the 1686 treaty made with William Penn, agreed that, "if it appeared that those Purchases were actually made, they must be honest and content with the Bounds and Limits thereof." In early 1735, Nutimus and Tishcohan met with Logan at Pennsbury to confirm their boundaries but found to their surprise that the Forks of the Delaware had been added to the proprietary claims. Teedyuscung, who arrived with his two uncles, remembered both meetings with disgust. He noted that the Delawares had never been "paid for the Lands they agreed to sell" at the 1686 treaty conference. As for conceding the land that they now occupied, Teedyuscung and his uncles refused. Logan, however, bullied the Delaware chiefs, insisting that the land belonged to the English and threatened to cut off trade. The Delawares tried to appeal to the Six Nations for support on their position, but, instead of aiding them, the Iroquois joined forces with Logan to assure that their own political needs were met.[25]

---

the Delaware and Shawanese Indians, 22; Michael N. McConnell, "Pisquetomen and Tamaqua: Mediating Peace in the Ohio Valley," in Grumet, ed., *Northeastern Indian Lives,* 277; McConnell, *A Country Between: The Upper Ohio Valley and Its Peoples, 1724–1774* (Lincoln, Nebr., 1992), 13.

25. Jennings, *Ambiguous Iroquois Empire,* 312–313; Logan to John Penn, Dec. 6, 1727, Copy of the proprietors' journey to Durham, Oct. 7, 1734, Penn Papers, Official Cor-

FIGURE 3. *Tishcohan, Delaware Leader.* By Gustavus Hesselius. 1735. Courtesy, The Historical Society of Pennsylvania, Philadelphia [1834.1]. *Tishcohan, also known as Captain John, originally lived at the Forks of the Delaware on land that became Nazareth and Allentown. Under pressure from James Logan and the Six Nations, he, Nutimus, and other Delaware leaders signed the Walking Purchase deed of 1737, eventually ceding 500,000 acres of land to the Pennsylvania proprietors. Five years later, he petitioned the governor of Pennsylvania to set aside land for permanent Indian use.*

Contended memories can be powerful weapons, especially when wielded by powerful players. Just as nineteenth-century Scots-Irish evoked the tale of Hay's Spring to serve their needs of the moment, the Six Nations and the Pennsylvania proprietors together used their own versions of the past to create the fiction of Delaware subordination to dispossess Indians of land. The result of this alliance would be the Walking Purchase of 1737, which became the center of political unease in Pennsylvania, generating a number of land-based myths that would be revisited often over the next half-century. First, Iroquois claimed ownership of Pennsylvania territory based on the assertion that they had conquered the Susquehannocks in the late seventeenth century. Although there was no evidence of military conquest, the Six Nations thought that, by claiming control over Pennsylvania land, they could use it as leverage to maintain their authority over Delawares and their alliance with Pennsylvania. Over the preceding decades, the Iroquois had slowly become less relevant to Indian trade and politics in the region; control over land could restore their relative importance. Second, the proprietors turned to a questionable treaty that was supposed to have taken place in 1686 between William Penn and Indians living at the Forks of the Delaware. After Nutimus and Tishcohan had expressed skepticism at Pennsbury, in 1736 Logan produced the treaty deed, which vaguely described an intended cession of land that could be traversed in a day-and-a-half walk, and pressed the Iroquois to confirm the purchase. By October, the Iroquois had signed a deed releasing all land from the Delaware River to the Susquehanna, "from the mouth thereof as far Northward or up the Said River as that Ridge of Hills call'd the Tyoninhasachta or endless Mountains; Westward to the Setting of the Sun." The following year, Pennsylvania used the Iroquois deed to force Delaware leaders, including Nutimus and Tishcohan, to affirm and sign the "Walking Purchase Deed" at Philadelphia, for which they received an insignificant sum. Finally, the walk itself took place in September 1737 and encompassed far more land than could have been covered in the time allowed. According to Delawares and their supporters, the walk was exe-

---

respondence, I, 311, II, 243, HSP. Nutimus and Tishcohan had sold four square miles of land at Durham in 1726 to James Logan, who privately set up an iron forge. Perhaps the Penns used this earlier sale to convince the Delawares that they had promised to sell more. See Teedyuscung's speech at Easton, June 24, 1762, no. 105, Penn Papers, Indian Affairs, III, 1757–1772, HSP; Wallace, *King of the Delawares,* 21–24.

cuted in bad faith by hired men who had already marked off the "shortest and best course." They went at least thirty miles beyond the original boundary of earlier treaties, marking off five hundred thousand acres for concession to Pennsylvania.[26]

The Walking Purchase seemed to be a victory for English and Iroquois cooperative land policies. The Penns had acquired land for white settlement. The Iroquois, in turn, had established a political precedence for domination over "an unruly People" whom they hoped would acquiesce to them in the future. But political alliances also had their limits. The Iroquois were still deeply suspicious of Pennsylvania leaders, even as they worked to maintain ties. They knew that the balance of power could easily tip toward the colony. If they transferred all the land they claimed to control, they would eventually forfeit their political leverage. The Iroquois surmised that land had more value to the English than the goods worth three hundred pounds that they had received for the Walking Purchase. At a treaty in July 1742, after admonishing the Delawares for questioning their authority over land matters, the Onondaga speaker Canassatego turned to the Pennsylvania governor and exclaimed, "We know our Lands are now become more Valuable; the white People think we don't know their Value, but we are sensible that the Land is Everlasting, and the few

26. "Opinions regarding the Grant to William Trent," William Trent Papers, HSP; Richter, *Ordeal of the Longhouse,* 275; Jennings, *Ambiguous Iroquois Empire,* 322–323; [Thomson], *Alienation of the Delaware and Shawanese Indians,* 34, 42; Wapwallopen Historical Society, *A History of the Wapwallopen Region* (Nescopeck, Pa., 1964), 14; Copy of deed, Oct. 25, 1736, no. 40, Penn Papers, Indian Affairs, I, 1687–1753, HSP; Steel to Barefoot Brunsden, Aug. 16, 1737, Steel to Nicholas Scull, Aug. 27, 1737, Logan Family Papers, Misc. Vols., Steel's Letter Book, 1730–1741, XXXIX, 155, 157, HSP; Walking Purchase Deed, Aug. 25, 1737, *PA,* 1st Ser., I, 541; *MPCP,* VIII, 211. Nutimus, for instance, received the equivalent of forty-two dollars for his share of the Walking Purchase (Steel to proprietors, Nov. 28, 1737, Penn Papers, Official Correspondence, III, 63, HSP). One white man, John Knowles, recalled that the Indians "began to look sullen" as they came to the Forks of the Delaware the first day "and murmured that the Men walked so fast, and several Times that Afternoon called out, and said to them, You run; that's not fair, you was to walk" ([Thomson], *Alienation of the Delaware and Shawanese Indians,* 39–40). The proprietors hired men for the walk who had "Travelled and held out the best when they walked over the Land" before the date and told them "to chose the best Ground and Shortest way that can be found" (Steel to Solomon Jennings, Aug. 27, 1737, Steel to Timothy Smith, Aug. 27, 1737, Logan Family Papers, Misc. Vols., Steel's Letter Book, 1730–1741, XXXIX, 156, HSP).

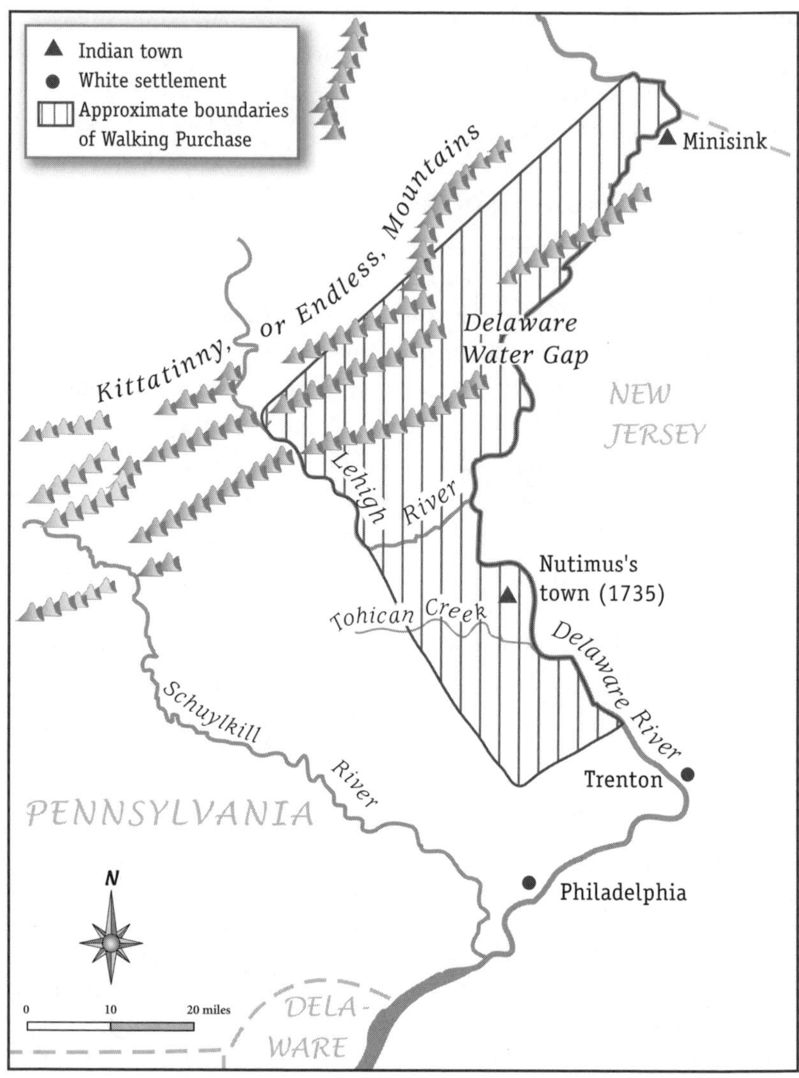

MAP 2. The Walking Purchase of 1737. *Drawn by Gerry Krieg*

Goods we receive for it are soon Worn out and Gone." Instead, the Six Nations warily laid out the conditions for further purchases: "For the future, we will sell no Lands but when Brother Onas is in the Country, and we will know before hand the Q[u]antity of Goods we are to receive." Rather than confirming their indelible power over Delawares, the Six Nations' ploy ultimately laid the groundwork for the English to take more Indian land; in essence, they had a foothold in Iroquoia.[27]

In 1742 and again in 1744, the Pennsylvania government and the Six Nations met to confirm the sale of Delaware territory, and together they demanded that the Delawares, whom James Logan simply called "those vile ones from the forks of Del[aware]," leave the region and "remove either over to Jersey again, or beyond the Hills." Asking Indians to leave and getting Indians to leave, however, were two different matters. For the next decade, Delawares remained at the Forks of the Delaware. Some, such as Nutimus, did move to the Susquehanna River valley, where he settled with three sons and their families at Wawhallopen and Nescopeck, just north of Shamokin. Those who remained, such as his nephew Teedyuscung, turned to new strategies for survival. The actions of Pennsylvania and the Six Nations had alienated Delawares politically. Indians, therefore, turned to the very communities with whom they competed for space to create new alliances. As English, Scots-Irish, and Germans ventured into the margins of empire during the early decades of the eighteenth century, they encountered Delawares, Nanticokes, and Shawnees who traveled through these landscapes. For better or worse, their futures lay along a common road.[28]

27. [Thomson], *Alienation of the Delaware and Shawanese Indians,* 45; Jennings, *Ambiguous Iroquois Empire,* 322–323; Richter, *Ordeal of the Longhouse,* 275; Witham Marshe, *Lancaster in 1744; Journal of the Treaty at Lancaster in 1744, with the Six Nations,* ed. William H. Egle (Lancaster, Pa., 1884), 4; *MPCP,* IV, 570.

28. Logan to Weiser, July 11, 1742, Logan to proprietors, July 12, 1742, Peters Papers, 1697–1845, I, pt. 2, HSP.

2

KINSHIP AND THE ECONOMICS OF EMPIRE

. . .

By the 1730s, new communities had sprouted along the Pennsylvania frontier. Complex relationships developed between these communities and with the colonial authorities to which they were loosely tied. Interactions among these groups were filled with contradictions. Whites sometimes displaced Indians, but they also shared space with them. Indians and whites became interdependent, but they also competed for material resources. Whether cooperating or competing, both groups needed to reach some kind of understanding about the boundaries of their relationships.

Trade became a particularly important point of contact. During the eighteenth century, native Americans and Euramericans actively participated in the transatlantic market economy. They established trade networks to exchange American furs for European goods and technology. Their common participation in and mutual dependence on a nascent capitalist economy often revealed disparate expectations and the power relations embedded in economic activities. Indians built ties of kinship, entailing hospitality, reciprocity, and gift exchange, that extended between communities. These kin alliances enabled individuals and families to fulfill mutual obligations and to obtain assistance during times of need. Euramericans, on the other hand, were beginning to separate economic exchange from personal relations and obligations. Although family ties and patronage were important factors in eighteenth-century colonial society, accumulating individual wealth and passing that wealth on through narrow channels of inheritance from father to son sometimes precluded the wider use of material goods for the community's benefit. Still, whites also recognized the close connection between economic obligations and kin relations, especially on the frontier, where families lived distant from town centers or urban areas and depended on kin and neighbors for assistance.[1]

For their own survival, then, Indians and whites, with comparable, if diverging, economic patterns, could and did create alliances with each other during the early eighteenth century. Although these associations were sometimes tension-filled and often self-serving, as long as the frontier remained relatively open Indians and whites found points of contact. Some whites, such as German Moravians, readily entered kinship connections with native Americans, forming new economic relations based on native precepts. Other whites participated in the fur trade or hired Indians to work for them, creating a sense of neighborliness. Native American women, in particular, negotiated these new community ties. Women held together Indian household economies and included nearby whites, especially other women, in their hospitality and customary kinship networks.

1. Portions of this chapter appear in Jane T. Merritt, "Cultural Encounters along a Gender Frontier: Mahican, Delaware, and German Women in Eighteenth-Century Pennsylvania," *Pennsylvania History*, LXVII (2000), 502–532. See Daniel H. Usner, *Indians, Settlers, and Slaves in a Frontier Exchange Economy: The Lower Mississippi Valley before 1783* (Chapel Hill, N.C., 1992), 6; Peter C. Mancall, *Valley of Opportunity: Economic Culture along the Upper Susquehanna, 1700–1800* (Ithaca, N.Y., 1991), xii. James A. Henretta, "Families and Farms: *Mentalité* in Pre-Industrial America," *William and Mary Quarterly*, 3d Ser., XXXV (1978), 3–32, contends that the market economy and the emergence of capitalism came to rural Pennsylvania in the early nineteenth century rather than the eighteenth century, sentimentalizing the subsistence activity and communal nature of farmers as opposed to the acquisitive, protocapitalist behavior of merchants and manufacturers. See also Allan Kulikoff, "The Transition to Capitalism in Rural America," *WMQ*, 3d Ser., XLVI (1989), 120–144; Christopher Clark, *The Roots of Rural Capitalism: Western Massachusetts, 1780–1860* (Ithaca, N.Y., 1990); and James A. Henretta, *The Origins of American Capitalism: Collected Essays* (Boston, 1991). I take it as a given that most colonists, whether merchant or farmer, engaged in some part of existing commercial markets as producers, investors, or consumers. Instead of being distinctively different, frontier dwellers and eastern merchants found common ground for economic activity. For a challenge to Henretta, see Winifred Barr Rothenberg, *From Market-Places to a Market Economy: The Transformation of Rural Massachusetts, 1750–1850* (Chicago, 1992). For a good critique of the debate as a whole, see Naomi R. Lamoreaux, "Accounting for Capitalism in Early American History: Farmers, Merchants, Manufacturers, and Their Economic Worlds" (paper presented at the annual conference of the Society for Historians of the Early American Republic, Lexington, Ky., July 15–18, 1999). See, generally, Stephen Gudeman, *Economics as Culture: Models and Metaphors of Livelihood* (London, 1986).

As they made daily decisions about household organization, production, and consumption, Indian women exercised an "adaptive capacity" that typified native response to the increasing presence of white settlers.[2]

Although kinship alliances brought economic opportunity to both Indians and whites, participation in the fur trade and the transatlantic market system also had profound effects on Indian societies. Neighborliness did not preclude conflict. The new social and economic networks that brought Indians and whites into contact also rearranged the power dynamics between them, created new possibilities for misunderstanding, and even changed the physical world. White traders sometimes precipitated conflict. They provided goods to Indians on credit at the beginning of the hunting season, then undervalued furs at the end, extracting the remaining debt from future sales. Sometimes they illegally sold alcohol to Indians or used it to cheat hunters of their skins. Yet Indian hunters also contributed to the imbalances in their communities. Young men placed great value on British trade goods and the personal status certain items brought and killed increasing numbers of beaver and deer to acquire more. They demanded alcohol for consumption in social and ceremonial occasions, then struggled with the profound effects of drunkenness on their social relations. Certainly, by the mid-eighteenth century, the emphasis in economic exchange for Indians had begun to shift from the reproduction of social relations to the production of wealth.[3]

As long as alliances and the conflicts they generated were between individual trade partners or communities, Indians and whites managed to find mutually acceptable ways of dealing with the potentially violent consequences of misunderstanding, especially during the early decades of the

2. Kathleen M. Brown, "The Anglo-Algonquian Gender Frontier," in Nancy Shoemaker, ed., *Negotiators of Change: Historical Perspectives on Native American Women* (New York, 1995), 30.

3. Mancall, *Valley of Opportunity,* xiii–xiv, 54–55; Richard White, *The Middle Ground: Indians, Empires, and Republics in the Great Lakes Region, 1650–1815* (New York, 1991), 139; White, *The Roots of Dependency: Subsistence, Environment, and Social Change among the Choctaws, Pawnees, and Navajos* (Lincoln, Nebr., 1983), 146; Usner, *Indians, Settlers, and Slaves,* 27; Francis Jennings, "The Indian Trade of the Susquehanna Valley," in APS, *Proceedings,* CX (Philadelphia, 1966), 415–416; Eric Hinderaker, *Elusive Empires: Constructing Colonialism in the Ohio Valley, 1673–1800* (New York, 1997), 46. Carol Devens, *Countering Colonization: Native American Women and Great Lakes Missions, 1630–1900* (Berkeley, Calif., 1992), 15–17, contends that the shift to a market economy began to unbalance the equity between men and women in native societies.

eighteenth century. Euramericans even learned Indian protocol, using kinship terms and condolence ceremonies to compensate for their sometimes aggressive behavior. But the obligations of kinship did not always translate well to the imperial market, where broader political and economic alliances between nations shaped the nature of economic exchange. By the 1740s and 1750s, Pennsylvania expanded its boundaries and sphere of interest into the Ohio Valley, competing with the French for access to trade. Even though the Pennsylvania government used kinship terms and gift exchange to cement economic agreements with Ohio Indians, they did not recognize the need for reciprocity to build interdependent networks. Instead, the provincial government used Indians' growing economic dependence as a tool of empire to force political capitulation and cession of western lands.

Indians did not ignore the failure of Euramericans to understand the obligations of social and economic relations in a broader context. As colonial powers tried to turn Indian dependence to their own advantage, new Indian leaders emerged in opposition. Young warriors and hunters, who had come to power and had formed new bonds between Shawnee, Delaware, and Iroquois communities in Ohio, kept Pennsylvania officials at arm's length. They adeptly played European nations against each other, searching for the best trade prices and terms for political alliance. Even older Indian leaders, who had remained with their people on the Susquehanna River, mustered their rhetorical skills to manipulate the balance of power in trade. They denounced whites as hypocrites, attempting to shame them into fulfilling their obligations to Indian partners. As long as the frontier remained a relatively inclusive site of negotiated relationships that drew on metaphoric, if not actual, kinship networks to maintain accord, Indians held the balance of power over local economies. At midcentury, the equilibrium began to shift. Increasingly, colonial authorities controlled land, Indian access to markets, and, by consequence, their means of existence, further raising the possibility of open war.

To native Americans in the eighteenth century, kinship relationships were open for interpretation and continually renegotiated and renewed. They entailed a combination of male and female authority that was exercised in specific arenas and over specific people. Since Mahicans and Delawares in Pennsylvania lived in matrilineal societies, grandmothers, mothers, aunts, and sisters dominated social relations within households and communities. They owned their houses, managed material and agricultural resources, and passed on clan affiliation—the basis of kinship identity—to their children. Within these matrifocal communities, the relationship between siblings was most important to sustaining native households. Sisters and their families often lived together and shared the responsibilities of food procurement and preparation and child care. Marriage tended to be a flexible institution, where the husband and wife both had the freedom to leave the other if dissatisfied, and it did not concern the legal rights that men had over women and the children they bore. A child's most important family relationship was thus to the mother and her clan, especially the mother's sisters and brothers, who acted as "little mothers" or "little fathers."[4]

Although women had authority within households and clans, at other levels of social organization—the village, the district, and the tribe—men still wielded political power. Yet only together, through consensus, could women and men create and sustain communities. The relationship between sister and brother was far more important than between wife and husband. Consequently, brothers usually had authority over decisions affecting the political life of the family, and their sisters' sons generally succeeded them to positions of power. The agony over Sassoonan's successor indicates the significance of this lateral descent of authority. In June 1745, Moravians noted the Delaware chief's concern about who would take his place as leader. "His sister's sons are either dead or worthless," wrote August Gottlieb (Joseph) Spangenberg, the leader of the Moravian commu-

4. Robert Steven Grumet, "Sunksquaws, Shamans, and Tradeswomen: Middle Atlantic Coastal Algonkian Women during the Seventeenth and Eighteenth Centuries," in Mona Etienne and Eleanor Leacock, eds., *Women and Colonization: Anthropological Perspectives* (New York, 1980), 46; Ives Goddard, "Delaware," and William N. Fenton, "Northern Iroquoian Culture Patterns," both in William C. Sturtevant, gen. ed., *Handbook of North American Indians,* XV, Bruce G. Trigger, ed., *Northeast* (Washington, D.C., 1978), 225, 312; Paul A. W. Wallace, *Indians in Pennsylvania* (1961; reprint, Harrisburg, Pa., 1975), 55. Mahicans and Delawares ordered their households in much the same way as Iroquois did. See Elisabeth Tooker, "Women in Iroquois Society," in Michael K. Foster, Jack Campisi, and Marianne Mithun, eds., *Extending the Rafters: Interdisciplinary Approaches to Iroquoian Studies* (Albany, N.Y., 1984), 109–114; J. N. B. Hewitt, "Status of Woman in Iroquois Polity before 1784," in *Annual Report of the Board of Regents of the Smithsonian Institution Showing the Operations, Expenditures, and Condition of the Institution for the Year Ending June 30, 1932* (Washington, D.C., 1933), 475–488.

nity at Bethlehem, "hence it is not known on whom the Kingdom will descend." Women and men had separate jurisdictions, just as they had separate social roles. Thus, the balance of power in native communities most likely rested on subtle tensions between female clan lineages and male political needs. Potential for conflict between the two was always present and probably expanded as interactions with white immigrants multiplied.[5]

Kinship in Pennsylvania native communities included more than those people born or married into a family. Indians recognized the importance of turning strangers into "either actual or symbolic kinspeople" to strengthen political alliances or increase access to available resources. During the first half of the eighteenth century, Pennsylvania Indians created kinship networks that crossed ethnic and racial boundaries. Indians often adopted white or other native captives and refugees into their families to replenish community populations. Captives most often replaced specific individuals who had died in war or by disease. Robert Eastburn noted that, when he met his new family, "the Indians appeared very sad, and my Mother began to cry, and continued crying aloud for some Time, and then dried up her Tears, and received me for her Son." James Smith, taken in 1755 by Caughnewagas, learned that he had been "adopted into a great family, and now received with great seriousness and solemnity in the room and place of a great man." "After what has passed this day," they told him, "you are now one of us by an old strong law and custom." The first lessons that many white captives learned after running the gauntlet, being washed of their "white blood," or being reclothed and marked as

5. John W. Jordan, ed., "Spangenberg's Notes of Travel to Onondaga in 1745," *Pennsylvania Magazine of History and Biography,* II (1878), 430; [Richard Smith and Richard Wells], "Notes of a Tour to the Head of Susquehannah in the Year 1769," June 3, 1769, folder 1, Pierre Eugene Du Simitiere Papers, Library Company of Philadelphia; Grumet, "Sunksquaws, Shamans, and Tradeswomen," in Etienne and Leacock, eds., *Women and Colonization,* 30. Regula Trenkwalder Schönenberger, *Lenape Women, Matriliny, and the Colonial Encounter: Resistance and Erosion of Power (c. 1600–1876): An Excursus in Feminist Anthropology* (Bern, Switzerland, 1991), 16, 59–60, and Devens, *Countering Colonization,* 13, imply that a benign egalitarianism existed between men and women. Consensus politics should not be confused with idealized notions of democracy. Native groups were not always egalitarian. There were the enslaved and other nonpersons who did not participate in decision making. Threats of revenge, retaliation by witchcraft, or public ostracism could be used effectively to manipulate consensus.

Indians concerned kinship and their relative position in a native family. Hugh Gibson's adoptive Delaware brother, Pisquetomen, a nephew of Sassoonan, addressed him the first day: "'I am your brother,' and pointing to one after another in the company, added, 'This is your brother, that is your brother, this is your cousin, that is your cousin, and all these are your friends.'"[6]

Although captive adults at times rejected the offer of new family relations, maintaining a clear distinction between themselves and the Indians who adopted them, children easily absorbed the lessons of kinship. Some of these children, returned to white communities at the end of the Seven Years' War, could no longer speak the language of their original homes. In August 1762, when Indians returned five boys and two girls to Lancaster, Pennsylvania, the clerk keeping records simply noted: "Children's names unknown, as they cannot speak English, or give any account from whence they were taken." The returned captives often could not remember where they had been born, and many were reluctant to leave their Indian families. Adolescents who had been part of native communities for five or ten years had not just received different names, such as "Nosewelamh," "Wapatenequa," or "Neculissika," and replaced native family members; by learning new languages, habits, and traditions from their adoptive families, these young people had become Indians.[7]

6. White, *Middle Ground,* 15; Robert Eastburn, *A Faithful Narrative of the Many Dangers and Sufferings, as Well as Wonderful Deliverances of Robert Eastburn, during His Late Captivity among the Indians . . .* (Philadelphia, 1758), 19, 22; "An Account of the Captivity of Hugh Gibson among the Delaware Indians of the Big Beaver and the Muskingum, from the Latter Part of July 1756, to the Beginning of April, 1759," Massachusetts Historical Society, *Collections,* 3d Ser., VI (Boston, 1837), 143; James Smith, *An Account of the Remarkable Occurrences in the Life and Travels of Col. James Smith, during His Captivity with the Indians, in the Years 1755, '56, '57, '58, and '59,* ed. William M. Darlington (1799; reprint, Cincinnati, Ohio, 1870), 16; Daniel K. Richter, *The Ordeal of the Longhouse: The Peoples of the Iroquois League in the Era of European Colonization* (Chapel Hill, N.C., 1992), 65–66; Francis Jennings, *The Ambiguous Iroquois Empire: The Covenant Chain Confederation of Indian Tribes with English Colonies from Its Beginnings to the Lancaster Treaty of 1744* (New York, 1984), 95. By the late seventeenth century, non-Iroquois people made up nearly two-thirds of some Iroquois villages in western New York. See also John McCullough, "Preliminary Draft of Captivity Narrative," in *A Selection . . . of Outrages Committed by the Indians* (Carlisle, Pa., 1808), n.p., microfilm, Pennsylvania State Archives, Harrisburg; [Jean Lowry], *A Journal of the Captivity of Jean Lowry and Her Children . . .* (Philadelphia, 1760), 11.

7. *MPCP,* VIII, 148, 750; McCullough, "Preliminary Draft of Captivity Narrative,"

For Indians, their position within and affinity to a kinship group depended largely on their circumstances, which might change drastically over the course of their life. They often received a new name to mark these changes. Names had power and could set the course of one's future or refashion an individual into another person. Most males received at least two names during their lifetime. Among the Delawares, for instance, a father would give a child a name at age six or seven, saying "it has been suggested to him in a dream." The family performed a ceremony of song and sacrifice that they repeated when the person received another name as an adult. These names sometimes described great feats, bestowed honor, or indicated specific social roles for the recipients. The Iroquois attached great power to names, which went beyond simple titles and could designate a role within the clan or kin group that different individuals in succession might fulfill. In this way, names of honor passed from generation to generation, bringing with them particular responsibilities.[8]

What did it mean, then, when Indians and whites renamed one another? Perhaps, as Greg Dening suggests of encounters between Pacific Island natives and the English in the nineteenth century, accepting a new identity, at least in the guise of a name, could be read as "the greatest gift" that Indians and whites could give each other, "to let them make him

---

in *A Selection . . . of Outrages,* Pa. State Arch. See also Quaker Journal (attributed to Susanna Lightfoot), Easton, Pa., 1761, 7–8, William L. Clements Library, University of Michigan, Ann Arbor; George Croghan to General Thomas Gage, May 12, 1765, enclosure, General Thomas Gage Papers, American Ser., XXXVI, Clements Library; John W. Jordan, ed., "Journal of James Kenny, 1761–1763," *PMHB,* XXXVII (1913), 178.

8. George Henry Loskiel, *History of the Mission of the United Brethren among the Indians in North America,* trans. Christian Ignatius La Trobe (London, 1794), pt. 1, 62. Delaware language suggests the ease in which multiple names and social roles could be accepted by individuals. According to John Heckewelder, personal identifiers in Unami, such as "I am," did not refer to an interior identity; it indicated "I am the body of a man" or "my body is a Lenape." See John Heckewelder to Peter Du Ponceau, Apr. 8, 1819, John Heckewelder Letters, 1816–1822, APS. See also Frank G. Speck, *The Tutelo Spirit Adoption Ceremony: Reclothing the Living in the Name of the Dead* (Harrisburg, Pa., 1942), 75; C. A. Weslager, "Delaware Indian Name Giving and Modern Practice," in Herbert C. Kraft, ed., *A Delaware Indian Symposium,* Anthropological Series No. 4 (Harrisburg, Pa., 1974), 137–138; Richard White, "'Although I am dead, I am not entirely dead. I have left a second of myself': Constructing Self and Persons on the Middle Ground of Early America," in Ronald Hoffman, Mechal Sobel, and Fredrika J. Teute, eds., *Through a Glass Darkly: Reflections on Personal Identity in Early America* (Chapel Hill, N.C., 1997), 409–411.

like themselves." Like adoption, renaming played a role in creating kinship between Indians and whites, although often in metaphoric, rather than literal, terms. Indians renamed whites to help them feel welcome while living in native society. In June 1745, when Moravian missionaries traveled to Onondaga, the Iroquois gave them Mohawk names, since, according to August Gottlieb Spangenberg, "ours were too difficult for them to pronounce." Spangenberg became *T'gerhitonti,* or "a row of trees"; Joseph Bull was called *Hajingonis,* "one who twists tobacco"; and David Zeisberger became known as *Ganousseracheri,* translated as "on the pumpkin." In this case, renaming was no mere matter of phonetics. Spangenberg noted in his diary that, "if [the Iroquois] give someone a name, then they give him their kinship as they did to us." For their part, the Moravians seemed willing to explore the deeper meanings of this relationship. Bishop John Christopher Frederick Cammerhoff, on a journey to Onondaga in June 1750, mused while at a Cayuga town on the upper Susquehanna: "My Indian name being Gallichwio in the Gajuka [Cayuga] language, I sometimes felt like saying to myself: I am dwelling among my own people, and when I shall be able to say that in its true meaning, my heart will rejoice." Conversely, Euramericans sometimes conferred names on Indians both formally and informally, and, by most accounts, native Americans accepted the names. A Delaware man, Depaakhossi, or "a belt of Wampum that is wide enough," was also called Joseph Growden by the English after a white lawyer who had successfully defended an Indian woman facing the death penalty. Quaker trader James Kenny, upon meeting a Delaware at Pittsburgh, noted that he "seemed very good Natur'd and having no English Name I gave him my Name which he said he would keep."[9]

9. Greg Dening, *Mr Bligh's Bad Language: Passion, Power, and Theatre on the Bounty* (Cambridge, 1992), 258; W[illia]m M. Beauchamp, ed., *Moravian Journals Relating to Central New York, 1745–66* (Syracuse, N.Y., 1916), 10–11, 35; "Wenn sie jemanden Nahmen geben, so geben Sie ihm gemeinigl. einen uns ihre Freundschafft"; see Spangenberg travel diary, June 10, 1745, *Moravian Records,* reel 30, box 223, folder 7, item 1; Bethlehem Register, Nov. 15/26, "Bethlehemisches Kirchen=Buch," I, 1742–1756, 99, Moravian Archives, Bethlehem, Pa.; Jordan, ed., "Journal of James Kenny," *PMHB,* XXXVII (1913), 13. Depaakhossi was later baptized by the Moravians and received yet another name, Christian Renatus. Names given to Indians, which were used by both whites and Indians, often described a tribe, residential location, or a personal characteristic, such as Delaware George, Shamokin Daniel, Seneca George,

Perhaps not as innocuous and "good Natur'd" as Kenny suggests, renaming people, like renaming the landscape, still entailed assumptions of dominance—that one had the power to rename another. Indians and whites used names to bind each other in kinship but also to manipulate each other politically. In August 1755, Lieutenant Governor Robert Hunter Morris told Kanuksusy, "the son of old Allaguipas," that "he was going to give him an English name." Presenting a string of wampum, Morris said, "I do in the most solemn manner adopt you by the name of Newcastle, and order you to be called hereafter by that name which I have given you, because in 1701 I am informed that your parents presented you to the late Mr. William Penn at Newcastle." With that name, Morris once more reminded Pennsylvania Indians of their connection to the memory of a Euramerican past, hoping that their fondness for the former proprietor would bind them to the present provincial administration. Conversely, that same loyalty to William Penn had created another potent name, a native one. Delawares called Pennsylvania's founder *Miquon,* most often rendered by the Iroquois term *Onas,* meaning "feather" or "pen." Beyond representing one person, the name denoted the responsibilities attached to that position of power, and Indians conferred the name to others after Penn's death, but only if they proved publicly worthy of the honor. In 1756, Scarouyady, an Oneida representative of the Ohio Indians visiting Philadelphia, collectively called the eighteenth-century Quakers who supported Indian rights Onas, likening them to William Penn and "the first settlers." He further stressed that, since Penn's death, no provincial governor had lived up to the name. In essence, Indians attached ideal characteristics to a title that would benefit their political goals; they then used it to coerce Euramericans to act by those ideals.[10]

Honest John, or Cut-finger Peter. The term *Freundschafft* has several implications in both the German records and as a translation of the Iroquois concept. Though it can be translated as "friendship," in early modern Germany *Freunde* or *Freundshaft* more often indicated people "who were related to an individual through marriage." See David Warren Sabean, *Power in the Blood: Popular Culture and Village Discourse in Early Modern Germany* (Cambridge, 1984), 31. The Moravians most often used the term in the latter sense.

Unless otherwise noted, all translations from the German are mine.

10. *MPCP,* VI, 588–589; Council at Israel Pemberton's, Apr. 23, 1756, Historical Society Collection, Miscellaneous Manuscripts, 1661–1931, Indians, HSP; Jennings, *Ambiguous Iroquois Empire,* 231 n. 19. James H. Merrell, *Into the American Woods: Negotia-*

The exchange of names during the first half of the eighteenth century indicated that Indians and whites wished to draw each other into alliances. Yet Indians and whites sometimes had problems reaching a mutually understood definition of those relationships and understanding their implications. Indians expected kinfolk to participate in the customary obligations of hospitality, reciprocity, and gift exchange. In social, economic, or political interactions, Indians extended hospitality to family members, to neighbors, or even to nonhostile strangers who passed through a village, and they expected the same hospitality in return. "They count it a most sacred duty, from which no one is exempted," remarked one Moravian writer. "Whoever refuses relief to any one, commits a grievous offence, and not only makes himself detested and abhorred by all, but liable to revenge from the offended person." Expectations of hospitality and reciprocity, like the exchange of names, expanded kinship networks, including intercommunity clan obligations, and assured that individuals could find material support among a variety of households as they worked or traveled abroad.[11]

Indians, therefore, insisted that hospitality, reciprocity, and gift exchange be part of their interactions with white neighbors and made these obligations central to the fur trade and their participation in the market economy of Pennsylvania. By the 1730s, trade between Indian communities on the Susquehanna and white communities to the east was frequent and brisk. In the early seventeenth century, Captain John Smith had already noticed a proliferation of European hatchets, knives, and pieces of iron among the Susquehannocks as he explored the upper Chesapeake Bay. Only in the early eighteenth century did French and English traders establish permanent posts along the Susquehanna River and in the Ohio Valley. At the turn of the eighteenth century, Conestoga was a major cen-

---

tors on the Pennsylvania Frontier (New York, 1999), 66, indicates that Newcastle had been named several times by white colonists. In Virginia, he went by "Colo Fairfax," whereas the Iroquois gave him a second name, Ah Knoyis. See Mary Jo Maynes et al., eds., "Introduction: Toward a Comparative History of Gender, Kinship, and Power," in Maynes et al., eds., *Gender, Kinship, Power: A Comparative and Interdisciplinary History* (New York, 1996), 14.

11. Loskiel, *History of the Mission,* trans. La Trobe, pt. 1, 15. See also Mancall, *Valley of Opportunity,* 51–53; John Phillip Reid, *A Law of Blood: The Primitive Law of the Cherokee Nation* (New York, 1970), 47–48.

ter for economic exchange in Pennsylvania, but by 1718 Shamokin had eclipsed other towns as the preferred site for trade. At these crossroads, Indians controlled the course of trade. Native hunters were not interested in merely accumulating goods. Instead, they created an exchange economy that enhanced customary social structures and hierarchies. Indians hoped to protect their access to European goods by making white traders dependent on them for food, transportation, shelter, and other services. In return, they expected traders to offer them gifts, negotiate partnerships, and keep the cost of trade items at a reasonable and constant level. Once their basic needs were met, gift exchange provided hunters the opportunity to gain status within their own communities. Moreover, Indians used European trade goods in ways that whites did not always intend. Often, native Americans adapted them for their own purposes and tastes. As consumers, Indians had immense influence over the kinds of commodities that traders offered, and they demanded both utilitarian and luxury items. They traded for glass beads, vermilion paint, Jew's harps, brass rings, and other decorative material alongside flints, knives, tomahawks, and kettles. Everyday items were sometimes reshaped for new uses. Indians cut brass kettles into pieces to decorate their clothing and bodies and often drilled holes in British coins to make ornaments rather than use them to purchase English goods.[12]

Some individual white traders learned the protocol of Indian alliances and became part of the growing network of trade and settlement, if only to assure their own economic success. In about 1705, John Harris established a post on the Susquehanna River near the mouth of Paxtang Creek, where he traded with Shawnees and other native inhabitants. By the 1720s, experienced men, such as "expatriate Canadians" James Le Tort, Martin

12. Barry C. Kent, *Susquehanna's Indians*, Anthropological Series No. 6 (Harrisburg, Pa., 1984), 26, 279; Jennings, "The Indian Trade of the Susquehanna Valley," in APS, *Procs.*, CX (1966), 409–411; Arthur J. Ray and Donald B. Freeman, *"Give Us Good Measure": An Economic Analysis of Relations between the Indians and the Hudson's Bay Company before 1763* (Toronto, 1978), 223, 225–226; Richter, *Ordeal of the Longhouse*, 84; Christopher L. Miller and George R. Hamell, "A New Perspective on Indian-White Contact: Cultural Symbols and Colonial Trade," *Journal of American History*, LXXIII (1986–1987), 313–316; Thomas McKee to Edward Shippen, Oct. 6, 1743, Shippen Family Papers, I, HSP; Journal, 1763–1766, Records of the Proprietary Government, Commissioners of Indian Trade Accounts, 1758–1766, RG-21, microfilm 0597, reel 1, Pennsylvania State Archives, Harrisburg.

FIGURE 4. New Sweden. *From Tomas Campanius Holm,* Kort beskrifning om provincien Nya Swerige uti America: som nu förtjden af the Engelske kallas Pensylvania *(Stockholm, 1702). Courtesy, The Library Company of Philadelphia. Regular trade between mid-Atlantic Indians and Europeans began in 1638, when the New Sweden Company established a trading post at Fort Christina in Delaware. They set a precedent for relatively peaceful economic interactions with New Jersey and Pennsylvania natives.*

Chartier, and his half-Shawnee son, Peter, dominated the fur trade in the Susquehanna region, but they also had turned their attention west, extending their network of trade to the Ohio Valley. They had connections to Pennsylvania officials that helped them to find commercial outlets for furs and skins. Le Tort and Chartier, for example, were deeply indebted to James Logan, who endeavored to control the economic life of the colony as much as the political life. Financed by Philadelphia mercantile firms or wealthy elites of eastern Pennsylvania, English traders, such as Edmund Cartlidge, Jonas Davenport, John Harris, George Gabriel, and Thomas McKee, were able to "goe 3 or 400 Miles back in the woods to trade with the Indians." These traders were often considered "as wild as some of the most savage Indians, amongst whom they trade for skins." Still, their success as traders more often rested upon a willingness to take risks and live among their best customers, gaining the Indians' trust, friendship, and even kinship. Blood relations, for example, gave Peter Chartier an advantage, for he knew "the Shawanise Tongue Very perfectt and [was] well Looktt upon among them."[13]

Although crucial to the selection and adoption of captives as new family members, women also played an important role in creating links between individual traders and Indian communities. Through marriage, a native woman offered a white man access to resources and the skills and support of her clan. A Shawnee woman had married Thomas McKee, who by the 1740s built a trading post on the Susquehanna River below Shamokin. Although she spoke "but little English," she helped him to establish his reputation among her people and to maintain "a brisk trade with the Allegheny Country." She also kept up a household that became a hub for Indian and white travelers. According to Moravians, she received them "with much kindness and hospitality."[14]

13. Edmund Cartlidge to Gov. Patrick Gordon, May 14, 1732, *PA,* 1st Ser., I, 328; Shippen to William Cam, Dec. 4, 1733, Shippen Family Papers, box I, APS; Witham Marshe, *Lancaster in 1744; Journal of the Treaty at Lancaster in 1744, with the Six Nations,* ed. William H. Egle (Lancaster, Pa., 1884), 15; Charles A. Hanna, *The Wilderness Trail; or, The Ventures and Adventures of the Pennsylvania Traders on the Allegheny Path* (New York, 1911), 176. French trader James Le Tort lived with the Shawnees at Paxtang by 1707 and traded as far west as the Alleghenies and in Shamokin (John H. Carter, *Early Events in the Susquehanna Valley . . .* [Millville, Pa., 1981], 128). By the mid-1720s, Le Tort, Chartier, and Cartlidge were indebted to Logan for £300–650 each (Hinderaker, *Elusive Empires,* 22–25). See also Michael N. McConnell, *A Country Between: The Upper Ohio Valley and Its Peoples, 1724–1774* (Lincoln, Nebr., 1992), 37–38.

14. John W. Jordan, ed., "Bishop J. C. F. Cammerhoff's Narrative of a Journey to Shamokin, Penna., in the Winter of 1748," *PMHB,* XXIX (1905), 169. McKee's wife might have been a white woman raised by a Shawnee family, but she was always identified as Shawnee by the sources. More privately, the Moravians suspected that McKee might have beat his wife. "John sagte: er hätte gehört, daß Thomas [McKee] seine Frau geschlagen hätte, er müste gehe u. zustehen obs wahr sey"; see Shamokin diary, Feb. 8, 1750, *Moravian Records,* reel 6, box 121, folder 5, item 2.

Beyond their ability to establish new alliances through marriage, native women participated in all aspects of economic exchange in Pennsylvania. Sometimes they managed land and established their own trade relationships with whites. James Le Tort, who lived in the Susquehanna Valley during the first decade of the eighteenth century, had an Indian "Land Lady at the Cannois" who owed him one fox skin for a looking glass. Besides McKee's wife, we know that Sassoonan's wife, Sheeckehnichan, actively traded, doing business with James Logan in the 1720s. At Shamokin in September 1745, Madame Montour, a French-Huron interpreter and cultural broker, lodged and entertained visiting kin, including her sister's daughter, who had come nearly four hundred miles from the Allegheny River on her way to Philadelphia to sell deer skins, "with which they have loaded 10 Horses." As fur processors and traders, women made most of the decisions about household consumption. A man often left deer skins and furs in the hands of his wife, "who sells or barters them away to the best advantage for such necessaries as are wanted in the family; not forgetting to supply her husband with what he stands in need of." They incorporated innovative technologies into their societies, such as labor-saving devices—needles, awls, cloth, and kettles—that had an impact on the daily lives of their communities. As agents of change, native women expanded their role as household provider into one of active participant in the Atlantic market economy. By the mid-eighteenth century, they used their own labor and production to regain a degree of independence that had been curtailed by the growing importance of male hunting in the fur trade.[15]

15. "Petition and List of Indian Debts Kept by James LeTort," 1704, no. 4, Logan Family Papers, 1664–1871, XI, Indian Affairs, HSP; Albright Gravenor Zimmerman, "The Indian Trade of Colonial Pennsylvania" (Ph.D. diss., University of Delaware, 1966), 85; Martin Mack's travel diary, Sept. 19, 1745, *Moravian Records*, reel 28, box 217, folder 12B, item 1; Merrell, *Into the American Woods*, 54–55; John Heckewelder, *History, Manners, and Customs of the Indian Nations, Who Once Inhabited Pennsylvania and the Neighbouring States*, rev. ed., ed. William C. Reichel (1876; facsimile reprint, Bowie, Md., 1990), 158; Jordan, ed., "Cammerhoff's Narrative," *PMHB*, XXIX (1905), 168. Claudio Saunt, "'Domestick . . . Quiet being broke': Gender Conflict among Creek Indians in the Eighteenth Century," in Andrew R. L. Cayton and Fredrika J. Teute, eds., *Contact Points: American Frontiers from the Mohawk Valley to the Mississippi, 1750–1830* (Chapel Hill, N.C., 1998), 172, examines the effects of the new economy on gender roles in the late eighteenth and early nineteenth century. Creek women had lost their importance within the male-dominated fur trade but adapted an entrepreneurial spirit to recapture their economic independence.

Women might have controlled the economic life of households, but the best-documented economic exchanges occurred between men and generated a different dynamic. Individual white traders with established posts could work within native kinship alliances, especially if tied by marriage to native families. When hunters and traders came into contact, however, most often in the woods or at an Indian's hunting cabin, they had to negotiate more temporary partnerships and test the boundaries of their relationships. But these encounters also tested the ability of colonial leaders to control the behavior of frontier inhabitants. Commercial exchange, often fraught with tension, could just as easily lead to violence, prompting Indians and whites to search for common ways to administer justice.

Alcohol often had a featured role in trade, affecting the dynamics between Indian and white men. Mutual drinking cemented trade alliances, indicated goodwill, or celebrated success at trading posts or treaty negotiations. Although a sense of initial trust made these encounters possible, alcohol could quickly turn amity into enmity. Ghesaont, speaking for the Iroquois in July 1721, complained to governor William Keith of Pennsylvania that traders carrying goods up the Susquehanna River treated their young warriors badly: they "use them with ill Language, and call them Dogs, etc. They take this unkindly, because Dogs have no Sense of understanding: whereas they are men, and think that their Brothers should not compare them to such Creatures." Finally, Ghesaont's young warriors decided to retaliate for the insults: "They seiz'd a Cag of Liquor, and run away with it." The rough camaraderie between cultures, heightened by alcohol, often hung on a thin line over an abyss of stronger emotions. Eating, laughing, drinking, backslapping might shift suddenly into more ambiguous actions, as it did on a quiet evening in September 1727 at Snaketown, forty miles above Conestoga, when some white traders and Indians "were drinking near the House of said [John] Burt, who was Si[ng]ing and dancing with the indians after their manner." Indians were imitating traders, drinking hard, and, in exchange, traders danced like Indians. At what point did the scene change? Was it an elbow in a face during a misstepped antic? Or perhaps a hat grabbed in jest off a trader's head? Was it a fresh insult or brooding, pent-up anger given focus by the alcohol? Whereas Ghesaont's warriors had merely exchanged curses with Pennsylvania traders before taking their keg, John Burt chose a more direct approach. He "fill'd his hands with his own Dung and threw it among the Indians." A fight broke out, and Thomas Wright, another trader, was killed.[16]

Indian leaders hoped to prevent violent fraternization between white traders and Indian hunters, but their attempts to control the liquor trade were complicated by the growing importance of alcohol to Indian culture and their economy. Seen as a powerful force that could control an individual's will, alcohol, at times, became an agent for dream visions and spiritual powers. By the eighteenth century, a variety of native rituals involved alcohol consumption. Iroquois women petitioned William Johnson in the 1750s for rum "for Christenings, Weddings, Dreams, Burials etc." Native women, in particular, profited greatly from the alcohol trade. With the encouragement of town leaders, they exchanged goods for liquor in white communities and brought alcohol home to sell. In August 1731, Delaware chief Sassoonan asked the Pennsylvania government whether "some Rum may be lodged at Tulpyhockin and Pextan, to be sold to them, that their Women may not have too long a way to fetch it." Once home, women sold liquor to Indian hunters, who, for a drink, might trade "even their rifles on which they depend for subsistence." Its ceremonial and economic importance notwithstanding, Indians complained of increasing sales and use of liquor in their towns and turned to the Pennsylvania government to help regulate liquor at the seller's end. In 1734, Conestogas asked the governor to limit the number of trade licenses they issued, hoping to decrease the availability of liquor and the social disruption it engendered.[17]

16. "Particulars of an Indian Treaty between Sir William Keith and the Deputies of the Five Nations, July 5, 1721," 5–6, APS; *MPCP,* III, 285–286. For the fate of John Burt, see William Henry Egle, ed., *Notes and Queries, Historical and Genealogical: Chiefly Relating to Interior Pennsylvania,* I (1894; reprint, Baltimore, 1970), 10.

17. James Sullivan et al., comps., *The Papers of Sir William Johnson,* 14 vols. (Albany, N.Y., 1921–1965), IX, 629; Abraham H. Cassell, comp., "Notes on the Iroquois and Delaware Indians: Communications from Conrad Weiser to Christopher Saur, 1746–1749 . . . ," trans. Helen Bell, *PMHB,* I (1877), 322; Beauchamp, ed., *Moravian Journals,* 208–209; John Bartram, *Travels in Pensilvania and Canada* (Ann Arbor, Mich., 1966) (originally published as *Observations on the Inhabitants, Climate, Soil, Rivers, Productions, Animals, and Other Matters Worthy of Notice . . .* [London, 1751]), 15–16, 54; Richter, *Ordeal of the Longhouse,* 86; *MPCP,* III, 365, 406; Archer Butler Hulbert and William Nathaniel Schwarze, eds., "David Zeisberger's History of the Northern American Indians," *Ohio Archaeological and Historical Publications,* XIX (1910), 90. See also Mack's travel diary, Oct. 31, 1745, in English, *Moravian Records,* reel 28, box 217,

Pennsylvania authorities were happy to comply; they, too, wanted to control the liquor trade among frontier inhabitants. Although seen as a necessary part of sociability (even survival in regions without potable water), liquor's effects often raised broader questions about social divisions and rank-appropriate behavior. Some whites during the eighteenth century considered liquor a beverage for gentlemen, and certain forms, like brandy and wine, were associated with the affluent. The drinking behavior of carousing traders who came to town after months in the woods or garrisoned soldiers away from their families stepped over a boundary of civility. For the Pennsylvania elite, regulating alcohol went hand in hand with controlling the deficient nature and potential disorderly actions of the "lower sorts," including servants, the enslaved, and Indians, whom they banned from public houses. Within a few years of the Conestogas' request, the provincial Council forbade the sale of "Rum, Brandy, or other strong Liquors, mixed or unmixed, to or with any Indian within this Province, under the Penalty of their forfeiting Ten Pounds."[18]

The combined efforts of Indian leaders and the Pennsylvania provin-

---

folder 12B, item 1, Shamokin diary, Oct. 31, 1745, reel 6, box 121, folder 2; M. [Pierre] Pouchot, *Memoir upon the Late War in North America, between the French and English, 1755–60; Followed by Observations upon the Theatre of Actual War, and by New Details concerning the Manners and Customs of the Indians; with Topographical Maps,* ed. and trans. Franklin B. Hough, 2 vols. (Roxbury, Mass., 1866), II, 237; Beauchamp, ed., *Moravian Journals,* 146–147, 173; Letter from Conestoga, May 1, 1734, *PA,* 1st Ser., I, 425; Peter C. Mancall, *Deadly Medicine: Indians and Alcohol in Early America* (Ithaca, N.Y., 1995), 59–60.

18. Capt. Reynolds to William Parsons, Aug. 12, 1756, Timothy Horsfield Papers, II, APS; David W. Conroy, *In Public Houses: Drink and the Revolution of Authority in Colonial Massachusetts* (Chapel Hill, N.C., 1995), 13, 22; Mancall, *Deadly Medicine,* 19–20; Colin G. Calloway, comp., *North Country Captives: Selected Narratives of Indian Captivity from Vermont and New Hampshire* (Hanover, N.H., 1992), 64, 65; John Harris to Joseph Shippen, July 24, 1756, Edward and Joseph Shippen Papers, Miscellaneous Correspondence, APS; *MPCP,* IV, 87. When serving on the Pennsylvania frontier during the Seven Years' War, white officers took great care to have their own wines and liquors delivered to them, whereas the soldiers received a ration of rum (Peter Thompson, *Rum, Punch, and Revolution: Taverngoing and Public Life in Eighteenth-Century Philadelphia* [Phildelphia, 1999], 36). Orders against the sale or use of liquor among the soldiers were common. See *General Orders of 1757 Issued by the Earl of Loudoun and Phineas Lyman in the Campaign against the French* (1899; reprint, Freeport, N.Y., 1970), 14; Capt. Ourry, Journal kept at Bedford, Jan. 16, 1759, in S. K. Stevens et al., eds., *The Papers of Henry Bouquet* (Harrisburg, Pa., 1951–), III, 65.

cial government to control frontier trade and the consequences of alcohol-induced violence only went so far. They were unable to eliminate the use of liquor or its importance as a trade item, and, although they attempted to employ each other's systems of justice to negotiate mutually acceptable solutions, their cooperation was limited. Governor Patrick Gordon assured Pennsylvania natives that the government would "not suffer any Injury to be done to the Indians without punishing the Offenders," but Indians "must do the same Justice on their Parts." Indian leaders, however, feared that the English might zealously persecute Indian troublemakers, while ignoring the violent actions of their own countrymen. Whereas Indian communities provided a system of compensation and condolence for accidental deaths or murder—the perpetrator offering gifts and trade goods to the family of the victim—Indians wondered whether this system would be understood or accepted by whites. Tagotolessa, the Conestoga leader known as Civility by the English during the early eighteenth century, knew that "if one Indian should kill another they have many ways of making up such an Affair," but he was uneasy "lest a Christian should be ill used by any Indian intoxicated with that Liquor [rum]."[19]

Instead of insisting that whites think or act like Indians when dealing with cross-cultural justice, native leaders more often pressured colonial leaders to comply with their own colonial laws. Kinship metaphors and the obligations that they implied provided the Pennsylvania government with guidelines for diplomacy, but kinship only went so far to promote cooperation between native American and Euramerican leaders. In May 1728, Governor Gordon admonished white settlers, not to provoke "our Friends" the Indians, but to treat the neighboring Delawares, Conestogas, Conoys, Shawnees, and Iroquois "with the same civil Regard that they would an English Subject." Beyond friendship, he assured the Iroquois in August 1732 that Indians and whites in Pennsylvania shared familial bonds. He reminded them that, some years before, "when two fool-

19. *MPCP,* III, 364; Gordon to Henry Smith and John Petty, *PA,* 1st Ser., I, 229; White, *Middle Ground,* 76–77; Reid, *Law of Blood,* 73–112. See James H. Merrell, "'The Customes of Our Countrey': Indians and Colonists in Early America," in Bernard Bailyn and Philip D. Morgan, eds., *Strangers within the Realm: Cultural Margins of the First British Empire* (Chapel Hill, N.C., 1991), 142–146, for the shift in the balance of power from the dominance of native custom, including legal custom, to the dominance of Euramerican political systems and their effects on Indian cultural practice.

ish People had shott two of our Delaware Women Indians and a Boy, the [white] Men that did it were tried and hang'd for it, in the same manner as if they had killed their own sisters, of the same Mother." Indians could not be sure that the governor or colonists fully understood the implications of those kinship metaphors, but they did use his implied familiarity to press for their own forms of justice. When reports of the murder of a Seneca Indian by two white traders, John and Edmund Cartlidge, reached the Pennsylvania Council in early March 1721, they sent James Logan and Colonel John French to investigate. Delaware, Conestoga, and Conoy witnesses corroborated the rumors, recalling that everyone had been drinking hard, and, when Sawantaeny, a Seneca, asked for more rum, a prolonged fight ensued. Edmund Cartlidge struck the Seneca "three Blows on the Head" while John stripped him of his clothes and kicked him "on the side and broke two of his Ribs." Although many of the details were disputed, a local sheriff arrested the Cartlidges and took them to Philadelphia for trial. James Logan, accommodating native protocol, held a condolence ceremony to placate the Iroquois. There the provincial Assembly presented wampum to "Wipe away [the] Tears" of the grieving family. The Iroquois accepted this meager gesture but were disappointed that the Pennsylvania government did not travel the extra miles to present the gifts at Onondaga, the central council fire of the Six Nations. Eventually the Iroquois insisted that the Cartlidges' lives be spared. They were less concerned about the murderers' guilt or innocence than the larger context of their trade agreements. To them, the punishment of a few drunk and violent individuals would have little impact on improving trade relations. Instead, they demanded that the Pennsylvania government create and enforce harsher laws "against selling Rum to the Indians, which will prevent such Mischiefs for the future."[20]

20. *MPCP*, III, 151, 164, 194–195, 308, 436. See also Merrell, *Into the American Woods*, 115–121. A similar situation occurred in May 1728, when Walter Winter and John Winter were arrested for killing several Indians, including two women. The provincial government made reparations to the dead Delawares' families and also took the two white men into custody for trial and execution. See examination of Walter Winter, *PA*, 1st Ser., I, 219–220; *MPCP*, III, 304, IV, 91–92; James Logan to John Penn, May 15, 1728, Penn Papers, Official Correspondence, II, 9, HSP. Merrell, *Into the American Woods*, 42–53, examines the killing of John Armstrong by a Delaware, Mushemeelin, after which the parties sought what they thought was mutual justice rather than the truth of the incident.

During the early decades of the eighteenth century, individuals at central trading posts along the Susquehanna or deep in the woods, exchanging furs for British goods, created alliances based partially on the precepts of native kinship obligations. Although Indian hunters and white traders sought personal economic advantage within their alliances, under pressure from colonial leaders they managed to make concessions to keep the peace when disagreements arose. Still, these tended to be temporary relationships; accommodation often lasted only until they parted company. As white settlement increased, the possibility of sustained interactions between communities also grew. In the 1740s, whites who traveled to Indian communities, distant from the center of Pennsylvania provincial authority, found that they, too, like earlier traders, had to conform to Indian social and economic customs as much as Indians were expected to adapt to theirs. Here, kinship and the reciprocity and gift exchange it entailed played an important role in describing the parameters of social and economic alliances and the power dynamics between Indians and whites.[21]

No Euramerican group in Pennsylvania had more opportunity for sustained interactions with Indians in their communities than Moravian missionaries. The Moravians, or United Brethren, were a Protestant Pietist sect who had migrated from the German province of Saxony in 1740 and settled on land north of Philadelphia, where they established the towns of Nazareth and Bethlehem. Besides forming their own religious communities free from the persecution they had experienced in central Europe, the Moravians hoped to proselytize Indians in the colony. In September 1742, Count Nikolaus Ludwig von Zinzendorf, the Moravian spiritual and secular leader, made contact with native Americans at Shamokin, knowing that this multiethnic trade town was key to their religious mission. He asked Shickellamy, the Iroquois representative and overseer at Shamokin, for permission to preach among the Delawares and other Indians on the Susquehanna River. Zinzendorf assured Shickellamy that he "was specially and intimately acquainted with the Great Spirit, and asked them finally to permit me and the Brethren simply to sojourn in their towns, as friends, and without suspicion, until such time as we should have mutu-

21. Merrell, "'The Customes of Our Countrey,'" in Bailyn and Morgan, eds., *Strangers within the Realm*, 117–156.

ally learned each other's peculiarities." Shickellamy granted the Moravian request, perhaps less from his own interest in Christianity than for the potential economic and political alliances between the Iroquois and their German neighbors to the southeast that would further legitimize the Six Nations' authority in Pennsylvania. And what better way to determine another's motives or "peculiarities" than to carefully observe their actions in one's own community?[22]

Ambivalent but persistent characterized the relationship that developed between Moravians and the Shamokin Indians. The former, unused to the way of life and rituals of Indian peoples, even disgusted by them, fearfully described Shamokin as "the very seat of the Prince of darkness." The Moravians thought its inhabitants were at best a "blissful nation," who lived like gypsies, unaware of their own poverty. At worst, the Indians were "almost always drunck Day and Night," "so drunk, that they roar'd like Beasts." Some natives at Shamokin, themselves suspicious of the Moravians, threatened them, as one man "full of Fury" entered their host's hut at midnight, "Snatch'd a great Fire Brand out of the Fire, and said he wo.d burn the white People." Still, the Moravians found friendship in the community and actively sought economic and social ties with its inhabitants, if only to further their religious agenda. Almost all the missionaries cultivated a craft or skill to serve their potential converts and to support themselves. Indeed, Moravians selected missionaries as much for their artisanal skills as for their pious spirit. At one of their mission towns, there was a gardener, a cutler, a blacksmith, a linguist who also taught school, a farmer, a carpenter, and a shoemaker. Bishop John Christopher Frederick Cammerhoff, in Shamokin during 1748, planted turnips and distributed them among Indians. "Shikellmy . . . is always delighted with a

22. Vernon H. Nelson, ed. and trans., "Peter Boehler's Reminiscences of the Beginnings of Nazareth and Bethlehem," Moravian Historical Society, *Transactions*, XXVII (Nazareth, Pa., 1992), 2–3; W. C. Reichel, *A Register of Members of the Moravian Church, and of Persons Attached to Said Church in This Country and Abroad, between 1727 and 1754*, ed. Abraham Reincke (Bethlehem, Pa., 1873), 60, 46; Count Nikolaus Ludwig von Zinzendorf to European Brethren, Sept. 29, 1742, in William C. Reichel, ed., *Memorials of the Moravian Church*, I (Philadelphia, 1870), 65. For general works about Moravians in colonial America, see Gillian Lindt Gollin, *Moravians in Two Worlds: A Study of Changing Communities* (New York, 1967); Beverly Prior Smaby, *The Transformation of Moravian Bethlehem: From Communal Mission to Family Economy* (Philadelphia, 1988); and Daniel B. Thorp, *The Moravian Community in Colonial North Carolina: Pluralism on the Southern Frontier* (Knoxville, Tenn., 1989).

present of some," he remarked about his gardening efforts, "and in return treats us to venison." While the German men helped to cultivate crops and build structures for Indian towns, the women missionaries often took in washing, sewed clothing, or gave haircuts to local inhabitants. They tried to use this informal daily exchange of goods and services with the Susquehanna Indians as the basis of more formal alliances, which might, in turn, lead to a permanent mission.[23]

Moravians might have thought that "the Great Spirit" would guide them to native souls, but in truth Indians, Iroquois in particular, called the shots. Shickellamy had initially invited Moravians to visit Shamokin, but he wanted very specific conditions met before he allowed them to become permanent residents. In 1742, soon after their first trip, he demanded that the Moravians provide Shamokin, sometimes known as Schachenaméndi ("where we get our gun-barrels made straight, when they are bent"), with the services of a blacksmith. Although he did not promise that his people would accept their religious teachings, the Moravians struggled to accommodate the request. After five years of careful negotiations and after permission from the Pennsylvania governor, missionary Martin Mack and Nathanael, a Mahican convert, arrived at Shamokin in April 1747 to complete the deal with the local governing council. By this time, Moravians had found Delawares somewhat receptive to their religious message, but at Shamokin the Delaware leader Sassoonan and his family had little political power. Instead, Shickellamy controlled the balance of power. His council, which consisted of himself, his three sons,

23. Martin Mack's journey to Shamokin, September 1745, in Reichel, ed., *Memorials of the Moravian Church,* I, 66; Shamokin diary, Sept. 29, 1742, *Moravian Records,* reel 6, box 121, folder 1, Mack's travel diary, Nov. 2, 1745, reel 28, box 217, folder 12B, item 1, Shamokin diary, July 11, 1747, reel 6, box 121, folder 3, item 1 (Shickellamy came to the mission house to ask the women to cut his hair ["auf indianische art"]), Shamokin conference minutes, Aug. 20, 1747, reel 6, box 121, folder 9, item 3(1), Oct. 26, 1747, reel 6, box 121, folder 3, Shamokin diary, Dec. 30, 1747, reel 6, box 121, folder 3, item 3, Report from Br. Kunz at Shamokin, 1749, reel 26, box 211, folder 19, item 1; Loskiel, *History of the Mission,* trans. La Trobe, pt. 2, 37; Jordan, ed., "Cammerhoff's Narrative," *PMHB,* XXIX (1905), 173. For the names and occupations of the ten white Moravians at Gnadenhüutten during the 1750s, see Reichel, ed., *Memorials of the Moravian Church,* I, 201n. James H. Merrell, in "Shamokin, 'the very seat of the Prince of Darkness': Unsettling the Early American Frontier," in Cayton and Teute, eds., *Contact Points,* 16–59, interprets the Shamokin encounters between Moravians and Indians as darkly ominous, foreboding, and mutually incomprehensible.

and three other Iroquois, held the final negotiations, presenting a string of wampum to Martin Mack for Bethlehem's leader, August Gottlieb Spangenberg. Shickellamy told him: "T'gerketonti, my brother . . . I have wished a long time for a blacksmith to live here. I want to love him as my own flesh." He cautioned, however, that there were many warriors traveling through Shamokin to participate in the recurrent raids against the Catawbas and Flatheads to the south, and, if a blacksmith worked there, he would have to fix their guns for free, "since they have nothing to pay." The missionaries, both men and women, were expected to offer hospitality to warriors passing through. In return for the blacksmith's services, Shickellamy would protect him from unruly Indians, give his family a piece of land to use as they wished, and offer the Moravians a chance to preach in the community.[24]

Although the Moravians were reluctant to fix warriors' weapons because of their pacifist principles, within a month the Moravians had capitulated to the demands of Indian economic exchange, since it was essential to their missionary efforts. For them, economic relationships were less about profit and more about producing goodwill among the natives whom they wished to convert. They reasoned, since "the Warriors make use of their Guns to shoot Deer with, and support themselves therefrom," then the blacksmith could repair them with a clear conscience and should "take nothing of them when they go to War." By July 1747, the Moravians returned with Anton Schmidt, the first of several blacksmiths, and before the council they introduced him to Shickellamy and requested permission for him to live in Shamokin. In their speech, the Moravians confirmed not just an economic arrangement for the services of a blacksmith but the mutual ties and responsibilities of kinship as well. "My brother

24. "Ich habe einen lange Zeit gewünschten wann ein Schmidt hier wohnen wolte; ich wolte ihn lieb haben wie mein eigen Fleisch"; see Mack's journey to Shamokin, Apr. 21, 1747, *Moravian Records,* reel 6, box 121, folder 9, item 2; Jordan, ed., "Spangenberg's Notes," *PMHB,* II (1878), 429; Maurice C. Jones, "Memorandum of the Names and Significations Which the 'Lenni Lenape,' Otherwise Called 'the Delawares,' Had Given to Rivers, Streams, Places, etc., within the States of Pennsylvania, New Jersey, Maryland, and Virginia . . . Taken from the Papers of the Rev. John Heckewelder . . . ," HSP, *Proceedings,* I (Philadelphia, 1847), 127; Richter, *Ordeal of the Longhouse,* 220–221 (the governments of New France and New York also sent blacksmiths and gunsmiths as resident craftsmen to native towns); Carter, *Early Events in the Susquehanna Valley,* 93; and Reichel, ed., *Memorials of the Moravian Church,* I, 67.

Spangenberg and all my other brothers have given me a greeting to our brother Shickellamy and his brothers," Christian Heinrich Rauch intoned, invoking the relational forms of address that were familiar to both Iroquois and Moravians, "I am sent from my brother to bring to you our brother the smith and his wife and brother Hagen's wife."[25]

As Rauch implied, men were not alone in making formal and informal arrangements for social and economic exchange. Native women also negotiated with Moravians, since they would be the ones to offer hospitality and perform many of the rituals of kinship. Indeed, when whites came to Indian communities or Indians traveled to white communities, women often made the first efforts to communicate with each other. At Shamokin, a young Mahican woman had provided translation services for the blacksmith treaty proceedings. She had "translated everything that was spoken on both sides," since the German men could not understand Iroquois but could speak Mahican and she could speak both. Interpretation was not an unusual activity for native women. By the eighteenth century, most Indian communities in Pennsylvania were interethnic—a mix of refugees, adoptees, or remnant groups—and Indian women, who presided over these diverse households, often understood and spoke several native dialects. As Euramericans became neighbors or economic allies, native women just as ably learned their languages. This linguistic accommodation helped them to incorporate strangers, such as the Moravians, into their communities.[26]

White women also contributed to intercultural communication, since they often interacted with native women in their homes and communities as captives, traders, missionaries, or neighbors. The Moravians realized early that they had to show goodwill to Indians by making the effort to communicate clearly. Bishop Cammerhoff, overseeing negotiations with

25. Various Indian speeches, May 26, 1747, in English, *Moravian Records,* reel 35, box 323, folder 8, item 4, Christian Heinrich Rauch's journey to Shamokin, Aug. 2, 1747, reel 29, box 221, folder 5, item 1 ("Mein br. Tkerkedonit [Spangenberg] u. alle meine anderen Brr: haben durch mich einen gruß mit gegeben, an unser Br: Shikellemy u. seine Brr: u. ich bin von meinen Brr: geschükt, den Schmit u. seine fr. u. Br. Hagens fr: u. euch unsern Brr: zu bringen").

26. "Sie ist eine gebohrne Mahikanderin, und hat alles übersezt, was auf beiden Seiten ist gesprochen worden: weil weder ich noch Nathanael konten was verstehen"; see Mack's journey to Shamokin, Apr. 21, 1747, *Moravian Records,* reel 6, box 121, folder 9, item 2; Diarium von Bethlehem, Feb. 22/Mar. 5, 1749, reel 4, Van Pelt Library, University of Pennsylvania, Philadelphia.

Indians in Shamokin, claimed, "Our meetings attract them." "But," he added, "what strikes them the most, is our desire to learn their language." Many German missionary women spoke at least one native language. Jeanette Mack, having grown up in the New York backcountry along the Hudson River valley, had learned some Mohawk, Delaware, and Mahican at a young age. Because of her language skills, she could readily offer a "prayer in Mahican" at the bedside of an ailing person or upon the baptism of a young Indian.[27]

Jeanette Mack's communication skills opened the way to meaningful interactions, as Indian women amicably incorporated their Moravian neighbors into the rituals, activities, and community patterns that formed the core of their lives. The same Mahican woman who translated economic and political negotiations at Shamokin mourned the death of her child in 1748. She asked Jeanette Mack, a resident missionary, for materials to build a coffin. She confided her concern about her daughter's soul, asking whether Jeanette thought it might go to the Christian heaven. After a long discussion about the nature of God, death, and children, however, the Mahican woman prepared the young girl for an Indian afterlife, filling the coffin with the traditional items for housekeeping—"a blanket, several pairs of mocassins, buckskin for new ones, needle and thread, a kettle, two hatchets, and flint, steel, and tinder." Yet she also acknowledged the comfort and assistance that the German woman had given her. After the burial, she "presented Sr. Mack with a *quart tin,* saying: 'This belonged to my daughter—accept it in remembrance of her.'" This gesture, the distribution of the personal effects that were not buried with a corpse, was reserved for family and friends—another sign that some Indians at Shamokin wanted to incorporate the Moravians into their community as kin.

27. Bishop John Frederick Cammerhoff to Count Nikolaus Ludwig von Zinzendorf, Feb. 10–16, 1748, John Christopher Frederick Cammerhoff, 1721–1751, Letters, 1747–1748, copied by John W. Jordan, HSP; John W. Jordan, ed., "Rev. John Martin Mack's Narrative of a Visit to Onondaga in 1752," *PMHB,* XXIX (1905), 343; *Moravian Records,* Sept. 28, 1742, reel 6, box 121, folder 1, Dec. 7, 1742, reel 1, box 111, folder 7, item 7, Feb. 13, 1743, reel 1, box 111, folder 1. Margarethe Büttner Jungman, who worked at various mission towns from 1742 to 1785, could speak Mahican and Delaware; see Katherine M. Faull, ed. and trans., *Moravian Women's Memoirs: Their Related Lives, 1750–1820* (Syracuse, N.Y., 1997). See also Johann Jacob Schmick, "Miscellanea linguae nationis Indicae Mahikan dicta cura suscepta," 2 vols., [ca. 1760], APS.

Jeanette Mack's acceptance of the gift also implicated the Moravians in the daily rituals of Indian life.[28]

Kinship alliances and kinship metaphors, to some degree, provided a common basis for relations between individuals and communities on the frontier. By the early 1750s, however, when translated to broader trade and diplomatic agreements between nations, kinship alone could not always sustain alliances. Especially in the western parts of Pennsylvania, internal colonialism shaped the struggle for power over the fur trade, which fueled the economics of empire. Colonial leaders in Pennsylvania used annual gifts as tribute for encroachment on native territories and to smooth the way to future economic cooperation, if not future land purchases. But the fur trade with Indians was more about empire building than about interdependence. Western Indians, in turn, relied little on colonial authorities. Although cooperative among themselves, Ohio Valley Indians were suspicious of the Six Nations' attempts to dominate them and slow to establish trade alliances with the Pennsylvania government. Emerging as powerful and autonomous groups, a new generation of hunters and warriors dominated the political leadership in the west, transforming the nature of internal Indian politics as well as Indian-white diplomacy. Neither "dead" nor "worthless" as the Moravians contended, Sassoonan's remaining nephews (his sister's sons)—Pisquetomen, Shingas, and Tamaqua (the Beaver)—had settled on the Allegheny River with nearly fifty families at Kittanning by the early 1730s and commanded authority among the western Delawares. Also embittered by the Six Nations' hold on Indian politics in eastern Pennsylvania, Shawnees had moved west to establish Logg's Town on

28. Shamokin diary, Nov. 21, 29, 1747, *Moravian Records,* reel 6, box 121, folder 3; Jordan, ed., "Cammerhoff's Narrative," *PMHB,* XXIX (1905), 173–174; Beauchamp, ed., *Moravian Journals,* 183; "The Journal of Andreas Hesselius," Historical Society of Delaware, *Delaware History,* II (Wilmington, Del., 1947), 100. Notes on archaeological excavations, site 36 Lu 43, Wapwallopen, Pennsylvania State Museum, Harrisburg, indicates that Pennsylvania Indian graves were often filled with beaded clothing, shell or glass pendant necklaces, and brass bells or jinglers placed on people's legs and feet. In other words, they were dressed in their finest clothing for the afterlife. John Heckewelder notes that native women played an important role in preparing funeral rites and were treated with equal respect when buried. Heckewelder, *History, Manners, and Customs,* 270–271.

the Monongahela River. Finally, a group of Iroquois, who had separated from the confederacy, settled south of Lake Erie at Kuskuski. By the fall of 1747, with nearly two thousand warriors and their families living in the Ohio Valley, the Delaware, Shawnee, and Iroquois villages had become a loosely confederated network of ethnically separated towns whose power systems were localized and kin-based. They created a council fire at Logg's Town and agreed on a representative, Scarouyady, an Oneida, to act as liaison with colonial powers to the east.[29]

Ohio Indians quickly dominated the fur trade, becoming an important economic and diplomatic force in Pennsylvania. Beginning in 1746, annual exports of furs and skins from the colony began to increase dramatically, both in comparison to previous years and in comparison to other fur-trading colonies, such as New York. In 1752 alone, Pennsylvania exported furs worth £14,428, nearly half the value of all goods the colony shipped to London. Ohio hunters contributed significantly to the increase of trade and, therefore, could often dictate the terms of economic exchange. As England and France vied for their loyalties and, thus, control over the Ohio Valley, Indians learned to play one nation against the other to get the best terms of trade. In 1747, for instance, the Ohio Indians became unhappy with the price French traders offered for their furs and with their mistreatment of Indian hunters. The French had begun a campaign to remove Pennsylvania settlers from the Ohio and Mississippi River valleys. In retaliation, Ohio Indians patronized English traders, preferring the price of their goods. Still, Ohio Indians used the threat of a French alliance to get what they needed from the English. During conferences with the governor and his Council at Philadelphia in the fall of 1747 and at Lancaster in 1748, the Ohio representative Scarouyady demanded that Pennsylvania reopen direct exchange with them, which had been interrupted by the imperial

29. Michael N. McConnell, "Pisquetomen and Tamaqua: Mediating Peace in the Ohio Valley," in Robert S. Grumet, ed., *Northeastern Indian Lives, 1632–1816* (Amherst, Mass., 1996), 273–294; McConnell, *A Country Between*, 21–46, 61, map on 116–117; Wallace, *Indians in Pennsylvania*, 177; Kent, *Susquehanna's Indians*, 90–91; *MPCP*, V, 463. In 1748, Conrad Weiser counted 789 "fighting men" in Ohio, including 163 Senecas, 162 Shawnees, 100 Wyandots, 40 "Tisagechroanu" [Hurons?], 74 Mohawks, 15 Mahicans, 35 Onondagas, 20 Cayugas, 15 Oneidas, and 165 Delawares; see Conrad Weiser's journal of tour to Ohio, Sept. 8, 1748, in Reuben Gold Thwaites, ed., *Early Western Travels, 1748–1846*, I (Cleveland, Ohio, 1904), 30–31.

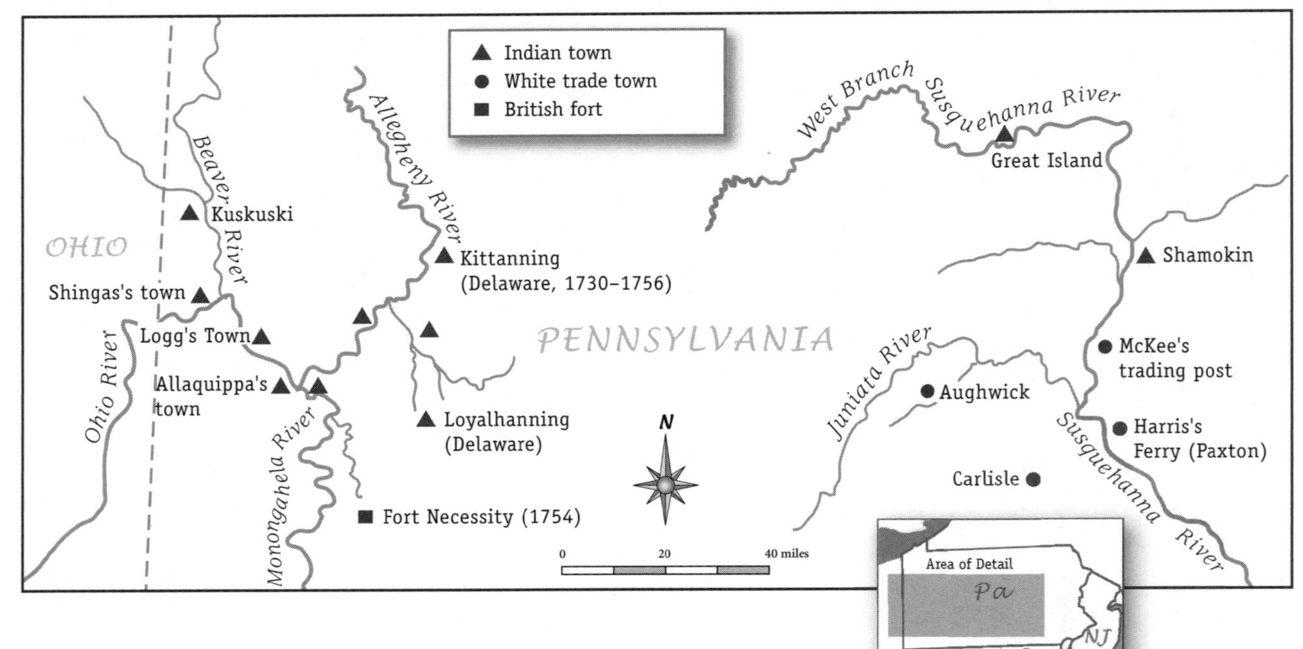

MAP 3. Ohio Valley Indian Communities to 1756. *Drawn by Gerry Krieg*

trade war. He implied that Ohio hunters could just as easily return to their French trade partners if Pennsylvania did not comply.[30]

The Pennsylvania government faced conflicting demands, trying to reconcile the power struggle between Indian groups with the imperial rivalry between Great Britain and France. They wanted to accommodate the Ohio confederacy, but they were also bound by their alliance with the Six Nations in New York, which led to confusion over the course of Indian diplomacy. Conrad Weiser, the provincial interpreter and longtime friend of the Iroquois, encouraged the colony to deal with western Indians as subordinate to the Six Nations. The Iroquois leadership insisted that western Indians were not "Counsellors, but Hunters, and would take it amiss to leave them treated with in any other manner than as people depending upon them." Ohio Indians, however, refused to recognize the council at Onondaga as a political authority. Even colonial officials began to sense that the Six Nations were losing "their influence and Character every Day" over Pennsylvania Indians. Consequently, in September 1748, Weiser agreed to meet with Tanaghrisson (the "half king"), a Seneca compatriot of Scarouyady's, and presented him with gifts worth nearly twelve hundred pounds as a sign of Pennsylvania's goodwill toward the Ohio Indians. Weiser realized the wisdom of a separate peace agreement even more after the death of the Onondaga chief and leader among the Six Nations, Canassatego, in 1750. Some thought he had been poisoned by French-allied Iroquois, and, indeed, the new head of the council was "a professed Roman Catholick and altogether devoted to the French." Weiser and his confidant, provincial secretary Richard Peters, warned the proprietors that Iroquois leaders sympathetic to the French would undermine their diplomatic efforts in the Ohio.[31]

30. Stephen H. Cutcliffe, "Colonial Indian Policy as a Measure of Rising Imperialism: New York and Pennsylvania, 1700–1755," *Western Pennsylvania Historical Magazine*, LXIV (1981), 240–244. Hinderaker, *Elusive Empire*, 33–34, contends that the income from the fur trade was "insignificant," but its political worth for undermining French colonial claims was significant. See also McConnell, *A Country Between*, 67, 83–88; Mancall, *Valley of Opportunity*, 38; White, *Middle Ground*, 201.

31. Peters to proprietors, Dec. 8, 1749, James Hamilton to Thomas Penn, Oct. 13, 1750, Penn Papers, Official Correspondence, IV, 265, V, 69, HSP; Weiser to Peters, Oct. 4, 1750, Conrad Weiser Papers, I, Correspondence, HSP; McConnell, *A Country Between*, 73–75. See also Weiser journal to Onondaga, Sept. 17, 1750, Penn Papers,

Although Weiser still hoped to patch together new supporters among the Six Nations, the task of negotiating broader political and economic alliances with the Ohio Delawares instead fell to George Croghan, who was better suited for the role. He began his long career as an Indian trader in 1741 and developed tremendous influence over the course of English trade in Pennsylvania because of both his extensive lines of credit and his cachet with the native population. A competitor lamented to Thomas Penn that the Indians "so well esteemed" Croghan "that if he has asortable Cargo not one Trader in the Woods at the Indian Towns can sell anything till he has done." Croghan even moved west of the Susquehanna to land on Aughwick Creek, which became a way station for Ohio Indians traveling to Philadelphia or seeking refuge from trade wars in the west. Like many traders and cultural brokers before him, Croghan married a Mohawk woman, the daughter of chief Nickas, giving him further access to native resources and trust.[32]

From 1750, Croghan, as the provincial go-between in the west, met regularly with Delawares, Shawnees, Wyandots, and Twightwees at Logg's Town and used well-known Indian protocol—reciprocity and gift exchange—to create kinlike alliances. He condemned the attempts of France to force English traders from the Ohio Valley. In exchange for their loyalty, he promised Indians trade goods at a better price. More important, Croghan used familiar kinship terms to cement these agreements. In May 1751, Croghan addressed a group of chiefs at Logg's Town: "Friends and Brethren:—I am sent here by your Brother the Governor of Pennsylvania with this Present of Goods to renew the Friendship so long subsisting between Us, and I present you these four strings of Wampum to clear your Minds and open your Eyes and Ears that you may see the Sun clear, and hear what your Brother is going to say to you." After assuring them of their status as "Brothers," Croghan invoked other images of family and told of their potential ill fate if the Delawares were to ally with the French, who, according to Croghan, would "impoverish You and keep your Wives and Children always naked by keeping the English Traders at a Distance."[33]

Indian Affairs, I, 1687–1753, HSP; Weiser to Peters, Sept. 30, 1750, Peters to the proprietors, Oct. 15, 25, 1750, Penn Papers, Official Correspondence, V, 63, 73, 101, HSP.

32. Richard Hockley to Thomas Penn, Feb. 15, 1749/50, Penn Papers, Official Correspondence, IV, HSP.

33. Thwaites, ed., *Early Western Travels*, I, 63, 68.

Croghan and Ohio Indians might have addressed each other by relatively equal kin terms to assure mutually beneficial trade relations, but the political alliance that had so many personal consequences for the Ohio Indians had a far different meaning for the Pennsylvania government. Whereas Indians considered gifts of provisions and clothing for their families as the compensation they deserved for their loyalty, proprietors and governmental agents thought that Indians' demands simply depleted the limited resources of the colonial treasury. Instead of reciprocity in kind, the provincial government expected obedience, even subordination, in return for their protection and alliance. Indeed, they used the gift exchange as a tool of empire, first to create dependence on English trade goods, then to control Indian populations, and, finally, to force cessions of western lands. Since the Walking Purchase in 1737, the proprietor Thomas Penn had growing contempt for what he called the "worthless Indians" of Pennsylvania and thought that perhaps the colony did not need to purchase land outright. Instead, they could give Indians items from "a List of Goods, to the value of two or three hundred pound Currency every three years forever, not money but the Goods specyfyed, this will preserve a kind of dependence on us." After creating a need for British goods, the government could then take advantage of Indians by drawing up vague deeds that "would not have it in words too particular, but to extend to the Northern Boundary of the province of Pennsylvania, without any mention of a degree, and will be a release of their claim to all the Land within that Province." Although William Penn had once voiced more personal admiration for Indians, in many ways his son Thomas was his father's political heir. Both wanted to dominate trade in the province, control the purchase and distribution of land, and make subjects of native peoples.[34]

Indians, however, saw the situation quite differently. They rejected insinuations that their loyalty or land could be bought by gifts, that the English had somehow saved them from poverty by their generosity, or that Indians were dependent on Euramericans for their survival. In 1744 at Lancaster, Canassatego reprimanded the English, whose "young men" arrogantly told them "that we should have perished if they had not come into

34. Thomas Penn to Robert Hunter Morris, July 2, 1755, in Julian P. Boyd, ed., *The Susquehannah Company Papers*, 10 vols. (Ithaca, N.Y., 1962–1971), I, 290; Gregory Evans Dowd, "'Insidious Friends': Gift Giving and the Cherokee-British Alliance in the Seven Years' War," in Cayton and Teute, eds., *Contact Points*, 138.

the Country and furnished us with Strowds and Hatchets and Guns and other things necessary for the Support of Life." "But," he said, "we always gave them to understand that they were mistaken, that we lived before they came amongst us, and as well or better." Many Indians remembered another scenario when whites first came to the mid-Atlantic region. At the Albany Conference, Mahicans told English colonial leaders that, contrary to white memory, the Indians had helped the early traders and explorers find shelter and clothing, since the new immigrants needed to secure the friendship of the Indians to survive. It was, after all, the Indian woman of Northampton County who offered the Scots-Irish settlers cool water and showed the newcomers its source. By the 1750s, after providing personal and community assistance to Euramericans for nearly a century, Indians were angry that English leaders would not fulfill their end of the bargain "now the Case is altered."[35]

Once more a contested past provided the stage for debate over the present course of Indian-white relations. In the 1730s, the Pennsylvania proprietors and the Six Nations had used their versions of prior treaties to dispossess Delawares of land. Twenty years later, Indians, now entangled in social-economic alliances with white Pennsylvanians, called upon their own memories of the past to critique the imperial policies of the provincial government and the deteriorating relationship between their peoples. Even as Pennsylvania Indians asserted their political independence from the Six Nations, they recognized that they were becoming more dependent on British trade and, to some extent, British protection. By the 1750s, Ohio Indians, in George Croghan's words, had placed "thire hole Depenance on this government." But they also grasped the profound contradictions embedded in Euramerican actions: while professing to be economic partners or kin, whites manipulated this dependence to take their land. In midcentury, native Americans continually confronted whites with their own hypocrisy, reiterated whites' own terms of the encounter to remind them of their current obligations as allies and kin, and challenged them to apply to their relationships with Indians the rules of fairness that supposedly governed their own societies.[36]

Shawnees in Ohio, for example, invoked memories of the past as well as new kinship alliances to criticize the effects of the imperial market. In Feb-

35. *MPCP*, IV, 707–708, VI, 95.

36. George Croghan to Morris, Dec. 2, 1754, *PA*, 1st Ser., II, 209.

ruary 1752, they sent a message to the Pennsylvania government, recalling a long history of economic and cultural entanglements and their bitter end result. First, the speaker presented a picture of common humanity, although separated by color and geography: "It is a great while ago since You, our Brothers the English, and We, Your Brothers the Indians, were both made by one God that made all things; and when he made you white and Us black he placed You on the Ground beyond the Great Sea and us on the Ground on this side that Sea." Next, the Shawnee reminded them that, when whites had "come over the Great water to visit us your poor Brothers," Indians had seen their ship, and "we took hold of her and was glad to see you our eldest Brothers." Although employing relational metaphors such as younger "Brother" that implied Shawnee subordination, the speaker manipulated white understanding of that familial hierarchy to demand the assistance and protection of their "eldest Brothers." He recalled sardonically that, soon after their arrival, whites "gave us Books, and told us we should pray, and we thought we would do so, but in a short time we got in debt and the Traders told us we must pay them, so we quitted praying and fell to hunting." Using the logic of Euramericans, the Shawnees concluded that, since they had been forced to turn away from their own God, who had previously provided for all their needs, and subsequently had been forced to give up "praying" to a Christian God to participate in the market economy, "you our eldest Brothers" should instead "take care of us and advise us for the best."[37]

As the Shawnees' critique pointedly suggests, by the 1750s the meaning of economic exchange had changed for Indian communities, at great cost to their societies and social relations. Attempts at sharing resources through interdependent alliances gave way to growing dependence on European trade goods. In turn, colonial leaders manipulated this dependence to force capitulation of land and political autonomy. Trade between Indians and whites in Pennsylvania had less to do with hospitality, reci-

37. *MPCP,* V, 569. See also Weiser to Morris, Mar. 1, 1755, *PA,* 1st Ser., II, 259, for similar demands and reprimands by Shawnees who returned to the Susquehanna River in the spring of 1755. Nancy Shoemaker, "An Alliance between Men: Gender Metaphors in Eighteenth-Century American Indian Diplomacy East of the Mississippi," *Ethnohistory,* XLVI (1999), 251–252, looks at ways in which Cherokees and the English used the metaphors of younger and elder brothers to negotiate relative power in the 1720s and 1730s. See Chapter 6, below, for further discussion of kinship metaphors and diplomacy.

procity, or gift exchange and more to do with credit and debt within a market economy. Indians did not ignore these effects. Indeed, they became a springboard for soul-searching opposition among native American leaders. By the 1740s, a new group of cultural critics emerged in Pennsylvania to reform and revitalize Indian communities. Mostly prophets and preachers, the leaders of the reform movement condemned whites who had changed the economic conditions and practices of native peoples. Reformers tried to correct native ways of life, especially practices perceived as vices associated with white behavior, and hoped to guide their people back to an Indian-centered society. Criticism came in two forms. First, they blamed whites for corrupting Indians through unfair trade practices and the proliferation of alcohol. But, implicitly, they also criticized Indians for the breakdown of traditional native political authority, which led to the social ills of a new economy.

One of the most important of these reformers in Pennsylvania was Papunhank, a Munsee spiritual leader who was uniquely positioned as a vocal critic of both Indian and white communities. In 1752, he had settled with about three hundred followers on the Susquehanna River at Wyalusing, between the Six Nations and Shamokin. According to Moravian minister Christian Frederick Post, Wyalusing was "an Indian town newly laid out, where there are a company together all of the Munsee (Mennissing) Indians, a sort of religious people." Papunhank, as a neutral leader, had the ear of Indians and provincial agents and openly criticized both. He decided that economic alliances with colonial governments had become a burden to Indians rather than a boon. At Philadelphia in July 1760, Papunhank refused Pennsylvania's offer of presents. "I will tell you the Reason why I say I am frighten'd; should I lay my hands on your presents," he told Governor William Denny. Then directing his comments to the attending Indian leaders, Papunhank pointedly continued: "It would raise a Jealousy in the Breasts of those round about me, who transact the publick Business and are wont to receive Presents on such Occasions. It would, moreover, be apt to corrupt my own mind, and make me proud, and others would think I wanted to be a great Man, which is not the case." He had seen how gifts had seduced the Iroquois to sell Delaware land in Pennsylvania in a piecemeal fashion over the previous three decades and knew that others had succumbed to petty bickering among themselves as they vied for favors from colonial powers. Instead of confirming the mutual obligations of allies, gifts simply "spoil and corrupt the receivers of them." "Many have misbehaved after they have received them, and many, I am afraid, came only for the sake of Receiving them."[38]

Papunhank decried the shifted meaning of the gift exchange, especially when the gifts were given by colonial governments. Kinship alliances, perhaps, had worked too well, creating an economic dependence that ultimately dismantled the local partnerships between frontier inhabitants. Yet Papunhank simultaneously engaged the governor in a new kind of economic dialogue, hoping that Indians would regain control over their trade relations with whites. Like Civility before him, like the Shawnee speaker, Papunhank cast the points of conflict in terms that Euramericans might better understand; instead of an alliance of mutual obligations based solely on networks of kin, trade relations could be ordered by the same ethical and moral principles that governed Christian behavior in white communities. Papunhank called upon God to shame the English into acting properly when dealing with Indians. He reprimanded the governor for allowing traders to continually alter the prices they paid for skins: "God can not be pleased to see the prices of one and the same thing so often altered and changed." When prices fluctuated so wildly, young Indian men soon learned how to cheat by soaking their furs to add weight. "You do wrong in altering your prices," he lamented, and, in turn, "the Indians do wrong in bringing skins with so much badness on them." Only through the reform of economic relationships would the harmony between their two peoples be restored in God's eyes and in theirs.[39]

Even as they found ways to cooperate, to create kin alliances and exchange goods for subsistence, Indians and whites competed to dictate the nature of those relationships. Whites saw Indians as increasingly dependent on colonial powers, even subordinate to their economic authority. Indians, in turn, manipulated their dependence, sometimes rhetorically, to criticize whites, but sometimes they managed to demonstrate economic clout if their threats carried political consequences. Still, faced with a rapidly intensifying frontier, Indians had to be especially resourceful. Kinship was the glue that held Indian communities together. If they could not

38. In Post's words: "an Inschan taun nuly layd out, war der ar a Companie to gader all of da Manyssing Indeans, a sord of raleceous poepel"; see "Relation by Frederick Post of Conversation with Indians, 1760," *PA*, 1st Ser., III, 742–743; *MPCP*, VIII, 488. For population figures, see Quaker Journal, Easton, Pa., 1761, 1, Clements Library.

39. *MPCP*, VIII, 489.

rely on their new white neighbors to fulfill the economic obligations implicit in their alliances, Indians had to find other strategies to strengthen and unify their communities. As Papunhank suggested, Indians had to look within to understand how their world had changed and what they might do to make it whole. Kinship and the market economy might have dictated the ways people interacted daily in a material world. But religion and one's spiritual relationship to a higher power also provided a compass for the future.

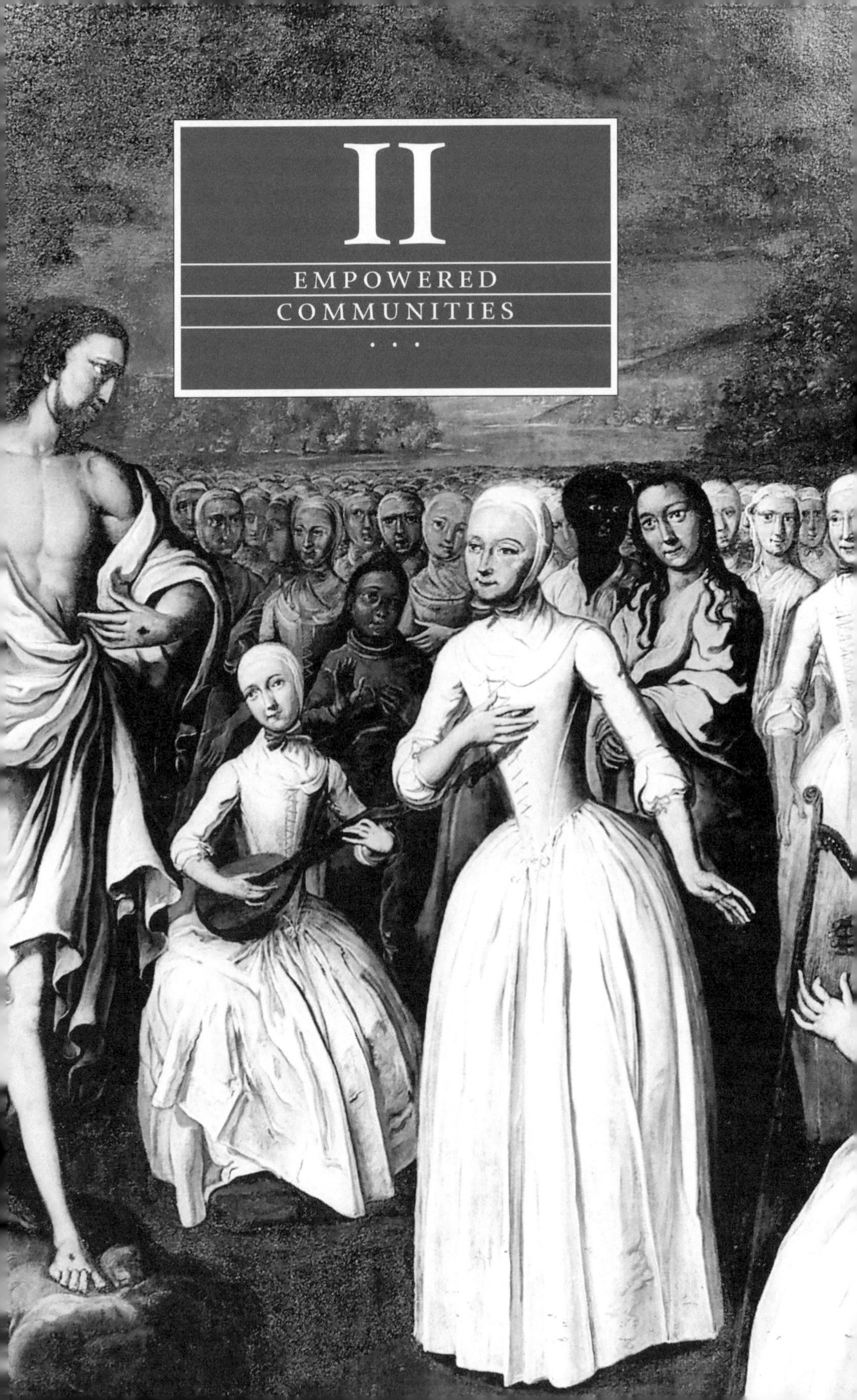

II

EMPOWERED COMMUNITIES

. . .

3

THE INDIAN GREAT AWAKENING

• • •

In December 1747, Joshua, a Mahican Christian, told a Moravian missionary at Gnadenhütten, Pennsylvania, that he had seen "many Indians in a dream, who asked him to say something to them about his God." When Joshua told the dream Indians about "the Lamb who was hung on the Cross for their sins" and about Christ's sacrifice of blood, one of their leaders urged his followers to pay close attention and remember Joshua's words. Several weeks after Joshua related his dream, the missionary Christian Heinrich Rauch noted in his journal that a Delaware arrived from the nearby village of Meniolagomekah, asking to hear about the Christian Savior.[1]

That a dream vision foretold a meeting between Christian Mahicans from Gnadenhütten and non-Christian Delawares from Meniolagomekah was perhaps less remarkable than it seems. For several decades, the latter village had been the home of an extended network of New Jersey Delawares who had kinship ties to natives along the Susquehanna River at Shamokin, Nescopeck, Wapwallopen, and the Wyoming Valley. The Moravian leader, Count Nikolaus Ludwig von Zinzendorf, foreseeing the importance of neighborly relations with Indian communities in the region, had first visited the small Delaware village in July 1742, when he toured the

1. This chapter is a revised version of Jane T. Merritt, "Dreaming of the Savior's Blood: Moravians and the Indian Great Awakening in Pennsylvania," *William and Mary Quarterly*, 3d Ser., LIV (1997), 723–746. On Joshua, see *Moravian Records*, Dec. 10, 1747, reel 4, box 116, folder 2 ("Daß er so viele Indianer im Traum gesehen die ihn gefragt, Er solte ihnen was sagen von seinem Gott," "Er ihnen mit einen solchen warmen Herzen gesagt von dem Lämmlein, das am Creuz wäre aufgehänget worden vor die Sinn der und habe sie mit seinem Blut erkauft"), Jan. 1, 1748, reel 4, box 116, folder 3, no. 7.

Pennsylvania countryside in preparation for the migration of Moravians and their mission work. By 1743, the Delawares had begun to trade and socialize with the Moravians, since their village was only a few days journey from the Moravian community at Bethlehem. The captain of Meniolagomekah, twenty-seven-year-old Memenowal, even visited occasionally, curious about Moravian religious practices. Certainly, by the time of Joshua's dream, the Delawares knew about the local Christian Mahicans, who, in turn, had most likely encountered their Delaware neighbors. Still, dreams were powerful signs, noted and interpreted by Indians and missionaries, by Christians and non-Christians alike, and dreams, like roads and kinship alliances, were particularly important in connecting frontier communities.[2]

The meaning of dreams, however, and the influence they had on native American society and religion in the eighteenth century did not always promote the peace and cooperation suggested by Joshua's vision. Other, more troubling images also informed Indian spiritual life. In February 1749, more than a year after Joshua's dream, a strange Indian came by way of Meniolagomekah to Gnadenhütten and described, as he probably had to the Delaware village, a recent dream that had come to a Nanticoke along the Susquehanna River. The Nanticoke had become ill the summer before and had disappeared. When found two days later "in the bush," he said he had been to heaven "and had been with God and had seen him and spoke with him." God revealed to the Nanticoke that "he had made brown and white people." "To the brown, he gave the Sacrifice, which they were to offer to him if they had not acted properly. . . . To the white people he had given the Bible." Both Indian and white people had strayed from their proper ways, however, and God "was not at peace with either." Further, God told the Nanticoke that Indians and whites should not "go the same way," especially since "the white people were very cunning, and had a large mouth." "If [Indians] associated with them, [the white people] would devour all of them." To show his disapproval and anger, God had caused a recent spate of epidemics and famine among the Indians of the region.[3]

2. "Annalen der Amerikanischen Brüdergeschicte," July 24, 1742, 1734 to 1857, comp. Levin T. Reichel, 1850–1857, Northampton County Papers, HSP.

3. "Und gesagt er wäre bei Gott gewesen und hatt ihnen gesehen und mit Ihm geredet." "Gott hätte gesagt, Er hätte braune und weiße Menschen gmacht. Den braunen hätte Er die Opffern gegeben, daß sie offern solten, wenn sie nicht recht gethan hätten . . . darum wär er gar nicht zu frieden mit, sie hätten auch sehr böße

Rather than driving a wedge between Pennsylvania Indians and whites, as the Nanticoke dreamer perhaps intended, this revelation, and many like it, sparked serious debates within Indian communities about native spirituality and the efficacy of Christianity in particular. They lived in a world permeated by crisis. Native populations had been reduced by epidemic diseases, white settlements crowded their customary hunting grounds and villages, and the market economy slowly replaced customary forms of gift exchange and reciprocity. Indians yearned to revitalize and reorient their communities, to address the social problems that punctuated their lives. For many, the answers lay within. Indians wanted to readjust the relationship between themselves and the spiritual realm. As the Nanticoke dream suggested, the Delawares at Meniolagomekah faced a choice between at least two different spiritual paths. They could accommodate "the Lamb" and the new Christian God, or Indians could separate themselves from white religious practices, denounce the Book, and return to the "Sacrifice" to appease native manitous. But religious enlightenment did not come simply by choosing one or the other. As Indians' circumstances changed during the first half of the eighteenth century by the presence of new technologies, diseases, and foreign peoples, they adopted new strategies, often a range of responses that combined old and new beliefs. During the 1740s, native Americans began to experience an "Indian Great Awakening," a revival and revitalization of native religiousness that included the adaptation of Christianity.[4]

Whether they attempted to find new spiritual focus for their communities or to relieve individual distress in the face of social disruption,

---

gelebt." "Den Weißen menschen hätten Er die Bibel gegeben danein hätte Er viele schone Sachen setzen lassen, sie thäten es aber auch nicht. Nun wolte Er nicht haben, daß den braunen und weißen Menschen solten einerlei weg gehen, . . . denn die weiße Mschen waren sehr kluge, und hatten einen großen Maul, wenn sie sich mit Ihnen ein ließen, wurden sie sie alle verschlingen"; see *Moravian Records,* Feb. 18, 1749, reel 4, box 116, folder 5.

4. Patrick Frazier, *The Mohicans of Stockbridge* (Lincoln, Nebr., 1992), 240–242; James H. Merrell, "The Indians' New World: The Catawba Experience," *WMQ*, 3d Ser., XLI (1984), 539; Mechal Sobel, "The Revolution in Selves: Black and White Inner Aliens," in Ronald Hoffman, Sobel, and Fredrika J. Teute, eds., *Through a Glass Darkly: Reflections on Personal Identity in Early America* (Chapel Hill, N.C., 1997), 173; Gregory Evans Dowd, *A Spirited Resistance: The North American Indian Struggle for Unity, 1745–1815* (Baltimore, 1992), 23–46; Jean M. O'Brien, *Dispossession by Degrees: Indian Land and Identity in Natick, Massachusetts, 1650–1790* (Cambridge, 1997), 51–60.

Indian leaders controlled their peoples' initial encounters with Christians. Some effectively used religion as a political tool to protect their communities' independence from the Iroquois through alliances with white Christians. For others, Christianity became an alternative way to express their faith in supernatural beings. In either case, leaders looked to what might best benefit their kin group and community. For instance, Memenowal, before he requested baptism as Augustus in April 1749, weighed Christianity's spiritual and political consequences against the Nanticoke's alternative vision of a separate existence from whites. He insisted that the Moravians extend the sacrament to his wife, siblings, and other adults related through marriage before inviting missionaries to live permanently in Meniolagomekah. During the 1740s and 1750s, Christianity helped some Indians reorient themselves during a time of crisis. But Indians also altered Christianity to fit their own spiritual needs. During the same period, Indian prophets and shamans attempted to revitalize native religions and rally support for Indian-initiated social reforms in their communities. They, too, however, had to grapple with Christianity. To debate or counter its effects, nativist reformers had to understand Christianity's concepts. In doing so, these ideas seeped into the language and beliefs of spiritual leaders. Indians did not merely shed their old practices and embrace new religious habits offered by Protestant missionaries or nativist reformers. In the religious climate of the 1740s and 1750s, individuals and communities reframed their spiritual past to help them order their present immaterial as well as material needs. Still, their search for revitalized faith, even their dreams, increasingly reflected the defining terms of that which they embraced or resisted: white Christianity.[5]

5. Bethlehem Register, Feb. 27/Mar. 10, 1749, "Bethlehisches Kirchen=Buch," I, 1742–1756, 110, Moravian Archives, Bethlehem, Pa.; *Moravian Records*, Mar. 31, Apr. 1, 1749, reel 4, box 116, folder 5; James Axtell, "Some Thoughts on the Ethnohistory of Missions," *Ethnohistory*, XXIX (1982), 35–37. Anthony F. C. Wallace with the assistance of Sheila C. Steen, *The Death and Rebirth of the Seneca* (New York, 1970), traces the advent of the Handsome Lake religion among the Iroquois at the turn of the nineteenth century. James P. Ronda, "'We Are Well As We Are': An Indian Critique of Seventeenth-Century Christian Missions," *WMQ*, 3d Ser., XXXIV (1977), 66–82, and Harold W. Van Lonkhuyzen, "A Reappraisal of the Praying Indians: Acculturation, Conversion, and Identity at Natick, Massachusetts, 1646–1730," *New England Quarterly*, LXIII (1990), 396–428, contend that eighteenth-century Indian religions included the influence of both native and Christian traditions. Charles E. Hunter, "The Delaware Nativist Revival of the Mid-Eighteenth Century," *Ethnohistory*, XVIII

Between the 1740s and 1760s, a general revival of Protestantism in the British North American colonies affected religious thought and practice from New England to the Carolinas and provided a backdrop for new religious movements among Christian and non-Christian Indians. Partly influenced by German Pietism and Protestant revival movements in central and eastern Europe, the proponents of religious awakening emphasized the importance of personal faith rather than conformity to doctrine as the path to salvation. Enthusiastic itinerant ministers, such as George Whitefield and Gilbert Tennent, stirred up a renewed sense of spiritual urgency among a largely youthful audience, offering a deeply personal relationship with God to any who chose to participate.

The revivals were particularly successful in frontier regions, where communities could not always support permanent church establishments. People welcomed ministers of any persuasion and accommodated diverse religious practices. In Pennsylvania, William Penn's legacy of ethnic and religious tolerance allowed for an eclectic mix of practices and creeds. At Lancaster in 1744, Witham Marshe, an official from Maryland engaged in treaty negotiations with the Indians, encountered Dutch Calvinists, Lutherans, and Anglican clergymen as well as "great numbers of Irish Presbyterians and several Jews . . . with divers others that neither themselves nor any one else can tell what sect they follow or imitate." By the 1740s, "outbreaks of revivalism in Pennsylvania" accompanied the increasing migration of Scots-Irish Presbyterians. Itinerant ministers sent by the Presbytery formally served Craig's Settlement and Donegal, but, in the patchwork of frontier settlements, they preached to Germans, Irish, and Indians alike. Conversely, Scots-Irish inhabitants would listen to a Baptist or Methodist minister if a Presbyterian were not available. German Moravian ministers in Nazareth also tolerated diversity among the local population. On March 23, 1746, they noted that "Eight strangers attended Preaching, viz the wife and daughter of our neighbor Le Febre, the two daughters of our Holland neighbor van Bogert, the wife of an English Minister—Dan. Burr, who had come into our vicinity from the country about Checomeco, and 3 Indian boys, relatives of our Gottlieb, who had been

(1971), 40, on the other hand, argues that native American religious revivals of this period were not "an outgrowth of indigenous tradition, but rather . . . a basically European innovation expressed in native idiom."

baptised by the Presbyterians." This array of worshipers and their participation in the inclusive spiritual revivals of the mid-eighteenth century set the tone for religious encounters between whites and Indians.[6]

Evangelical revivals affected native American communities in a variety of ways. If Indians had already accepted Christianity in these towns, the Great Awakening sometimes intensified existing religious practices. Many of the Protestant denominations experiencing revitalization supported ministers and missionaries who worked among Indians, especially in New England and the mid-Atlantic colonies. Eleazar Wheelock, David Brainerd, Joseph Fish, John Sargeant, Gilbert Tennent, and even Jonathan Edwards spent time preaching to native communities in Massachusetts, Connecticut, New Jersey, and Pennsylvania. In August 1745, while working among Christian Delawares in New Jersey, Brainerd described the emotional response of his audience, which resembled that of any revivalist congregation: "Most were much affected and many in much distress; and some could neither go, nor stand; but lay flat on the ground as if stab'd at heart: Crying incessantly for mercy. Several were newly awakned: and it's remarkable; that as fast as they came from remote places round about; the Spirit of God, seem'd to seize them, with Concern and distress for their Souls."[7]

When preaching to non-Christian Delawares on the Susquehanna, Brai-

6. Witham Marshe, *Lancaster in 1744; Journal of the Treaty at Lancaster in 1744, with the Six Nations,* ed. William H. Egle (Lancaster, Pa., 1884), 10–11; Marilyn J. Westerkamp, *Triumph of the Laity: Scots-Irish Piety and the Great Awakening, 1625–1760* (New York, 1988), 14; New Brunswick Presbytery, Minutes, 1738–1798, Presbyterian Historical Society, Philadelphia; [John Cunningham Clyde], *The Scotch-Irish of Northampton County, Pennsylvania* (Easton, Pa., 1926), 276; James H. Smylie, *Scotch-Irish Presence in Pennsylvania* (University Park, Pa., 1990), 17; "Register of Inhabitants of Nazareth" (extracts from Nazareth Diary, English translation), Mar. 23/Apr. 3, 1746, Church and Meeting Collection, HSP.

7. David Brainerd's journal, Aug. 7, 1745, APS. See also James Axtell, "Dr. Wheelock and the Iroquois," in Michael K. Foster, Jack Campisi, and Marianne Mithun, eds., *Extending the Rafters: Interdisciplinary Approaches to Iroquoian Studies* (Albany, N.Y., 1984), 51–64; William S. Simmons and Cheryl L. Simmons, eds., *Old Light on Separate Ways: The Narragansett Diary of Joseph Fish, 1765–1776* (Hanover, N.H., 1982); and William S. Simmons, "Red Yankees: Narragansett Conversion in the Great Awakening," *American Ethnologist,* X (1983), 254. Daniel Mandell, *Behind the Frontier: Indians in Eighteenth-Century Eastern Massachusetts* (Lincoln, Nebr., 1996), 127, dismisses the first Great Awakening as ineffectual or inconsequential for Massachusetts Indians.

nerd more often confronted polite attention tempered by skeptical reserve. In their own communities, Delawares, Mahicans, and Iroquois carefully controlled the actions of missionaries and determined whether and when they could speak. Still, Christian revivalism intrigued these Indians. In the fall of 1744, Brainerd visited Wapwallopen with his interpreter, Moses Tattamy, and two other Delawares. After he told the local chief his business, their council met and decided that he could hold a meeting. Brainerd recalled: "The Indians gathered, and I preached to 'em. And when I had done, I asked if they would hear me again. They replied that they would consider of it; and soon after sent me word that they would immediately attend, if I would preach." Perhaps their interest in the spectacle gave Brainerd false hope. He returned again to the Susquehanna in 1745 and 1746, with less luck. At Juniata Island, following an afternoon of native powwowing, Brainerd attempted to "discourse with [the Indians] about Christianity; but they soon scattered and gave me no opportunity for anything of that nature."[8]

Moravian missionaries also hoped to make spiritual inroads among Pennsylvania Indians. After establishing Bethlehem in the early 1740s, the Moravians appointed August Gottlieb (Joseph) Spangenberg as director of Indian missions. Missionary work, like most of their earthly activities, was meant to draw Moravians closer to God. They recognized cultural differences between themselves and the natives they sought to convert but downplayed the inequalities that other Euramericans emphasized. They believed that Indians were one of the ten lost tribes of Israel who simply needed to be reintroduced to their ancient habits and brought back into the Judeo-Christian tradition. Since everyone could and should have a personal relationship with God, they felt morally obligated to reconnect Indians with the church and give them access to salvation. They never expected large numbers to convert, nor did they think it wise to baptize Indians en masse, but they strove to have a few sincere disciples. To this end, they sent missionaries to Mahican communities in New York in 1742, and, by 1745, they had initiated work among natives on the Susque-

8. Jonathan Edwards, *The Life of David Brainerd,* ed. Norman Pettit (New Haven, Conn., 1985), 268, 328. See also Thomas E. Burke, Jr., *Mohawk Frontier: The Dutch Community of Schenectady, New York, 1661–1710* (Ithaca, N.Y., 1991), 82; Richard White, *The Middle Ground: Indians, Empires, and Republics in the Great Lakes Region, 1650–1815* (New York, 1991), 23.

hanna River and around the Forks of the Delaware and Lehigh Rivers. From the 1740s to the 1760s, the Moravians established five mission communities for Mahican and Delaware Indians in New York, Connecticut, and Pennsylvania. They began their work in the Mahican town of Shekomeko, New York, but soon turned their attention to Pennsylvania, inviting nearly sixty baptized Mahicans to Bethlehem. Subsequently, the Mahicans settled on 197 acres of land near the mouth of the Mahoning Creek, above the Lehigh Water Gap, where in the spring of 1746 Moravians built the town of Gnadenhütten, the keystone to their Pennsylvania missionary efforts.[9]

The Moravians' sincerity and concern for Indian souls did not always mitigate the impact of their presence on the region. Their methods and attitudes toward Indians sometimes precipitated the displacement of native inhabitants. Spangenberg believed that Indians would remain true to Christianity only if they lived together in a mission town, closely controlled by Moravians. He agreed with Governor George Thomas that large-scale Indian conversion might come only when "the whites are so much increased that the Indians are Cooped up into a narrow Compass and Subdued." Consequently, the Moravians had little remorse when they settled Nazareth in May 1740 on land purchased from evangelical minister George Whitefield that already supported a "fairly large Indian town." Intent on clearing and developing the land for themselves, their leader,

9. Kenneth G. Hamilton, ed. and trans., *The Bethlehem Diary,* I, *1742–1744* (Bethlehem, Pa., 1971), June 13/24, 1742, 15–16; William C. Reichel, ed., *Memorials of the Moravian Church,* I (Philadelphia, 1870), 34, 57; Synod on Moravian Indian Missions, Feb. 1–6, 1748, Northampton County, Pa., Miscellaneous Pamphlets, V, 25, HSP; Jon F. Sensbach, *A Separate Canaan: The Making of an Afro-Moravian World in North Carolina, 1763–1840* (Chapel Hill, N.C., 1998), 36, 182; "Extract from the Instructions or Rules, for Such of the United Brethren as Are Used as Missionaries or Assistants in Propagating the Gospel among the Indians," *Moravian Records,* reel 34, box 315, folder 3, item 7; George Henry Loskiel, *History of the Mission of the United Brethren among the Indians in North America,* trans. Christian Ignatius La Trobe (London, 1794), pt. 2, 7; Alfred Mathews and Austin N. Hungerford, *History of the Counties of Lehigh and Carbon, in the Commonwealth of Pennsylvania* (Philadelphia, 1884), 573; "Annalen der Amerikanischen Brüdergeschicte," Aug. 21, 1742, 1734 to 1857, comp. Levin F. Reichel, 1850–1857, Northampton County Papers, HSP. According to Zinzendorf, the "ancient habits" of Indians included male circumcision. The eighteenth-century Bethlehem graveyard, although separated by gender, was racially mixed.

Count Zinzendorf, offered to pay the proprietors for "preference in the next Indian purchase of a large body of land," and, in 1742, they received permission from the governor "to dispossess the Indians in Nazareth."[10]

The Indians, however, resisted eviction. One Delaware resident, Tishcohan, whom the Moravians called Captain John, refused to leave. The Moravians complained that he and his extended kin group, including his nephew Teedyuscung, had "made themselves Masters of our purchased Land in Nazareth." The Moravians came up with what to them seemed a compromise:

> If the Government can convince the Indian at Nazareth, called Captain John, that that Land, which has been purchas'd and warranted to us, is the Honourable Proprietor's: We are willing that the said Captain continue his Habitation on our Land, and that he enjoy the Use of all the Land he has hitherto cleared. We will also consider him as our Tenant, but without any Payment of Rent to us, because the said Place has been a Settlement of his Forefathers; and we will not drive any body from such a Right, was it only a simple Imagination.

Tishcohan would not give up easily. His clan had struggled for decades to keep control of their lands at the Forks of the Delaware. The Pennsylvania government confiscated 500,000 acres when they enforced the questionable Walking Purchase of 1737. Faced with the possible loss of their homes, Tishcohan and their Delaware neighbor Moses Tattamy petitioned the governor of Pennsylvania in November 1742, arguing that, because they had "embraced the Christian Religion [Presbyterianism] and attained some small Degree of Knowledge therein, they are desirous of living under the same Laws with the English, and praying that some place might be allotted them where they may live in the Enjoyment of the same Religion and Laws with them." The provincial secretary Richard Peters,

10. Charles Brockden to Joseph Spangenberg, *Moravian Records*, in English, May 4, 1746, reel 26, box 211, folder 4, item 2, Spangenberg to Brockden, in English, May 11, 1746, reel 30, box 223, folder 11, item 1; Vernon H. Nelson, ed. and trans., "Peter Boehler's Reminiscences of the Beginnings of Nazareth and Bethlehem," Moravian Historical Society, *Transactions*, XXVII (Nazareth, Pa., 1992), 2–3, 12; Richard Peters to Thomas Penn, Nov. 21, 1742, in Reichel, ed., *Memorials of the Moravian Church*, I, 16; Diarium von Bethlehem, June 22/July 3, 1742, in English, reel 1, Van Pelt Library, University of Pennsylvania, Philadelphia.

who had broad powers over the Land Office of Pennsylvania, denied their request; he was incredulous that "those rascals" had the "impudence to subscribe themselves, 'Your Honour's brethren in the Lord Jesus.'" The Pennsylvania government hoped that Delawares would instead acknowledge the authority of the Six Nations (as Canassatego had reminded them recently when confirming the Walking Purchase in 1742) and move to their designated settlements at Shamokin or the Wyoming Valley.[11]

The Moravians, Peters, and the Pennsylvania government might have wished them away, but Indians at the Forks of the Delaware and Lehigh Rivers faced the challenge of Christian intrusion with persistence. Tishcohan agreed to move away from the white settlement at Nazareth, receiving some compensation for his improvements on the land. He continued to live in the area, however, and visited the Moravians, even sending his son to be educated by them. Although the Moravians thought his attachment to the land "a simple Imagination," they could not ignore their real dependence on his presence, for the Delaware hunted "very diligently," providing venison and other game for their table. Thus, Moravians continued to have unbaptized Indians as neighbors—perhaps an uncomfortable reminder that they had displaced the original inhabitants even as they relied on their skills and resources. Others in Tishcohan's kin group thought that a direct religious alliance with Christians through baptism provided a possible tool for survival; it promised to strengthen their political ties with white settlers and the Pennsylvania government. In turn, these alliances could help them preserve customary communities threatened by white settlement and the political pressures from the Six Nations to the north.[12]

11. Diarium von Bethlehem, June 22/July 3, 1742, in English, reel 1, Van Pelt Library; *MPCP*, IX, 624; [Charles Thomson], *Causes of the Alienation of the Delaware and Shawanese Indians from the British Interest* (Philadelphia, 1867) (originally published as *An Enquiry into the Causes of the Alienation of the Delaware and Shawanese Indians from the British Interest . . .* [London, 1759]), 35, 39–40; Draft of statement accompanying a deed by the Six Nations to the Pennsylvania proprietors, October 1736, no. 25, Logan Family Papers, 1664–1871, XI, Indian Affairs, HSP; Copy of deed, Oct. 25, 1736, no. 40, Penn Papers, Indian Affairs, I, 1687–1753, HSP; Peters to Thomas Penn, Aug. 25, Nov. 21, 1742, in Carl Van Doren and Julian P. Boyd, eds., *Indian Treaties Printed by Benjamin Franklin, 1736–1762* (Philadelphia, 1938); Letter Book V, Apr. 23, 1743, Richard Peters Papers, 1697 to 1845, HSP; Peters commission, Oct. 26, 1737, *PA*, 1st Ser., I, 545.

12. Diary of Nazareth, Dec. 26, 1742, June 20, 1747, English translation, Moravian Hist. Soc., Nazareth, Pa.; Reichel, ed., *Memorials of the Moravian Church*, I, 127.

FIGURE 5. Baptism of Indians in America. *From David Cranz,* Kurze, zuverlässige Nachricht . . . *(Halle, 1757). Courtesy, The Library Company of Philadelphia. Delaware and Mahican converts and candidates for baptism gather at Bethlehem, Pa., to witness the ceremony. Like the Moravian congregations, separation by sex was common.*

The Delaware kin group of Tishcohan and Teedyuscung encountered the Moravians in Bethlehem and the Christian Indians at Gnadenhütten at the height of the Moravians' missionary activities in the 1740s. Even though the Delawares had lost a portion of their land to the Moravians, or perhaps because they had, the Delawares calculated that an alliance might be useful. Where Presbyterianism had failed to convince the governor of their claims, perhaps they thought German Pietism would succeed. In October 1743, with most of the family settled at Buchkabuchka, a day's journey from Bethlehem, they first "requested that the brethren should come and preach to them occasionally." Teedyuscung's half-brother Weshichagechive, called Joe Evans by the English, was the first in the family to discuss his spiritual state with the Brethren. He was impressed that the

Christian Indians at Gnadenhütten "were very happy and contented in their Hearts, and that they liv'd no longer like other Indians, doing bad Things." Perhaps he simply reiterated a formulaic confession similar to those that other Delawares had made before him when he told the Moravians at Bethlehem that "he had lead an extraordinary wicked Life and drank very hard." Yet he insisted on baptism and assured them that "his Heart had begun to feel that which he heard of our Savior."[13]

The Moravians, for their part, considered Weshichagechive's request for baptism with skepticism, wondering "if it was now the right Time for this Man, upon whom we have so long had an Eye." Yet they, too, considered the political potential of this sacrament, noting that, with the Delaware's baptism, "we break into a quite new Family, out of which the Lamb will yet gather many to his Wounds." Although their success in baptizing Indians often led to conflict with their white neighbors, the Moravians hoped that the prospective communicants might help justify their missionary efforts to the European Brethren. Indeed, the Moravians were often so eager for converts that they bypassed the usual channels of spiritual decision making. In order to baptize or marry community members, Moravian elders traditionally used the lot, in which they directed a question to the Lord and picked a marker from a jar that indicated his answer—"yes," "no," or "ask again." Among Indians in Pennsylvania, the Moravians used the lot far less. After some discussion with Bethlehem leaders, Bishop John Christopher Frederick Cammerhoff rather quickly "found that the Lamb, as we had believed, had appointed the bloody side-Holes Bath" for Weshichagechive, and he baptized the Delaware as Nicodemus in June 1749. Nicodemus's baptism in the wounds of Christ opened the way to kin conversions, including his wife, four of his sons and some of their wives, a niece, and his sister's son. In January 1750, Nicodemus's half-brother, Young Captain Harris, and his wife were baptized as Petrus and Theodora. Only in March 1750, after his brothers had placed their souls in the care of the Moravians, did Teedyuscung consent to be baptized. The Moravian minister who gave Teedyuscung the name Gideon thought he was "a great sinner" but baptized him and his immediate family all the same. The three

13. Hamilton, ed. and trans., *Bethlehem Diary,* Oct. 23, 1743, I, 169; Bethlehem Register, "Bethlehemisches Kirchen=Buch," I, 1742–1756, 114, Moravian Archives; Extract from the Bethlehem journal, June 1749, in English, *Moravian Records,* reel 26, box 211, folder 19, item 1.

Delaware brothers and their families, then, came together as Christians at the mission town of Gnadenhütten in 1750, perhaps to combat the dissolution of their family and community, perhaps to use the connections of the Moravians with other whites to strengthen their claims on land at the Forks of the Delaware, and perhaps to express what they felt in their hearts.[14]

Moravians, of course, hoped that Indians would experience the latter, a heartfelt longing for connection to Christ. To that end, they attempted to create strong emotional and personal attachments with Pennsylvania natives. As a Pietistic faith, Moravianism stressed that potential converts did not need to focus on or necessarily understand the Scriptures as a sign of election by God; they simply had to profess their faith and love of Christ. Zinzendorf insisted that the Brethren "learn nothing of their Conduct out of Books"; instead, the "Holy Ghost seizes the Heart, which has an Inclination, a Love, a Desire to the Thing." When the Moravians bap-

14. Extract from the Bethlehem journal, June 1749, in English, *Moravian Records,* reel 26, box 211, folder 19, item 1; Bishop John Christopher Frederick Cammerhoff to Count Nikolaus Ludwig von Zinzendorf, Mar. 8–23, 1747, John Christopher Frederick Cammerhoff, 1721–1751, Letters, 1747–1748, copied by John. W. Jordan, HSP; Peters to Thomas Penn, Feb. 17, 1749, Penn Papers, Official Correspondence, IV, 195, HSP; Bethlehem Register, "Bethlehemisches Kirchen=Buch," I, 1742–1756, 121, Moravian Archives. I use the German spelling for all native and baptismal names when available. Although I cannot begin to guess whether Delawares and Mahicans used their Moravian baptismal names with each other in the privacy of their own homes, they did use their given names when communicating with the Moravian missionaries or sending formal messages to other native mission communities or the Brethren in Europe. I will give a native name if it is known but will generally use baptismal names when speaking about Christian Indians in the mission towns to distinguish them from non-Christian Indians. It is clear from diplomatic sources that, by the Seven Years' War, many of the Moravian Indians who left the mission communities preferred to use their native names first, but they still included their Moravian names on documents. See Chapter 7, below.

During the late 1740s and early 1750s, the Moravians baptized several other large Delaware kin groups at the same time. Among the Indians in Pennsylvania, Moravians did not always use the lot for baptismal decisions, but they did for promotion to communicant status. Indians often pressured Moravians to baptize their children and other family members, which they also did sometimes without consulting the lot. Sensbach, *A Separate Canaan,* 107–110, notes that Moravians used the lot when deciding to baptize the African enslaved. Moravians had a very different relationship with the enslaved, however, some of whom they owned.

tized the first Delaware couple in April 1745, the diarist noted that they did not need "the Knowledge and Understanding of the Truths; but only to be sensibly touch'd with and convinced of ones Miserable Condition, that one has no Rest, and would gladly be delivered and that one has a hunger and thirst after our Savr. that he may in Grace have Mercy on one." To get their message across, most of the missionaries learned native languages, into which they translated hymns, the Scriptures, and prayers. From these translations they converted Indians, who could then preach the Moravians' message in native communities. The missionaries, usually married men and women, also moved to Indian towns, where they took part in the daily social and economic life of the inhabitants. Presbyterian David McClure observed of a western Pennsylvania mission town: "The moravians appear to have adopted the best mode of christianizing the Indians. They go among them without noise or parade, and by their friendly behaviour conciliate their good will. They join them in the chace, and freely distribute to the helpless and gradually instil into the minds of individuals, the principles of religion."[15]

Moravian women, who were actively involved in mission work during the 1740s and 1750s, proved critical to the missionaries' success. Because the Moravians divided their own religious community into a "choir" system, holding separate worship services for women and men, German women, as leaders among their sex, had a fair amount of spiritual authority. They trained as lay ministers and worked closely with their native counterparts in mission communities. Moravian women's participation led to more Indian baptisms than any early Protestant missionary effort in the colonial northeast, especially among women. Between 1742 and 1764, the Moravians baptized at least 276 Delaware and Mahican women and girls, and many more expressed interest in Christianity. During the

15. Henry Rimius, *A Candid Narrative of the Rise and Progress of the Herrnhuters, Commonly Call'd Moravians, or Unitas Fratrum . . .* (London, 1753), 44–45 n. 9; *Moravian Records,* Apr. 15/26, in English, reel 34, box 319, folder 5, item 1, n.d., in English, reel 34, box 315, folder 3, item 7; John Heckewelder, *History, Manners, and Customs of the Indian Nations, Who Once Inhabited Pennsylvania and the Neighboring States,* rev. ed., ed. William C. Reichel (1876; facsimile reprint, Bowie, Md., 1990), xvii; Johann Jacob Schmick, "Miscellanea linguae nationis Indicae Mahikan dicta cura suscepta," [ca. 1760], APS; David McClure, *Diary of David McClure, Doctor of Divinity, 1748–1820,* ed. Franklin B. Dexter (New York, 1899), 51. See also Earl P. Olmstead, *Blackcoats among the Delaware: David Zeisberger on the Ohio Frontier* (Kent, Ohio, 1991), 5, 36.

same period, 229 men and boys were baptized. Numbers alone, however, give us little insight into the reasons native Americans chose to become Moravian, nor was baptism ultimately a sign that Indians fully accepted Christian doctrine. Still, Indian women responded to the emotional elements of Pietism that Moravian women expressed and used baptism (or at least their interest in Moravian religiousness) to build ties between their communities. "They love my wife much and are Glad of all opertunities to speak with her," Brother Gottlob Büttner said of a group of Indian women visiting Bethlehem in October 1742. "She had likewise great love for them." Büttner had once surreptitiously gazed through the cracks of a wall at the service his wife held for 20 "Savage women." Büttner noted, the women "were all much moved, and sighed, and fell on each others necks." Native women did appear to be "much moved" by their experiences with Moravian women. And these first impressions became the basis for adopting Christianity as well as lasting friendships. An Indian woman who had traveled to Philadelphia in the fall of 1745 returned to Shamokin and "c[oul]d not express with w[ha]t great love she had been reced by our People [the Moravians] in Phila: but particularly th[a]t the Women had kiss'd her." "She said; it had made a great Impression on her Heart, for she had never before been treated in th[a]t manner by white People."[16]

Besides Moravianism's unique emotive qualities, Indian women found Christianity and Moravian religious practices in particular a source of power that could enhance their spiritual authority rather than diminish it. Among Algonquians, women often acted as the spiritual centers of their households, passing on gods, totems, and traditions to their daughters.

16. The years 1749 and 1750, in particular, witnessed the greatest religious activity, with sixty-six and twenty-one females baptized respectively. In comparison, David Brainerd had baptized only forty-seven Indians (twenty-three adults and twenty-four children) by 1745 (David Brainerd's journal, Nov. 4, 1745, APS). Ethnohistorians estimate that there were about five hundred Mahicans in 1700 and about thirty-two hundred Delawares (Unamis and Munsees) in 1779; see T. J. Brasser, "Mahican," and Ives Goddard, "Delaware," in William C. Sturtevant, gen. ed., *Handbook of North American Indians,* XV, Bruce G. Trigger, ed., *Northeast* (Washington, D.C., 1978), 206, 214. I estimate that 10 percent to 20 percent of the Delawares and Mahicans in Pennsylvania were baptized by the Moravians. I do not equate baptism with conversion to Christianity. See Br. Gottlob Büttner to Br. Anton Seiffert, October 1742, in English, *Moravian Records,* reel 26, box 211, folder 5, item 6, Martin Mack's travel diary, Oct. 22, 1745, in English, reel 28, box 217, folder 12B, item 1.

Delaware and Mahican women in the northeast also assisted shamans or powwows, and, as herbalists or physicians, they performed healing rituals themselves. Moravian missionary John Heckewelder noted that there were both female and male physicians among the Delawares. German women working at Indian towns took every opportunity "to apply to the female physicians, for the cure of complaints peculiar to their sex, [and] experienced good results from their abilities." When Delaware and Mahican women encountered new religious practices at Moravian mission towns, they found ways to assert themselves through what Natalie Zemon Davis has called "Christian forms and phrases" while still framing their spirituality within familiar native contexts. Some baptized Delaware and Mahican women became elders (Arbeiter Schwestern) in native congregations, a role similar to that of a lay minister. Already a forceful social presence within matrilineal kinship groups, they proselytized to unconverted neighbors, blessed newly baptized children, and listened to and translated other native women's professions of faith. Christianity also gave native women new authority as spiritual advisers, even over men. In February 1745, the Moravian missionaries found Esther, a Mahican woman, deep in conversation with an unconverted man. After much debate over the nature of Jesus, about whom "he had examined her closely," Esther seemed confident that he would choose to be baptized.[17]

17. Robert Steven Grumet, "Sunksquaws, Shamans, and Tradeswomen: Middle Atlantic Coastal Algonkian Women during the Seventeenth and Eighteenth Centuries," in Mona Etienne and Eleanor Leacock, eds., *Women and Colonization: Anthropological Perspectives* (New York, 1980), 53–54; Heckewelder, *History, Manners, and Customs*, 229; *Moravian Records*, Dec. 6/17, 1750, reel 5, box 117, folder 1; Diarium von Bethlehem, Feb. 27, 1745, reel 1, Van Pelt Library. See also Gladys Tantaquidgeon, *A Study of Delaware Indian Medicine Practice and Folk Beliefs* (Harrisburg, Pa., 1942), 26, 29, 30. Although a twentieth-century study of traditional herbal remedies, Tantaquidgeon's work confirms that Delawares used gender-specific remedies for "weakness and debility in women," "to strengthen the female generative organs," "to increase fertility," for "displacement of womb," and "for suppressed menstruation." Natalie Zemon Davis, "Iroquois Women, European Women," in Margo Hendricks and Patricia Parker, eds., *Women, "Race," and Writing in the Early Modern Period* (London, 1994), suggests that seventeenth-century Iroquois women used Christianity "to find a voice beyond that of a Shaman's silent assistant" (254). See also Nancy Shoemaker, "Kateri Tekakwitha's Tortuous Path to Sainthood," in Shoemaker, ed., *Negotiators of Change: Historical Perspectives on Native American Women* (New York, 1995), 49–71, which explores ways that Indian women embraced and adapted Catholicism.

TABLE 1. *Moravian Baptisms of Pennsylvania Delawares and Mahicans during the Eighteenth Century*

Dates	Women	Men	Total
1742–1748	64	56	120
1749–1750	86	79	165
1751–1757	69	54	123
1758–1764	34	20	54
Unknown	23	20	43
Overall	276	229	505

Sources: Carl John Fliegel, comp., *Index to the Records of the Moravian Mission among the Indians of North America,* 4 vols. (Woodbridge, Conn., 1970); *Moravian Records.*

Perhaps Esther and other Indian women found some spiritual authority in the Christian teachings of the Moravian Church because of its theological underpinnings and use of female imagery. Within the choir system, single sisters, for instance, lived and worked separately. They took communion together and spoke of themselves, Christ, the Virgin Mary, and the Holy Ghost in ways that celebrated femaleness. They likened themselves to brides of Christ, their "eternal husband." Yet they also identified with the virginal state of his mother, Mary, and her creative powers in giving birth to Christ. Perhaps most important to this female piety, the Moravians portrayed the Holy Spirit as Mother. All these representations gave women avenues to express their personal piety and gave Mahican and Delaware women a powerful religious language to express theirs.[18]

Native American women and men accommodated Christianity for a variety of political, social, and spiritual reasons, but Moravians also adapted. As missionaries established social alliances with Indians and struggled for their souls, they had to make sense of Indian religious prac-

18. Beverly Prior Smaby, "Female Piety among Eighteenth Century Moravians," in Nicholas Canny et al., eds., *Empire, Society, and Labor: Essays in Honor of Richard S. Dunn,* special supplemental issue to *Pennsylvania History,* LXIV (1997), 153–154. See also Amy C. Schutt, "Forging Identities: Native Americans and Moravian Missionaries in Pennsylvania and Ohio, 1765–1782" (Ph.D. diss., Indiana University, 1995), 50; Craig D. Atwood, "Blood, Sex, and Death: Life and Liturgy in Zinzendorf's Bethlehem" (Ph.D. diss., Princeton Theological Seminary, 1995), 158–162.

tices. In understanding, even trying to eradicate, older customs, the Moravians unavoidably participated in the religious lives of natives. During the 1740s and 1750s, missionaries listened to, recorded, and interpreted dreams, blessed hunters and their lodges, dispensed magical medicines, performed rituals over the dead and dying, and offered personal spiritual power through the blood of Christ. As they incorporated native idioms and rituals into their attempts to bring Indians into a common Christian faith, Moravian missionaries, perhaps unwittingly, acted more and more like shamans, their native counterparts. Although each borrowed language and concepts from the other, in many ways Indians absorbed Moravians, rather than vice versa.[19]

Dreams, especially, became a point of entry into this overlapping spiritual world. On the Pennsylvania frontier, whites, Indians, Christians, and non-Christians intently analyzed dreams that bore striking resemblance to one another. Many involved the presence of a male god figure, a prophecy, or instructions on correct forms of religious life. In the Nanticoke's dream, which stirred so much debate in Meniolagomekah and Gnadenhütten, God revealed that he had created both whites and Indians but insisted they live separately. Other dreams envisioned a world of common worship. In December 1747, for instance, a Paugusset (Wampanosch) at Gnadenhütten woke one morning to the cock's crow, and, as he dozed off again, he saw a luminous kraal (a livestock enclosure) that held the manger and Christ child, descending from heaven to earth. As the brightly lit manger came to rest on the ground, the entire community of Bethlehem—Germans and Indians—knelt to pray before the child.[20]

19. *Moravian Records*, Mar. 28, May 26, Nov. 21, 1752, reel 5, box 117, folder 3, July 23, 1753, reel 5, box 117, folder 4. See also Daniel K. Richter, *The Ordeal of the Longhouse: The Peoples of the Iroquois League in the Era of European Colonization* (Chapel Hill, N.C., 1992), 113.

20. *Moravian Records*, Dec. 27, 1747, reel 4, box 116, folder 2. Sobel "The Revolution in Selves," in Hoffman, Sobel, and Teute, eds., *Through a Glass Darkly*, 185, contends that, in the early modern period, Euramericans were reevaluating the self, and they projected their own negative characteristics onto alien others, such as native Americans. Dreams, which revealed these inner anxieties, were at times evidence of "othering."

The people whom Moravians identified as Wampanosch were most likely Paugussets, rather than Wampanoags. Though perhaps related to Mahicans in language and sometimes intermarriage, they had patrilineal rather than matrilineal kin structures. Far fewer Paugussets than Mahicans from Shekomeko migrated to Pennsylvania mis-

Although their dreams contained similar elements, Pennsylvanians, whether Indian or non-Indian, Christian or non-Christian, found different meanings in dreams and in the act of dreaming. At times these dreams came from external sources to provide internal inspiration and life direction. In both Iroquois and Delaware culture, the vision quest was one of the most important rites of passage for young men. Sometimes they entered a sweat lodge to induce visions that led them to the spirit world, where they could find supernatural assistance. John Heckewelder recounted that the Delawares prepared young males "so as to excite dreams and visions; by means of which they pretend that the boy receives instructions from certain spirits or unknown agents as to his conduct in life, that he is informed of his future destination and of the wonders he is to perform in his future career through the world." Far from pretense, Indians prepared themselves carefully to find and understand the prophetic meaning carried by these spirits. At other times, dreams acted as personal messages for the dreamer, emerging from within but still presenting instructions for future action. Many eighteenth-century Delawares asked, "Ta hatsch léke rechdelungawamoagan untschi?" ("What will become of his dreams?"), or, "Kocuhatsch w'delungwamoagana lapémquattowi?" ("What benefit will he derive from his dreams?"), suggesting that they, like the Iroquois, pursued the fulfillment of dreams, reading them as "desires of the soul" that they had to satisfy to avoid unwanted consequences.[21]

Even though some Euramericans scoffed at Indians' "silly fancies about

---

sion towns. See Franz Laurens Wojciechowski, *Ethnohistory of the Paugussett Tribes: An Exercise in Research Methodology* (Amersterdam, 1992), 45–47, 85–88; Kathleen J. Bragdon, *Native People of Southern New England, 1500–1650* (Norman, Okla., 1996), 21. I am grateful to Amy Schutt for these references.

21. Heckewelder, *History, Manners, and Customs,* 245; Abraham H. Cassell, comp., "Notes on the Iroquois and Delaware Indians; Communications from Conrad Weiser to Christopher Saur, 1746–1749 . . . ," *PMHB,* I (1877), 320; John Heckewelder to Peter S. Du Ponceau, Oct. 9, 1821, in John Heckewelder Correspondence, 1816–1822, APS. See also Tantaquidgeon, *A Study of Delaware Indian Medicine,* 4–5; Wallace and Steen, *Death and Rebirth of the Seneca,* 59–75; Matthew Dennis, *Cultivating a Landscape of Peace: Iroquois-European Encounters in Seventeenth-Century America* (Ithaca, N.Y., 1993), 25; Richter, *Ordeal of the Longhouse,* 25–28; Karen Anderson, *Chain Her by One Foot: The Subjugation of Women in Seventeenth-Century New France* (New York, 1991), 178–183; Iris Anna Otto, *Der Traum als Religiöse Erfahrung: Untersucht und Dargestellt am Beispiel der Irokesen* (Wiesbaden, Germany, 1982).

spirits, about their dreams, and their sorceries," they, too, listened intently to astrological forecasts, accounts of prophesies, and dreams to find meaning and purpose in their own lives. Often a fine line lay between magic and religion. Evangelical ministers of the 1740s such as the Tennents tapped into a world of miracles and apparitions to evidence the power of God. William Tennent, Jr., became seriously ill before his ordination—so ill that he died. After he had been "laid out on a board" and funeral arrangements had been made, he unexpectedly came to life. James Kenny, a Quaker trader at Pittsburgh, carefully recorded his dreams, whether they produced the devil, who "appear'd to have Frederick Posts ficognomy and Dress," or the "Appearance of a Glorious Person Possited over me like toward the firmament the attire of his head looked bright a shining Star on his forehead." Moravians also looked to the meanings of dreams as a portent of the supernatural. The elders at Nazareth, for example, voiced concern when a young German girl got "into a queer way of thinking, dreaming and speaking much about the devil." "She describes him to the other children as a black man, who is going to burn them unless they love the saviour." After all, the Moravians had not questioned whether a shrouded figure claiming to be God had appeared to a Nanticoke in a dream at Wyoming. They accepted supernatural phenomena and the power of the dream visions that it implied within their own Christian context. They questioned only whether the apparition was generated by God or the devil.[22]

In the Christian native communities of Pennsylvania, dreams still marked significant life changes and foretold life courses, infusing old

22. Cassell, comp., "Notes on the Iroquois and Delaware Indians," trans. Bell, *PMHB*, I (1877), 319; Jon Butler, *Awash in a Sea of Faith: Christianizing the American People* (Cambridge, Mass., 1990), 185; John W. Jordan, ed., "Journal of James Kenny, 1761–1763," *PMHB*, XXXVII (1913), 191; James Kenny, "A Journal to the Westward, 1758–1761," HSP; "Register of Inhabitants of Nazareth" (extracts from Nazareth Diary, English translation), Apr. 14/15, 1746, Nov. 12 / Dec. 2, 1746, Church and Meeting Collection, HSP. For other Kenny dreams, see Jordan, ed., "Journal of James Kenny," *PMHB*, XXXVII (1913), 12, 153, 176, 184. See also [Isaac Childs], *The Vision of Isaac Childs, Which He Saw in the Year 1757, concerning Pennsylvania, the Land of His Nativity* ([Philadelphia], 1766); "Prophecy and Dream" (ca. 1757), small handwritten book of verse and prophecy, HSP; David D. Hall, *Worlds of Wonder, Days of Judgment: Popular Religious Belief in Early New England* (Cambridge, Mass., 1989), 71–94; Richard Godbeer, *The Devil's Dominion: Magic and Religion in Early New England* (New York, 1992), 24–25, 122–123.

forms with new meaning. After baptism, adult Mahicans and Delawares often related to the Moravians their life stories *(Lebenslauf)*, usually an account of the spiritual crisis that led to their conversion and commitment to the Moravian faith. Many of the older baptized men had been chiefs, doctors, or religious leaders of their communities, and they described to the Moravians the dream visions they had as young men. By recounting these tales, Indians could refashion themselves; they could examine, even exorcise, past evils and project a better, perhaps saintly, future. Keposch, an old Delaware who was baptized as Salomo when in his seventies, described one such vision in January 1749. Years before, when he was a young chief at the Forks of the Delaware, he had insulted another Delaware leader by persuading his wife to leave him. The man then bewitched Keposch so that he "died after a long illness." In his deathlike state, Keposch had a vision in which he met "a man in a bright white robe floating in the air, who called to him and said: you shall not die, but live, and be called after my name, Tammekappei." He was "lifted up to the man in the air, and saw the world below him as a small ball in a large child's playground, in which white, brown, and black people" lived together. The Godlike man then "showed him how evil the people of the world acted and what gruesome sins they committed." He warned Keposch to "be a good influence and not fall into the wickedness of the world, and therefore he should not die prematurely, but live until his proper time would come." Finally, Keposch "saw that he was not dead and he believed that he was awarded with life with which he could become acquainted with the Lord, and might be baptized with his blood."[23]

We may wonder whether the Moravian missionary recording the newly baptized Keposch / Salomo's life story changed the meaning of his tale from a dream vision, by which young Indian males received life instructions, to a Christian Redemption story that predicted baptism in the blood of Christ. No doubt missionaries often interpreted such dreams in a Chris-

23. Bethlehem Register, Jan. 13/24, 1749, "Bethlehemisches Kirchen=Buch," I, 1742–1756, 105–106, Moravian Archives. Sobel, "The Revolution in Selves," in Hoffman, Sobel, and Teute, eds., *Through a Glass Darkly*, 173–174, suggests that these collected testimonials came through submission to the authority of the Christian church, even indicating that native Americans or Africans accepted the religious ideology of that church over their traditional beliefs. I argue that native Americans already participated in situational refashioning and were, therefore, comfortable reframing the past in a new context but not rejecting their customary religious beliefs.

tian context and read significance into them, hoping to redirect the spiritual energies of Pennsylvania Indians toward Christ. For Moravians, who widely distributed copies of Indian confessions and Lebenslauf among their own communities, these dreams also provided ways to reconceptualize Indians, to make them acceptable as Christians. But were they evidence of native piety? In some ways, the distinction between dream vision and Redemption story hardly matters here, for Keposch had probably seen enough similarity in the Christian stories of Resurrection, Redemption, and renewal to use them to make sense of his own youthful visionary experience as he entered a new phase of his life. Even though his vision, retold many decades later, supposedly predicted Christian conversion, we know that Keposch lived for many years as Tammekappei before he chose to be baptized as Salomo. Indians often took on new names, personae, and social roles at significant junctures in their lives, and baptism, with the bestowal of a Christian name, could be yet another milestone. To become Christian, then, an Indian did not have to let go of the past but instead could merely reframe it as a new, yet familiar context for the present.[24]

Besides dreaming, other rituals provided a place where spiritual lives intersected and where native forms accommodated Christian meaning. For native Americans, hunting rituals had great religious significance, since game was a primary source of food. They recognized a social relationship between animals and humans, the outcome of which could be manipulated to their advantage through a variety of religious rites. Hunters often performed rituals of sacrifice and made appeals for supernatural assistance. After the first kill of a hunting expedition, individuals might prepare ritual offerings and a feast. They sometimes appeased animal spirits by setting out tobacco by a carcass as a gift or by blowing smoke from a pipe into the throat of a dead animal, which "conjures the departed Spirit not to resent the injury done his body" or interfere with future hunting.[25]

24. Loskiel, *History of the Mission,* trans. La Trobe, pt. 1, 62; Frank G. Speck, *The Tutelo Spirit Adoption Ceremony: Reclothing the Living in the Name of the Dead* (Harrisburg, Pa., 1942), 75; C. A. Weslager, "Delaware Indian Name Giving and Modern Practice," in Herbert C. Kraft, ed., *A Delaware Indian Symposium,* Anthropological Series No. 4 (Harrisburg, Pa., 1974), 137–138. For a dream experience of a non-Christian Indian that is strikingly similar to Keposch's, see *Moravian Records,* Sept. 2, 3, 1755, in English, reel 28, box 217, folder 12 B, item 4.

25. Richard White and William Cronon, "Ecological Change and Indian-White

Hunting did not lose its material or spiritual significance when Indians became Christian. For Moravian Indians, the hunting lodge remained an important site of religious activities, baptisms, and conversations, and missionaries joined in ritual appeals for supernatural assistance. As one of the most successful hunters of the Delaware community at Meniolagomekah, Memenowal (baptized as Augustus) spent much of his time at his hunting lodge, especially in the fall. In November 1752, missionary Johann Jacob Schmick joined Augustus and his brother Joshua at their hunting lodge, where "they passed their time in the evening with beneficial discourse, and often thought about the gratifying love of the Lord and their predestination." One wonders whether Schmick made any connection between native rituals and Christian contexts when he further noted: "Morning and evening they sing verses. In hunting they are considerably fortunate." The Delaware hunters no doubt associated their own success with the new hymns and prayers they used. The Lamb of God provided the same sacramental focus for Augustus as deer or bear spirits. Just as Indian dreams could have Christian meaning, Indian rituals could encompass the Christian God's providence.[26]

Relations," in Sturtevant, gen. ed., *Handbook,* IV, Wilcomb E. Washburn, ed., *History of Indian-White Relations* (Washington, D.C., 1988), 419; W[illia]m M. Beauchamp, ed., *Moravian Journals Relating to Central New York, 1745–66* (Syracuse, N.Y., 1916), 184; John Bartram, *Travels in Pensilvania and Canada* (Ann Arbor, Mich., 1966) (originally published as *Observations on the Inhabitants, Climate, Soil, Rivers, Productions, Animals, and Other Matters Worthy of Notice* . . . [London, 1751]), 25; "So gar die beine wurden ins feur geworfen, damit sie kein Hund fresen solten"; see *Moravian Records,* June 4, 1749, reel 6, box 121, folder 5, item 2. See also David Brainerd journal, Sept. 19, 20, 1745, 31–32, APS; Peter C. Mancall, *Valley of Opportunity: Economic Culture along the Upper Susquehanna, 1700–1800* (Ithaca, N.Y., 1991), 44–46; Tantaquidgeon, *A Study of Delaware Indian Medicine,* 42; Dowd, *Spirited Resistance,* 29; Paul A. W. Wallace, *Conrad Weiser, 1696–1760, Friend of the Colonist and Mohawk* (1945; reprint, New York, 1971), 88; William A. Hunter, ed., "John Hays' Diary and Journal," *Pennsylvania Archaeologist,* XXIV (1954), 79.

26. *Moravian Records,* Dec. 14, 15, 1745, reel 1, box 111, folder 1, Dec. 30/Jan. 10, 1750, reel 5, box 117, folder 1, Nov. 24, 1752, reel 5, box 117, folder 3 ("Ihre Abdzeit haben sie mit nuzlichen Discursen zu gebracht, u[nd] oft an die erfreunl. liebe des Hlds und ihrer Gnadenwahl gedacht. Morgens u[nd] Abends singen sie Versgen. Im jagen sind Sie zieml. glückl."), Jan. 26, 1754, reel 5, box 118, folder 1. Goddard, "Delaware," in Sturtevant, gen. ed., *Handbook,* XV, Trigger, ed., *Northeast,* 220, asserts that, if someone dreamed of their own guardian spirit, which was usually an animal or bird, it was also considered fortunate for the hunt.

Dreams and rituals contained multiple meanings in mission communities and crossed the boundary between Indian and white worlds. Other religious metaphors also brought Christian and non-Christian peoples together. In political arenas, native Americans always symbolically cleansed the body, washing the eyes, ears, throat, and heart before public speaking; thus, they prepared disputing parties to approach negotiations with open minds. Similarly, the body was a central metaphor for religious expression. In 1752, an Onondaga asked the Moravians to preach at their town, for he believed that, if spiritual men learned to communicate with them and vice versa, they might "tell one another the thoughts of our hearts." Zinzendorf also emphasized the heart as the center of religious experience, the place where faith resided because "love institutes the very life and soul of belief" in true religion. Though some Euramerican Protestants strove to overcome the needs and desires of the body, the Moravians made their bodies and the body of Christ and its corporeality their focus. For most Protestant groups, the blood of Christ remained metaphoric and its power a symbol of his sacrifices and promised salvation. Moravians, in contrast, brought a sensual and emotional quality to their worship of Christ's wounds and blood, and Indians found these images most compelling. In their own worship and their teachings to native Americans, Moravians focused on the wounds of Christ, especially the side wound and the blood that flowed from his body.[27]

The power inherent in the body and blood of Christ seemed to be what most attracted Indians to the Moravian faith. Native Americans were drawn to, yet cautious of, the crucified and bleeding Christ. Blood was powerful: even outside the spirit world, Indians perceived blood as enigmatic or dangerous. The images and rhetoric of blood, however, had different meanings for women and men. For men, the imagery of a bleeding Christ might have evoked certain connections to the powers of warriors who stoically withstood torture and the curing properties of the sweat lodge. Nanticoke and Shawnee warriors, visiting Bethlehem in March

27. John W. Jordan, ed., "Rev. John Martin Mack's Narrative of a Visit to Onondaga in 1752," *PMHB*, XXIX (1905), 355; Gillian Lindt Gollin, *Moravians in Two Worlds: A Study of Changing Communities* (New York, 1967), 11; Beverly Prior Smaby, *The Transformation of Moravian Bethlehem: From Communal Mission to Family Economy* (Philadelphia, 1988), 28–29. The word for death that Moravians used during this period was "Seitenhölchenfahrt," or "journey into the sweet side wound" (ibid., 29). See also Atwood, "Blood, Sex, and Death," 101–104, 220.

1753, examined pictures of the crucified Christ in the Single Brothers' House and responded with awe: "Do but look, how many wounds he has! how much blood flows forth! I have also heard lately from the Brethren, th[a]t he was very sick, and prayed, and then sweat very much; th[a]t his sweat ran like blood from his body." Few images could be as powerful to these young men as the Crucifixion. Here was a spiritual leader captured by the enemy and nailed to a cross, sweating blood and silently defying torture, whose body, blood, and spiritual powers were then distributed to his followers for consumption through communion. The warriors' awe at the number of wounds, the powerful image of a man sweating blood to heal himself and his followers, and their own ideals of stoicism under torture all suggest that they saw Christ as the ultimate warrior captive.[28]

For women, the imagery of Christ's blood also had physical implications. When their bodies bled every month, native women did not simply come into contact with a potentially powerful being; they became powerful beings. Menstruating women were therefore isolated from their families and forbidden to prepare food or take part in community ceremonies. Native men avoided coming in contact with menstruating women for fear the women's potent energy might damage their own power. Although mediated by the pen of a Moravian missionary and formulaic in nature, the religious testimonies of Delaware and Mahican women who chose baptism provide an oblique window into their understanding of blood theology and its personal significance. Many women expressed a deep longing to partake in the Moravian rituals of blood—baptism in the wounds of Christ and communion. When the newly baptized Delawares of Meniolagomekah visited Gnadenhütten in the summer of 1749, the women exclaimed how they were "right hungry after the Savrs. Blood." Anna Benigna, Augustus's first wife, admitted that "her Heart lov'd the Side Hole very much, and wish'd to sink yet deeper into it." Another Delaware woman, Verona, had been feeling ill that week, but, when she heard they would travel to Gnadenhütten, she brightened: "'We shall certainly have the Blood of our Savr. there.' Upon which she got up imediatly and set out

28. *Moravian Records,* Mar. 20, 1753, in English, reel 40, box 3500, folder 16; Richter, *Ordeal of the Longhouse,* 36; Wallace and Steen, *Death and Rebirth of the Seneca,* 30–33, 44–45. See also Dowd, *Spirited Resistance,* 15–16; and Frank G. Speck, *A Study of the Delaware Indian Big House Ceremony* (Harrisburg, Pa., 1931), 74. For Christian Indians, the sweat lodge, like the hunting cabin, also provided a place to hold spiritual discussions (*Moravian Records,* Jan. 1, 1748, reel 4, box 116, folder 3).

on the Way, came along right well and lost her Sickness." One unbaptized woman who had come with her family lamented that "she c[oul]d not bear any longer to be without our Savr.'s Blood; and that particularly since she had seen *Sophia,* Gottlieb's Daughter, baptis'd in Gnaden=Hütten, her Heart long'd Day and Night after that Blood."[29]

Native women in Pennsylvania experienced conversion in physical terms—as hunger, thirst, longing, trembling—and usually expressed this piety to the German women who shared their communities and could empathize with their common bodily experiences. In 1755, a young Mahican woman spoke with missionary Anna Mack after communion (called a Love Feast) and said: "Sister you spoke to me true words, namely when one feels the Lord and his blood, then one continues to feel hunger and thirst. It is true; I had such an experience this week. My heart was at peace. I was in the woods making baskets and there I felt within me such a hunger for the Lord that I nearly trembled. The Lord was very near to me." A Paugusset woman, baptized as Rachel, the first wife of Moravian missionary Christian Frederick Post, most eloquently combined her joy at taking communion and having her first child. "I must let thee know How I felt myself at the Lord super," she wrote to Maria Spangenberg in 1746:

> When I was in Checomeco, and I saw Children, I wept always because I had none: Now I thank our Savr. Continually, th[a]t he has given me one, and I think always, Onéwe, Onéwe pachtomawas, i.e. I thank thee, I thank thee O my dr. Savr. I am right happy, it was so with me as if I had seen the Angels how they rejoiced with us. . . . Then it was clear to my Heart . . . Muchree honiseso pachtomawas onéwe onéwe Kia utachwonen Uctomsee. . . . I can't express how it was with me when I reced that Blood.

29. Extract from Bethlehem diary, June 4/15, 1749, in English, *Moravian Records,* reel 26, box 211, folder 19, item 1; Milo Milton Quaife, ed., *The Western Country in the Seventeenth Century: The Memoirs of Lamothe Cadillac and Pierre Liette* (Chicago, 1947), 132–133; Dowd, *Spirited Resistance,* 6; Tantaquidgeon, *A Study of Delaware Indian Medicine,* 14; Speck, *Delaware Indian Big House Ceremony,* 91. See also Mary Douglas, *Implicit Meanings: Essays in Anthropology* (London, 1975), 61. White, *Middle Ground,* 516, uses the example of Tenskawatawa, who, after failing to conquer the Americans at Tippecanoe in 1810, "blamed the failure of his power on the menstruation of his wife." "Unclean, she had polluted his medicine and sapped his strength."

FIGURE 6. *Doubting Thomas.* By Johann Valentin Haidt. 1758. From the collection of the Moravian Historical Society, Nazareth, Pa.
Moravians believed deeply in the power of Christ's wounds and blood. The side wound, in particular, was seen as a place of reverence and refuge, meant to restore one's faith.

Yet she did express it, whether in Paugusset or German or English, that the release of childbirth, the joy of having a child—her own power of creation in blood—was simultaneous with, inseparable from, perhaps even a consequence of her spiritual deliverance through the blood of Christ. Indian women in Pennsylvania could readily connect the female imagery of Mary, Christ's mother, and the communion of Christ's sacrifice with their own understanding of the power and physicality of blood to create a new religious identity that combined their own traditional values with Christian theology.[30]

According to these women's recorded statements, their hearts longed and their bodies hungered for the creative (even procreative) powers of Jesus' blood. But they also acknowledged the fragility of the human body or the tenuous nature of human life and sought ways to heal themselves. Whereas many Europeans understood illness in terms of a physical imbalance of the body, Indians and Moravians shared assumptions about the deep connections between spiritual and physical well-being. In native communities, shamans or Indian doctors looked after the spiritual as well as physical health of their patients. In mission towns, the Moravians did the same. Christian native communities accepted the bloodletting of Christ as a means of spiritual renewal. By way of communion, this source of power could be incorporated into Indians' own bodies. Because the Moravian ministers officiated at the rituals of baptism and communion, they acted as powerful shamans who dispensed the body of Christ and

30. *Moravian Records,* reel 5, box 118, folder 4 ("Schwester, du hast mir lezthen wahren Worte gesagt, neml. wenn man die Hld u. sein Blut fühle, so spure man doch noch immer hunger u. durst nach ihm ihn noch mehr zu fühlen. Es ist wahr, ich habe diese Woche so erfahren, es war mir recht wohl in meinem Herzen ich war im Busch Korbe zu machen, u. da fühlte ich meinen solchen Hunger nach dem Hld., daß ich fast gezittnet habe; der Hld war mir recht nahe"), Rachel Post to Maria Spangenberg, (1746?), reel 34, box 319, folder 2, item 1. Susan Juster, *Disorderly Women: Sexual Politics and Evangelicalism in Revolutionary New England* (Ithaca, N.Y., 1994), 67, describes similar religious sensibilities among New England women in the mid-eighteenth century. It is, perhaps, a sad irony that Rachel Post died a year later during a premature birth. She had been quite ill when "a son came from her, with which she was six months pregnant, . . . It was laid in her arms in the coffin with her" and buried in the Bethlehem cemetery ("In den lezten zugen, ginng ein Söhnlein, womit sie 6 monath schwanger gewesen, von ihr und hatte schon sein Huttlein verlassen. Es wurde in ihren Arm in Sarg gelegt und also mit ihr um"); see Bethlehem Register, Dec. 15/26, 1747, I, Sterbe=und Begrabniß=Register, 187, Moravian Archives.

created a link between Indians and the spirit of th
like their native counterparts, also provided medici
the sick. August Gottlieb Spangenberg, while a min
studied medicine at the University of Halle and tr
Like his contemporaries, he learned that a person's
the fluids, or humors, in the body—blood, phlegn
choly. One of the most common medical practices
moral balance of an individual was bloodletting. Moravians performed bleeding operations with the same kind of reverence they felt for the wounds of Christ. In April 1746 at Nazareth, "Br. Rauch performed venesection on Sarah." "The operation came off quite successfully—thank God—whilst Abm. sung verses." They let the blood of humans and animals alike. In May, the "calves and horned cattle [at Nazareth] had venesection performed upon them." Bloodletting was thought to cure a variety of ailments, including fevers, convulsions, and the complications of pregnancy. Still more significant, Moravians believed that it could ward off smallpox.[31]

Perhaps Moravians' belief in bloodletting's protective powers explained why Indians in Pennsylvania thought it could be a potent cure. Native communities in the northeast had been devastated by smallpox, and they welcomed new medicines and medical practices that might help

31. Charles A. Waltman, *Eighteenth Century Bethlehem Medical Practices* (Bethlehem, Pa., 1986), 5, 19; Colin G. Calloway, *New Worlds for All: Indians, Europeans, and the Remaking of Early America* (Baltimore, 1997), 32; Laurel Thatcher Ulrich, *A Mid-Wife's Tale: The Life of Martha Ballard, Based on Her Diary, 1785–1812* (New York, 1991), 55–56. Purging was particularly popular in the eighteenth century. See Peters to Conrad Weiser, June 4, 1744, Richard Peters Papers, 1697–1845, II, pt. 1, HSP: "Dr. Grame sends you a vomit gentle and easy, just to clean your stomach." Indians also prescribed herbs that induced purging. On April 14, 1727, Conrad Weiser again was given medicine by his host at Onondaga, which "made a strong impression on my stomach and bowels, succeeded by a violent vomiting" (William M. Beauchamp, *The Life of Conrad Weiser as It Relates to His Services as Official Interpreter between New York and Pennsylvania, and as Envoy between Philadelphia and the Onondaga Councils* [Syracuse, N.Y., 1925], 25). See also "Register of Inhabitants of Nazareth" (extracts from Nazareth Diary, English translation), Apr. 2/13, Apr. 17/28, May 24/June 4, July 7/18, 1746, HSP; *Moravian Records*, Aug. 23, 1751, reel 5, box 117, folder 2, Dec. 5, 1751, reel 5, box 117, folder 3; William Parsons to Timothy Horsfield, June 9, 1757, Northampton County Papers, Bethlehem and Vicinity, Miscellaneous Manuscripts, 1741–1886, HSP.

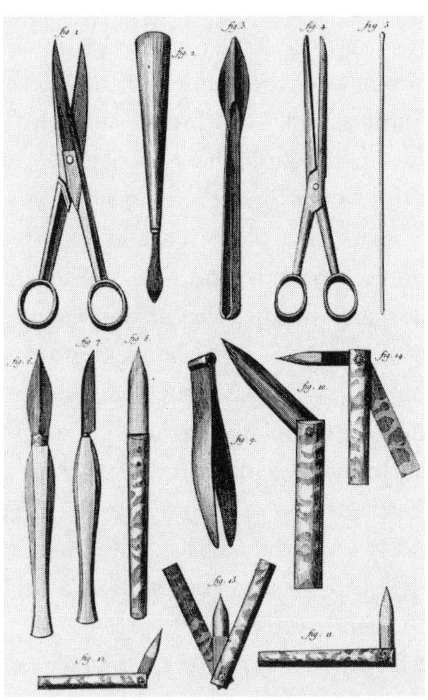

FIGURE 7. Bloodletting. *(left)* Bloodletting Procedure. *By Prosper Alpini. 1718. (top) Medical Instruments. (bottom) Bloodletting Procedure. By Hermann Peters. 1900. All courtesy, National Library of Medicine, Bethesda, Md.*
Like their European ancestors, Moravians and other Euramerican colonists commonly used bloodletting to treat illness during the eighteenth century.

alleviate its symptoms or prevent it altogether. At the Forks of the Delaware in the summer of 1746, an epidemic struck both Indian and white communities. "Within 5 hours time," wrote the Bethlehem diarist on July 17, "3 of our brown Brethren [died] of the smallpox in the house." By August, more had died, and many more were sick. That summer twenty-two baptized Indians died in Bethlehem, Nazareth, and Gnadenhütten. Perhaps in search of healing purification and guiding visions that usually came through ritual sweating, Christian Indians—both the sick and the dying—instead turned to white missionaries for assistance, assurance, medicine, and ritual bleeding. Moravians and Indians traveled great distances to bleed patients and to be bled. Indeed, so many Indians came to the Brethren for bloodletting during the 1740s that the Moravians decided to place restrictions on its use. In January 1748, the elder's conference in Shamokin determined that "blood letting to the Indians should be performed rarely and only in the case of urgent need."[32]

Epidemic diseases so overwhelmed frontier inhabitants that even non-Christian Indians clamored for the supernatural assistance of the Moravians. The spiritual rites of communion and the healing rituals of bloodletting helped to bridge gaps between Christian and non-Christian worlds. When missionaries visited native communities along the Susquehanna, for example, bloodletting offered a diplomatic way to preserve goodwill between whites and Indians. On a trip in June 1745, Spangenberg bled cultural broker Andrew Montour's sister in Shamokin, and, upon reaching the Iroquois in Onondaga, he "let the blood of our house host, the King

32. "Daselbst ginngen in 5 Stunden Zeit 3 von unsern Braunen Geschw. an den Blattern aus der Hutte"; see Diarium von Bethlehem, July 17/28, 1746, reel 2, Van Pelt Library. The count of those who died from smallpox did not include unbaptized kin and the native peoples along the Susquehanna, who were also suffering from epidemics and famine that summer. "Den Indianer Ader laßen soll so selten als auf geschehen und nur ohne dringende Noth"; see *Moravian Records,* Jan. 4/15, 1748, reel 6, box 121, folder 9, item 3, May 10, 1763, reel 6, box 124, folder 4. Moravians were equally concerned about the safety of the operations and decided to keep their medical knowledge a secret (June 26, 1748, reel 6, box 121, folder 9, item 3). Benjamin Rush, "An Inquiry into the Natural History of Medicine among the Indians of North-America . . . ," in *Medical Inquiries and Observations,* 2d American ed., I (Philadelphia, 1794), 32, notes that Indians in late-eighteenth-century Pennsylvania still used bleeding as common medical practice along with sweating and purging. See also Julius Friedrich Sachse, trans., *Falckner's Curieuse Nachricht von Pennsylvania* . . . (Philadelphia, 1905), 137–139.

[Canassatego]." "There also came many sick people and demanded some medicine from Br. Joseph, which he also gave them, and the Lord blessed it." Six days later, when Spangenberg returned to Onondaga, Canassatego saw him approaching by boat and "built a fire, and prepared food." "When Bro. Spangenberg landed, he requested him to bleed him." What an intriguing scene: an Iroquois chief seeking the services of a white missionary (shaman) by offering a ritual feast and the missionary making blessings or incantations over medicines to cure white illnesses. Epidemic diseases did not necessarily shatter native belief systems, but they did often push Indians to find innovative solutions. Indians, faced with the horrors of smallpox and other illnesses carried by white men, adapted some of the spiritual principles and healing rituals that Moravian missionaries offered, and they found comfort in them. Rather than abandon their religious practices under the pressures of colonialism, native Americans found creative ways to borrow Christianity as they revitalized their spiritual lives.[33]

Not all Indians invited Moravians or Christianity into their lives. Some were deeply suspicious of the new religion and the missionaries who introduced it. Even some families who welcomed their presence, such as Teedyuscung and his kin group, experienced contention and factionalism over the Moravians. In particular, Teedyuscung's uncle Nutimus, who by the late 1740s had moved from the Forks of the Delaware and settled among unconverted kin at Nescopeck on the Susquehanna River, objected to Teedyuscung's interest in Christianity and soon after his nephew's baptism tried to "bring him back to the old Indian Way." Nutimus distrusted the Moravians' motives; the diarist at Gnadenhütten hastily scrawled that the whole "affair was very complicated, and filled with the usual arguments against the Brethren and their intentions among the Indians."

33. "Br. Joseph ließ unserm Hauß wirth den König zur Ader, es kamen auch viele kranke u. begehrten etwas Arzney vom Br. Joseph, welche er ihnen auch gab, u. den Heyl. seegnete es"; see Spangenberg travel diary, June 20, 1745, *Moravian Records,* reel 30, box 223, folder 7, item 1; John W. Jordan, ed., "Spangenberg's Notes of Travel to Onondaga in 1745," *PMHB,* II (1878), 430; Beauchamp, ed., *Moravian Journals,* 14. See also Jordan, ed., "Journal of James Kenny," *PMHB,* XXXVII (1913), 46; Bruce G. Trigger, "Ontario Native People and the Epidemics of 1634–1640," in Shepard Krech III, ed., *Indians, Animals, and the Fur Trade: A Critique of Keepers of the Game* (Athens, Ga., 1981), 30.

FIGURE 8. *A Method of Bloodletting among Native Americans.* By Lionel Wafer. 1699. Courtesy, National Library of Medicine, Bethesda, Md.
Although the setting looks fanciful, many colonists, such as Benjamin Rush, note that Indians did use bleeding as a common medical practice well into the late eighteenth century.

Others besides Nutimus considered Christianity dangerous to Delawares. On one level, the Moravians acted as political links to the Euramerican world, but, on another, they represented a rival group of spiritually powerful men. Accordingly, shamans sometimes feared that their own spiritual powers might be damaged or depleted through contact with Christians. Or, conversely, Indians who considered Christian conversion feared that shamans might poison or enchant them in retaliation. In July 1760, a baptized Delaware called on a visiting Indian doctor to cure his ill son at a Moravian mission town. After a few attempts at conjuring the proper spirits for a healing ceremony, the doctor returned the gun with which the father had paid him and said, "I can't cure your son, because he and his heart are always there in the small church, where I have no power to perform my business."[34]

The Brethren, of course, underestimated the strength of conviction among native religious leaders. For every Indian doctor who laid down his rattle in the face of Christianity, several more struggled even harder to practice their craft. Just as Nutimus attempted to recapture the allegiance of his nephews, shamans attempted to bring their own communities "back to the old Indian Way." Beginning in the late 1730s, a religious alternative emerged in Pennsylvania Indian communities that closely paralleled the Nanticoke's dream in Wyoming. By the 1740s, a nativistic movement to revitalize Indian religions and to reform Indian communities had gathered momentum. The reform movement was not so much a coordinated reaction to Christianity in the small communities between the Forks of the Delaware and the Susquehanna River as it was a response to whites who

34. *Moravian Records,* Dec. 30/Jan. 10, 1750, reel 5, box 117, folder 1 ("Ihn wieder auf den alten Indianer Weg zu bringen. Die Sache war sehr weitläufftig u[nd] mit den gewöhnlichen Argumenten gegen die Brüder u[nd] ihre Intentionen unter den Indianern angefüllt, und zugleich hatte er ihn invitiren laßen, daß Gideon doch nur einmal nach Nesgopeke kommen solte, da er als denn weiter mit ihm reden wolte"), July 20, 21, 1760, reel 6, box 124, folder 1, item 3 ("Ich kan deinen Sohn nicht Curiren den er ist mit seinen Hertzen dort immer in der kleinen Kirche, da zu habe ich selber keine Kraft hier meine Sachen aus zu führen"). Gloria Flaherty, *Shamanism and the Eighteenth Century* (Princeton, N.J., 1992), sees a similar pattern among Greenland and Siberian natives, where shamans either practiced underground in the face of the increased activity of Christian missionaries or incorporated Christian elements into shamanistic rituals (56–57). See also Edwards, *Life of David Brainerd,* ed. Pettit, 265–266; Jordan, ed., "Journal of James Kenny," *PMHB,* XXXVII (1913), 19; David Brainerd's journal, Aug. 26, 1745, 26–27, APS.

had changed the material conditions of native peoples' lives. Like their critique of new economic relationships, reformers also tried to revitalize indigenous religious practices and correct native ways of life, especially practices perceived as vices associated with white behavior. They blamed white traders and settlers for introducing alcohol and its ill effects to Indian communities. They admonished Indians for abandoning their past moral standards to indulge in these new vices.[35]

Native American reformers began to define the traditional moral behavior of Indians by reference to the immoral actions of whites, whom they blamed for Indian degeneracy. They especially criticized the seeming hypocrisy of whites who extolled the virtues of Christianity while displaying unchristian behavior. In their critique of the white world, however, Indians described their own spiritual state in terms that echoed the rhetoric and moral tone of their Christian neighbors. In July 1744, an Indian traveling through Bethlehem said "that he wanted to have nothing to do with [Christian] teaching." "For he saw that even if many Indian and white people observe the Sabbath, they were still just as wicked as them." The following summer, when Delaware Indians visited Bethlehem, one remarked that he had once wished to be baptized and even had lived among white people, but he soon realized that, although they praised the virtues of the Bible, "they still lived as badly as the Indians." A Delaware chief asked David Brainerd why he wanted "the Indians to become Christians, seeing the Christians were so much worse than the Indians are in their present state." "The Christians, he said, would lie, steal, and drink worse than the Indians. 'Twas they first taught the Indians to be drunk." Such phrases—"as wicked as them," "as badly as the Indians," and "worse than the Indians"—are conspicuous in their reproaches. Pennsylvania Indians used the moral terms of Christianity to critique white Christians and in doing so placed themselves along that same moral continuum. By the 1750s, native spiritual leaders seemed to be less concerned with what the Nanticoke dreamer had called the "Sacrifice," the ritual manipulation and appeasement of gods and spirits that composed part of traditional Indian religions. As they struggled to save Indians from degeneracy, reformers became more and more preoccupied with questions of morality and sin.[36]

35. Peter C. Mancall, "Men, Women, and Alcohol in Indian Villages in the Great Lakes Region in the Early Republic," *Journal of the Early Republic*, XV (1995), 442–446.

36. Diarium von Bethlehem, July 8, 1744, reel 1, Van Pelt Library ("Daß er nichts

With threats of imminent disaster, native preachers admonished Indians to reform their moral behavior. But they also offered new paths to salvation. In the early 1760s, a prophet appeared in western Pennsylvania and the Ohio Valley among the Delawares. Neolin, known as the Impostor by the English, envisioned a radical separation from white society. He advocated that Indians in Ohio "learn to live without any Trade or Connections with the White people, Clothing and Supporting themselves as their forefathers did." According to Quaker trader James Kenny, Neolin introduced "new devotions" that included "Dancing, Singing and sometimes all Kneeling and praying (its said) to a little God who carries the petitions and presents them to the Great Being, which is too High and mighty to be Spoke to by them; this little God lives in some place near them."[37]

Even in isolation from white people, however, Indian ministers and reformers borrowed from white cultures as they reformulated and revitalized native religious practices. Not only did Neolin introduce new devotions, whose deity structure resembled that of Christianity (the little God could have parallels to Jesus); he also employed recently introduced religious paraphernalia, a prayer book with "the Image of the Son or Little God at the top of it." As early as the seventeenth century, Jesuits had offered books or calendars of religious feast days to their Indian converts. By the mid-eighteenth century, similar kinds of books, charts, and other written works were becoming more common even among non-Christian Indian worshipers. In the 1750s, Indian religious leaders in Pennsylvania sometimes distributed books or charts of rules for religious behavior. In the Wyoming Valley in 1754, the Moravians encountered an Indian preacher who carried a book that "contained everything that they should know about God, about the world, about Men, about deer, about hunting, and about other things."[38]

---

möchte mit unsern Lehren zu thun haben. Denn er sähe, daß viele Indianer und weise Leute wenn sie gleich den Sontag feierten, doch eben so schlimm wären wie sie"), June 15/26, 1745 ("Er sagte er hatte sich auch ein mahl bekehren wollen u. er hatte auch unter Weisse Leute gewohnt, die hatten das große Buch gahabt, hatten aber doch so böse gelebt wie die Indianer"); Edwards, *Life of David Brainerd,* ed. Pettit, 576; White, *Middle Ground,* 280–281; Hunter, "The Delaware Nativist Revival," *Ethnohistory,* XVIII (1971), 42–45; Ronda, "'We Are Well As We Are,'" *WMQ*, 3d Ser., XXXIV (1977), 68–70.

37. Jordan, ed., "Journal of James Kenny," *PMHB,* XXXVII (1913), 171–173.

38. "Der habe ein indianische Buch gebracht, und vorgeben, es wäre alles drin,

Although native religious leaders adopted books of images and written works, hoping to revitalize traditional native practices, these new devices also changed the nature of their religions. The distribution of such books and images helped to standardize local and diverse practices, in which kin groups passed down their family spirits, totems, talismans, and rituals from generation to generation. Before his baptism by the Moravians, for instance, a Mahican man from New York complained about having to worship the god his mother-in-law had inherited from her grandmother; because "she was the oldest she gave it to be worship and we ded it so long tell our [teacher] came and told ous of the lamb of god." The adoption of religious books, whether pictorial or written, may indicate that Indians had accepted European writing as a means of organizing and disseminating the spiritual. Yet Indians also acted on more customary impulses. Because Protestant missionaries used reading and writing as primarily religious activities, Indians, perhaps, thought written words in and of themselves had supernatural powers. Books, then, could be wielded like totems that reinforced older spiritual practices. Still, whether absorbed into customary native beliefs or indicative of a new religious direction, the presence of Euramerican spiritual concepts and icons in non-Christian native communities indicates how impossible complete isolation from white society had become.[39]

Even those religious leaders who were sympathetic with whites, who insisted that peaceful coexistence was possible—even necessary—like their isolationist counterparts appropriated some pieces of Christianity while they attempted to create a new native spiritual life for their followers. One of the most important of these accommodationists was Papunhank, the Munsee spiritual leader who had reprimanded the Pennsylvania governor so handily about gift exchange and the colony's role in destroying the economic life of native Americans. Papunhank had been

was sie wißen solten, von Gott, von der Welt, von den Menschen, von Hirschen, von jagen, u. von andre dingen"; see John Martin Mack's trip to Wyoming, July 5, 1754, *Moravian Records,* reel 28, box 217, folder 12, item 4. In June 1760, Pennsylvanian John Hays met an old Indian preacher on the upper Susquehanna who carried "A Book of Pickters whish he Maid him Self"; see Hunter, ed., "John Hays' Diary and Journal," *Pa. Arch.,* XXIV (1954), 76–77. See also White, *Middle Ground,* 279.

39. *Moravian Records,* 1741, in English, reel 34, box 319, folder 1, item 1; James Axtell, "The Power of Print in the Eastern Woodlands," *WMQ*, 3d Ser., XLIV (1987), 306.

"called to preach" among the Indians at Wyalusing on the Susquehanna River in 1752 and was soon joined by two or three more preachers who promoted what some visiting Quakers described as "true Piety which they apprehended to be an inward work by which the heart is chang'd from bad to good which they express'd by the heart becoming soft and being fill'd wth good." The Munsees also professed a certain pacifism and refused to ally themselves with Indians who were at war with the English. Where Quakers saw a familiar piety, or "inner light," some Moravians, such as Christian Frederick Post, thought Papunhank and the Munsees strictly adhered to "the ancient Customs and Manners of their Forefathers." What neither recognized or realized was the complex way in which Indian religious eclecticism could embrace both customary practices and Christian beliefs. Moments after Post observed the Indians' "ancient Customs," the Munsees requested that he "keep a Meeting for them," after which Post preached a text of Christian peace to an attentive audience of Papunhank's followers.[40]

For reformers like Papunhank, religious syncretism had purposes beyond the revival of native spiritual expression. To understand Christianity and its moral precepts gave Indian leaders a powerful language to urge white immigrants to live up to their own principles when they interacted with Indians. Reformers might have become preoccupied with the sins and morality of their own people, but they knew exactly where that behavior came from. Papunhank especially took to task white religious pretensions. When speaking with Quakers in 1761, Papunhank wondered why "white people were very wicked, as they had so great an advantage of that book [the Bible], and lived so contrary to it." Although he criticized Christianity and its proponents, Papunhank could not deny the increasing interpenetration of Christian and Indian religious terms and concepts that marked his world. By the mid-eighteenth century, the fate of Indians in the northeast, spiritual and otherwise, was entangled with white Christians on many levels. Even those like the Nanticoke dreamer who believed that God "made brown and white people" separate, with distinct religious sacraments, envisioned their sharing a common deity, if not humanity. As

40. "An Account of a Visite and Conference of Some Indians (of Penselvania) Mostly of the Minisink Tribe," July 1760, Misc. MSS, 1661–1931, Indian Affairs, HSP; Christian Frederick Post, Journal, May 19, 1760, Apr. 1–June 30, 1760, contemporary copy, HSP.

Indians rethought and reinterpreted their religious lives before the Seven Years' War, they did not necessarily become susceptible to white cultural dominance or embittered by a sense of cultural loss. Instead, the diverse religious identities that emerged provided a means to engage Euramericans in dialogue without yet resorting to violence. Compelled by colonialism to find new ways to exercise local power over their economic and religious lives, native leaders and their communities borrowed cultural precepts from their Euramerican neighbors, using legal forms, the market economy, even Christianity as strategies of survival.[41]

41. *An Account of the Behavior and Sentiments of Some Well Disposed Indians, Mostly of the Minusing Tribe* . . . (Stanford, N.Y., 1803), 10–11; *Moravian Records,* Feb. 18, 1749, reel 4, box 116, folder 5; Nancy Shoemaker, "How Indians Got to Be Red," *American Historical Review,* CII (1997), 627. Moravians used the terms "Weißen" and "Braunen Brüdern" to describe members of their white and Indian congregations. Among Indians they more often distinguished between Christian "Braunen Bruder" and non-Christian "Wilden Indianern." In other words, although "brown," Christian Indians were at least "brothers."

4

MISSION COMMUNITY NETWORKS

• • •

In the spring of 1746, a group of baptized Mahicans from the Moravian mission at Shekomeko, New York, migrated to land near Bethlehem, Pennsylvania. Among those who moved were Tawaneem, baptized as Bathseba in August 1743, and her first husband, Jonas. At Shekomeko, they had lived with Jonas's mother, but for several years she had been threatening to throw them out of her house if they continued to take communion with the Moravians. Other circumstances also made life in New York difficult for Bathseba and Jonas. White settlers in the Hudson Valley, who had long coveted the Indians' land, pressured them to sell it cheaply. English clergymen, who disliked and distrusted the Moravians, urged the Mahicans to join their congregations instead. Non-Christian Mahicans in nearby Westenhuc implored the Shekomeko residents to join them in an alliance against both the Moravians and the English communities. And the Iroquois, as they had since the 1730s, demanded that the Mahicans move to the upper Susquehanna River under their watchful eye. Baptized Indians realized that, if they stayed in New York, competing pressures might compel them to give up their land, their religious practices, perhaps even their livelihood. Instead, upon the Moravians' invitation, a group of baptized Mahicans decided to resettle in Pennsylvania.[1]

1. Portions of this chapter appear in Jane T. Merritt, "Cultural Encounters along a Gender Frontier: Mahican, Delaware, and German Women in Eighteenth-Century Pennsylvania," *Pennsylvania History,* LXVII (2000), 502–532; *Moravian Records,* June 18, 1743, reel 1, box 111, folder 2, Dec. 9, 1743, reel 1, box 111, folder 3, item 7, Dec. 23, 1744, reel 1, box 112, folder 5, item 3, June 1, 1745, reel 1, box 111, folder 1; Diarium von Bethlehem, Apr. 27, 28, 29, May 22, 1745, reel 1, Van Pelt Library, University of Pennsylvania, Philadelphia; George Henry Loskiel, *History of the Mission of the United Brethren among the Indians in North America,* trans. Christian Ignatius La Trobe, pt. 2,

The native immigrants, however, faced a series of crises in their new home. Native and white communities in Pennsylvania experienced illness during the summer of 1746, but Indians bore the brunt. Jonas, along with two small sons, died of smallpox only four months after reaching Bethlehem. With Bathseba's consent, the missionaries quickly arranged her remarriage to another Mahican, Josua, and in January the new couple received the use of land at the Lehigh Water Gap in the mission community of Gnadenhütten, a day's journey from Bethlehem. Within a few years, two of Bathseba's sisters, Schauwabeam and Noossawahnema, recently baptized as Catharina and Judith, joined her. Following the patterns of matrilineal clans, Judith, a widow of four years, along with her still-unbaptized sixteen-year-old son moved into her sister Bathseba's home. They joined an already extended household that included a young son from Bathseba's first marriage as well as several of Josua's children, an adopted boy, and another Mahican couple. Bathseba's other sister, Catharina, and her husband, Joachim, settled in a house nearby, which they shared with their three children. By 1749, their families reunited and healthy, Bathseba and her sisters settled into creating life anew at the Moravian mission town.[2]

But cultural communities are never simply recreated or reproduced. Although they brought all the habits that came with birth, clan affiliation, and native society, the Mahican sisters entered an unfamiliar environment, a different context for their lives. In the mission towns, Moravians initially controlled community social structures. They introduced new ideas about kinship, marriage, sexuality, proper gender roles, and economic order, which potentially put customary native social systems at risk. Christian Indians were still Indians, however, and, as they had with spiritual practices, they responded to their new circumstances with a remarkable "adaptive capacity." They drew upon familiar kin and household strategies, combining male and female authority to refashion life in Pennsylvania. Kinship and economic alliances connected Christian Indians to

---

27–28, 31, 80–81. Some New Yorkers distrusted the Mahicans from Shekomeko. One Mahican surmised that whites feared the Indians "might some day, joined to the Moravians, return [to New York] to invade the Country" ("Register of Inhabitants of Nazareth" [extracts from Nazareth Diary, English translation], June 7/18, 1746, Church and Meeting Collection, HSP).

2. *Moravian Records,* Feb. 6, 1750, reel 4, box 116, folder 7.

a vast network of people that spread north to New York and west to the Susquehanna River. During the 1740s and 1750s, the mission communities at Gnadenhütten and Meniolagomekah stood at the nexus of social, economic, and political activities between Christian and non-Christian peoples. Travelers found rest and refuge on their road north to the Wyoming Valley or south to Philadelphia, and hunters and traders sold their wares at the mission store. Women and female kin networks were most important to maintaining these cultural crossroads. Indeed, just as women were key to new native religious identities, they created a complex web of relations that included Moravians but extended beyond the mission communities as well. Native men, too, adapted Moravian social and economic structures to fill traditional needs. Some found ways to use Christian values and Moravian regulations to consolidate their own powers of leadership. They could manipulate Christian principles to maintain community integrity, which sometimes included ethnic segregation. New market economies also provided ways to fulfill older kinship obligations.[3]

Although flexibility and creative adaptation helped Indian communities to negotiate the new circumstances without completely abandoning their past, the changes wrought by accommodation also exposed many social fractures that threatened their stability and contributed to growing hostilities on the frontier. Gender differences, generational conflicts, and ethnic animosities, all exacerbated by the presence of white missionaries and the encroachment of white settlers, challenged native leaders' ability to maintain unity within their societies. By the early 1750s, the Six Nations also began to apply increasing pressure on Christian Indians to move north into their sphere of influence. Internal factionalism and external coercion signaled the decline, though not the extinction, of the Moravian mission towns. In 1754, many baptized Indians moved away from the Moravian mission towns, resettling among non-Christian natives on the Susquehanna River. Although most did not abandon their new religious practices nor sever their ties to the Brethren, these Indians chose to return to native-centered communities, an act that would eventually draw them into war.

3. Kathleen M. Brown, "The Anglo-Algonquian Gender Frontier," in Nancy Shoemaker, ed., *Negotiators of Change: Historical Perspectives on Native American Women* (New York, 1995), 30.

In mission towns, such as Gnadenhütten where the three Mahican sisters moved, Moravians struggled to make strange Indians into Christian kin. They carefully planned the social and economic order of the mission towns to make a place for everyone but also to keep everyone in their place. Between 1746 and late 1755, the small town of Gnadenhütten, about forty miles northwest of Bethlehem near the Lehigh Water Gap, grew from 197 to 1,382 acres. With the assistance of other Germans in the region, the resident Indians built a gristmill and sawmill, a blacksmith shop, a thirty-one-foot meetinghouse, a bakehouse, a kitchen and washhouse, a stable and barn, a storehouse, eighteen log houses, and twelve less-permanent "Indian cabins." Fences kept animals out of fields but also marked off land for use by particular people, separating the missionaries' crops from those of their converts. On the side of a little hill above the Mahoning Creek, the Indian houses stretched out in an arch with the meetinghouse as the keystone. These houses filled as newly baptized Delawares and Mahicans joined the community. Further up the nearby hill, beyond the farm buildings and Indian houses, was "an orchard, and on the summit, the grave-yard." Moravians hoped that Gnadenhütten, in particular, would become central to the Christian Indian world because of its location at a crossroads of communities. "The place is well adapted for Indians," Bishop John Christopher Frederick Cammerhoff assured Count Nikolaus Ludwig von Zinzendorf in 1747, "for they can hunt, as only a very few whitemen live north of the Mountain, and the Proprietary lands, as yet, extends only a few miles N.W. of us." He noted, "Furthermore the Wyoming Path is here, and many strange Indians pass over it, and are thus brought to Gnadenhütten—they frequently attend our meetings."[4]

4. Diarium von Bethlehem, May 10/21, 1746, reel 2, Van Pelt Library; William C. Reichel, ed., *Memorials of the Moravian Church,* I (Philadelphia, 1870), 34n, 222–223; *Gnadenhütten, Mahony,* undated map [early 1750s], no. 15, folder 8, drawer VII, Moravian Archives, Bethlehem, Pa.; Bishop John Frederick Cammerhoff to Count Nikolaus Ludwig von Zinzendorf, May 22–24, 1747, John Christopher Frederick Cammerhoff, 1721–1751, Letters, 1747–1748, copied by John W. Jordan, HSP. At Gnadenhütten, the white missionaries separated the fields of the "white people" from the Indians (*Moravian Records,* Nov. 1, 1747, reel 6, box 119, folder 1, item 2). When the Moravians moved west and established another town called Gnadenhütten in the Ohio Valley in about 1783, they also separated "der Weissen Geschwister Plantage und Garten"

MAP 4. Missionary Activity at the Forks of the Delaware and Lehigh Rivers, 1740s–1760s. *Drawn by Gerry Krieg*

Whereas Gnadenhütten arose at an uninhabited spot on a small river, Meniolagomekah, another cornerstone of the Moravian mission, was already a well-established Delaware town eight miles away. Less ambitious about molding the physical landscape, the Moravians nonetheless sought to introduce their version of economic and social order to that community as well. Ten Indian huts surrounded the missionaries' meetinghouse,

---

from "Welche von den Indianer Plantagen" (*Gnadenhütten an Huron River oberhalb Detroit,* map, ca. 1783, no. 14, folder 8, drawer VII, Moravian Archives).

and, by 1752, they had built fences to separate and protect cornfields. Since many unbaptized kin lived in these households or nearby, however, the Delawares at Meniolagomekah managed to control their social and economic life more than their neighbors at Gnadenhütten. In June 1749, the diarist noted that there were sixty Indians in Gnadenhütten, not including those from Meniolagomekah or those living "over the Lehi," who often joined them for services. By 1754, both towns housed more than two hundred baptized and unbaptized Delawares and Mahicans, who had fashioned far-reaching kin and economic ties among various inhabitants between the Delaware and Susquehanna Rivers.[5]

Like the encounters between Susquehanna Indians and Moravians in the early 1740s, kinship provided a point of contact for natives at the Forks of the Delaware and missionaries from Bethlehem but also set the stage for misunderstanding and conflict. The two groups could not always reconcile their ideas about how individuals should behave within the community or who should be considered kin. Moravians wanted to modify Indian concepts of personal and household relations in the mission towns, to break down old bonds of kinship and create new ties based on a common Christian faith. They believed that "whoever does the will of my Father, they are my mother, and they are my brothers and sisters." They thought that Indians were too attached to household clans and told them that true kinship came, not from common ancestry or kin alliance, but through faith in one God. This new metaphor for kinship was meant to cross racial and ethnic boundaries as well. They proclaimed to baptized Indians: "We brown and white, Mahican and Delaware are not to be considered except as one nation."[6]

5. *Moravian Records,* May 18, 1752, reel 6, box 122, folder 2; Reichel, ed., *Memorials of the Moravian Church,* I, 36. For mission population figures, see "Extract Out of the Bethlehem Congregation Journal 1749," June 4/15, 1749, in English, *Moravian Records,* reel 26, box 211, folder 19, item 1, Dec. 17/28, 1749, reel 6, box 119, folder 2, item 1, January 1752, reel 6, box 119, folder 3, item 2, August 1752, reel 6, box 119, folder 2, item 4, January 1754, reel 6, box 119, folder 2, item 6. John Heckewelder, *A Narrative of the Mission of the United Brethren among the Delaware and Mohegan Indians, from Its Commencement, in the Year 1740, to the Close of the Year 1808 . . .* (1820; reprint, New York, 1971), 38, asserts that five hundred Indians lived in Gnadenhütten in 1749.

6. *Moravian Records,* Mar. 12, 1754, reel 6, box 119, folder 1, item 10.13 ("Denn wir braune u. weisse Mahicander u. Delaw. sind nicht ander als eine Nation anzusehen, dazu hat uns der l. Hld. mit s. Blute gemacht"), Aug. 24, 1754, reel 5, box 118, folder 3 ("Wer den Willen meines Vater thut, der ist meine Mutter, & das sind meine Brr. u.

Although they appropriated Moravian articles of spiritual faith, Christian Indians often frustrated Moravians' attempts to redefine their social relations. They could certainly understand and appreciate the Moravians' deemphasis of the nuclear family. In Bethlehem, for instance, married couples often lived in separate houses with their infant children, but the Moravian choir system put single and widowed individuals of similar sex and age together to work and worship. Native American families also encompassed more than a husband, wife, and children. But, unlike Moravians, Indian households, such as Bathseba's, which combined individuals and families, never segregated by sex. Sibling families, usually sisters, lived together with their children as well as with adopted or single clan members. Christian Indians wanted to maintain their own social, ethnic, and clan divisions, but, since they needed to expand their chances of survival, they were willing to extend alliances to others, Moravian and Indian alike.[7]

Along with concepts of Christian kinship, Moravian missionaries introduced different lessons about proper marriage practices at the mission towns, hoping to reshape personal relations between Indians. For Moravians, marriages guided individual men and women toward Christ; together a couple could help each other focus on their relationship with the Savior. In their own communities, the Moravian elders planned and directed marriages between church members. Throughout their married life, couples came under the scrutiny of the church. The Moravian council might keep husbands and wives from partaking in communion "because they do not agree well together" or "on account of the indifference of their hearts." If a sister had an "unreasonable deportment towards her husband" or a "shameless face," or a married brother displayed "levity and improper deportment towards his wife," the church elders would not allow them to participate in communal or spiritual activities until they admitted remorse. Even within a marriage, there was a particular hierarchy of love and power. Johann Jacob Schmick carefully translated their ideas about marriage into Mahican so Indian congregations would understand them: "A man must love his wife, like the Saviour does his flock." In

---

Schwestern"). See also Diary of Nazareth, May 3, 1755, January 1740–December 1806, English translation, Moravian Historical Society, Nazareth, Pa.

7. Beverly Prior Smaby, *The Transformation of Moravian Bethlehem: From Communal Mission to Family Economy* (Philadelphia, 1988), 9–23.

turn, a wife must show obedience to her husband. Although the husband and wife were to create a strong bond based on common faith, Schmick cautioned that "no one must love their wife more than the Lord."[8]

Like the Moravians, native Americans also considered marriage an important part of community formation, though not with overt spiritual ends. Marriage provided economic and political alliances between families and clans, which increased available resources, widened support networks, and eased potential conflicts between neighboring ethnic groups. Unlike Euramerican marriage, however, the union of Indian men and women was not a legal arrangement that had to be recognized by political or religious institutions to be legitimate. Customarily, marriage was a matter of agreement between two individuals as well as a matter of negotiation between two kin groups. Moravian John Heckewelder noted that, when a Delaware man and woman were attracted to each other, the man's mother would bargain with the other family, and the couple exchanged food and clothing items. If everyone agreed to the marriage, the couple set up a household together, the man usually moving in with his wife's kin. Since Mahicans, Iroquois, and Delawares in Pennsylvania traced their family lineage through female kin, the marriage relationship did not concern the authority that men had over women and the children they bore. Rather, native marriages emphasized mutual reciprocity between men and women.[9]

In Gnadenhütten, Indian elders often heeded the advice of Moravian missionaries, who repeatedly discussed the Christian idea of marriage with new couples who united and with those Indian couples who already

8. "Register of Inhabitants of Nazareth" (extract from Nazareth Diary, English translation), Feb. 28/Mar. 11, Apr. 6/17, Apr. 26/May 7, 1746, Church and Meeting Collection, HSP; "Ein Mann muß seinen Frau lieben, wie der Heiland seine Gemeine. Aber es muß niemand seine Frau mehr lieben als den Hld"; see Johann Jacob Schmick, "Miscellanea linguae nationis Indicae Mahikan dicta cura suscepta," 2 vols. [ca. 1760], APS.

9. See John Heckewelder, *History, Manners, and Customs of the Indian Nations, Who Once Inhabited Pennsylvania and the Neighboring States,* rev. ed., ed. William C. Reichel (1876; facsimile reprint, Bowie, Md., 1990), 161–162; Gottlieb Mittelberger, *Journey to Pennsylvania,* ed. and trans. Oscar Handlin and John Clive (Cambridge, Mass., 1960), 65; Elizabeth Tooker, "Women in Iroquois Society," in Michael K. Foster, Jack Campisi, and Marianne Mithun, eds., *Extending the Rafters: Interdisciplinary Approaches to Iroquoian Studies* (Albany, N.Y., 1984), 120.

had long-term relationships. When arranging marriages between baptized natives, Indians also thought it important that two potential mates display a similar level of Christian virtue. But Christian Indians still applied their own criteria for the suitability of partners. The couple had to be from different clans, for example, allaying the fears of marrying someone too closely related. The Moravians did not always take the nature of clan membership into consideration when they suggested unions, making the possibility of forbidden marriages more prevalent. Augustus, the Delaware leader who had brought the inhabitants of Meniolagomekah into the Moravian faith, complained several times that some of the marriages that the Moravians recommended crossed over the Indians' boundaries of incest.[10]

Rather than giving up traditional social connections for Christian values, in many ways Indian leaders forced Moravians to adjust to theirs. They drew missionaries into deliberations about kin relations in ways that Moravians never anticipated. In 1751, for instance, after his first wife died, Augustus planned to marry a Mahican woman, Esther, whom the missionaries had suggested. Not surprisingly, the bride's kin, especially her mother and brother, figured prominently in the negotiations. In June, Augustus brought a deputation of missionaries and Indian Brethren to Esther's village to speak with her family about the possibility of marriage.

10. "Consecration of Marriages Dating from Pre-Christian Past," Mar. 14, 1743, *Moravian Records*, reel 1, box 111, folder 2, item 3, Dec. 4/15, 1750, reel 5, box 117, folder 1, Johann Jacob Schmick to Joseph Spangenberg, May 19, 1755, reel 5, box 118, folder 5, item 8. From a database of 734 native Americans who lived in or visited Moravian mission communities between the 1740s and 1760s, there were 167 baptized and married couples. Of these couples, 57 had their prebaptism marriages confirmed by the Moravians. Karen Anderson, *Chain Her by One Foot: The Subjugation of Women in Seventeenth-Century New France* (New York, 1991), 98, argues that Indians accepted Christian marriage only as a last resort. Carol Devens, *Countering Colonization: Native American Women and Great Lakes Missions, 1630–1900* (Berkeley, Calif., 1992), 26–27, contends that native women in the Great Lakes region resisted monogamous marriage practices because it was not to their advantage. After his second wife Esther (see following discussion in text) died in March 1754, Augustus wanted to marry a third time. Naomi, the mother of Augustus's first wife, Anna Benigna, proposed that a female relative of hers from the Susquehanna be considered as the bride, since she was not of the turtle clan, which was Augustus's phratry (Schmick to Spangenberg, July 24, 1755, *Moravian Records*, reel 5, box 118, folder 6, item 6; see also July 13, 1755, reel 5, box 118, folder 6, item 2).

The Moravians first spoke with Augustus and Esther, asking whether they found it in their hearts to marry each other. Esther replied that "she had nothing against it, if it was also the same with her Mother." Her mother, Hanna, had no objection to the marriage, but, according to Indian custom, insisted that they speak with Esther's brother Benjamin, "without whose determination she could not entirely decide the matter." For several days, Hanna and Benjamin haggled with the visitors about the marriage. Hanna did not mind that her daughter would be marrying a Delaware; Benjamin, however, had reservations. He insisted that he loved Augustus and had nothing against the marriage, but he feared that the Delawares, "a jealous nation," would not allow a Mahican to marry into their clans. The Moravians reminded Benjamin that Augustus and Esther planned to live among the Brethren, "not among the Wild Indians," and, thus, ethnic differences should not be a factor. Benjamin, not so certain, left the house in anger. The next day, when Hanna realized that the Brethren were preparing to return home, "resolved herself to give up her daughter." The Moravians, serving as kin, had successfully completed eight long days of negotiation; Esther and Augustus were to marry, and both mother and daughter cried as they parted.[11]

Although native Americans acted in customary ways within the context of Moravian mission communities, Christianity provided a catalyst for social change. Benjamin, for instance, struggled with the new categories of identity that Moravians introduced: Christian Indians were supposed to act different from "Wild Indians." He had grown up in a world where Mahicans and Delawares harbored enduring animosities toward each other, distinctions that Moravian ideals of a common Christian faith could not entirely erase. As a brother, Benjamin knew that he had the

11. "Sie nichts dar gegen hette wen es ihrer Muter auch so währe so," "Auf Benjamin das sie ohne deßen Willen die Sache nicht ganz auß machen könte"; see Diary of Joachim Sausemann, June 8, 1751, *Moravian Records,* reel 3, box 114, folder 3. For a similar example of the Moravians' negotiating marriage, see Nov. 4, 5, 1753, reel 3, box 114, folder 8. See also *Moravian Records,* June 15, 1751, reel 3, box 114, folder 3 ("Weil die Delawar Nacion eine neidische nation währe, so fürchte er nur das, das sie der Ester den Augustus nicht gönnen würden und sie bald aus den wäge zu renuen [ruin?] suchen würden wor auf wir ihr ant: daß sie nicht unter Wilde sondern unter Geschw: zu wohnen käme, und daß ich von ihr nichts mehr begärt als von 2 Worten eines daß solte Ja der eine seÿn den ich könte die 3 Brüder nicht langer mehr auf halten"), June 16, 1751 ("Sie sich nun resolvieret hete ihre Tochter zu über geben u. sie solte gleich mit unß reisen ging darauf gleich im Busch und holte ihre pferdt").

duty to protect his sister and the family's best interest. In his eyes, an alliance with a Delaware did not serve them well. As a Christian, however, Benjamin recognized that new criteria might now affect decisions of the household. Torn between customary Mahican ways and new Christian ways, he found he could not exercise his traditional role of authority over Esther's marriage and instead washed his hands of the whole business.[12]

Like Benjamin, many Christian Indians turned their backs on the Moravian social values with which they did not agree. They did not completely reject the structures that missionaries put in place, however, nor did they abdicate power over their social relations. Instead, they ignored what they thought incompatible with their lives and manipulated those principles that served them. Moravians created a hierarchy of community leadership in mission towns that tended to be patriarchal in nature. They insisted that not a house could be built, nor a piece of land assigned for planting, nor a baby baptized without the express approval of August Gottlieb (Joseph) Spangenberg, the Moravian leader at Bethlehem, or the male-dominated Council of Elders. Even more powerful and charismatic was European aristocrat Count Zinzendorf, who, soon after the Moravians migrated to North America, appointed himself bishop of the Moravian Church, chairman of the Helpers Conference, and chairman of the Communal Council. Still, the Moravians tempered their focus on male authority, encouraging female piety and spiritual life and insisting that women participate fully in the day-to-day business of the community. Christian Indians used the familiar pattern of combined male and female authority as a point of reference, a place where Indian and Moravian ideas of kinship and community could come together. Christian Indian men and women joined the weekly and monthly meetings at the mission towns to discuss all aspects of their economic and social lives and to make decisions together. Although Moravians tried to control the ways that Christian Indians exercised authority and the outcome of their decision making, the community councils gave Indian leaders a legitimate avenue through

12. Of the 167 married couples at the Moravian mission towns between the 1740s and 1760s, only 32 couples, whose marriages had been arranged by the combined efforts of families, Indian elders, and Moravian missionaries, were of mixed ethnic backgrounds, ironically including Benjamin, who married a Delaware in 1753. Mixed marriages were not rare. Shawnees married Delawares, even whites married various Indians, but Mahicans and Iroquois had long-standing suspicions of Delawares. See Chapter 5, below, for further discussion.

which to run their communities as they saw fit. Men and women could bend or manipulate the rules to achieve their own ends.[13]

Sexuality provides a prime example of how Indian women and men exercised traditional authority by selectively rejecting or manipulating Moravian social values. Native American sexual behavior and its consequences sorely tested the Moravian conception of intimacy. The native practices of premarital sex, serial monogamy, and polygamy appalled the Moravian missionaries. Sexuality did have a revered place in the Moravian social order. Zinzendorf emphasized to his followers that the human body was "sacred as the temples of the holy spirit." However, sexuality had no legitimacy outside of marriage; it was in "the Conjugal Bed, where two Persons, of whom one represents for a Time the Husband of all Souls, and the other the whole Congregation of Souls, keep a daily Worship." To avoid the temptations of premarital sex, Moravians had their young people live and worship separately in boys' and girls' choirs.[14]

On the other hand, native Americans accepted sexual experimentation even at a young age. Captain Pierre Pouchot of the French army in North America during the mid-eighteenth century noted: "Sometimes at six or eight years of age, they [young Indian girls] have lost their virginity in play-

13. Smaby, *Transformation of Moravian Bethlehem*, 23–30; Gillian Lindt Gollin, *Moravians in Two Worlds: A Study of Changing Communities* (New York, 1967), 34–35. The Brethren nearly deified Zinzendorf and portrayed him as a saint, even an object of worship, to the baptized Indians, who often wrote adoring letters to him or celebrated his birthday with elaborate rituals.

14. English diary of Joseph Powell, Feb. 4, 10, 1748, *Moravian Records*, reel 6, box 121, folder 4, item 1 (see references to "Polyandry," Apr. 14/25, 1745, reel 2, box 112, folder 15, and "Marriage regular procedure not observed at Wyoming," May 1745, reel 2, box 112, folder 11, item 2). "Register of Inhabitants of Nazareth" (extracts from Nazareth Diary, English translation), Sept. 3/14, 1746, Church and Meeting Collection, HSP; Henry Rimius, *A Candid Narrative of the Rise and Progress of the Herrnhuters, Commonly Call'd Moravians, or Unitas Fratrum* . . . (London, 1753), 48 n. 6. According to Zinzendorf, the first wound of Christ was his circumcision, which rendered the penis a "holy member." Women were to "honour that Member, by which we resemble Christ, with the utmost Veneration." "His first holy Wound attracts to us (the Men) an eternal Respect from them, in the married and unmarried State, and if they had another Motive for respecting us, taken from ourselves, and not on Account of our resembling the little Man Jesus, it would be an Injury to their eternal Husband" (ibid., 49 n. 7). See also Smaby, *Transformation of Moravian Bethlehem*, 151–152, 163–164.

ing with other children. Their parents have nothing to blame, saying that every one is the master of his or her own person." Unlike Euramericans, it was not unusual for native women to take the initiative in setting the boundaries of sexual encounters. Young women might follow men to their homes, or a man might enter a woman's cabin where she had the power to accept or reject his sexual advances. Native women also could choose to be part of a temporary sexual relationship with a hunter or trader to provide assistance and companionship during travel. John Bartram, while journeying through Pennsylvania with Conrad Weiser, observed in August 1743 that one "night our fellow traveller lodged with his occasional wife in a corner of our cabin, and in the morning would have taken her with him at our expence." Bartram and Weiser found "it intolerable that an intruder should gratifie his private inclinations to the shortning of our necessary provisions, already insufficient." Bartram did not explain whether his fellow traveler was white or Indian, but, most certainly, the "occasional wife" was a native woman who accompanied the man and shared his bed, maybe receiving some support for her family in return.[15]

Even with the introduction of Euramerican sexual mores in Christian Indian communities, women continued to follow customary sexual behavior. They still exercised the power to accept or reject sexual activity. In November 1743, Bathseba's sister Catharina announced to the Chris-

15. M. [Pierre] Pouchot, *Memoir upon the Late War in North America, between the French and English, 1755–60; Followed by Observations upon the Theatre of Actual War, and by New Details concerning the Manners and Customs of the Indians; with Topographical Maps,* ed. and trans. Franklin B. Hough, II (Roxbury, Mass., 1866), 195–197 (quotation on 195); James Smith, *An Account of the Remarkable Occurrences in the Life and Travels of Col. James Smith, during His Captivity with the Indians, in the Years 1755, '56, '57, '58, and '59,* ed. William M. Darlington (Cincinnati, Ohio, 1870), 140–141; John Bartram, *Travels in Pensilvania and Canada* (Ann Arbor, Mich., 1966) (originally published as *Observations on the Inhabitants, Climate, Soil, Rivers, Productions, Animals, and Other Matters Worthy of Notice . . .* [London, 1751]), 67; Sylvia Van Kirk, *Many Tender Ties: Women in Fur-Trade Society, 1670–1870* (Norman, Okla., 1980), 4–5. Although the Mahicans and Delawares of Pennsylvania often tolerated a wide range of individual sexual behavior, other native peoples farther west, the Illinois and Miamis, for example, restricted the sexual behavior of married women. Miami men would shave their adulterous wives' heads, cut off their noses and ears, and turn them out, or a husband might take his wife to the village center and have her publicly raped (Milo Milton Quaife, ed., *The Western Country in the Seventeenth Century: The Memoirs of Lamothe Cadillac and Pierre Liette* [Chicago, 1947], 70, 119).

tian Mahican congregation at Shekomeko that she believed Joachim, the son of the first two Mahican converts, was the father of her unborn child, compelling him to marry her. Many other Christian Indian women had similar sexual encounters outside marriage that resulted in pregnancies or, at least, in reprimands. A single mother, Regina, lived with her daughter Eva in Gnadenhütten before she married a man who could have been the father. Another Delaware woman, Benigna, married a baptized man in 1755, though she had conceived a child some years earlier with an unbaptized Delaware living on the Susquehanna River at Nescopeck. In January 1758, this child, then sixteen years old, was publicly accepted into the community at Gnadenhütten through baptism and placed under the guidance of white and Indian godparents. Many of the baptized Delaware and Mahican women accused of scandalous behavior, bigamy, sexual misconduct, or similar charges left the mission towns for at least a brief time, some for good.[16]

Whereas some Christian Indians ignored Moravian sexual values, others manipulated the new morality to exercise power within the community. For instance, in January 1748, the Indian workers' conference (Mitarbeitern Conferenz) met to discuss the case of a Delaware woman named Tschanxehs who had been caught fornicating with some Indians visiting Gnadenhütten. The Indian elders, angry that Tschanxehs had used their newly built barn as a "place of whores" to commit "the evil deed," recommended she be sent away from the community along with two other strangers. Tschanxehs's offense was serious, but the Mahican leaders allowed her to explain her actions. She said she had come to hear about the new religion from the local Indians, which had interested many people living in communities on the Susquehanna River. Intriguingly, Tschanxehs apologized for her behavior and even admitted to committing a "sin": "My evil heart has seduced me. I believe I was very wretched. The Devil took me by the hand." Still, merely learning the forms of Christian confession was not enough to elicit forgiveness from the mission community. After a lengthy reprimand, the Moravian Indians told her to leave Gnadenhütten by morning.[17]

16. *Moravian Records,* Feb. 13/24, 1744, reel 2, box 112, folder 6, item 1; Bethlehem Register, Jan. 8, 1758, "Bethlehemisches Kirchen=Buch," II, 11, Moravian Archives. Anderson, *Chain Her by One Foot,* 18, suggests that Indian women flaunted their sexuality in the face of restrictive moral codes and, thus, rejected Christianity.

17. "Mein böses Herz hat mich verführt. Ich glaube, ich bin sehr unglücklich ge-

On the surface, these Mahicans appeared to have accepted Moravian Christian practices, dismissing from their midst an unbaptized woman who misbehaved sexually. However, they allowed to remain other baptized and unbaptized inhabitants at Gnadenhütten who ignored the Moravians' teachings on sexuality. After all, the product of Catharina and Joachim's premarital affair, their son Akoan, remained unbaptized, yet he lived in their house. Similarly, in December 1748, the Indian congregation accused a twenty-four-year-old widow, Maria, of being a whore and expelled her from town. But, once she asked forgiveness from both the community and the Lord, they allowed her to remain. In fact, the Mahicans were probably not that concerned about Tschanxehs's sexual behavior. Despite her confession and regret, which would have been sufficient for exoneration in other cases, the Mahican majority in Gnadenhütten had more pervasive reasons to exclude her from the community: she was a Delaware stranger. By wielding the same standards that they bent or ignored among their own, Mahican leaders could control the membership of their community.[18]

Although native men found an outlet for their traditional leadership roles through the Moravian system of community conferences and elders councils, women, who also participated at these meetings, more often turned to customary channels to exercise authority. Moravians might have hoped to replace native matrilineal kinship structures with patriarchal religious authority, but female networks still operated at the household and family level, where daily decisions about social life were made. Indian and white women formed attachments with each other similar to those among sisters that became key to negotiating cross-cultural values. At the Forks of the Delaware, native and white women shared personal circumstances and emotional bonds that strengthened alliances between their two communities. Delaware and Mahican women in Gnadenhütten and Meniolagomekah, for example, asked white women to assist them during childbirth. Missionaries Anna Rauch and Anna Mack at various times attended native women in labor. They provided a medical service for these women and offered blessings and prayers for the new baby. Between 1746 and 1755, a continual stream of women from Bethlehem and other

---

wesen. der Teufel habe sie bey der Hand gekriegt"; see Mitarbeitern conference, Jan. 8/19, 1748, *Moravian Records,* reel 6, box 119, folder 1, item 3.

18. *Moravian Records,* Dec. 4, 1748, reel 4, box 116, folder 4.

white communities at the Forks of the Delaware visited native communities, conducted religious services, taught schools, prepared meals, brought gifts, and dressed and buried the dead for Indian women and their families at Gnadenhütten and Meniolagomekah. Native women expressed the joy of finding other women with whom they might share their household responsibilities and spiritual lives. Indeed, female converts indicated a certain sense of gender loyalty at the mission communities. In September 1752, a young candidate for baptism, when asked whether she would remain obedient to the Lord and the Gnadenhütten congregation, exclaimed "with tears" that she would "remain with the Lord and the Sisters."[19]

For Indians, extending female networks to include Moravians provided alternative systems of support. At the mission towns, for example, German Moravians introduced the practice of godparenting, an important institution in their own communities. When an Indian child was baptized, missionaries and members of the Indian congregation became godparents to provide Christian guidance and education for the child's welfare. When the Delaware Maria's infant daughter was born in Bethlehem in March 1756, she was baptized as Christiana, "under the Litany of the humanity of Jesus, in his death." Two German women, Johanna Schmick and Anna Rosina Anders, and three Mahicans, Bathseba, Esther, and Johanna, all became godparents to the girl. Indians, who recognized the responsibility of the entire community in raising children, could understand godparenting as another way to create and use kinship connections. Indians associated the Moravian duties of a godparent with the obligations of a mother's sister or a mother's brother. Indians at Gnadenhütten and Meniolagomekah frequently sent their children to be cared for in the homes of kinfolk. In 1750, for example, Bathseba and Josua adopted a young boy of eight or nine years who was probably Bathseba's nephew. Since she was considered the boy's "little mother," she took responsibility for his welfare as if she were his biological parent. Indians could call on these extended female networks, asking Moravian women to adopt and raise their children. In February 1748, Zippora and Benjamin felt they were unable to care prop-

19. *Moravian Records,* Dec. 8, 1747, reel 4, box 116, folder 2, Feb. 3, 1749, reel 4, box 116, folder 5, Dec. 31, 1750, reel 5, box 117, folder 1, Sept. 25, 1752, reel 5, box 117, folder 3 ("mit Thränen . . . ich will beim Hld u. den Schwestern bleiben"). There are many more examples of this kind of assistance as midwives or as observers. See Nov. 8, 1748, reel 4, box 116, folder 4, Dec. 7, 1750, reel 5, box 117, folder 1, Mar. 13, 1754, reel 3, box 114, folder 9. Anna Mack married Martin Mack after Jeanette's death.

FIGURE 9. *The 24 Single Sisters Choirs.* By Johann Valentin Haidt. 1751. Courtesy, Unity Archives, Herrnhut, Germany.
Female networks proved key to Moravian missionary work but also flourished because of women's respected place within Moravian society. Although separated from men in worship, individual women had authority within the church. Here Anna Nitschmann (who some thought to be the consort of Count Nikolaus Ludwig von Zinzendorf) presents the Single Sisters' Choirs to Christ. The native American woman standing prominently behind her represents the native women who became elders (Arbeiter Schwestern) in their communities.

erly for their daughter, Salome, when Marie Werner, a woman in Bethlehem who had no children, promised to raise her as her own. The following month, Anna Rauch was "named mother" of a little Mahican girl in Gnadenhütten and took her into her home.[20]

Indian women also relied on female networks to negotiate more personal problems, especially within their marriages. Customarily, when conflict arose between incompatible spouses, Indians in the northeast could leave a marriage without further consequences or obligations to their partner. Although the leaders of the Moravian church in Bethlehem were firmly opposed to separation of an Indian marriage and Christian doctrine encouraged lifelong monogamous unions, Christian Indians still turned to customary methods of handling domestic strife. If a spouse was abusive or unable to support the family or there were irreconcilable differences, native women sometimes left the household and returned to non-Christian kin either temporarily or permanently. Augustus and his second wife, Esther, for instance, might have overcome his brother's opposition to their marriage, but Esther soon found she not only missed her family at Wechquatnach but also needed time away from Augustus. She moved back to her mother's house for three months at the end of 1752 and again in 1753 after the death of an infant girl. Esther was finally reconciled to her husband and taken back to Meniolagomekah in mid-August 1753.[21]

20. Bethlehem Register, "Bethlemisches Kirchen=Buch," I, 1742–1756, 4–65, Moravian Archives ("Geburts=und Tauff=Register derer zur Bruder Gemeine gehörigenund bald nach ihrer lieblichen Geburt in der Tod Jesu getauften"), Mar. 6, 1756, 63 ("Unter der Litaney der Menschheit Jesu, in Seinen Tod"); *Moravian Records,* Feb. 1, 10, 1748, reel 4, box 116, folder 3, Mar. 3, 4, 1748, reel 4, box 116, folder 3. There were also many unbaptized Indian children in the mission communities. Often the older children of baptized adults remained unbaptized. Newly born infants of baptized adults, however, were often baptized soon after birth. Between 1742 and 1763, at least 186 boys and girls under age eleven were baptized (91 girls, 95 boys), most receiving both German and Indian godparents.

21. Heckewelder, *History, Manners, and Customs,* 162; *Moravian Records,* Aug. 11, 14, 1753, reel 5, box 117, folder 4, Aug. 14, 1753, reel 6, box 122, folder 3, "Zeugniße von den Geschwistern in Meniowolagamekah," August 1753, reel 34, box 319, folder 4, item 17, Apr. 29, 1755, reel 5, box 118, folder 5, item 14. Of the 334 married people living in and around the Moravian mission communities between the 1740s and 1760s, at least 51 had discernible and repeated problems with their marriages. See, for example, Apr. 24, 1748, reel 4, box 116, folder 3, Feb. 13, 1754, reel 6, box 122, folder 3, May 20, 1756, reel 4, box 115, folder 6. See also Anderson, *Chain Her by One Foot,* 18.

The presence of Moravians provided Indian women with options other than leaving the community. The Moravian choir system created separate living spaces for single and widowed women and men where they supported themselves and practiced a similar religious piety. The Moravians encouraged Indian women to take refuge in the separate quarters, especially the Single Sisters' and Widows' Houses, when they experienced trouble at home. In early 1747, shortly after moving to Gnadenhütten, Bathseba and her second husband Josua began to quarrel. Josua first complained that his wife "took much pleasure in speaking out against him." A month later, although her husband objected, Bathseba moved into the Widow's House at Bethlehem, and, by the end of March, she had left the region altogether. In June 1747, after Bathseba's return, Jeanette Mack "spoke with Josua in the presence of Martin [her husband] and asked him with tears if he shall proceed with better behaviour toward Bathseba." We cannot be certain what their specific conflict was because the Moravian diarist was so discrete. However, that autumn Bathseba again "ran away from her husband," for which Martin Mack "could find no real fault" with Josua. We might wonder whether Jeanette Mack or the other German women in town thought the same, for it was to them that native women turned when domestic problems (even violence) occurred.[22]

Whether they found alternative ways to establish interhousehold alliances, applied new social criteria to maintain customary ethnic divisions, or extended female kin networks to help with child care and marital problems, Christian Indians actively sought to preserve their communities. Just as they had accommodated Christian religious and social principles to

22. *Moravian Records*, Jan. 8, 1747, reel 4, box 116, folder 1 ("Martin redte mit Josua wegen Fr. Bathseba, weil sie sich sehr ins vergnugt gegen ihn bezeugt"), Mar. 28, 1747, reel 4, box 116, folder 1 ("Bathseba in schlecten umständen wäre und der Satan suche sie zu verfuhren, sie wäre sehr gegen ihn eingenommen"), June 16, 1747, reel 4, box 116, folder 1 ("Die Aennel [Jeanette Mack] sprach mit Josua in Gegenwart Martins, und bat ihn mit Thränen, er solte doch seiner Bathseba mit einem bessern Wandel vorgehen"), Oct 1, 1747, reel 4, box 116, folder 2 ("Es lief heute die Bathseba von ihren Mann dem Josua. Wir konten bey Ihm keine rechte Schuld finden. Sie bliebe des Nachts bey der Esther und dachte Morgens drauf nach Bethlehem zu gehen"), Feb. 10/21, 1748, reel 4, box 116, folder 3; Diarium von Bethlehem, Mar. 31/ Apr. 11, 1747, reel 2, Van Pelt Library. For examples of domestic violence, see *Moravian Records*, Feb. 25, 1748, reel 6, box 121, folder 4, Apr. 24, 1748, reel 4, box 116, folder 3, Feb. 8, 1750, reel 6, box 121, folder 5, May 20, 1756, reel 4, box 115, folder 6.

some degree, mission Indians also tailored new economic practices to fit their current needs and to fulfill the customary obligations of their communities. How they adapted to the market economy, however, sometimes clashed with Moravian demands, creating disagreements between native community leaders over the use of resources. By the 1750s, Christian Indians began to experience growing disunity that threatened the very stability they had worked so hard to establish.

In the mission towns of Gnadenhütten and Meniolagomekah, Moravians tried to reproduce their own economic model with mixed results. Like many Euramericans, they thought that Indians were "idle when they should work, and when they have any Thing to eat, they mispend it and are prodigal, and then suffer Hunger again." Although Moravians negotiated alliances with some non-Christian Indian communities—such as Shamokin—based on the reciprocal precepts of native kinship obligations and gift exchange, they believed that Indians should eventually learn Euramerican economic habits for their ultimate survival. They hoped to train baptized Indians "to regular Labour, viz.: to plant, hunt, fish and do every thing in the right Season—to keep good House with every thing they have, to tend their Corn well and to make provision for their Families and also their Cattle in the right Season." In their own communities, Moravians had a highly regulated economy. Under the leadership of August Gottlieb Spangenberg, for instance, Bethlehem was planned as a general economy to which all individuals would devote their time and labor and from which they would receive their daily needs of food and clothing. Between 1742 and 1761, no individuals owned property; rather, they exchanged labor for the use of land and goods owned by the community. Moravian leaders hoped that by participating in a communal economy individuals would think less of worldly concerns and more of their relationship with God. "We are here as Brethren and Sisters, who owe themselves to the Saviour," stated the Brotherly Agreement of 1754, "and for whom it is, indeed, a token of grace that they may do all for His sake. We declare therefore, . . . that we do not for this time nor for the future pretend to any wage or have reason to pretend to any." Ideally, they would work for God and the greater good of the community.[23]

23. "Extracts from the Instructions or Rules, for Such of the United Brethren as Are Used as Missionaries or Assistants in Propagating the Gospel among the Indians," *Moravian Records*, n.d., in English, reel 34, box 315, folder 3, item 7; "Brotherly

FIGURE 10. *Joseph, alias Augustus Gottlieb Spangenberg.* By Herline and Hensel, Philadelphia. Courtesy, The Library Company of Philadelphia. *Despite strong connections between females in the local communities, the Moravian Church still saw itself as a patriarchy. Joseph (more often called Augustus Gottlieb) Spangenberg became the director of Moravian Indian missions in North America and the community leader of Bethlehem in the early 1740s. He set the strict rules that governed the social and economic structure of German, Delaware, and Mahican congregations.*

The economic community that Moravians attempted to create and how Christian Indians responded to new economic choices did not always coincide. Perhaps they assumed that Indians would equate the Bethlehem communal economic model with their own tendencies to organize eco-

Agreement," 1754, paragraph 3, Moravian Archives; Gollin, *Moravians in Two Worlds,* 99, 142.

nomic activities around kin networks. Christian Mahicans and Delawares, however, saw the two very differently and adamantly preferred the latter. They did not reject communalism per se, but each ethnic group within the mission community, even individual bands, wanted to control their own resources and were reluctant to pool them with each other. In the fall of 1747, for instance, shortly after Mahicans and Paugussets (Wampanosch) from Shekomeko and Pachgatgoch (in present-day western Connecticut) had migrated to Gnadenhütten, many complained about the Moravian communal economy. One core group decided to return to their town in Connecticut. Another band of Paugussets from Pachgatgoch, most of them unbaptized except a few leaders, insisted that the missionaries "give them land at Nazareth forever, as they wish to settle there permanently." Like Teedyuscung's clan, the Paugussets wanted to assure their economic future by demanding equal access to property now being purchased and settled by whites. Only ownership would "assure that their children and their children's children" had a legacy of land. The Moravians, however, refused to deed land to Indians and did not want to create an Indian town at Nazareth, but they eventually conceded that all the mission communities would work better with separate household economies, if just to keep their converts under their spiritual care. At Gnadenhütten and Nazareth, Moravian leaders assigned individual households land to plant, warning them that "it would be expensive to those who lived by themselves," and agreed to divide "all the low land among them" as well as to distribute a few bushels of wheatmeal to each family. The Indians also had to "prepare to cook, plant, eat, and work for themselves." Moravians might have considered separate household economies prone to failure, but they probably worried more about the spiritual effects of Indian economic independence.[24]

24. "Weil wir gehört hatten, daß es ihnen lieber wäre, wer sie vor sich wohnten, wir ihnen zu helffen willig wären und hätten also beschlaßen, alles Low land unter sie in Gnadenhütten zu theilen, . . . und über diß solle auch eine jede Familie ein Paar Buschel Weizen Mehl zugetheilt bekommen. Dahero solten sie sich also einrichten, daß sie vor sich kochen, pflanze, eßen und arbeiten solten"; see *Moravian Records*, Sept. 6/17, 1747, reel 4, box 116, folder 2; "daß Ihren Kindern u. Kindes Kindern zum Besitz versichert würde"; see Diarium von Bethlehem, June 20/ Oct. 1, 1747, Appendix A, July 1747, Sept. 20/ Oct. 1, 1747, reel 3, VI, 1747, Van Pelt Library. See also Bishop John Christopher Frederick Cammerhoff to Count Nikolaus Ludwig von Zinzendorf,

Christian Indians, on the other hand, saw independence as key to their survival. They used strategies of their past to control their economic future. They still worked in seasonal cycles of hunting and planting, women were central to household economic activities and consumption, they relied on kin networks as a means of organizing economic activities, and, more important, they maintained economic obligations that bridged the gap between Christian and non-Christian Indian communities. Clan-based households, including husbands and wives with their brothers, sisters, and children, coordinated efforts to support their families. In the fall, brothers would hunt together, and sisters would travel to nearby towns to trade for goods. By late winter, when food supplies were often low, women searched the surrounding woods for available resources, including "Haccle Berries," chestnuts, blackberries, wild honey, and hemp, to supplement their meals or to sell at markets in the area. The Delawares at Meniolagomekah were particularly active. In the spring of 1753, "Naomie, Verona and her son Levi went out to gather cranberries, which they sell to the white people." Native women used traditional economic activities to connect with Euramerican neighbors, allowing them to share foodstuffs, as they would with kin, and to participate in the market economy.[25]

Although subsistence activities such as hunting and gathering natural resources continued to be important in the Christian native communities, Indians also drew on a range of economic strategies that differed from that of their ancestors. Traditionally, native women were thought to be "the Truest Owners" of land in the northeast. They labored in fields and produced much of the basic food sources for households. In mission towns,

---

Nov. 17, 1747, John Christopher Frederick Cammerhoff, 1721–1751, Letters, 1747–1748, copied by John W. Jordan, HSP.

25. Gnadenhütten Account Book, September 1747–May 1749, Generalia, Accounts and Inventories, 1747–1795, *Moravian Records,* reel 33, box 311, folder 1, Bernhard Grube's diary, Apr. 4, 1753, reel 6, box 122, folder 3 ("Naomie, Verona und ihr Sohn Levi gingen aus Cramburey samlen die sie hernach verkauffen an die Weißen Leüte"), Aug. 6, 1753, reel 6, box 122, folder 3, Oct. 9, 1753, reel 6, box 122, folder 3, Oct. 23, 1753, reel 5, box 117, folder 4. See also Carl John Fliegel, comp., *Index to the Records of the Moravian Mission among the Indians in North America,* 4 vols. (Woodbridge, Conn., 1970), 1260–1263; Heckewelder, *History, Manners, and Customs,* 155–157; Jay F. Custer, "Late Woodland Cultures of the Lower and Middle Susquehanna Valley," in Custer, ed., *Late Woodland Cultures of the Middle Atlantic Region* (Newark, N.J., 1986), 139–141.

Moravians surveyed and distributed land for native American use and aggressively introduced agriculture as a male responsibility. By the 1750s, Christian Indian men became increasingly active in cultivating land, especially cash crops of corn, rye, wheat, barley, and flax. "Jonathan and David [two Delawares] from Gnadenhitt wass here to help hoe Corn," a missionary at Meniolagomekah noted in July 1752. However, women, too, received land to plant if their husbands had died, abandoned them, or were living elsewhere. Sara received one acre but told the Brethren that she might want more if her husband, David, returned; otherwise, she would let the Moravians use the land if she decided not to plant. Maria was given land in Gnadenhütten in 1749 after her husband left. Moravians even recognized previous claims to land use, if not ownership, by native women. Naomi owned and worked a plantation at Meniolagomekah, which had probably been in her family for several generations.[26]

Other activities that became part of the Christian Indian economy brought significant change to the ways that Indians valued goods and their own labor. Groups of Delawares still might have gone to "the woods a hunting," as many native families had done for years, but by the mid-eighteenth century manufacturing and wage labor rivaled hunting and agriculture as a primary means of support. Some Indians no longer performed services simply as reciprocity for another's act of hospitality but relied on cash to purchase material goods that they needed. Wage work was increasingly important to survival in Christian Indian communities, and women as much as men performed a variety of tasks, usually for white neighbors. The women of the mission towns traveled as far as Nazareth, Christiansbrunn, Bethlehem, Broadheadville, and the Delaware Water Gap to work for nearby German and Scots-Irish settlers. In October 1753, for example, "Naomi and Amalia with their children went to the Jerseys to work to supply themselves with Winter clothing." Like many Indian women, they probably pulled flax and turnips, reaped oats, or gathered pine knots, for which they usually received the going rate for women's labor, one shilling a day. Native men had a wider range of work available to them, such as reaping, carting, thrashing, working on roads, and

26. Iroquois Cayenquiragoa, Mar. 10, 1763, in James Sullivan et al., comps., *The Papers of Sir William Johnson,* 14 vols. (Albany, N.Y., 1921–1965), IV, 56; "Indianische Conferenz," Oct. 31, 1747, *Moravian Records,* reel 6, box 119, folder 1, item 2, Sept. 2, 1749, reel 6, box 119, folder 1, item 2, July 14, 1752, in English, reel 6, box 122, folder 2, June 23, 1754, reel 5, box 118, folder 1.

floating lumber to the mill, for which they received better wages. During the 1750s, Delaware men from Gnadenhütten helped to open up the roads through the Kittatinny, or Endless, Mountains. Some Delaware and Mahican men at the Moravian mission towns also were skilled laborers, such as canoe makers or coopers. In the mid-1750s, Indian men usually received about two shillings a day for their work. These figures were on par with the general wages for the white population in the backcountry and in urban regions closer to Philadelphia. With a labor shortage in Pennsylvania, workers of any kind, whether white or Indian, were in high demand and could command decent wages—at times 30–100 percent higher than in England.[27]

The introduction of wage labor and a cash economy during the mid-eighteenth century dramatically changed how Indians subsisted. More significant, the new economy had the potential to rearrange gender dynamics within Indian communities. Women's status as economic providers was threatened. Their right to property was not recognized by the Pennsylvania provincial government. As laborers, they received less than

27. Schebosch's diary, Sept. 1, 1752, in English, *Moravian Records,* reel 6, box 122, folder 2, April 1753, reel 5, box 117, folder 4, Oct. 5, 1753, reel 6, box 122, folder 3 ("Die Naemie, und Amalia mit ihren Kindern gingen nach der Jerseys, Arbeiten, da mit sie sich Winter kleider anschaffen können"), June 25, 1754, reel 5, box 118, folder 1, June 28, 1754, reel 5, box 5, folder 1; Marshall J. Becker, "Hannah Freeman: An Eighteenth-Century Lenape Living and Working among Colonial Farmers," *PMHB,* CXIV (1990), 249–269. During the late 1750s, when the British military presence increased, they continued to use Indian labor. In the fall of 1758, the Forbes Road crew at Loyal Hanna included fifty-four to seventy-three Indians, depending on the day. See Thomas Donnellon, Sept. 19, 20, 1758, Burd-Shippen Papers, Letters, APS; "Benjamin Lightfoot's Notes of a Survey of a Road from Fort Henry to Shamokin," Mar. 14, 17, 18, 1759, HSP. Beginning in 1751, baptized Indians were doing roadwork. See *Moravian Records,* Sept. 28, 1751, reel 3, box 114, folder 4, Apr. 2, 1753, reel 5, box 117, folder 4, Gnadenhüutten Account Book, 1755, Generalia, Accounts and Inventories, 1747–1795, reel 33, box 311, folder 3; William Buchanan, Advertisement, May 1755, box 1, Burd-Shippen Papers, Letters, APS. On wages, see Gary B. Nash, *The Urban Crucible: The Northern Seaports and the Origins of the American Revolution,* abridged ed. (Cambridge, Mass., 1986), 121; James T. Lemon, *The Best Poor Man's Country: A Geographical Study of Early Southwestern Pennsylvania* (Baltimore, 1972), 179; Mary M. Schweitzer, *Custom and Contract: Household, Government, and the Economy in Colonial Pennsylvania* (New York, 1987), 51–52. Forge laborers might be paid as much as three shillings a day. Schweitzer suggests that Indian laborers were sometimes paid slightly less than white workers, depending on the job, time, and place.

men. By the 1750s, native women were also becoming less relevant to the fur trade. Rather than accepting a diminished role in the production of resources, however, native women found new avenues to exercise their economic powers. They turned to entrepreneurial activities to help support their households; besides selling the food they gathered outdoors, they manufactured goods for sale. Probably like their seventeenth-century grandmothers, Delaware and Mahican women used the winter season to manufacture items for home use. Unlike past generations, however, in the eighteenth century women increasingly manufactured these items specifically for sale to neighboring white communities. "Maria went to Christianbrunn and wants to work several days and make brooms," a missionary noted in July 1752. Native women produced these brooms as well as baskets, wooden spoons, bowls, and sleeping mats to exchange for any number of trade goods or cash. Brooms might bring in three pence a piece, bowls, four pence. Although perhaps not as lucrative as selling deer skins, which commanded about six shillings, or half the price of a warm winter blanket, native women managed to maintain their economic independence and continued to contribute to household subsistence.[28]

Even though Moravian Indians, like their non-Christian neighbors to the west, grew increasingly dependent on the Euramerican market system for their livelihood, the relative economic stability brought on by the sale of manufactured goods and consistent wage labor also gave Christian Delawares and Mahicans the wherewithal to fulfill older obligations to kin. Moravian missionaries often expressed a concern for the "great poverty" or "extreme poverty" in which they found some Christian Indians. They could not understand why their converts, who had been given land to plant and lessons in thrift and economy, did not plan ahead more carefully about their winter and spring needs. They encouraged Indians to produce enough excess crops to take them comfortably through times

28. Claudio Saunt, "'Domestick . . . Quiet being broke,': Gender Conflict among Creek Indians in the Eighteenth Century," in Andrew R. L. Cayton and Fredrika J. Teute, eds., *Contact Points: American Frontiers from the Mohawk Valley to the Mississippi, 1750–1830* (Chapel Hill, N.C., 1998), 167–170; Gnadenhütten Account Book, September 1747–1752, Generalia, Accounts and Inventories, 1747–1795, *Moravian Records*, reel 33, box 311, folders 1, 2, Schebosch's diary, July 17, 1752, in English, reel 6, box 122, folder 2, Bernhard Grube's diary, Feb. 25, 1753, reel 6, box 122, folder 3 ("Maria ging nach Christb. und will etl. Tage dort Arbeiten und Bärseim machen"), Mar. 14, 1753, reel 6, box 122, folder 3.

of starvation. According to Euramerican standards, these Christian Indians were barely surviving. The mission Indians were actually better off than the Moravians perceived, however, at least among native frontier communities. Even as they struggled for economic survival, the residents of Gnadenhütten and Meniolagomekah used their meager wealth to strengthen political and economic alliances between themselves and non-Christian Indians who turned to them for assistance in times of need.[29]

During the 1740s, starvation had threatened Indians along the Susquehanna River, and they often entreated white trade partners in Tulpehocken or Moravians at Bethlehem for help. By the 1750s, native Americans, caught within the developing imperial conflict between England and France, found it increasingly difficult to conduct regular trade in Pennsylvania; their hunting grounds were endangered. In the spring and summer of 1752, many Susquehanna natives, left with little food for the year, sought the assistance of Gnadenhütten residents, who had relatives in Nescopeck, Wapwallopen, and the Wyoming Valley. Paxnous, the Shawnee leader from Wyoming, arrived at Gnadenhütten in July with a delegation of sixty-five, presented a belt of wampum, and described their situation: "The entire trip they and their children have had nothing to eat but huckleberries and several of the old people are already without strength. . . . They first wanted to go as far as Bethlehem, but since they were very weak from hunger" they instead begged the Indians at Gnadenhütten for aid. To the Indians at Wyoming, "Gnadenhütten had a great name," and

29. *Moravian Records,* Nov. 25, 1751, reel 5, box 117, folder 2, Jan. 12, 1752, reel 5, box 117, folder 3, Jan. 16, 1752, reel 5, box 117, folder 3. See also Cronon, *Changes in the Land,* 41. Native cycles of feast and famine were not so different from Euramerican consumption patterns. According to Carole Shammas, *The Pre-Industrial Consumer in England and America* (Oxford, 1990), American colonists spent 50–60 percent of household budgets on food. But people were not necessarily eating a lot or even enough. "When working people had extra money they often spent it on food, and when they had less income, they cut back," thus treating food as a luxury (145). Real starvation was not common, but they were "resigned to a certain level of malnourishment" (148). The relative economic success of the mission community at Gnadenhütten can been seen in a 1755 inventory. Besides the building structures, they owned 2 mares, 2 horses, 3 colts, 14 cows, 7 heifers, 7 calves, 17 oxen, 65 bushels of oats, 11 loads of hay, 2 loads of steeped flax, 1 load of hemp, 5 loads of wheat, 4 loads of rye, 1 load of barley, 500 pounds of butter, 10 bushels of meal, 12 bushels of buckwheat, 3 bushels of Indian corn, 1 and a half bushels of flaxseed, 4 bushels of beans, 6 bushels of salt, and 24 pounds of beeswax (Reichel, ed., *Memorials of the Moravian Church,* 222–223).

they considered an alliance with these well-connected clans important to their survival. Yet more than simple need brought Paxnous to the mission town. His request would also act as a way to reintegrate Christian Indians into an Indian power structure. Since the late 1730s, the Six Nations had attempted to force Pennsylvania Indians into their sphere of influence. By the early 1750s, the Iroquois were hard-pressed by the struggle for economic power in the region. They had lost their influence over Indians in the Ohio Valley and now hoped to exercise their control over Delawares and Mahicans in the east. Still, to make this possible, they relied on nonpartisan leaders, such as Paxnous, to sow the seeds of an alliance. At the end of the conference in July 1752, the Delawares and Mahicans at Gnadenhütten gave the Nanticokes and Shawnees a symbolic gift of "a dressed deer skin, with which they should repair their children's shoes," thus building a bridge between them. More substantially, they presented sixty bushels of meal and eighty pounds of tobacco to "divide among themselves, which they accepted with great acclamations."[30]

Christian Delawares and Mahicans could assist their non-Christian kin and neighbors precisely because they participated in the market economy and had accumulated enough excess wealth to offer these gifts. Yet the gift exchange and the political alliance it represented also drew Christian Indians back into a set of traditional alliances that would place their commu-

30. Bethlehem Diary, Feb. 21, 1745, reel 1, Van Pelt Library; *Moravian Records,* June 22, 1747, reel 6, box 121, folder 3, July 24, 1747, reel 29, box 221, folder 5, item 1, June 15, 1751, reel 6, box 121, folder 5, July 15, 1752, reel 35, box 323, folder 1 ("Die ganze Reise vor sich und ihre Kinder nichts als Heidelbernt zu eßen gehabt, wobey einige Alte schon kraftlos sind," "daß sie willens gewesen erst nach Bethlehem zu gehen, weil sie aber von Hunger sehr matt sind, so wollen sie ietzo nur hierher kommen. . . . Gnadenhütten einen grosen Nahmen bey ihnen hätte, darum wären auch ihre alte Leute mitgekommen, Gnadenhütten zu sehen, und sie hoffen in einem halben Jahr bekannter mit uns zu werden"), July 18, 1752, reel 35, box 323, folder 1 ("Ein zubereitetes Hirsch=fell: sie solten damit ihrer Kind Schuh, die veilleicht auf dem Weg zerreißen, flicken. Sagten ihnen auch, daß 60. Buschel Mehl und 80. lb. Tobac zum Present vor sie da wären, die sie unter sich vertheilen konten, welches sie mit großen Acclamationen annahmen"); "An Account of the Famine among the Indians of the North and West Branch of the Susquehanna, in the Summer of 1748," *PMHB,* XVI (1892), 432. Peter C. Mancall, *Valley of Opportunity: Economic Culture along the Upper Susquehanna, 1700–1800* (Ithaca, N.Y., 1991), 58, speculates that the famine of 1748 was caused by traders, who "destabilized communities and disrupted economic rhythms."

nities at risk. Although many native families in the region had moved to the Susquehanna River or they had fled west of the Alleghenies, avoiding Iroquois authority entirely, Christian Indians were among the few who remained in eastern Pennsylvania, holding onto relative political autonomy. The alliance that Moravian Indians had confirmed through a gift exchange with Nanticokes and Shawnees from Wyoming gave the Six Nations a new source of leverage with which to pry the baptized Indians away from white missionaries. A year after they received aid from mission Indians, the Wyoming delegation returned to Gnadenhütten under specific Iroquois direction and made a reciprocal offer. The Iroquois in New York wanted the mission Indians, both Delawares and Mahicans, to move north to the Wyoming Valley, to live under the protection of their "Uncles," the Six Nations, to once more become subordinates, or props of the Longhouse, and to act as a buffer between them and the increasing numbers of white settlers moving into the frontier. Addressing the Mahicans and Delawares as equal "cousins," Partrik told them that the Shawnees had made room in Wyoming for the Christian Indians and now expected them to move. The Six Nations promised a permanent place of residence and protection, and they threatened retribution if the offer was not accepted.[31]

The Christian Indians were torn about their response to the Shawnee and Iroquois proposal. The Mahicans, who formed a dominant element in Gnadenhütten, led the discussion. Their leader Shabash, baptized by the Moravians as Abraham a decade earlier, insisted that the Mahicans should accept the proposal to move, since they, at least, had specific obligations to their neighbors to the north that could be traced back more than a century. Not only had they created new kinship bonds with Nanticokes and Shawnees in the summer of 1752 by extending gifts to them, but, according to Abraham, "Our ancestors made an alliance and clung fast to the same." He had a harder time convincing the Christian Delawares at Gnadenhütten, however, who had grown wary of Mahican leadership, to follow suit. At the April 1753 council meeting, Abraham modified the usual format of prayerful discussion and turned instead to native diplomatic protocol to persuade the Delawares. First, he laid out four strings and four belts of wampum and symbolically cleansed the eyes, ears, and hearts of

31. *Moravian Records,* Mar. 18, 1753, reel 5, box 117, folder 4, Mar. 22, 1753, in English, reel 40, box 3500, folder 15, Speech of Wyoming Shawnees to Mahicans and Delawares, March 1753, reel 35, box 323, folder 1, item 3, letter E.

the Delawares: "Until now your eyes have been dark. I will wash them out so that you can see nothing but the good. I will cleanse your ears so that you can hear nothing but the good. I will make your inner heart clear and take out everything that is evil." "My Grandfather heard that we Mahicans and Delawares had once made an alliance in Menninsing," Abraham recalled. "That fire is dead. . . . Now we want to renew the alliance with you and have a fire together." Abraham repeated these words before the Nanticoke and Shawnee delegates, making clear that it was the wish of their uncles, the Iroquois, to have them all renew their alliances and rebuild the council fires that had been extinguished and to consider again the proposed removal. The mission community, however, divided along ethnic lines and, under increasing pressures from Moravians to break their ties with non-Christian kin, delayed a formal decision about the offer.[32]

In the spring of 1754, Abraham once more reminded the Christian Indians and German Moravians at Gnadenhütten about their promises to the Iroquois, Nanticokes, and Shawnees, which had been confirmed in annual conferences during the previous two years. "The Brethren know that it is a great matter, what we discussed with the Nanticokes and what we have promised them," Abraham reprimanded. "It was also not one of us who dealt with them, but all of us, white and brown Brethren." All of them, whites and Indians, Susquehanna and Forks of the Delaware communities, had developed and maintained personal, economic, and political ties that had endured for ten years. Christians and non-Christians had come together repeatedly to celebrate their spiritual lives—as Moravians traveled to Shamokin and beyond and Nanticoke warriors pondered the por-

32. "Unser Vorfahren haben ehedem einen Bund gemacht, und derselben fest gehalten," "Bis hero sind eure Augen dunkel gewesen ich will sie euch aus wischen, daß ihr lauter gutes sehen könnt. Eure Ohren will ich reinigen, daß ihr lauter guts hören könnt, Eure inwendiges Herz will ich rein machen und alles böse heraus nehmen," "Mein GroßVater hört wir Mahikander u. Delewar haben einmal einen Bund in Menninsing gemacht. Da war auch ein groß feuer und Schatten. Das feuer ist Todt. . . . Nun wollen wir mit euch den Bund verneueren und ein feuer zusammen haben"; see Conferenz, Apr. 5, 1753, *Moravian Records,* reel 6, box 119, folder 1, item 9. Perhaps Abraham was referring to a century-old alliance that New York Mahicans had made with the Mohawks. After years of war (1624–1628), Mohawks made peace with Mahicans and, along with the Dutch, confirmed trade links between the three parties (Francis Jennings, *Ambiguous Iroquois Empire: The Covenant Chain Confederation of Indian Tribes with English Colonies from Its Beginnings to the Lancaster Treaty of 1744* [New York, 1984], 49–50, 54–47).

trait of a bleeding Christ. They had negotiated marriages across ethnic and religious boundaries. They had traded with each other and labored together. Now, as Abraham reminded them, the Christian community was obligated to fulfill the demands of the Susquehanna Indians. Despite the Moravians' attempts to redefine the meaning of native kinship and despite their attempts to dissuade an exodus of their converts, many Christian Indians chose, as the Germans phrased it, to return "to heathenish manners." In April 1754, Abraham, his wife Sara, and son Joachim as well as many other Mahicans and their families announced their move to Wyoming. Several Delaware households, including Teedyuscung and his kin, followed suit and migrated to the Susquehanna River. By the end of 1754, nearly ninety Delawares and Mahicans, just fewer than half of the mission population, had moved from Gnadenhütten and Meniolagomekah to various parts of the Susquehanna, some to the Wyoming Valley and some to kin at Nescopeck.[33]

The renewed alliances between communities, which were intended to extend and strengthen kinship networks and their attendant support systems, had instead precipitated the Pennsylvania mission communities' decline. In particular, the debate over the Iroquois offer highlighted the many social fractures within households and between clans that had lain beneath the surface for many years and contributed to out-migration. The encroachment of whites onto Indian land and the continuing political tensions generated by the Six Nations and Pennsylvania government probably exacerbated these intercommunity conflicts. As early as 1749, Richard Peters, the provincial secretary, had claimed land on the Aquanshicola Creek that encompassed the Delaware village of Meniolagomekah. In April 1754, he "demanded that the Indian Brethren evacuate his land,"

33. "Zur Heidenischen Lebens=Art," Oct. 18, 1753, *Moravian Records,* reel 6, box 119, folder 1, item 10.1, Mar. 11, 1754, reel 6, box 119, folder 1, item 10.9 ("Drum wißen doch die Brr. daß es eine große Sache ist, wo von wir mit den Nantigogs geredt u. was wir ihnen versprochen haben. . . . Es hats auch nicht einer von uns mit ihnen davon gehandelt, sondern wir alle, wiese u. braune Brr"), Apr. 18, 1754, reel 5, box 118, folder 1. Individual Christian Indians had moved to the Susquehanna River throughout the preceding decade, but the first mass migration occurred in 1754. See, for instance, "Register of Inhabitants of Nazareth" (extracts from Nazareth Diary, English translation), Aug. 10/21, 11/22, 1746, Church and Meeting Collection, HSP. Gottlieb and Maria, the first Delaware couple to be baptized, left Nazareth "in a very dark mood" and "with a brazen face" returned to the Susquehanna River (*Moravian Records,* Dec. 31, 1754, reel 5, box 118, folder 2).

promising a token five pounds for the improvements. Pushed from their homes of half a century, about forty-nine of the Delawares joined families in Gnadenhütten; others went to the Susquehanna to live.[34]

Some of the social fractures emerging at the mission communities cut along gender lines. During this time of crisis, Indian women faced difficult choices between their husbands' or their fathers' wishes and the kinship networks they had established with other women, including the German Moravians. Abraham might have convinced some Mahicans and Delawares to act on older native political alliances and move to the Wyoming Valley, but he had a harder time with his own family. Abraham's son, Jonathan, agreed that the political obligations of Mahicans were important and that he, too, would move to the Wyoming Valley. Jonathan's wife, Anna, however, did not want to leave and hoped to remain in Gnadenhütten with her children for their safety. She begged Jonathan to consider her side of the matter, and, in the end, he went to the Susquehanna, and she stayed behind. "If I should live in Wyoming," she confided to the Moravians the following year, "I already know beforehand, it will go badly for me and my children." "We would suffer hunger there. . . . I wouldn't have what I have here; that distresses me." Sara, Anna's mother-in-law, had similar concerns about leaving her home at Gnadenhütten but went to Wyoming with her husband nonetheless. Unlike Anna, Sara no longer had to worry about small children. But she, too, was less than happy about the move. She maintained close ties with Moravian sisters and in August 1754 wrote to Johanna Spangenberg through a visiting missionary, "I greet you lovingly." Though she felt "very poor here in Wyoming," Sara beseeched,

34. "Nachmittag kam Br. Josuas Frau die Agnes von Meniol. mit der Nachricht, daß der Eigenthums Mann (referring to Peters) dasiges Landes in Meniol. sein Land von den Ind. Brüdern zu räumen verlange"; see *Moravian Records*, Apr. 26, 1754, reel 5, box 118, folder 1. Peters might have made claim on this land in the early 1740s, assuming it was part of the Walking Purchase. See "Acct. of Lands Unsold in Northampton Co.," Dreer Collection, Pennsylvania Surveys, 1742–1765, Lands in Lancaster, Bucks, York, Cumberland, and Philadelphia Counties, HSP (111/145/41 and 109/72 are a "warrant for 500 [acres] March 11, 1742 above the Forks of Delaware on the Western Branch. Another for 200 Ac. of Dec. 6, 1744 adjoining the Cedar Swamp on Aquanskikalo"); Reichel, ed., *Memorials of the Moravian Church*, I, 35n; J. Max Hark, "Meniolágoméka: Annals of a Moravian Indians Village an Hundred and Thirty Years Ago" (paper presented at the annual meeting of the Moravian Historical Society, Sept. 15, 1880, 16).

"My sister, remember me to the Lord, I need it, for I am among Indians who still live in sin."[35]

Generational differences, even more than gender differences, created destructive tensions within the mission communities during the early 1750s. Those Indians who had chosen baptism as adults had challenged the social conventions of their families. The younger generation growing up in the Moravian mission towns now questioned the choices of their parents. As the children of Christian Indians, they were placed in a milieu of family relationships, sexual attitudes, economic interactions, and religion that reflected both customary native practices and Moravian social lessons. The boundaries of kinship had shifted to include white missionaries and unrelated Christian Indians of various ethnic origin. Although their parents had consciously selected this new context for their lives, the younger generation expressed frustration with the restrictions of the mission communities. Some young Indians rejected their parents' world and reinvented another kind of Indian past.

In the mission towns, the Moravians tried to teach the social lessons of Christian communities to native children. By the mid-1740s, the Moravians established boys' and girls' schools in Frederickstown and Nazareth, respectively. Moravians were concerned about the impressionable nature of young Indians and created the separate programs to focus on the children's needs. John Heckewelder insightfully commented that "Old converted Warriors make the *best* Christians—Some *few* born of converted Parents, and who have received instruction from their infancy lead an exemplary life—others take delight in the Heathenish ways, and must often be admonished, and reprimanded." Many baptized Indians sent their young children to the schools, sometimes for religious education to assure their salvation. More often, they hoped that the Moravians

35. *Moravian Records*, Jan. 8, 1754, reel 5, box 118, folder 1, Jan. 9, 1754, reel 5, box 118, folder 1, Schmick to Spangenberg, Apr. 29, 1755, reel 5, box 118, folder 5, item 14 ("Wann ich soll in Wajomick leben, ich weißes schon zum voraus, es wird mir und meinen Kindern schlect geh wir werden dort hunger leiden . . . ich dort auch nicht das, was ich hier habe; das thut mir wehe"), Sara to Johanna Spangenberg, Aug. 31, 1754, reel 34, box 319, folder 4, item 9 ("Ich bin sehr arm hier in Wajomik, der Heiland thut sich aber doch zu mir, und ich halte mich an Ihnen." "Ich bitte dich meine Schwester, denk vorm Heiland an mich, ich habe es nöthig, denn ich bin unter Indianern die noch in Sünden leben").

might protect their children from epidemics and the hard conditions that plagued Indian villages.[36]

The children of native converts had ambivalent feelings about being taken from their families and placed in a strange setting with white children. The Moravians attempted to educate, but Indian children were more often alienated. In early 1746, young Mahican girls from the mission towns were sent to Nazareth to learn to read, write, and speak German and to prepare for baptism in the Moravian Church. However, they did not always respond to their education in ways their parents or the missionaries expected. Faced with a different environment and new playmates, the young girls became very conscious about the boundaries between themselves and the white children around them. They struggled with their own sense of self and their place in their parents' new world. In May 1746, the German girls at Nazareth greeted two Mahican sisters, six and nine years old, and another young Indian with great joy and proclaimed them a "gift" from the Savior. The attentive white girls gave the three young Indians endearing names—little worm (Würmchen), little dove (Täubchen), and little chicken (Hühnchen)—and at first treated them like exotic playthings. The Mahican girls clung together for support. The Moravian sisters noted that they held "special meetings in Indian, the little Dove leading in prayer—they often sing Ind. hymns together." One wonders whether the youngest girl, "affected to tears during meetings," cried for the Lord, as her teachers interpreted it, rather than sheer loneliness. "Little worm," the head mistress admitted, "often weeps for her mother." By summer, however, other native girls joined them, and they seemed to adjust to their new surroundings.[37]

Ironically, physical affliction, which their parents had hoped the girls would escape, changed their experience and response to the school. By late July, about eighteen of the girls, both Indian and white, became seriously

36. "Questions Put to Friend Heckewelder," box 1, folder 27, Heckewelder Papers, 1755–1822, HSP; *Moravian Records,* January 1747, reel 34, box 319, folder 3, items 1, 3, 4, Sept. 3, 1747, reel 4, box 116, folder 2, Feb. 1, 10, 1748, reel 4, box 116, folder 3.

37. "Register of Inhabitants of Nazareth" (extracts from Nazareth Diary, English translation), May 15/26, June 5/16, June 24/July 5, 1746, Church and Meeting Collection, HSP; "Kinder Diaria," excerpt from the Nazareth diary, in English, May 21, 1746, Moravian Archives. The girls' names came from the titles of Moravian religious societies—little fools, little worms, baby chicks, little bees—at Herrnhaag and Herrnhut in Germany and at Bethlehem. See Gollin, *Moravians in Two Worlds,* 12.

ill with smallpox. "Little chicken" succumbed immediately and lay ill for fifteen days, with an "Unpleasant odour around her; her ulcers alive with maggots." The Moravians marveled at the surprising change that came over her: "Formally she used to be like a little wild kitten; now in her sickness she is still as a lamb." The young Mahican adopted a pious tone during her illness, instructing the other girls on proper Christian behavior and affirming that "the Saviour is going to come for me." She died on August 8, 1746, after being baptized as Beata. The Moravian sisters praised her courage, since she had shown "not the least fretfulness, or impatience; though suffering many and dreadful pains." The Moravians exaggerated the memory of Beata's brief stay and the effects of her illness as a saintly lesson for other children.[38]

Beata might have learned the language of Christian piety to deal with her pain, but the Indian girls who survived had a more devilish response to their near-death experience. Nine-year-old Martha became very wary of the white students. The Moravian sisters "had formerly given cause, to think her ashamed of her Indian descent; but now after her sickness she seeks the company of [the Indian girls] Maria and of little dove in preference of all others, and would like to recover the Ind[ian] language." Like Martha, other girls wished to revive a sense of their own Mahicanness, separate from the white community. By the end of the summer, some of the remaining Indian girls, sullen and homesick, "conceived the idea of running away." In September 1746, Anne "watched her sister, 'the little dove,' as she went on the privy, and asked her to come along to Checomeco." The two girls also met with Maria, "urging her to come to Checomeco" with them. The following month, the Moravians wondered "how to manage the young Indians in our sisters house." "The question is how on the one hand to keep them under check sufficient to prevent them from acting the mistresses, and on the other hand, to keep them encouraged, and in humor of making exertions to learn something useful." Susanna finally ran away in September but was brought back by force. One of the elders at Nazareth complained that Maria, who had been adopted by the Spangenbergs in Bethlehem after the death of her mother Ruth, "acts some times as if possessed of an evil spirit" and "like a fury, threatening to strike and stab the sisters, and stirring up the other Ind. girls to be refractory."

38. "Register of Inhabitants of Nazareth" (extracts from Nazareth Diary, English translation), Aug. 7/18, 1746, Church and Meeting Collection, HSP.

Their defiance had nothing to do with evil spirits; the native girls, experiencing acute linguistic and social isolation, reacted to the unwelcome restraints of the Christian school.[39]

Similarly, young men struggled to make sense of their lives as Christian Indians and rebelled against their Moravian upbringing. A group of Mahican boys, in particular, who had attended boys' school together in Frederickstown between 1745 and 1750, had great difficulty adjusting when they returned to live with their parents in Gnadenhütten. During the early 1750s, when non-Christian Nanticokes and Shawnees began to visit the town, the boys encountered traditional Indian rituals and customs for the first time. In January 1754, the young men tried their own hand at reviving "pagan practices" by holding feasts and plucking the hairs from their heads to form scalplocks. Josua, Jr., after being reprimanded for his behavior, unconvincingly confessed to the council of missionaries and Indian elders: "It is true, it is already over a year that my heart was wounded. The wound is still not entirely healed and since that time it's gone bad with me." He assured the Brethren that, since the New Year, he and the other young men had agreed again "to live for the Lord and also to be entirely with our white brothers." Two months did not find the young men any happier with the mission town. The Moravians thought Abraham's sons were "still poor miserable spoiled Souls and are only suffered to continue there for their Parents sake." One elder complained that "the young people have frankly acknowledged that they have lived their time badly here." Further, the community feared that the occasional visit of "painted Indians" would continue to seduce or harm their children. Although baptized Indians wanted to provide their children with security and expanded opportunities for survival through a Moravian way of life, they only succeeded in making the alternative look attractive. Their children, isolated from traditional native ways and frustrated with the rules of Christian living, sought to create their own Indian identity.[40]

39. Ibid., Aug. 29/ Sept. 9, 1746, Sept. 10/21, 1746, Sept. 24/ Oct. 5, 1746, Oct. 8/19, 1746, Nov. 3/14, 1746, Nov. 5/16, 1746.

40. "Extract Out of the Bethlehem Congregation Journal, 1749," *Moravian Records*, in English, reel 26, box 211, folder 19, item 1, Jan. 14, 1754, reel 5, box 118, folder 1 ("Ja das ist wahr, es ist schon über ein Jahr, daß mein Herz wundt geschoßen ist; die Wunde is noch nicht ganz wieder heil, u. seit der Zeit ists schlect mit mir gegangen." "für den Hld zu leben, u. auch mit unsern weisen Brudern ganz zu seyn"), Mar. 9, 1754, reel 6, box 119, folder 1, item 10.7 ("Die jungen Leute habens gestanden, daß die

Whether owing to gender or generational differences, the mission towns tended to magnify growing community fractures. The more Moravians attempted to eradicate conflict and neutralize older disagreements among Indians to create a unified community of faith, the more they provoked discord. The Delawares and Mahicans who remained at Gnadenhütten began to argue about whether they should or should not entirely give up "the old Indian Way." No problem proved more enduring than the animosities between Mahicans and Delawares, which surfaced throughout the 1740s but coalesced by the early 1750s. Sometimes disagreements were minor. Mahicans refused to marry Delawares. Delaware children teased their Mahican playmates, calling them names. The situation worsened after Moravian elders moved Gnadenhütten across the Lehigh River in 1754, and Delawares from Meniolagomekah joined the predominantly Mahican town. At the new town site, Delawares demanded that their houses be built away from Mahicans. A public road divided the community and even became contested space, where sullen inhabitants confronted each other. In February 1755, a Mahican, Johannes Peter, "in a gloomy disposition," suspected the Delaware Nicodemus of some unknown offense and "gave him a blow on the arm with his stone jar." Johannes Peter finally apologized to Nicodemus, but ethnic hostilities remained.[41]

If Christian Mahicans and Delawares who chose to live together under the protection and tutelage of the Moravians found it hard to transcend the anger of the past, how would Indians and whites on the frontier fare? As long as peace prevailed, Indians in Pennsylvania built roads between different, but interdependent, communities through cultural adaptation. In turn, they found protection, economic stability, and a certain politi-

---

die Zeit her schlect gelebt u. manchen zum Angewiß gewesen sind"), Apr. 6, 1755, reel 5, box 118, folder 5, item 12.

41. *Moravian Records,* May 29, 1753, reel 5, box 117, folder 4, May 26, 1754, reel 5, box 118, folder 1, Schmick to Spangenburg, Jan. 10, 1755, reel 5, box 118, folder 5, item 4, Feb. 23, 1755, reel 5, box 118, folder 4 ("hatten wir zwischen 2 Brr. Joh: Peter den Mahik. u[n]d Nicodem. den Delaw. ein Versöhnungs Stündgen," "Ersterer hatte,/ etwa vor ein paar Monathen/, in einer Düsternheit seines Gemüths u[n]d genommen Argwohn den br. Nicodem. auf öffentl. Straße mit sr. Kruke einen Schlag auf den Arm gegeben"), Feb. 28, 1755, reel 5, box 118, folder 4, June 30, 1755, reel 5, box 118, folder 5, item 26, Sept. 22, 1755, reel 5, box 118, folder 6, item 13; Loskiel, *History of the Mission,* trans. La Trobe, pt. 2, 152–155.

cal autonomy from the Six Nations. By 1755, however, the face-to-face negotiations that sometimes brought Indians and whites together in kinship, in worship, and in work could not always mitigate the tensions that came with such close encounters. As the competition for land and resources increased and the clash between France and Great Britain over North America intensified at midcentury, Indians and whites more often confronted each other at the crossroads, stone jar in hand.

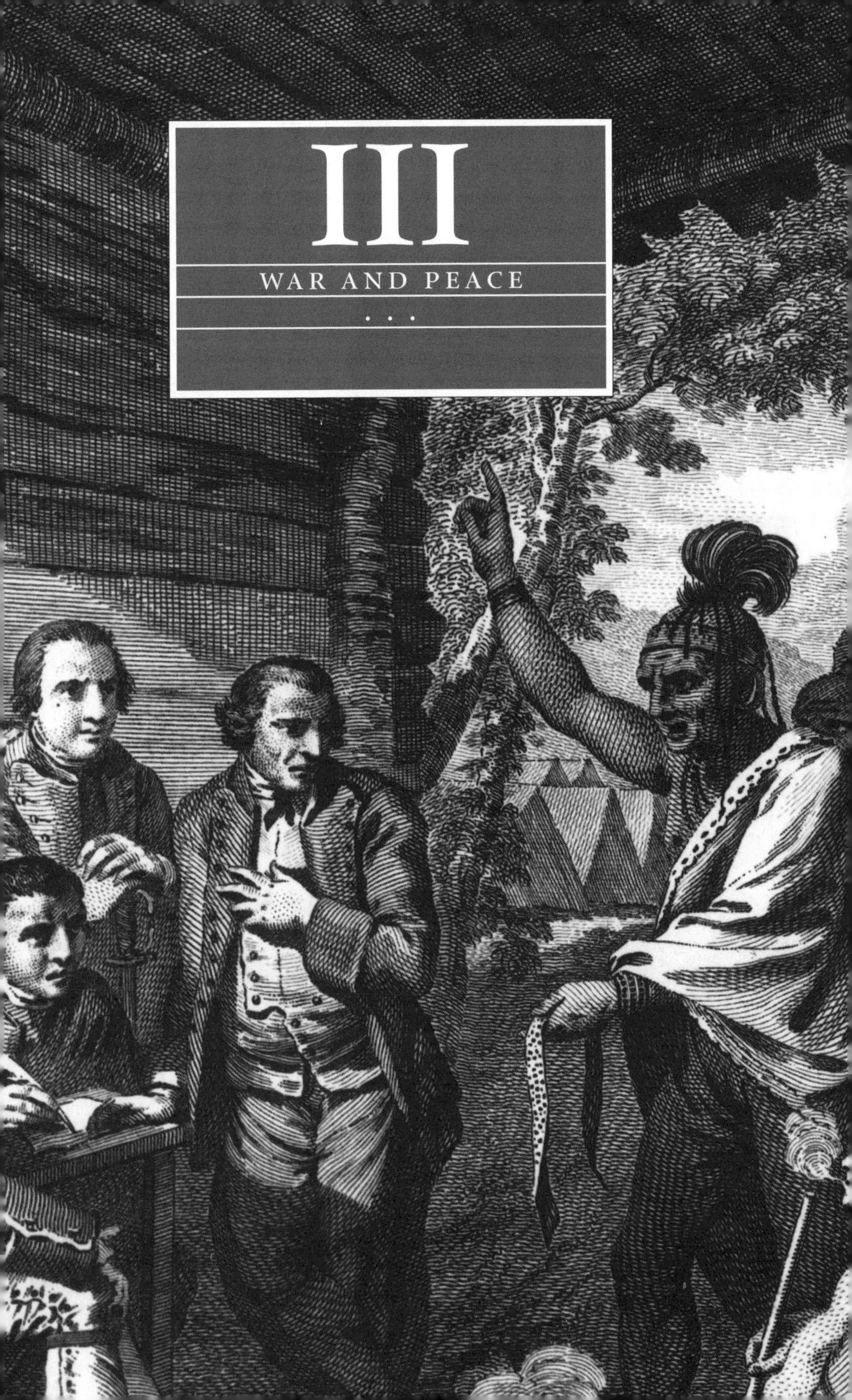

III

WAR AND PEACE

. . .

5

DEMONIZING DELAWARES

• • •

The Seven Years' War did not necessarily create differences between Indians and whites, but it aggravated already existing divisions. Frontier alliances often involved delicate balances of power among participants, and colonialism had shaken the equilibrium of many relationships. White and Indian communities experienced as much internal discord as cross-community conflict, and these hostilities intensified as colonial powers vied for control of their respective dependent populations. The Pennsylvania government, for instance, feared that the "lower sort" of white frontier settlers and Indians might ally themselves against government agents to overturn Pennsylvania land policies. Similarly, the Six Nations feared that alliances between Indian and white communities, such as the Moravians, would further undermine their authority over Delawares and Shawnees and their ability to manipulate European imperial powers as war drew nearer. Delawares, in particular, felt caught between colonial powers and the growing white frontier population. They had watched silently while the Iroquois and the English had negotiated for their land. From the 1720s, they had slowly given way to German and Scots-Irish settlers. In addition to losing territory, they lost political ground as well. They had not benefited from broader diplomatic agreements made between Pennsylvania and the Six Nations but remained subordinates to a relatively distant political authority.

Although much of the imperial posturing between Great Britain and France occurred far to the west of the Forks of the Delaware and the Susquehanna River valley, these events also affected interactions between communities east of the Alleghenies. The Seven Years' War began in May 1754, when Lieutenant Colonel George Washington's Virginia troops confronted a French delegation lead by Ensign Joseph Coulon de Villiers

Jumonville near the Great Meadows. With ten French soldiers dead and open hostilities initiated, war and rumors of war rearranged social relations and the daily patterns of frontier inhabitants' lives. Violence broke out between Indians and whites on the Pennsylvania frontier in 1755, involving not only the international rivalries of two European nations and the regional machinations of colonial powers but also the rivalries between and within families and communities. It pitted whites against Indians, Christians against non-Christians, strangers against kin, and Iroquois against Delawares. This was a war that tore families apart, divided loyalties, provoked ethnic animosities, and laid the foundation for new racialized boundaries of difference.

Land was central to the imperial conflict brewing in the Ohio Valley by the late 1740s. France and England had fought over colonial territory for decades. The Ohio Valley, a region of rich natural resources, attracted traders, potential settlers, and political agents from both countries. All sought to make alliances with Indians in order to control land distribution and the fur trade. Land was also a major factor in the continuing struggle for local power. The Six Nations and the Pennsylvania government vied for control of frontier regions, even as they attempted to maintain their alliance with each other and their tentative hold on increasingly restive populations. As the imperial conflict converged with the contest to dominate the region, Pennsylvania peoples of all kinds were pressured to declare loyalties and realign themselves for battle.

As white settlers spread into the frontier of Pennsylvania by the late 1740s, the Six Nations worried most about their ability to influence native politics and the Indian population. The Iroquois expressed grave misgivings "about the white people's Setling beyond the Endless mountains on Joniady, on Sherman's Creek and Else where." In the spring of 1749, some thirty white families lived on Indian lands, most just west of the Susquehanna "along the path that leads to Ohio." The Six Nations assured Pennsylvania that they would not "sell this part of the Country to the Virginians" or any other colony claiming jurisdiction over land. In return, the Iroquois wanted the province to evict white squatters from their territory, "forbidding the Settlement of any Lands not purchased by the Indians." Visiting Philadelphia in August 1749, Canassatego implored the council to "use more vigorous measures" to "forcibly remove" white settlers from the Juniata and Susquehanna Rivers. The Six Nations had their own political purposes in mind. Publicly, they alluded to the personal and sacred nature of the land in the Wyoming Valley and at Shamokin, insisting that "our Bones are scattered there, and on this Land there has always been a great Council Fire." Canassatego also pointed out that Pennsylvania would enjoy the economic benefits if Indians retained their "hunting Country," "for all we kill goes to You, and you have the profit of all the Skins." Yet the Iroquois more often used land to exert power over other Indians. After being instrumental in selling land in eastern Pennsylvania to the provincial government, they attempted to force Delawares, "who shall deserve to be in our Alliance," to live in the Wyoming Valley or at Shamokin under their supervision.[1]

White immigration to the frontier also worried the Pennsylvania government, but for different reasons. Individual families who moved to Indian land threatened Pennsylvania's colonial security because they often ignored laws restricting where they could settle, they refused to pay quitrents to the proprietors, and they sometimes quarreled with the Indian inhabitants. In many ways, the elite leadership preferred that Indians under the control of the Iroquois live on their frontiers rather than "the lower sort of People who are exceedingly loose and ungovernable." Government agents, such as Richard Peters and Conrad Weiser, worried that white settlers, beyond their ability to elude Pennsylvania law, might find common cause with their Indian neighbors. Whereas the Six Nations argued for an end to illegal occupation of Indian lands, local Indians did not always insist on the eviction of white settlers. Indeed, some Indians had invited whites to reside west of the Susquehanna, for which the Indians were paid rents or other goods for the use of the land. By the spring of 1754, for example, Andrew Montour, the son of cultural broker Madame Montour and Oneida warrior Currundawanah, had "already sold some of the Land on Sherman's Creek or Juniata, which the Indians of Ohio gave him, and had setled several Others upon it as his Tenants." Four years earlier, magistrates and sheriffs sent by Peters had cleared this same region of white settlers on the insistence of the Iroquois. They shut down communities in Sherman's Valley, the Path Valley, and the Big Cove, where, according to Peters, "the worst sort of Irish had been to mark places." At the

1. Conrad Weiser to Governor James Hamilton, Apr. 22, 1749, *PA*, 1st Ser., II, 24; Richard Peters to Thomas Penn, May 16, 1749, Peters to proprietors, July 5, 1749, Penn Papers, Official Correspondence, IV, 213, 219, HSP; *MPCP*, V, 401, VI, 116.

Juniata settlements, "thro which the new Indian Traders Road passes to Allegheney," the officials "burnt their Houses and sent the chief Mutineer to Jayl," and they shipped the rest of the settlers back east. The ambiguities of Indian-white relations, however, weakened provincial control, and, without local Indian cooperation, the Pennsylvania government could not keep white settlers from the region.[2]

Both the provincial government and the Six Nations struggled to subordinate frontier dwellers, but they also relied on each other to achieve their own goals. The Pennsylvania government needed the cooperation of the Iroquois to purchase Indian land and to assure future control of the frontier region. From Canassatego's death in 1750, however, the Six Nations had become wary of their English alliance. Consequently, in early 1753, Peters recruited Conrad Weiser, who had always been considered "a friend of the Iroquois," to reinvigorate the accord between nations. Weiser thought it best to solicit the help of Shickellamy's sons—John (T'hachnechtoris), James Logan (Tahgahjute, the lame one), and John Petty (Sagogeghyath)—who had succeeded their father as overseers of the native population at Shamokin, to persuade the Onondaga council to sell Pennsylvania "the Lands in the Coves, Path and Valley, and as far Westward as to the Allegheny Hills." Weiser, more interested in his own claims to Indian land, berated, bribed, and flattered the Shickellamy brothers, saying, "If they did not now stir, Others would bring it about, and they would then be obliged to sit and kill Lice and Fleas, and repent their Backwardness and Folly." He warned them that, if they did not act soon, Sir William Johnson, the British superintendent of Indian affairs, would secure the land in the Susquehanna River valley for the settlement of New England people or his own friends instead of those sympathetic to Indian inhabitants. John Shickellamy, dispatched to negotiate in the spring of 1754, must have persuaded the Six Nations. In June at the Albany Con-

2. Peters to proprietors, July 5, 1749, Peters to proprietors, July 12, 1750, Peters to proprietors, July 20, 1750, Penn Papers, Official Correspondence, IV, 219, V, 29, 39; Weiser to Hamilton, Apr. 22, 1749, *PA,* 1st Ser., II, 24; *MPCP,* V, 408; Weiser to Peters, May 2, 1754, no. 9, Penn Papers, Indian Affairs, II, 1754–1756, HSP. In Richard Peters's report to the provincial Assembly, he implied that some settlers cooperated in their own evictions; they "very chearfully and voluntarily took everything out of their Log Houses and assisted in burning them" (*MPCP,* V, 448). Elsewhere, the settlers confronted the sheriffs with loaded guns and threatened to kill them if they came near (*MPCP,* V, 443).

ference, even though Canadagaia, the Mohawk representative, grumbled that "there are writings for all our Lands, so that we shall have none left, but the very spot we live upon," he and the other Iroquois council members agreed to sell seven million acres in western Pennsylvania for four hundred pounds. The Albany Purchase included established Indian communities in the Ohio Valley. In July 1754, the Six Nations and the Pennsylvania governor formally signed an agreement and deed of purchase, after which a new boundary line was run between provincial and Indian lands, opening up the west to land claims by Pennsylvania leaders.[3]

Although the two colonizing powers had come to an agreement about the sale and distribution of Pennsylvania land, Delawares remained suspicious of Iroquois motives and the presence of provincial government agents in their communities. Delawares were particularly incensed by the Albany Purchase because they had been neither consulted nor invited to attend the conference. The Six Nations had already sold land at the Forks of the Delaware through the 1737 Walking Purchase, forcing the native inhabitants to move from established communities. Again, in 1749, with the cooperation of the Iroquois, the Pennsylvania government bought an additional 1,500,000 acres that cut a swath from the Delaware River to Thomas McKee's trading post on the Susquehanna River, just south of Shamokin. Now, with the Albany Purchase and renewed imperial conflict in the west, Ohio Delawares, in particular, wondered "where the Indian's Land lay" if "the French claimed all the Land on one side the River Ohio and the English on the other Side." They feared that, like their land, their liberty would soon be gone.[4]

3. Peters to Weiser, Feb. 6, 1753, Weiser to Peters, Oct. 12, 1754, Conrad Weiser Papers, I, Correspondence, HSP; Peters to Weiser, Apr. 17, 1753, Richard Peters Papers, 1697–1845, III, pt. 2, HSP; Weiser to Peters, May 2, 1754, no. 9, Council at Albany, June 27, 1754, no. 12, Penn Papers, Indian Affairs, II, 1754–1756, HSP. For John Shickellamy, see Julian P. Boyd, ed., *The Susquehannah Company Papers*, 10 vols. (Ithaca, N.Y., 1962–1971), I, 128; "Proprietaries of Pennsylvania Their Account with Richard Peters for the Indian Purchase," July 6, 1754, no. 6, Penn Papers, Indian Affairs, IV, 1733–1801, Indian Walk, HSP. Shickellamy was given £37 10s. for his assistance. See Anthony F. C. Wallace, *King of the Delawares: Teedyuscung, 1700–1763* (1949; Syracuse, N.Y., 1990), 179, for a map of of the purchase boundaries.

4. "Christopher Gist's First and Second Journals, Sept. 11, 1750–Mar. 29, 1752 . . . ," in Lois Mulkearn, ed., *George Mercer Papers Relating to the Ohio Company of Virginia* (Pittsburgh, Pa., 1954), 39; Indian deed signed by Canassatego, John Shikellamy, and

Caught between two empires, the western Delawares struggled to maintain good relations with Pennsylvania, especially because they were increasingly dependent on European trade goods. However, they also remained wary of the growing British military presence in the Ohio Valley. Shingas, their leader, had entreated the governor of Virginia, through colonial agent Christopher Gist, to build a fort for trade and protection near Logg's Town. Yet, when the Virginia military arrived in November 1753 under the command of Lieutenant Colonel George Washington, Delawares were reluctant to take orders from the young, inexperienced, and sometimes arrogant officer. Shingas even refused to meet with him at first, tendering the excuse "that his wife was sick." Despite pressure from Tanaghrisson, the Seneca "Half King" who acted as mediator between the Six Nations and the Ohio Indians, Shingas refused to accompany Washington to Fort Le Boeuf to negotiate a French withdrawal from the Ohio. Only through George Croghan's diplomatic intervention did Delawares finally agree to assist Washington when he returned to the Ohio Valley the following spring. By that time, the French had expelled English traders from western Pennsylvania and had built several strongholds against potential British retaliation. Warriors under the leadership of Shingas and Tanaghrisson helped Washington to kill Jumonville and nine of his small French detachment in May 1754, thus instigating a broader war. Delawares invested both men and honor to keep their agreement with the Virginian commander. In return, they experienced both defeat and insult. Washington, with a ragtag force of frontier dwellers of questionable ability, gave no gifts to Indian allies, nor did he take their advice, and the French easily pushed the Virginians back to the newly built, but soon abandoned, Fort Necessity. There, under siege in June 1754, Tanaghrisson complained bitterly that Washington treated "the Indians as his Slaves, and would have them every day upon the Out Scout and attack the Enemy by themselves," yet he refused to "take Advice from the Indians."[5]

Delawares Nutimus and Qualipaghack, 1749, *PA*, 1st Ser., II, 34; *MPCP*, V, 407. See the map in Wallace, *King of the Delawares*, 179.

5. Francis Jennings, *Empire of Fortune: Crowns, Colonies, and Tribes in the Seven Years War in America* (New York, 1988), 61; Michael N. McConnell, *A Country Between: The Upper Ohio Valley and Its Peoples, 1724–1774* (Lincoln, Nebr., 1992), 107–110; Fred Anderson, *Crucible of War: The Seven Years' War and the Fate of Empire in British North America, 1754–1766* (New York, 2000), 50–65; *MPCP*, VI, 151; "Copy of

Despite Washington's behavior, Ohio Delawares did not immediately lose faith in their military allies. They had put their economic future in English hands and acted accordingly. Whether from loyalty to the English, self-preservation, or dependence on British goods, some Indians returned east to the Susquehanna River in the fall of 1754 after the French defeated Washington at Fort Necessity. They resettled at places such as Shamokin, Croghan's plantation at Aughwick, or the Forks of the Delaware. Most of the refugees had little but the clothes on their backs and even feared to go hunting, lest their enemies kill them in the woods. Still, their young warriors joined white men in local militia units, as John Harris noted, "leav[ing] their Famileys" and setting off to fight the French "with all Cheerfulness Imagenable."[6]

Rather than gratefully accepting Indian assistance or using Indian skills and knowledge to help defeat the French, the British military managed to alienate their Indian allies further. When Major General Edward Braddock arrived in the colonies to attempt to retake Fort Duquesne in 1755, he, like Washington before him, had little experience with Indian warriors and did not understand how to nurture or maintain alliances. He failed to schedule a formal meeting with Ohio Indians living at Aughwick who were intending to join his westward march. Consequently, they gave him no intelligence on French movements in the west and "declined, if not refused, to attend the Comm[issione]rs to survey the country, in order to find out good Places for Roads." Braddock also treated the warriors' wives and families with contempt. Although his own men complained that Braddock spent "a Month idly, whoreing and feasting" at Will's Creek camp before heading to the Monongahela to fight the French, Braddock blamed the Indians for the delay. He issued orders forbidding them admittance to

---

Mr. George Croghan's Account of Indian Affairs from 1748/9 to General Braddock's Defeat," Penn Papers, Indian Affairs, I, 1687–1753, HSP. On Tanaghrisson, or Tanacharison, see Richard White, *The Middle Ground: Indians, Empires, and Republics in the Great Lakes Region, 1650–1815* (New York, 1991), 225 n. 4.

6. Robert Hunter Morris to Thomas Fitch, Nov. 20, 1754, in Boyd, ed., *Susquehannah Company Papers*, I, 163–164; George Croghan to Peters, Dec. 23, 1754, John Harris to Edward Shippen, Dec. 28, 1754, *PA*, 1st Ser., II, 218–219, 230. Aughwick was one of the major refugee communities for English-allied western Indians during the war. Tanaghrisson moved there and died there in October 1754. See Harris to James Hamilton, Oct. 5, 1754, Peters to Croghan, Dec. 10, 1754, *PA*, 1st Ser., II, 178, 214; *MPCP*, VI, 218.

the British encampment "and insisted with the Indians that their Women should be sent home."[7]

Angry at repeated insults from the military and increasingly suspicious of provincial motives for securing the Ohio Valley, western Indians finally turned their backs on the English. Scarouyady, the Oneida liaison for the Ohio Indians, scoffed at Braddock's defeat on July 9, 1755, saying it was his own fault. Though Braddock had died bravely in battle, his "pride and ignorance" had been his undoing. "He looked upon us as dogs," the Oneida speaker told the Pennsylvania governor with contempt, "and would never hear any thing what was said to him." "We often endeavoured to advise him and to tell him of the danger he was in with his Soldiers; but he never appeared pleased with us, and that was the reason that a great many of our Warriors left him and would not be under his Command." More troubling to the Delaware chief Shingas was Braddock's insistence that "No Savage Shoud Inherit the Land" after the English defeated the French. Ohio Indians plainly did not believe the British would leave their territory after the war. Shingas reasoned that "if they might not have Liberty To Live on the Land they woud Not Fight for it." Braddock, in turn, thought wrongly that he could defeat the French without Indian assistance. The subsequent fiasco of Braddock's defeat proved Scarouyady and Shingas right, but it also made Delawares vulnerable to retribution by the French and their Indian allies. Although the Delawares in western Pennsylvania preferred trade with the English, many Indians in the Ohio eventually chose to join the French or to remain neutral for "their Own Safety."[8]

By midcentury, Pennsylvania Indians feared that failed alliances and the actions of the English army would lead only to the further erosion of their territory. In response, they took out their anger on the white fron-

7. Peters to William Shirley, May 12, 1755, *PA*, 1st Ser., II, 308; John Rutherford to Peters, Aug. 13, 1755, Peters Papers, 1697–1845, IV, pt. 1, HSP; *MPCP*, VI, 397.

8. *MPCP*, VI, 589; Beverley W. Bond, Jr., ed., "The Captivity of Charles Stuart, 1755–57," *Mississippi Valley Historical Review*, XIII (1926–1927), 63, 64; White, *Middle Ground*, 225. C. Hale Sipe, *The Indian Wars of Pennsylvania . . .* (Harrisburg, Pa., 1929), 184–185, asserts that Braddock performed a condolence ceremony after his soldiers mistakenly shot Scarouyady's son. On some level, he might have understood certain native rituals as diplomatic gestures in Indian-white relations, but he made these gestures only when convenient or when they were to England's benefit. Scarouyady remained loyal to the English and an important go-between with the Delawares and Shawnees.

tier inhabitants who had been their closest neighbors. During 1755 and 1756, as imperial forces clashed on battlefields in the Ohio Valley and along the New York frontier, Delawares and Shawnees attacked white settlements in Pennsylvania. Within two years, they had killed at least 326 white settlers and had taken another 125 captive from their frontier homes. Like the dynamics that made personal alliances between Indians and whites possible, violence, too, had complex origins and revealed as much, if not more, about the nature of cross-cultural relationships. Rather than simply acting on the orders of French allies, whom they probably distrusted as much as the English, Ohio Indians, especially Delawares and their kin on the Susquehanna River, fought for their own reasons. They targeted specific communities that had repeated and prolonged contact with their own. Many of the Delawares who assailed white plantations between the Delaware and Susquehanna Rivers had traded with their white neighbors, had labored among the nearby German and Scots-Irish communities, had lived in mission towns, or had been baptized by the Moravians. Indians had become intimate with whites, but they also had been betrayed by that intimacy. Through violence, they sought to sever ties to individuals or families who had ignored the obligations that years of personal and economic alliances entailed. In particular, they attacked white settlements situated on land that they claimed as their own.[9]

Several decades of face-to-face interactions produced a casual familiarity between Indians and whites that surfaced during these violent encounters. Attackers and the attacked exchanged words and gestures that revealed a deep understanding of the other's language, family relations, economic activities, and habits. Indians used this knowledge to lure their intended victims but also to make their anger clear to whites. When Indians attacked the Kobel family in November 1755, they drove "the Children together, and spoke to them in High Dutch [German], '*be still, we won't hurt you,*'" then killed their parents. Another Indian addressed a white man "in proper high Dutch" before killing and scalping him. When

9. Hugh Mercer to James Burd, July 10, 1757, Shippen Family Papers, III, HSP. See "Lists of Pennsylvania Settlers Murdered, Scalped, and Taken Prisoners by Indians, 1755–1756," *Pennsylvania Magazine of History and Biography,* XXXII (1908), 309–319. Sir William Johnson secured the release of 338 white captives from Delawares and Shawnees at Fort Pitt between June 1759 and October 1761 (Sipe, *The Indian Wars of Pennsylvania,* 404).

William Fleming was captured in 1755, the Delawares "said to me in good English: I must go with them." Another young man captured just west of the Susquehanna noticed that his captors "mostly all Spake English, one spake as good English as I can." Indians spoke English or German in their rage. Conversely, whites knew their attackers by name (even their many names). After he escaped, Leonard Weeser listed the Delawares who took him captive from Smithfield township in Northampton County: "Teedyuscung alias Gideon alias Honest John, and three of his Sons, Amos and Jacob, the other's name he knew not. Jacobus and his Son, Samuel Evans and Thomas Evans were present; Daniel was present, one Yacomb, a Delaware, who used to live in his Father's Neighbourhood." In March 1756, Andrew Lycan, Ludwig Shut, and a young boy exchanged fire with a group of Indians in front of their house near Harris's Ferry. After several people were wounded or killed, there was a lull. Andrew and Ludwig then "sat down on a log to rest themselves, whilst the Indians stood a little way off looking at them. One of the Indians killed was Bill Davis, and two others they knew to be Tom Hickman and Tom Hayes, all Delawares and well known in those parts." However much imperial politics or economics drove the war, for Indians and whites on the frontier it was very personal.[10]

Just as white settlers believed they recognized their attackers, Indians knew exactly whom they captured, killed, or did not kill and why. Hostile Indians, disappointed that symbolic and actual kin alliances with whites had, for the most part, failed, used their knowledge of whites to redefine those relationships. They used particular acts of violence against the body to mark who was no longer friend or kin. Although Indian warriors took white women captive more often than not, they also killed and mutilated women to emphasize their rejection of the "common humanity" that women's bodies and their role as mothers represented. Native war-

10. Weiser to Morris, Nov. 24, 1755, *PA*, 1st Ser., II, 512, Examination of Leonard Weeser, Nov. 9, 1756, Examination of Henry Hess, December 1756, Deposition of Richard Baird, May 12, 1758, *PA*, 1st Ser., III, 45–46, 57, 397; James Young to Burd, Oct. 3, 1757, Shippen Family Papers, III, HSP; William Fleming, *Eine Erzehlung von den Trübsalen und der wunderbahren Befreyung so geschehen an William Flemming und dessen Weib Elisabeth Welche bey dem verwichenen Einfall der Indianer über die Einwohner imgrossen Wald (Grät Cov) bey Cannagodschick in Pensilvanien sind gefangen genommen worden . . .*, trans. W. Duglas (Philadelphia, 1756), 7; *Report of the Commission to Locate the Site of the Frontier Forts of Pennsylvania*, 2 vols. (Harrisburg, Pa., 1896), I, 93–94, 285–286; *Pennsylvania Gazette*, Mar. 18, 1756.

riors often targeted breasts and wombs—the reproductive organs that gave both Indians and whites life. Peter Williamson, taken captive in 1754, would say only that Indians had tortured and treated one woman "in such a brutal manner as decency will not permit me to mention." They probably had treated her body in the same manner as another woman living along the Schuylkill River, "who had been at a Plough" when Indians "shot thro' both her Breasts" and scalped her. Another woman was found in Cumberland County at the Great Cove, "lying killed with her Breast tore off and a stake run thro' her Body."[11]

Whereas violence against women's bodies struck at their power to reproduce and sustain life (in these cases, the life of the enemy who populated their land), violence against men targeted the organ of male sexual power, the penis, and the very center of male thought and reason, the brain. In November 1755, white settlers found Casper Springs dead at a Berks County farm, his "brains were beat out, that he had two Cuts in his breast, was shott with a bullet in his back, and his privities cut off and put into his mouth." Nearby, another man's "brains were out, his mouth much mangled, one of his Eyes cut out and one of his Ears gashed and had two knives lying on his breasts." Joseph Shippen told his father in August 1756 that a group of his men near Thomas McKee's trading post "found a man lying in the Road shott and scalped his Scull split open and one of the Provincial Tomhawks sticking in his private parts." Through these acts of emasculation, Indians manipulated white men's fears and flaunted their powerlessness to protect themselves and their families.[12]

Far from being arbitrary, gendered symbolic mutilation played a specific role in constructing Indian identity and resisting the occupation of Indian land. By killing men and women in such gruesomely intimate fashion at their homes and taking their scalps, Indians provided proof of their prowess and gained status as warriors. They showed that they had the

11. Wilcomb E. Washburn, comp., *The Garland Library of Narratives of North American Indian Captivities*, XXI, *Affecting History of the Dreadful Distresses of Frederic Mannheim's Family* . . . (New York, 1977), 32; "A Journal in 1754," June 30, 1754, *PA*, 1st Ser., II, 161; *MPCP*, VI, 707; [Jean Lowry], *A Journal of the Captivity of Jean Lowry and Her Children* . . . (Philadelphia, 1760), 4; White, *Middle Ground*, 388.

12. Deposition of Jacob Morgan, Nov. 18, 1755, no. 46, Penn Papers, Indian Affairs, II, 1754–1756, HSP; Joseph Shippen to Edward Shippen, Aug. 21, 1756, from Ft. Augusta, Military Letter Books of Joseph Shippen, 1756–1758, Shippen Family Papers, 1701–1856, HSP.

power to strike at the heart of an enemy's territory, to destroy body, family, and community. Frederick and Johanetta Hoeth, for example, lived on Walking Purchase land at the old Delaware settlement of Buchkabuchka and frequently visited the Delawares at Meniolagomekah. On December 12, 1755, as the family sat at supper, Indians attacked their plantation; they set fire to the house and stables, killed Frederick, and cut Johanetta's "belly open, and used her otherwise inhumanly." But they took the daughter captive. Even as native Americans killed adults to protest their role in the dispossession of land, they often appropriated their offspring, adopting them into their communities in the hope of repopulating that same land with Indians once the war ended.[13]

As the Hoeth family incident implies, Indians selectively destroyed kinship alliances, but they also selectively created new bonds, even in the midst of war. After all, they took captive nearly half as many settlers as they killed, and most of these captives ended up as family members. Indians used violence against or among captives to control those they wanted to adopt into their communities and to remind them of the treatment that nonkin could expect. For instance, in late October 1755, after taking captives at Penn's Creek, Delawares from Kittanning scalped and burned a woman who had attempted to flee. They made survivors witness her death to warn them against escape. Unexpected kindnesses sometimes followed brutal lessons. After taking captives from the Great Cove the same month, Delaware Captain Jacobs killed a small boy in front of William Fleming and said, "You shall never be free from death, except by your future good conduct." After this display of cruelty, he loosened Fleming's hands and treated him well, giving him food and a certain amount of free movement. The apparent incongruity in behavior and emotions—or, in Euramerican eyes, the lack of appropriate emotions—had a certain logic to native Americans. Indians used torture to ascertain the strengths of their enemies but also to avenge the death of a clan member. Thus, acts of torture often preceded the adoption of white captives as members of native families.[14]

13. *MPCP,* VI, 759. See also Col. John Reid to Henry Bouquet, July 26, 1764, in Sylvester K. Stevens and Donald H. Kent, eds., *The Papers of Col. Henry Bouquet,* XX (series 21650), pt. 2 (Harrisburg, Pa., 1943), 45.

14. "The Narrative of Marie Le Roy and Barbara Leininger, for Three Years Captives among the Indians," *PMHB,* XXIX (1905), 410; Fleming, *Eine Erzehlung,* trans. Duglas, 13; White, *Middle Ground,* 245; Gregory Evans Dowd, *A Spirited Resistance:*

Violence was not the only thing that marked strangers from kin. Sometimes Indians pointedly passed over the settlements of whites whom they considered friends or who had treated them with kindness. George Custar, whose wife spoke fluent Delaware, lived near Gnadenhütten and had a long-standing trade relationship with both the mission Indians and those living on the Susquehanna. Even though Custar brought land speculators to Gnadenhütten in 1751 and hosted Presbyterian missionary David Brainerd—acts that might have angered non-Christian Indians—Delawares did not harm him during a raid on other white settlements in the area. Warriors spared a German living on the road between Shamokin and Tulpehocken whom other whites suspected had "harboured [Army] Deserters and entertained Indians." Shawnees probably avoided attacking Arthur Buchanan and his family when they destroyed Fort Granville in July 1756, because their chief Kishacoquillas had befriended him. When Delawares captured Charles Stuart in 1755 at the Great Cove, two of them were determined to kill Stuart in an imaginatively brutal fashion. However, their leader, Shingas, stopped them, recalling that he and his people "Frequently Calld at my [Stuart's] House in their Passing and Repassing between Aughwicks and Fort Cumberland and had Always been supplied with Provisss and what they wanted Both for themselves and Creatures without Ever Chargeing them Anything for it." Instead, Shingas adopted Stuart into his family, further complicating the nature of frontier relations during war.[15]

The North American Indian Struggle for Unity, 1745–1815 (Baltimore, 1992), 15–16. Some popular historians and the media have insisted that scalping was a practice introduced by Europeans to Indians. Many Indians in the northeast traditionally wore a scalp lock, however, which was a "tuft on the crown of their [Indian males'] heads," enabling other warriors to take the scalp off more easily but also denying their enemy a full head of hair (John Heckewelder, *History, Manners, and Customs of the Indian Nations, Who Once Inhabited Pennsylvania and the Neighbouring States,* rev. ed., ed. William C. Reichel [1876; facsimile reprint, Bowie, Md., 1990], 215). See also James Axtell and William C. Sturtevant, "The Unkindest Cut, or Who Invented Scalping?" *William and Mary Quarterly,* 3d Ser., XXXVII (1980), 466–467.

15. *Moravian Records,* Nov. 28, 1748, reel 4, box 116, folder 4, Jan. 31, 1752, reel 5, box 117, folder 3, Sept. 3, 1752, reel 5, box 117, folder 3, Mar. 22, 1755, reel 5, box 118, folder 5; Journal of Joseph Shippen, the building of Fort Augusta, Aug. 12, 1756, no. 4, Shippen Family Papers, 1701–1856, HSP; Sipe, *The Indian Wars of Pennsylvania,* 296; Bond, ed., "The Captivity of Charles Stuart," *Miss. Valley Hist. Rev.,* XIII (1926–1927), 62. Buchanan supposedly gave Captain Jacobs his English moniker "because of his

Violence to the body conveyed personal messages; it erased a common humanity and demarcated the boundary between an enemy and those considered kin. But Indians also used violence to address broader political problems, especially to protest the sale of their land. Indians had often complained about questionable tactics for land cessions and unauthorized white encroachment on their territory. They suspected that the French and English might "join together at a certain time and squeese the Indians all to Death at once," dividing the country between them, as one rumor ran. During the first two years of war, 1755 and 1756, Delawares from the Susquehanna and the Ohio Valley and their Shawnee compatriots specifically targeted communities on disputed land. The first major attack on white settlers in Pennsylvania occurred at Penn's Creek, within twenty miles of Shamokin, in October 1755. By early November, Delawares and Shawnees had attacked several other frontier settlements. Shingas led at least ninety Delaware warriors to the Path Valley and Great Cove along the Blue Mountain Ridge far west of the Susquehanna River, and his brothers struck closer to Philadelphia at Tulpehocken and other communities previously inhabited by Delawares. Every one of these fall attacks took place at settlements within the recent Albany Purchase. Meanwhile, Teedyuscung and his Susquehanna warriors attacked plantations on the fringes of land at the Forks of the Delaware that Iroquois had ceded to the Pennsylvania government in the 1737 Walking Purchase. Delawares thus violently countered colonialism, repossessing that which had been previously taken from them.[16]

For several years, under the guise of protecting Indian land, the Pennsylvania government had evicted white squatters from the Susquehanna River valley only to lay down claims of their own. By the spring of 1755,

---

close resemblance to a burly German in Cumberland county" (*Frontier Forts of Pennsylvania*, I, 606–607).

16. "Indian Intelligence Report by Jo Peepy," Timothy Horsfield to Sir Charles Hardy, July 21, 1756, in James Sullivan et al., comps., *The Papers of Sir William Johnson*, 14 vols. (Albany, N.Y., 1921–1965), II, 512; Six Nations' speech to Col. Johnson, Sept. 10, 1753, Penn Papers, Indian Affairs, I, 1687–1753, HSP; Isaac Norris, speaker of the house, to the governor, Nov. 5, 1755, Deposition of Patrick Burns, Nov. 17, 1755, no. 44, Penn Papers, Indian Affairs, II, 1754–1756, HSP; *MPCP*, VI, 675; Morris to the neighbouring governors, November 1755, Conrad Weiser to Morris, Nov. 19, 1755, *PA*, 1st Ser., II, 450, 503; William Parsons to the constables of Northampton County, Dec. 12, 1755, Northampton County Papers, Miscellaneous Manuscripts, 1727–1758, HSP.

before the first attack at Penn's Creek, provincial agents and white settlers competed to possess lands for which Indians still claimed title. In early March 1755, Conrad Weiser's sons were checking on attempts to remove white squatters from Indian lands near Shamokin and George Gabriel's trading post. Along the Susquehanna River, "they saw some trees marked with 3 or 4 peoples names," indicating informal land claims. At Shamokin, they heard that a German from Philadelphia had been there a few days earlier and that he insisted the proprietor "had given him all Shomokin and that he would [settle] 40 familys there next spring he wrote his name on the Moravians House in the folowing Manner in German. *Jacob Beyerly from Philadelphia the 15th of february 1755 arrivd here the 21 of february forwarns every Body from this place.*" Even as they noted the names of those who made illegal land claims, the Weiser boys marked several thousand acres for their own father and the provincial secretary, Richard Peters, including the best piece of land, "the Island between the mouth of John Penns Creek and the Midle Creek." Indians had little recourse. They complained about the actions of both Beyerly and the Weisers, saying that the proprietors could not "give away their land which he never as yet had purchased." Their appeal fell on deaf ears; it did no good to complain to the very people who intended to supplant both white settlers and Indians.[17]

Seven months after the Weiser boys made their trip to the Susquehanna, Delawares from Kittanning, under the command of Shingas and Captain Jacobs, attacked a plantation near George Gabriel's trading post on John Penn's Creek on the west side of the river. There they took captives and carved their own signs of "repossession." After the two-day attack, white settlers nearby found the area scattered with dead and scalped men, older women, "and one Child of two weeks old." The Delawares had struck six families, killing fourteen people and capturing twenty-eight. They carried away the younger women and children as prisoners, including the wife and two children of Jacob Beyerly. "One Woman was found with a Chain about her Neck," and another dead man "lay on his back barbarously burnt and two Tomhawks sticking in his Forehead, one of the Tomhawks marked newly WD." Could it be that even the settler, who so perceptively detailed the choking chain and markings on a tomahawk, missed the ironic message behind them? If white men—whether poor

17. Weiser to Peters, Mar. 11, 1755, Peters Papers, 1697–1845, IV, pt. 1, HSP; Weiser to Peters, Mar. 8, 1755, no. 50, Weiser Papers, I, Correspondence, HSP.

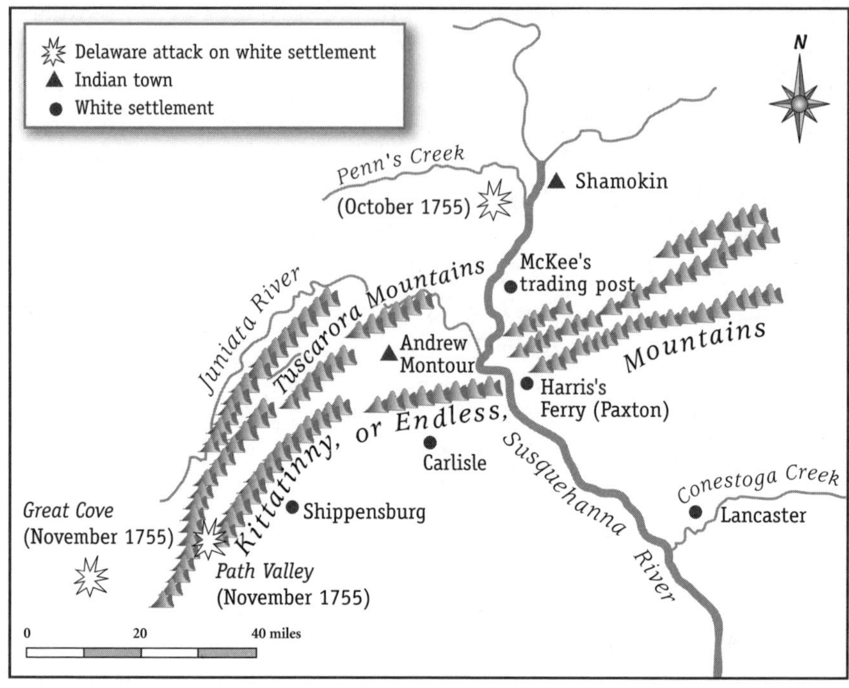

MAP 5. Frontier Attacks during the Seven Years' War, 1755–1757.
Drawn by Gerry Krieg

squatters or agents of a provincial proprietor—casually went around surveying with chains or carving their initials on trees to claim Indian land for their own, Indians would do no less, taking back disputed land by embedding their own marks on white bodies.[18]

If the attack at Penn's Creek epitomized an attempt to repossess land through violence on the bodies of white interlopers, the assault on Gnadenhütten in November 1755 could be read as an attempt to repossess the hearts and minds of Christian Indians through violence against their spiritual leaders. Baptized Indians, in particular, found themselves caught between their loyalty to native kin in the region and their newly expressed faith. Hoping that the Moravians would protect them, many Indians had

18. *MPCP,* VI, 647; Petition, Oct. 20, 1755, no. 32, Penn Papers, Indian Affairs, II, 1754–1756, HSP; Examination of Philip Wesa and Godfrey Resler, Nov. 10, 1755, Timothy Horsfield Letter Book, 1754–1755, HSP. The Penn's Creek settlers had arrived in 1754 on the heels of the Albany Purchase. See Sipe, *The Indian Wars of Pennsylvania,* 208.

remained at mission towns near Bethlehem, even as some families re moved to the Susquehanna. On the other hand, non-Christian Indians on the Susquehanna sometimes regarded the Moravians at Gnadenhütten with suspicion, despite the missionaries consistently peaceful relations with Indians in the region and their participation in Indian economies. For instance, the Delaware leader Nutimus, who had warned his nephew Teedyuscung against involvement with the Moravians in 1753, became an ardent supporter of hostile Indian warriors during the war, as did Teedyuscung. Delawares living between Shamokin and Wyoming aimed to change the relationship between Indian and white communities, doing by force what the Six Nations had advocated for decades, to terminate the alliances between white missionaries and Christian Indians, whether they were part of the Christian diaspora or under the protection of Moravians.

Susquehanna Indians first tried to quietly persuade those who remained in eastern Pennsylvania to join them by sending a message about the consequences of refusal. In mid-November 1755, a young Indian named Jemmy visited his mother and Jo Peepy, a Delaware interpreter for the Pennsylvania government living near Bethlehem, and told them that "the Gap of the Mountain was then open, and would remain so all the next Day, to give a free Passage for all the Indians in that Neighbourhood to return to their Friends at Neskopecka; but that if they refused this Invitation, they would meet with the same, nay worse Usage than the white People." The threat was real. A group of warriors, including Shawnees, Iroquois, Tuscaroras, and Delawares, stood ready to attack the white settlements at Minisink, the Forks of the Delaware, Tulpehocken, and all along the Endless Mountains. As the Susquehanna Indians intended, word of the imminent attacks spread to Gnadenhütten. A few days before the raid, "two strange Indian Men" arrived at the nearby house of George Custar. When the two men left the house, perhaps after warning Custar of the attacks, they approached two Christian Indian women pulling turnips in his fields and "told them not to stay there for that the French Indians were coming with intent to destroy the English, as the Women declared when they returned home whereupon many of the Indians at Gnadenhütten lodged and hid themselves in the Bushes."[19]

19. *Pa. Gaz.*, Dec. 4, 1755; Deposition of David Zeisberger, Nov. 22, 1755, no. 51, Penn Papers, Indian Affairs, II, 1754–1756, HSP. Moravian accounts also corroborate the threats made to Christian Indians and those allied with the English.

e warnings, the events of November 24, 1755, came as a sur-
the fourteen white Moravians who sat down to supper
ouse in Gnadenhütten. There was a knock on the door,
n standing on the stoop fired upon them. In the ensuing
the Moravians ran to adjoining rooms, others upstairs.
s set the barns and outbuildings near the missionaries' home on fire and shot and scalped several of the white Moravians. A few escaped, but the rest died in the burning house. As missionaries and Indians ran around and into and away from each other, a witness from another house insisted that the attackers "were Delawares, and that one of them had a French Match Coat on." Several who escaped the mission town reached a nearby settlement, and other survivors—"8 of the White People and between 30 and 40 of the Indians, Men Women and Children"—made their way to Bethlehem, from which "one did smell even the burning here because the wind was coming from that direction." A small group of Moravians returned the next day to Gnadenhütten with armed men but found only "a Blanket and a hat with a Knife stuck thro' them upon the Stump of a Tree," which Timothy Horsfield of Bethlehem had "heard is a Signal among the Indians, *'Thus much we have done and are able to do More.'* "[20]

This ominous warning—*"Thus much we have done and are able to do More"*—was aimed as much at the Christian Delawares and Mahicans who still lived in the mission town as at the German missionaries. Like the stark and brutal warnings against escape given to captives, the attackers cautioned both Moravians and their converts that anyone who did not live up to their obligations as kin or did not join them could expect violent retaliation. Pennsylvania Indians faced a dilemma. On one hand, they had become used to moving freely between Indian and white communities for kin visitation, trade, seasonal hunting, or hired work. Indeed, right before the attack some non-Christian Indians asked for permission to live in or near the mission towns, even as some Christian Indians moved to the Susquehanna River. Indian hunters traveling between the Susquehanna and the Moravian settlements during October and November of 1755, however, had become visibly shaken. They tried to avoid contact:

20. Diary of Nazareth, Nov. 24, 1755, English translation, Moravian Historical Society, Nazareth, Pa.; Horsfield to Morris, Nov. 27, 1755, Horsfield Letter Book, 1754–1755, HSP; Horsfield to Morris, Nov. 26, 1755, *PA,* 1st Ser., II, 521–522.

some ran "into the Woods to hide" from a passing missionary, or "walk'd so fast" to stay ahead of a white traveler, or "trembled with Fear" if one approached, or refused "to go among the White People" altogether. With the outbreak of war, Indians at the Forks of the Delaware, or any who still lived and worked among white people, were forced to reconsider their loyalties and even their associates.[21]

Indians reacted to frontier violence and the threat of hostility in a variety of ways, and the range of responses reflected the different survival strategies that had become common among native communities. Although belligerent Delawares on the Susquehanna insisted that Christian Indians owed them ethnic allegiance and therefore should turn against the English, some Indians instead acted upon new alliances created with their white neighbors, seeking their assistance accordingly. Between 1755 and 1758, Mahicans, Delawares, and Iroquois, both Christian and non-Christian, turned to the Moravian community or the Pennsylvania government for relief and refuge. After the attack on Gnadenhütten, thirty-five Mahicans and thirty-eight Delawares escaped and made their way to Bethlehem. Some had been separated from their families during the assault, such as Eva, who "lost herself from the Brothers and Sisters and was entirely alone in the woods" before arriving at the Moravian town. The surviving members of the mission congregation, once reunited, applied to the Pennsylvania governor for protection, insisting on their neutrality. They feared the threat of retaliation from Indians to the west. "None of us have any hand in the abominable murders lately committed by the Indians, but we abhor and detest them," assured Mahican leaders Josua and Jacob and Delaware leaders Augustus, Anton, and Jonathan. "It is our Desire, seeing we are perswaded that our Lives will be principally sought

21. Examination of John [Johann Jacob] Schmick and Henry Fry on their return from Wyoming, Nov. 15, 1755, Horsfield Letter Book, 1754, 1755, HSP. Apawachamunt applied for land in Gnadenhütten, Jo Peepy and his family moved to Bethlehem in late 1755, and Waapchan asked permission to stay near town (see *Moravian Records*, Mar. 20, 1754, reel 5, box 118, folder 1, May 12, 1754, reel 5, box 118, folder 1, May 19, 1755, reel 5, box 118, folder 5, item 18). Just days before the attack on the Moravians, a group of Indians from Nescopeck, probably Delawares with relatives at the mission town, had been at Gnadenhütten, exchanging "21 lbs. of deer flesh" for trade goods; see "Von den Nisckepacker Indianer 21 lb. hierschfleisch Empfangen," Nov. 19, 1755, Generalia Account Book, 1755, *Moravian Records*, reel 33, box 311, folder 3.

after, to put Ourselves as Children under the Protection of this Government." More emphatically, they pointed fingers at those responsible, the "Wicked People who serve the Devil have committed horrible Murders the Inhumanly Butchered even our own Brethren."[22]

As the war heated up, some baptized Indians who had become part of the Christian diaspora on the Susquehanna River also sought refuge either with neutral Shawnee leader Paxnous in the Wyoming Valley or with the Moravians. Jonathan, a baptized Mahican from Wyoming hoping to rejoin his kin at Bethlehem, wanted assurance from the governor that "Indians could safely come down among the White People, who they are afraid would suspect them for Enemies, if they should be several together." Similarly, Teedyuscung's brother Nicodemus and his nephew Christian "left Diahoga with a company of their Friends, Men, Women, and children, to the number of Fifteen." They stopped "a Day's Journey beyond Gnaden-Hutten," and, knowing that white settlers suspected them of hostilities as much as Teedyuscung, they made tentative overtures to peace, hoping to gain safe passage to Bethlehem. But rumors abounded that whites, even those who were once close friends, arbitrarily jailed or killed Indian refugees in Pennsylvania and New Jersey. In August 1757, Teedyuscung sent a string of wampum to Bethlehem to find out whether the Moravian Brethren "had cut the throats of all the Indians, put their heads in sacks and brought them to Philadelphia," as he had heard. Pennsylvania Indians rightfully wondered whom they could trust.[23]

22. William C. Reichel, ed., *Memorials of the Moravian Church,* I (Philadelphia, 1870), 210, 229–230; "Verlohr sich aber gleich von allen Geschw. und war ganz alleine im Busch"; see Bethlehem Register, Oct. 17, 1756, Nov. 18, 1758, "Bethlehemisches Kirchen=Buch," II, 238, 249, Moravian Archives, Bethlehem, Pa.; Address of Gnadenhütten Indians to the governor, *Moravian Records,* Dec. 9, 1755, reel 34, box 317, folder 1, item 7; "Poor Indians Address," Nov. 30, 1755, Horsfield Letter Book, 1754–1755, HSP. By 1756, a total of eighty-two Indians lived in Bethlehem (Bethlehem Register, Dec. 31, 1755, July 24, 1758, I, 241–242, II, 233–234; *PA,* 1st Ser., III, 76).

23. Deposition of David Zeisberger, Nov. 22, 1755, no. 51, Penn Papers, Indian Affairs, II, 1754–1756, HSP; *MPCP,* VII, 169; "Sie hätten allen Indianern die Hälse abgeschnitten, ihre köpfe in Säke getan, u. so nach Philadelphia gebracht. Dadurch wären um alle Indianer so erbittert worden, daß sehr viele auf gewesen, die Brüder Settlemente zu zerstören, u. alles umzubringen"; see Conversation between the Moravians and King Teedyuscung, *Moravian Records,* Aug. 27, 1757, reel 30, box 223, folder 10, item 1. See also Gregory Evans Dowd, "The Panic of 1751: The Significance

The war had disrupted the lives and livelihood of non-Christian Indians as well. Some had been informants, interpreters, or diplomatic go-betweens for the English, and they turned to men such as George Croghan or Conrad Weiser for assistance. Even larger groups of Indians who had lost the vital links of trade and the economic stability that came with peace solicited the help of their English trade partners. In July 1755, a group of Indians from Ohio moved east to John Harris's plantation at Aughwick, seeking protection from French aggression and joining other refugees from earlier trade wars. By late 1755 and early 1756, Indians from Shamokin and the Wyoming Valley who had not joined the hostilities now faced food shortages and dwindling supplies, and many fled south along the Susquehanna to Conestoga or Aughwick. John Shickellamy sent his sister and her children to Conestoga when the war began but soon sought asylum himself and, according to Thomas McKee, "Intends to live and Die with us." Sounding much like the white settlers who had also suffered from Indian attacks in the fall of 1755, the Indian refugees at Aughwick and Conestoga begged the governor and his council to "open all yr Eyes and ears and view yr slain People in this Land and put a stop to it immediately and come to their's and our Assistance without any Delay." Rather than acting the part of pleading dependents, however, these Indians sought to shame the provincial government into fulfilling its past promises to protect them and their communities. They presented a belt of wampum before the Council and reminded its members of the message it conveyed, "that the Proprietaries and your Honors would immediately act in Defence" of the Indians' land. They urged the governor to declare war against those nations that had broken "the old Chain of Friendship" and to help the refugees to return home once more. Although the governor assured equal protection to those natives he considered "friendly," Indians more often found themselves caught between hostile Delawares and an increasingly antagonistic white community.[24]

---

of Rumors on the South Carolina-Cherokee Frontier," *WMQ*, 3d Ser., LIII (1996), 527–560.

24. Harris to Peters, July 25, 1755, Peters Papers, 1697–1845, IV, pt. 1, HSP; "Indian Intelligence of December 1, [1756], by Auchkon [Akoan], a Young Indian Informer," II, Horsfield Papers, APS; Thomas McKee to Edward Shippen, Apr. 5, 1756, *PA*, 1st Ser., II, 616; John Shickellamy to Pennsylvania Council, Feb. 26, 1756, no. 75, Morris to Edward Shippen, Mar. 4, 1756, no. 75, Penn Papers, Indian Affairs, II, 1754–1756, HSP;

By the mid-1750s, the dynamics among frontier dwellers and their relationships to pervasive colonial powers had changed dramatically because of the war. While Indians scrambled to position themselves on one side or the other of an unclear political divide, white Pennsylvanians also wondered whom they could consider a friend or an enemy. Indians who had become Christian now burned missionaries and their towns—at least some did, but which ones? Non-Christian Indians, once aloof and living at a distance, now sought protection through the governor. Could they be trusted? For that matter, could settlers trust their white neighbors? For years, Scots-Irish and German settlers had been suspicious of the Moravians' close connections to Indians. When fighting began, they accused Moravians of fraternizing with French-allied Indians and then with Susquehanna Delawares implicated in the assaults of 1755 and 1756. Only after Indians killed Moravian missionaries at Gnadenhütten did the attitude of white settlers change to one of sympathy. They were less forgiving of the Pennsylvania government. White settlers had begged for military assistance, but they had found the predominantly Quaker Assembly unresponsive. The governor and Assembly members blamed white settlers for inciting Indian violence in the first place. Now the same government that had refused to secure their frontier plantations agreed to protect Indian lives.[25]

In many ways, white Pennsylvanians found it easier to define a broadly based enemy other than to ascertain which Indian was a friend or an ally. Often, they simply lumped friends and enemies together as adversaries. Settlers, enraged by Indian attacks on their homes, tended to aim their hatred at Indians close at hand rather than a faceless enemy in the west. When Conrad Weiser offered food and supplies to native women living near Shamokin in the summer of 1755, whites were "very malicious against our Indians; they curse and damn them to their faces, and say, must we feed you, and your husbands fight in the meantime for the French?" In mid-November 1755, Weiser went to Tulpehocken to investigate a recent attack and to meet with Indian allies. Most of the local white

---

Harris to Morris, Oct. 20, 1755, Records of the Proprietary Government, Richard Peters Account, 1755–1760, RG-21, microfilm 0597, roll no. 1, Pennsylvania State Archives, Harrisburg; *MPCP*, VI, 645, VII, 12.

25. Diary of Nazareth, Nov. 27, 1755, English translation, Moravian Historical Society.

settlers blamed the attacks on men like Weiser, who, to them, represented an ineffectual government that protected Indians while their own homes burned. They threatened to shoot him. Allied natives from Shamokin, whom Weiser escorted through Tulpehocken, elicited similar anger. Hundreds of armed men gathered on both sides of the road yelling, "Why must we be killed by the Indians and we not kill them! why are our Hands so tied?" Their solution to the Indian problem was simple. Forfeit Indian lives, "be they friends or enemies."[26]

Indeed, like the Delawares who had attacked white settlements in 1755 and 1756, white inhabitants felt deeply betrayed by Indians who had once treated them as neighbors. Consequently, they suspected those Indians who had been friends above all others. John Bartram, who traveled with Conrad Weiser on his diplomatic missions during 1756, seemed baffled by the "barbarous inhuman ungratefull natives weekly murdering our back inhabitants." Conflating the horror of hostile Indian actions with a paranoid uncertainty of ally intentions, Bartram further suspected that "those few Indians that profess some friendship to us are mostly watching for an opertunity to ruin us." Bartram remembered these "ungratefull natives" as "dayly familiars at thair houses" who shared food, drink, even "cursed and swore together." Indians had been "intimate play mates" who "now without provokation destroyeth all before them with fire ball and tomahawk." Whether or not Bartram accurately remembered the nature of past intimacies between Indians and whites, his assessment of present betrayals became the basis for creating an enemy other. All along the frontier, white refugees fled from their farms, crowded into the public houses at better-protected towns such as Bethlehem or Lancaster, and shared stories of their traumatic encounters with recent "familiars" and "intimate play mates." The collective memory of white victims and the vivid imaginations of white settlers helped to create an enemy that bore an uncanny resemblance to the Indian neighbors with whom they had recently interacted, and the image was most often Delaware.[27]

26. David B. Brunner, *The Indians of Berks County, Pa., Being a Summary of All the Tangible Records of the Aborigines of Berks County, with Cuts and Descriptions of the Varieties of Relics Found within the County,* 2d ed., rev. (Reading, Pa., 1897), 56, 68; Weiser to Morris, Nov. 19, 1755, in *Frontier Forts of Pennsylvania,* I, 73–74; Weiser to Morris, Nov. 19, 1755, Weiser to Morris, Nov. 24, 1755, *PA,* 1st Ser., II, 504, 511.

27. John Bartram to Peter Collinson, Feb. 21, 1756, John Bartram Correspondence,

Whites were not alone in targeting Delawares as the "real enemy among us." The Six Nations also found it politically useful to construct and manipulate an image of Delaware enemies to degrade and punish subordinates who refused to be submissive and to maintain their own status as political partners to Pennsylvania. Iroquois on the Susquehanna and at Onondaga became adept at spreading rumors, innuendoes, and carefully crafted images of Delawares that made them suspect in the eyes of white Pennsylvanians. Iroquois insisted that the Delawares, especially those at Nescopeck and beyond the Alleghenies at Kittanning, were at the center of frontier violence. They even implied that Delawares could be supernaturally dangerous. Iroquois had always demonized Delawares on some level, whether because of ethnic differences or as a justification for their political domination. In the communities they shared, Iroquois often accused Delawares of using witchcraft or other magical powers to harm them. At Shamokin, in the winter of 1748, the Mahican woman who befriended Moravian missionary Jeanette Mack insisted that her daughter had been killed by a Delaware sorcerer. During the following spring, her husband, John Logan, one of the elder sons of Shickellamy, "showed a great hostility toward the Delawares, since he believed they had conjured an evil spirit in him, and his child who died was bewitched, as was his wife." He wanted the Delawares to be dispersed as a band so they could no longer harm each other or the community. Within a month, the Iroquois in Shamokin had "beaten to death" the Delaware accused of sorcery, and his body had

---

ed. Edward E. Wildman, 1956, APS. Several years later, Brigadier General John Forbes voiced similar concerns when the Cherokees, who had promised military assistance, left for home after they became impatient with his delays. Forbes was "astonished and amazed" by their "villainous desertion." He accused the Indians of arriving "under the Cloak of Friendship," then robbing "us these several months, but that now having discovered themselves our private Ennemies, and having turned the Arms, put in their hands by us, against His Majesty's Subjects, which the Former parties have already done" (Gen. John Forbes to William? or James Burd, Nov. 19, 1758, in Alfred Procter James, ed., *Writings of General John Forbes Relating to His Service in North America* [Menasha, Wis., 1938], 256–257). See Gregory Evans Dowd, "'Insidious Friends': Gift Giving and the Cherokee-British Alliance in the Seven Years' War," in Andrew R. L. Cayton and Fredrika J. Teute, eds., *Contact Points: American Frontiers from the Mohawk Valley to the Mississippi, 1750–1830* (Chapel Hill, N.C., 1998), 114–150, for a discussion of misunderstandings between Cherokees and British over each others' behavior as military allies.

been "all cut to pieces and pierced," perhaps so he would do no further harm in the afterlife. In political settings, Iroquois used these images of supernaturally dangerous Delawares to further undermine Euramerican trust in them. In July 1756, at a treaty conference in Easton, Pennsylvania, Newcastle, a Seneca, came to the governor and complained "that the Delawares had bewitched him and that he should dye soon." He insinuated that Teedyuscung had threatened him, though "in a friendly manner," and "that two Delawares would put an End to his life by witchcraft." The following day, Newcastle was "seized . . . with a violent Pleurisy and thought to be in great danger," but he quickly recovered after bloodletting. He had no apologies for Teedyuscung.[28]

During wartime, Iroquois continued to draw attention to what they perceived as the dangerous and duplicitous actions of Delawares. After the attack on Penn's Creek, a group of forty-six white frontier inhabitants visited Shamokin to find out who had been responsible. They speculated that the main attackers had been Delawares, since several were "heard

28. Narration of incursions, December 1755, no. 34, Penn Papers, Indian Affairs, II, 1754–1756, HSP; *MPCP,* VI, 763; "Memorandum of Sundry Questions Asked Augustus / One of the Indian Messengers from Bethlehem / by Spangenberg," May 23, 1756, Northampton County Papers, Bethlehem and Vicinity, Misc. MSS, 1741–1886, HSP; John W. Jordan, ed., "Bishop J. C. F. Cammerhoff's Narrative of a Journey to Shamokin, Penna., in the Winter of 1748," *PMHB,* XXIX (1905), 173; Memorandum, July 27, 1756, Easton Council, Material Pertaining to Pennsylvania Indian Affairs, Collection of Treaties, deposited by Joseph Parker Norris, APS; Easton treaty Council minutes, July 27, 1756, *PA,* 1st Ser., II, 728. Delawares themselves were extremely concerned about witches and witchcraft and took great care to counter its effects (Gladys Tantaquidgeon, *A Study of Delaware Indian Medicine Practice and Folk Beliefs* [Harrisburg, Pa., 1942], 38). See *Moravian Records,* Apr. 26, 1749, reel 6, box 121, folder 5 ("Er ließ eine große Feindschafft merken gegen die Dellawares, weil er von ihnen glaubt sie hätten eine bösen zaubern Geist in sich, u. seine Kind daß gestorben ist bezaubert hätten, wie auch seine Frau"), May 31, 1749 ("des Morgens sehr früh hörten wir gleich daß David ein Dellaware Ind. diese Nacht Todt geschlagen sey worden von den Maquaischen, weil er ein großer Zaubere gewesen sey, u. viele Ind. vergeben habe. Sein Br. Daniel kam u. wolte gerne einen Sarg gemacht haben. . . ." "Und dann begruben sie ihn nach Indianischer Manier bey den Dellawar begräbniß Plaz. Er war sehr zerhauen u. zerstochen am ganzen leibe"). For other examples of Delawares accused of witchcraft by Iroquois and Mahicans, see Apr. 26, 1749, reel 6, box 121, folder 5, May 31, 1749, reel 6, box 121, folder 5, Mar. 9, 1754, reel 6, box 119, folder 1, item 10.7.

to talk that Language." When an Iroquois delegation met the white colonists at Shamokin to assist in the investigation, their leader, the Old Belt, "cry'd like a Child," according to Conrad Weiser. Others in the group, such as John Shickellamy, his brothers, and Andrew Montour, were "extremely concern'd and said that the Shawanese and Delawares are become our Enemy." Even Shawnees, at least those who maintained their neutrality, insisted that Delawares should carry the blame for destroying white plantations along the frontier. In early 1756, John Shickellamy met with Paxnous, the neutral Shawnee chief who acted as intermediary with the Delawares at Nescopeck. Paxnous informed the Iroquois go-between and, through him, the Pennsylvania Council that Delawares had abandoned their English alliance when General Braddock refused their advice before his defeat in July 1755. "From that Time," Paxnous concluded, "the Delawares were turned, and became another People and strangers to us."[29]

Neutral Shawnees and professedly loyal Iroquois insisted that once-friendly Delawares had become at the very least "strangers," if not outright enemies. Yet they, too, walked a fine line between neutrality and hostility, easily slipping into one camp or the other as it suited their purpose. After all, in the early 1750s, Conrad Weiser and the Pennsylvania government had been more concerned about Iroquois loyalties than the Delawares. In the fall of 1750, Weiser worried that the "friends of the English among the [Six Nation] Counsel are dead, and those that are at the Head of affairs now, are devout to the French, and confess it freely." Five years later, the Six Nations publicly proclaimed their allegiance to England and simultaneously questioned the loyalties of the Delawares to divert suspicions about their own actions, including those of a surprising number of Ohio Iroquois, or Mingo, warriors who had broken away from the Six Nations and joined frontier raiding parties during the war. John Shickellamy, for example, attempted to follow a narrow path between enmity and friendship with the English. In February 1756, when found among enemy Indians, he told Weiser that his family and friends had been "deceiv'd by the

29. Narrative on the incursions, Dec. 31, 1755, no. 34, Feb. 24, 1756, no. 74, Penn Papers, Indian Affairs, II, 1754–1756, HSP; *Pa. Gaz.*, Nov. 6, 1755; *MPCP*, VI, 658; Weiser to Morris, Oct. 31, 1755, Pierre Eugene Du Simitiere Papers, Library Company manuscript housed in HSP, 966.F 49 a-o; James H. Merrell, "Shamokin, 'the very seat of the Prince of darkness': Unsettling the Early American Frontier," in Cayton and Teute, eds., *Contact Points*, 50–56.

Delawares" while attempting to escape to Philadelphia. Shickellamy insisted that "the Delaware Indians would not let us go, and said the white People would certainly kill us." Perhaps Shickellamy was genuinely caught between a rock and a hard place, choosing survival among hostile Delawares rather than harm to his family. But, a month after this conversation, Shickellamy was again spotted in the company of eighty Delaware warriors, ready to set upon white settlements. Andrew Montour and Scarouyady, political go-betweens for Pennsylvania and the Ohio Indians, took Shickellamy aside, "upbraided him with his Ingratitude to this Government, which had ever been extreamly kind to his Father when alive." He once more insisted that Delawares had seduced him and his brothers into joining them, threatening to kill them if they did not fight the English. Shickellamy faced similar problems when he sought the protection of Thomas McKee near Conestoga. Instead of hostile Delawares, he felt the anger of nearby Scots-Irish settlers—"fearful ignorant people," according to Edward Shippen—who threatened to scalp him. Taking his chances with an enemy that he knew (or perhaps better understood) rather than an unpredictable ally, Shickellamy, by the end of April 1756, had "left his Gun, Cloaths, and all that he had" at Thomas McKee's and returned to the Wyoming Valley to seek protection in Paxnous's village.[30]

Shickellamy, white colonists, and the Six Nations blamed Delawares for instigating the violence of the mid-1750s, in part because the community-based alliances of previous decades had failed. Whether familiarity or economic competition bred contempt, white settlers, in particular, harbored suspicions of the Delawares who had become close neighbors. Even though many of these Indians had adapted some of the cultural practices of Euramericans, they feared that these similarities concealed more immutable differences beneath. When Delawares expressed their anger over broken promises by killing colonists who lived on disputed territory, white settlers felt betrayed for trusting Indians as friends. By demonizing Delawares, white Pennsylvanians denied that Indians could act as

30. Weiser to Peters, Oct. 4, 1750, Weiser Papers, I, Correspondence, HSP; Private conversation between Weiser and Shickellamy [or Tachneckdoras], Feb. 22, 1756, no. 73, Morris to Edward Shippen, Mar. 4, 1756, no. 75, Penn Papers, Indian Affairs, II, 1754–1756, HSP; Zeisberger to Horsfield, Sept. 2, 1756, no. 11, Penn Papers, IV, 1733–1801, Indian Walk, HSP. *MPCP,* VII, 65; Shippen to Morris, Apr. 19, 1756, *PA,* 1st Ser., II, 634.

kin and reasserted their right to take Indian land. Iroquois, too, emphasized Delawares as outsiders to enhance the Six Nations' position of political authority. They blamed insubordination for hostile Delaware actions, and they called on the military resources of the provincial government to retaliate. In early April 1756, Scarouyady reprimanded the Pennsylvania Council for "sitting with your Hands between your knees" while the Delawares took up the hatchet against them. He urged the province to actively target the Delawares, rather than their more distant enemy, the French.[31]

Although still reluctant to condemn the Delawares completely, even the Moravians, who had created close personal relations with them, conjured up monstrous images of Delawares to explain the failure of Moravian attempts to maintain strong religious and social alliances. Just before the war, when some Christian Mahicans and Delawares left the mission communities, Moravians found their faith in their converts shaken. The independence of these Indians made the Moravians sorely aware of their own secondary role in native decision making. When some baptized Delawares joined the hostile warriors who attacked white plantations, however, Moravians began to doubt the effectiveness of the entire missionary enterprise. August Gottlieb (Joseph) Spangenberg's dreams during the war revealed the unconscious ambivalence with which the Brethren now faced future Indian relations. While visiting a German couple at Quittaphilla, an old Indian town west of Philadelphia, Spangenberg fitfully dreamed of "a dark horrible mob moving quickly; and behind the mob moving just as quickly was a Red Dragon, which carried with him many people, close to his legs and feet were noisy people." As the dragon seized others to add to this mob, Spangenberg wondered "whether he would also come to me." Fearful and trembling as the dragon came closer, Spangenberg cried out: "Blood! Blood! Lamb's Blood! Jesus's Blood!" The dragon passed by, and "over the blood cries I awoke, as many around me slept on." Delawares might have once begged for Christ's blood to overcome their own spiritual demons, but now its power was invoked to rid Moravians of dragonlike Delawares. For Euramericans in the mid-Atlantic, whether white frontier settlers or missionaries or colonial leaders, the Seven Years' War unleashed cultural fears locked deep within. De-

31. *MPCP,* VII, 76, 79, 89.

monizing Delawares became the first step in creating a racialized image of all Indians that could be exorcized only through all-out war.[32]

32. Schmick to Mattheus Hehl, Nov. 5, 1754, *Moravian Records*, reel 5, box 118, folder 5, item 3, Dec. 31, 1754, reel 5, box 118, folder 2, "A Dream in Spittler's House," 1757, reel 40, box 3500, folder 1, item 1 ("Ich sahe am himmel von Nordwest her eine schwarze fürchterliche volke schnell fahren; und hinter der volke führ eben so schnell, ein Rother Drach, welcher viele Menschen mit sich führte, hinten bey seinen beinen und füssen waren lauten Menschen." "Und wie Er nahe kam, und wolte grad unter uns fahren. Da schrie ich aus aller macht, was ich schreyen kannte: Blut! Blut! Lammes=Blut! Jesu Blut! Und da fuhr Er schnell auf die seite vor uns Vorbey, Und über den Blut Geschrey wachte ich, und etliche die um mich schlieffen auf"). This dream presumably occurred before the June 19, 1757, attack on Quittaphilla, when nineteen people were killed, including Joseph Spittler (Sipe, *The Indian Wars of Pennsylvania*, 346).

6

QUAKERS AND THE LANGUAGE OF INDIAN DIPLOMACY

• • •

The Seven Years' War provoked parties to reassess the social and economic accommodations so carefully negotiated during the first half of the eighteenth century. The breakdown of Indian-white relations was at times physical, at times psychological. Hostile Delawares attacked frontier settlements on disputed land and aimed to separate those whites they now considered strangers from those they still accepted as kin. Disgruntled white settlers, fearful that even Indian friends had turned against them, demanded that Pennsylvania prepare to fight native peoples on the frontier. Pennsylvania governor Robert Hunter Morris and the Assembly officially declared war against the Delawares on April 14, 1756. By August, the Assembly agreed to fund a series of military posts along the frontier, which became staging areas for militia raids on Indian towns along the Susquehanna River and west of the Alleghenies. In September 1756, for instance, Colonel John Armstrong led an expedition into Kittanning, a major center of Delaware resistance in western Pennsylvania and Shingas's home. For white settlers, Kittanning symbolized native American betrayal of the personal ties that had been established over the past half-century. But it also exemplified the intimate nature of the frontier conflict and the myriad ways that Indian and white communities continued to be inextricably entangled. There Delawares had created a new home for many of their adopted white captives, perhaps "more than one hundred English Boys and Girls," as some estimated. Although the Kittanning expedition ended in disarray and only recovered eleven English captives, the militia destroyed the Delaware town.[1]

1. Petition, Robert Erwin to Robert Hunter Morris, Aug. 21, 1756, *PA,* 1st Ser., II, 757; William A. Hunter, "Victory at Kittanning," *Pennsylvania History,* XXIII (1956),

Yet, even in the midst of the intimate brutality of war, many Pennsylvanians still wanted to restore ties between their communities. War had sharpened the issues of conflict: growing economic dependence, landownership, and the future of Indian-white relations. Between 1756 and 1758, Delawares, Iroquois, Shawnees, and Euramericans articulated their concerns at treaty conferences, which became an important venue for reconciliation. But the war had also deeply affected the nature of authority in Pennsylvania and, thus, diplomacy. In the chaos of war, the balance of power had shifted away from the Six Nations and the provincial government and lay in the hands of those on the Pennsylvania frontier. The treaty conference, then, became a new arena of battle between colonial powers and the people they professed to dominate. The party that could control the present course of diplomacy could also define the terms of the future political alliance between Indians and whites.

Early in the war, the Ohio Delaware leader, Shingas, thought he knew how a new balance of power with the English could work. After his attack on the Path Valley and Great Cove in late 1755, he used captive Charles Stuart as a sounding board and a messenger to convey his vision of future coexistence to Governor Morris. Shingas insisted that the English "send 5 Men among the Indians who shoud live well at the Indians expence with them, But work for them without any other Pay." First, these men and their families would provide weapons and clothing directly to the Indians, eliminating the trader as middleman. They would engage in the "Makeing of Powder, Smelting of Lead from the Ore, . . . Weaveing of Blanketts—Makeing and Mending Guns." In addition to skilled white men, other

379; Morris to Richard Peters, Aug. 14, 1756, Simon Gratz Collection, French and Indian War, 1756, box 18, case 15, HSP; Rev. Thomas Barton to Peters, Aug. 22, 1756, "Manuscript Papers on the Indian and Military Affairs of the Province of Pennsylvania, 1737–1775," microfilm, APS; Deposition of John Baker, Mar. 31, 1756, no. 78, Penn Papers, Indian Affairs, II, 1754–1756, HSP. Morris estimated that three hundred English prisoners were being held in the west, "most of them at Shingas's Town" (Morris to William Johnson, Apr. 24, 1756, in James Sullivan et al., comps., *The Papers of Sir William Johnson,* 14 vols. [Albany, N.Y., 1921–1965], II, 443). Shingas estimated that forty of John Armstrong's men had been killed at Kittanning and only fourteen of his own, including Captain Jacobs ("An Account of the Captivity of Hugh Gibson among the Delaware Indians of the Big Beaver and the Muskingum, from the Latter Part of July 1756, to the Beginning of April, 1759," Massachusetts Historical Society, *Collections,* 3d Ser., VI [Boston, 1837], 143; Francis Jennings, *Empire of Fortune: Crowns, Colonies, and Tribes in the Seven Years War in America* [New York, 1988], 200).

Euramericans could also "Come and Settle among them with their Families and Promote Spinning for Shirts and In Genl shoud Bring all Kinds of Trades among them that they might be Supplied with what they want near home." Although Shingas agreed that Indians and "the English shou'd Live Together in Love and Friendship and Become one people," the promise of a peaceful alliance would come only after the Delawares received arms and trade goods and were taught skills that would assure their future independence. In other words, Shingas envisioned a world controlled by Indians.[2]

Strategies for postwar coexistence were not exclusively Delaware. A few whites also envisioned a future where Euramericans and Indians shared a limited space. In 1756, Thomas Pownall, before he replaced William Shirley as governor of Massachusetts, outlined a proposal for dealing with the Six Nations. Like Shingas, Pownall wanted to control the extent of economic interactions, but through the limits of a specific military alliance. He suggested that each of the Iroquois communities should be furnished "with Cabins sufficient for the whole Tribe, and Apartments for about twenty English Families, together with Storehouses for Indian Goods, Arms, Ammunition, and all kinds of Utensils for Farming, etc." In addition, he proposed that a blacksmith "with two Apprentices; one Armourer, one Carpenter, and one Taylor" be sent as well as a schoolmaster to teach both the English and Indian children. In Pownall's world, the English would provide Indians with skills, trade goods, and arms, but only if the Indians would serve the English as military allies. Indeed, Pownall insisted that Indian allies be closely monitored and identified with "proper Uniform, to distinguish them from one another, and from all other Indians: By this Means we shall be able to distinguish our Friends from our Foes." Through the course of the war, the English had reduced the Indian population to either dependent ally or independent enemy; there was little room in between.[3]

With several groups angling for military advantage and control of a postwar settlement, negotiating an immediate end to hostilities became trickier as the war progressed. Treaty conferences between Indians and

2. Beverley W. Bond, Jr., ed., "The Captivity of Charles Stuart, 1755–57," *Mississippi Valley Historical Review*, XIII (1926–1927), 65.

3. [Thomas Pownall], *Proposals for Securing the Friendship of the Five Nations* (New York, 1756), 3, 4, 7.

whites in the 1750s allowed those present to air their grievances and demand restitution for wartime injuries. But they also exposed deep-seated conflicts within each faction. For instance, the war had proved a vulnerable political spot for the otherwise pacifist Quakers of Pennsylvania. After they refused to address colonists' demands for military assistance on the frontier, the Quakers began to lose their political clout within the provincial Assembly. Although they made a principled and public withdrawal from politics, they were able to transfer their power to the supervision of Indian trade and diplomacy. Most Quakers felt strongly that Delawares, in particular, needed an advocate during treaty negotiations. Yet, at the same time, the Quakers used the Delawares to embarrass or criticize their political enemies, the proprietors and their supporters.

Indians, too, struggled with internal dissension and conflict. Throughout the eighteenth century, the Six Nations designated Delawares and Shawnees props of the Longhouse, who acted as buffers between Iroquois and their enemies to the south. In return, the Delawares and Shawnees were expected to welcome Iroquois supervision, protection, and dominance. While general peace prevailed, this political arrangement worked to the advantage of the Six Nations and the Pennsylvania government. The violent actions of Shawnees, Delawares, and even western Iroquois (Mingos) in 1755 and 1756, however, revealed that Iroquois control of these subordinates was tenuous at best. When Iroquois, Delawares, and Euramericans came together in common political spaces, the erosion of the old political order of Iroquois dominance became even more apparent. Shingas and other Delaware leaders, such as Teedyuscung, used the political forum as well as the support of Quakers to demand autonomy. They undermined the political and economic basis of Iroquois and Pennsylvania proprietary dominance by questioning the rights of these powers to sell and buy land.[4]

Competing factions, whether Indian or white, negotiated for different visions of peace and power based on a deeply contested past. In their attempts to control each other politically, to influence their future alliances, and to shape public memory of their relations, Euramericans,

4. Daniel K. Richter, *The Ordeal of the Longhouse: The Peoples of the Iroquois League in the Era of European Colonization* (Chapel Hill, N.C., 1992), 134–142, 241; Richter, "A Framework for Pennsylvania Indian History," *Pennsylvania History*, LVII (July 1990), 247–248. See also *MPCP*, VI, 342.

Iroquois, and Delawares harnessed the powers of language. They used common metaphors to assure some mutual understanding in treaty conferences. They learned what might be termed each others' "technologies of power"—the written word and wampum—through which they publicly debated the veracity of past treaty records and attempted to shape the current ones. Iroquois and Euramericans also constructed and manipulated ethnic representations of Delawares as enemies (some even with supernatural powers) and gendered images of Delawares as women to dominate them politically. By the late 1750s, diplomatic discussions focused less on the possibilities of realizing Shingas's vision of sharing common space where Indians and whites could "Become one people." Rather, Indians and whites bickered over who to blame for the demise of amicable interdependence. In the end, they saw no other solution than to create more permanent boundaries between communities.[5]

During the 1740s, Moravians had played an important role in maintaining diplomatic relations between Indians and whites in Pennsylvania. Their missionary enterprise and economic alliances with Indians at Shamokin allowed them access to a variety of native communities. The Pennsylvania governor and Assembly relied on Moravians, such as Count Nikolaus Ludwig von Zinzendorf and Christian Frederick Post, for information

5. Michel Foucault, "Truth and Power," in Foucault, *Power/Knowledge: Selected Interviews and Other Writings, 1972–1977*, trans. Colin Gordon et al. (New York, 1980), 125, asserts that technologies of power, such as writing, became important by the seventeenth and eighteenth centuries as part of new state policies and institutions (schools, police forces, armies, government administrations) that were created to control capital and the labor of men. Premodern technologies of power, on the other hand, included "signs of loyalty to the feudal lords, rituals, ceremonies and so forth, and levies in the form of taxes, pillage, hunting, war, etc" (125). Native Americans, with their focus on kinship relations, rituals of condolence, and retribution during war, would fit into Foucault's premodern category. The eighteenth century should be considered a period of crossover, however, where both modern and premodern technologies of power could be useful to both Indians and whites, depending on the circumstances. Greg Dening, *Mr Bligh's Bad Language: Passion, Power, and Theatre on the Bounty* (Cambridge, 1992), 222, puts these technologies in a broader context of the "signs of power" and argues that we cannot separate these signs from power itself. Certainly, if we look at power as a relationship between people, rather than as a separate and quantifiable thing, we can agree that "both those who exert power and those who bow to power manipulate its signs."

about tribal movements and the political situation among Susquehanna River Indians as well as the Iroquois in New York. At times the provincial government even used Moravians as interpreters. During the Seven Years' War, Bethlehem initially became a way station for Indians traveling to Philadelphia or Easton for diplomatic purposes. The governor asked Moravians to act as liaisons, "to receive into their Houses at Bethlehem all such friendly Indians as shall come to them and desire to be taken in, and to support and maintain them till they have my further orders." Moravians as a group were never intrinsically tied to Indian diplomacy, however, perhaps because they did not see themselves as political creatures beyond the governance of their own communities. They thus never became elected representatives to the provincial Assembly, and they never assumed official positions.[6]

Quakers, on the other hand, had been deeply involved in Pennsylvania politics for generations and, because of their reputation as peacemakers, believed it their right and duty to direct the course of Indian diplomacy and trade during the war. They had become suspicious of the Moravians' power to attract Indian converts and critical that the governor allowed the Brethren to "entertain such Indians as they please" during the 1750s. By late 1755, even as Quakers faced intense opposition for their refusal to send military assistance to protect frontier settlements, Friends in the Assembly moved to consolidate their control over Indian affairs. They helped to enact a bill that gave them authority to appoint commissioners to supervise provincial Indian agents, interpreters, and traders, even to set up their own trade posts. According to an angry provincial secretary, Richard Peters, the Quakers intended to exclude "the Governor out of all Transactions with the Indians," whether political or economic.[7]

6. *MPCP,* VII, 170. See also William C. Reichel, ed., *Memorials of the Moravian Church,* I (Philadelphia, 1870), 233, 255; Governor William Denny to Joseph Spangenberg, Dec. 2, 1756, Timothy Horsfield Papers, II, APS; Friendly Association Minutes, July 1756, Cox-Parrish-Wharton Family Papers, box 18, HSP.

7. Friendly Association Minutes, July 1756, Cox-Parrish-Wharton Family Papers, box 18, HSP; Peters to Thomas Penn, Nov. 13, 1755, Richard Peters Letter Book, HSP. By 1758, Quaker commissioners were recommending that Indians not go by way of Bethlehem. Because of "the extravagance of the Moravians' Accts they cannot entrust them with a General power of Providing for the Indians that may come in there; But are of Opinion the Indians having Business with this Government should be directed to come some nearer and more convenient way" ("Resolutions of the Commissioners

In the early months of 1756, Quakers continued to use their political position to dominate Indian relations over the growing protests of white colonists and, most important, the proprietors. As Assembly members, Quakers remained reluctant to declare war against Indians who had been "our steady Friends and allies" and begged the governor to suspend the rewards for scalps, which they thought "would encourage the blood thirsty Presbyterians" to arbitrarily kill Indians. But increased pressures from angry white settlers, who demanded money to support local defensive military efforts against Indians, and from proprietary agents, who accused Quakers of conspiring with Germans against the Church of England, forced several "sober Friends" to resign from the Assembly, leaving the province free to support the war against the Delawares. Quakers, however, did not drop out of politics altogether; they redirected their energies into other avenues of power. They managed to handpick many of their successors to the Assembly and keep their positions as commissioners of Indian affairs. In April 1756, under Israel Pemberton, a group of Philadelphia Quakers established the Friendly Association for Regaining and Preserving Peace with the Indians by Pacific Measures, whose stated purpose was to fulfill the legacy of William Penn's "Holy Experiment," including "preserving the Friendship of the Indians." In essence, the Friendly Association became an extension of the Quakers' former political powers. The group funded the activities of the commissioners of Indian affairs and allowed Quakers to effectively dominate Indian diplomacy and trade in Pennsylvania.[8]

Although the provincial governor censured the Quakers and their con-

---

to Supply Some Indians with Goods," July 14, 1758, "Manuscript Papers on the Indian and Military Affairs of the Province of Pennsylvania, 1737–1775," microfilm, APS).

8. Israel Pemberton to John Fothergill, July 19, 1755, James Pemberton to Fothergill, June 26, 1756, Frank M. Etting Collection, Pemberton Papers, 1654–1806, II, book 29, folders 2, 12, HSP; *MPCP,* VI, 705, VII, 735; Jennings, *Empire of Fortune,* 226, 242–243; Sally Schwartz, *"A Mixed Multitude": The Struggle for Toleration in Colonial Pennsylvania* (New York, 1987), 210; General Council of Cumberland County, Oct. 23, 1755, Lamberton Scotch-Irish Collection, I, 23, HSP; Alan Tully, "Quaker Party and Proprietary Policies: The Dynamics of Politics in Pre-Revolutionary Pennsylvania, 1730–1775," in Bruce C. Daniels, ed., *Power and Status: Officeholding in Colonial America* (Middletown, Conn., 1986), 78–79, 82, 87–88; Robert Daiutolo, Jr., "The Role of Quakers in Indian Affairs during the French and Indian War," *Quaker History,* LXXVII (1988), 10; Preamble for initial subscription, Friendly Association Minutes, 1756–1759, Cox-Parrish-Wharton Family Papers, box 18, HSP.

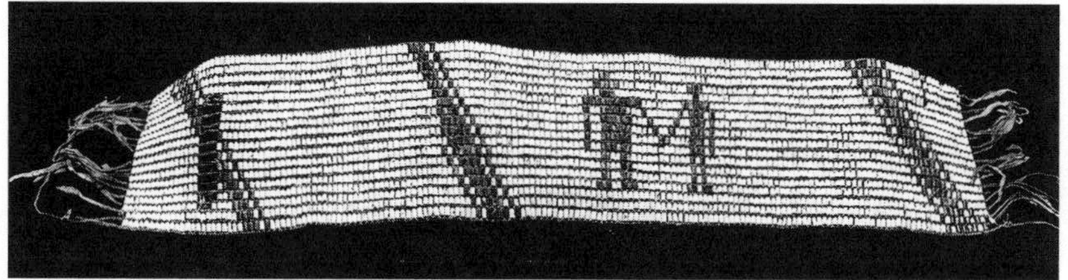

FIGURE 11. Wampum Belt.
Courtesy, The Historical Society of Pennsylvania, Philadelphia [1857.3]. This belt of wampum, presented to William Penn by Delawares in the seventeenth century, depicts an idealized history of English-Indian encounters, which the Quakers adopted as their legacy. Like a treaty document or deed, wampum belts could remind latter-day Pennsylvanians about the original intent of past alliances.

trol over Indian policy, he, too, relied on them as political tools in his own struggle for colonial power. The king had recently appointed William Johnson as British superintendent of Indian affairs in the northern colonies, supposedly superseding the proprietors' and governor's authority to negotiate with Indians. The provincial governor and Great Britain vied for control of Indian affairs in Pennsylvania, each trying to cultivate the favor of the Six Nations. Quakers, on the other hand, did not recognize the Iroquois as the political overlords of the Delawares and Shawnees at war. Instead, under the auspices of the Friendly Association, the commissioners of Indian affairs made initial overtures to negotiate directly with native leaders in the Ohio Valley and with the Susquehanna Delawares under the leadership of Teedyuscung. Pennsylvania Indians, in turn, helped legitimize Quaker authority when they preferred to deal with Quaker diplomats rather than representatives of a distant government in London. In April 1756, Quakers sounded out Scarouyady, an Oneida who acted as liaison for the increasingly powerful coalition of Ohio Indians, about the causes of the war and potential solutions. Scarouyady praised the Quakers for offering "to stand up as Wm Penn's Children" and for reviving "the old Principles of Peace and Love." "We thought that the People of that Profession had been all dead or bury'd in the Bushes or in the Ashes," he confessed, "but We are very glad there are some of the same Men living and that you offer to stand as Mediators between our Cousins the Delawares and this Government now at Variance." Because Indians recognized the Friendly Association as the heirs of Penn's peace policy, the Pennsylvania governor chose to co-opt Quaker diplomatic intervention to gain the support of Ohio Indian leader Scarouyady and, through him, to initiate negotiations with hostile Delawares. More to the point, the governor needed the additional financial resources that Quakers provided; as long as they remained involved in Indian diplomacy, he expected the Quakers to combine any gifts with those of the province for distribution at treaty conferences.[9]

Pennsylvania Indians also faced the problem of internal factionalism as they considered diplomatic solutions to frontier violence. The Six Nations, bolstered by official recognition from imperial agents such as William Johnson, maintained their innocence of hostilities, even as they professed to control Delawares involved in raiding activities. Not all Delawares had participated in attacks on white settlements, however. Shingas and Teedyuscung had reacted violently to increased encroachment on their lands in defiance of Iroquois authority, but some Christian Delawares, both in mission towns and those who now lived in the Christian diaspora on the Susquehanna, opposed participation in the war. In addition, neutral Shawnees and Christian Mahicans in the Wyoming Valley found themselves caught between these factions. Even though divided, by 1756 most Indian communities in Pennsylvania, whether neutral or hostile, thought it in their best interest to negotiate an end to the fighting.

Despite their acknowledged role as mediators, Quakers alone did not entice Indians to treaty conferences. Indians had their own reasons for

9. Peters to Thomas Penn, Oct. 30, 1756, Peters Letter Book, 1755–1757, HSP; Carl Van Doren and Julian P. Boyd, eds., *Indian Treaties Printed by Benjamin Franklin, 1736–1762* (Philadelphia, 1938), lxxvi; John R. Dunbar, ed., *The Paxton Papers* (The Hague, 1957), 15; "A Series of Conversations with Indians during Private Conference with the Quakers in Philadelphia," Apr. 19, 21, 1756, Friendly Association Minutes, July 29, 1756, both in Cox-Parrish-Wharton Family Papers, box 18, HSP; Council at Pembertons, Apr. 23, 1756, Historical Society Collection, Miscellaneous Manuscripts, 1661–1931, Indian Affairs, HSP. For an overview of the Quakers' role in peace treaties, see Jennings, *Empire of Fortune*, 254–281, 324–348; and Anthony F. C. Wallace, *King of the Delawares: Teedyuscung, 1700–1763* (1949; reprint, Syracuse, N.Y., 1990), 137–148. Governor Morris sent Newcastle, a Seneca, and Delawares Jagrea and William Lacquis to Wyoming to quell rumors that whites mistreated Indian allies: "I desire you will undeceive them and particularly I do charge Wm [Lacquis] to acquaint the Delawares, that those of their Tribe who live among us have not had any mischief done them but are treated with our usual kindness and are at Liberty and live in peace and plenty among us" (Friendly Association Minutes, Apr. 26, 1756, Cox-Parrish-Wharton Family Papers, box 18, HSP).

and manner of initiating diplomacy. More often, those native groups who wanted to negotiate with white Pennsylvanians enlisted the support of a network based on kinship and religious affiliation to compel hostile factions to the treaty table. Women with strong matrilineal clan ties acted as bridges between hostile and nonhostile Indians. By 1756, the Shawnee chief Paxnous had become a prominent and neutral mediator between the Pennsylvania government and Teedyuscung's band of Delawares on the Susquehanna. His Delaware wife Elisabeth, baptized by the Moravians in February 1755, most certainly encouraged Paxnous to accommodate peace between hostile Delawares and Euramericans. She had found comfort in the presence of Christian Indian women at Wyoming whom she could "love and discuss the Saviour with daily," she formed friendships with the German Moravian women she visited in Bethlehem, and she probably agreed with the Brethren's pacifist policies. Yet older kin connections also influenced efforts to initiate diplomacy. Her brother Benjamin, the son of Nutimus and the cousin of Teedyuscung, was among the perpetrators of frontier violence living at Nescopeck. He would have been more willing to listen to the pleas of Paxnous, his sister's husband, than anyone else. Elisabeth and her family were the reason Paxnous could "talk good Delaware," giving him the language skills for frontier diplomacy. In April 1756, Paxnous acted as host to Iroquois go-betweens and later as speaker for the Susquehanna Delawares when the Iroquois and Pennsylvania government first approached them to negotiate an end to their attacks on nearby white settlements.[10]

Indians also used the extended kin networks that spanned the Christian and non-Christian worlds to initiate treaty negotiations. Some Moravian Indians, who had fled to Bethlehem and the nearby town of Nain

10. Elisabeth Tooker, "Women in Iroquois Society," in Michael K. Foster, Jack Campisi, and and Marianne Mithun, eds., *Extending the Rafters: Interdisciplinary Approaches to Iroquoian Studies* (Albany, N.Y., 1984), esp. 114; Bethlehem Register, Feb. 17, 1755, "Bethlehemisches Kirchen=Buch," I, 1742–1756, 127, Moravian Archives, Bethlehem, Pa.; Bernhard Adam Grube to Mattheus Hehl, Aug. 4, 1753, *Moravian Archives*, reel 26, box 211, folder 16, item 1, Johann Jacob Schmick to Spangenberg, May 22, 1755, reel 29, box 221, folder 9, item 2 ("daß sie an ihr eine Schwester krigt, die sie lieb haben u. täglich mit ihr von Hld."); Trip to Wyoming, Friendly Association Minutes, 1756–1759, Cox-Parrish-Wharton Family Papers, box 18, HSP; *MPCP*, VII, 139–140; Memo on Newcastle's visit to Tioga, May 1756, no. 43, Logan Family Papers, 1664–1871, XI, Indian Affairs, HSP.

during initial attacks, acted as political go-betweens with Delawares on the Susquehanna River. Shortly after Pennsylvania declared war on the Delawares, Quakers attempted to diminish the damage of that belligerent act by enlisting the help of native negotiators. With Scarouyady's advice, they delegated two Ohio Iroquois, Newcastle and Jagrea, and a New Jersey Delaware, William Lacquis, to mediate between Pennsylvania and the Susquehanna Delawares. These three mediators requested that Christian Delaware leader Augustus join them because they thought he was "a man of good Judgement, of an honest Countenance, and well acquainted with the Woods up that way to Wajomick." Further, he had been "much regarded by His Nation formerly" and was considered "of a great Family." When the three negotiators traveled to Diahoga in June 1756 to convey another message to the Delawares from the governor, they again begged him "to procure Augustus the Indian, to go with them." They knew that Augustus would have influence on Teedyuscung, since both had been baptized by the Moravians in 1749, and several members of Teedyuscung's family—his mother-in-law, son Amos, daughter-in-law Juliana, and their children—had lived in Meniolagomekah with Augustus before Richard Peters took possession of the town in 1754. More important, the kinship connection between women proved significant to Augustus's mission; his third wife, Augustina, was the sister of Teedyuscung's wife.[11]

Given the tension between Iroquois and Delawares, it seems surprising that Newcastle and Jagrea requested Augustus as a fourth mediator. They might have suspected that the Delaware's potential malevolent powers

11. Roll of Meniolagomekah members, May 19, 1753, *Moravian Records,* reel 6, box 122, folder 3, Apr. 19, 1756, reel 35, box 323, folder 2, Spangenberg to Morris, May 2, 1756, reel 34, box 317, folder 1, item 7; Morris to Susquehanna Indians, Apr. 26, 1756, in Sullivan et al., comps., *Papers of Johnson,* II, 453; Spangenberg to William Logan, May 27, 1756, Northampton County Papers, Bethlehem and Vicinity, Miscellaneous Manuscripts, 1741–1886, HSP; Memo on Newcastle's visit to Tioga, May 1756, no. 43, Logan Family Papers, 1664–1871, XI, Indian Affairs, HSP; "Capt. Newcastle's Report," June 1, 1756, Horsfield Papers, I, APS; *MPCP,* VII, 166. Francis Jennings, *Empire of Fortune,* 270–271, implies that it was Conrad Weiser and the Iroquois intermediaries who convinced Teedyuscung to come to Easton, Pennsylvania, for peace negotiations. Historians focus on the role of Newcastle and Jagrea in this early meeting with Teedyuscung because their names appear on all the official reports given to the Pennsylvania Council. But the presence of Augustus and Lacquis proved pivotal because of their kinship affiliations with hostile Delawares.

could undermine the proceedings despite Augustus's kinship ties. Being from the Ohio, however, Newcastle and Jagrea had several reasons to rely on his assistance. According to their own assessment, Augustus was more familiar with the hilly terrain of eastern Pennsylvania and could help them find Teedyuscung in the Wyoming Valley. In addition, these Ohio Iroquois, like their Delaware neighbors to the east, struggled to maintain a political life independent of the Six Nations. When first commissioned for the task, Newcastle and Jagrea complained that Scarouyady had not consulted them—"We are not his vassals, nor to be treated in so haughty a Manner"—but they agreed to deliver Governor Morris's message. What appeared to be an unlikely partnership was yet another sign that the balance of power was shifting away from the Iroquois Confederacy; smaller native groups sought new avenues of cooperation with each other and ways to strengthen separate alliances with the English. Indeed, the Pennsylvania governor agreed to Augustus's presence in the peace delegation, perhaps foreseeing his potential powers of persuasion among the Delawares, but he also recognized the need to work with individual Indian leaders in the region.[12]

Oh, to be a fly on the wall when Augustus confronted Teedyuscung in Wyoming! Possibly they exchanged pleasantries about the family, one wife sending her sister an affectionate greeting. Augustus might have even berated the Delaware leader for abandoning his life as Gideon in Gnadenhütten and the Moravian spiritual life that Augustus had followed faithfully for seven years. Or was it strictly business? Teedyuscung must have confessed a good deal about his wartime activities, since, after his trip, Augustus concluded that Teedyuscung was, indeed, "the man that hath occasioned the late War." The latter had circulated "an exceeding large Belt of Wampum" among the Indians on the West Branch of the Susquehanna River and among the Cherokees, asking them to join in the war against the English. Imagine the scene of a younger man, in his prime, lecturing the older Teedyuscung on "the Custom amongst the Indians" to finish an affair that he began, and thus to take steps toward peace. Teedyuscung took to heart the instructions on how to "make all these things good again." He finally agreed to come to Easton in July 1756 for the first round of negotia-

12. James H. Merrell, *Into the American Woods: Negotiators on the Pennsylvania Frontier* (New York, 1999), 236–239; *MPCP,* VII, 105.

tions with the Pennsylvania government, thus establishing new public political alliances that went beyond the small trade agreements and petitions from native communities that typified relations with eastern Pennsylvania Indians during the first half of the eighteenth century. Teedyuscung had little trust "in the words of white people," however, assuming that the Pennsylvania government and their Iroquois allies would again deceive him.[13]

When whites and Indians came together in political arenas, they brought different assumptions about the form and function of these negotiations, rendering mutual trust or even understanding at times elusive. For eastern Algonquian cultures, as well as the Iroquois, the goal of treaty negotiations was to reach a consensus among parties through extensive discourse. If conflicts arose between individuals or families, those involved spoke their mind in council. Civil leaders would diplomatically arbitrate between differing opinions until they arrived at an appropriate judgment or decision that represented the "collective wisdom" of the community. Everything that unfolded during the conference became part of the agreement, and it was assumed that certain common problems such as land use, economic assistance, and political alliances, all important to community stability, would be renewed or renegotiated at regular intervals. Since native leaders had no formal means to coerce agreement, political power and authority rested on oral traditions, memory, and particular speech forms used for persuasion. Ritual language was a means of appropriating personal power and obtaining spiritual assistance to influence other people and the situation at hand. Indians customarily used strings and belts of wampum to perform and remember these rituals and to send messages between communities. In many ways, wampum, being a record of formal council proceedings, served as written language and as a symbol of authority; similar to a commission, it gave an individual power to speak, and its form—color, size, and design—indicated its function. For instance, Augustus told Teedyuscung at their first meeting that the Delaware leader had to send a specific wampum belt, "at least five or six feet long and twelve Rows broad," to all hostile Indian leaders. Only

13. Minutes of Indian conferences at Easton, July 30, 1756, July and November 1756, 20, APS; "Information about the Delaware King Teedyuscung Delivered by Jos. Spangenberg Who Reced It from a Delaware Indian 30 July 1756," no. 98, Penn Papers, Indian Affairs, II, 1754–1756, HSP.

FIGURE 12. *The Indians Giving a Talk to Colonel Bouquet . . . in Octr. 1764*
By Benjamin West. From William Smith, *An Historical Account of the Expedition against the Ohio Indians, in the Year 1764 . . .* (London, 1766).
Courtesy, The Library Company of Philadelphia.
As part of native American political ritual, wampum strings and belts preserved a record of conference proceedings and, depending on the size and appearance, gave Indian representatives the authority to speak in council. Oratory and persuasive powers were important to native political culture, but, as this engraving also suggests, the English incorporated these oral presentations into their own written records of treaty conferences, thus contributing to the hybrid nature of eighteenth-century Indian-white relations.

with these belts and twelve strings of wampum "to confirm the Words he sends" could Teedyuscung seek native consensus to "make all these things good again."[14]

Like their Indian neighbors, whites also sought conflict resolution, friendship, and material assistance when negotiating with strangers. Instead of seeking consensus or the fluidity of a continuing dialogue about mutual problems, however, they generally used a treaty conference to negotiate for and to claim absolute legal control over land, resources, labor, or groups of people. In their world, where the emphasis lay on particular legal principles and the formal structures of government, neither resonance of voice, presentation of gifts, nor wampum was a key factor. The written word was all important. Deeds, commissions, receipts, petitions, ordinances, legislation, and court records embodied the power of political language for Europeans. Within the political forum, written documents were meant to capture the presumed permanence of an agree-

14. Spangenberg to the Pennsylvania Council, July 30, 1756, Minutes of Indian Conferences at Easton, July and November 1756, APS; "Information about the Delaware King Teedyuscung," no. 98, Penn Papers, Indian Affairs, II, 1754–1756, HSP; Richter, *Ordeal of the Longhouse,* 45; Robert Steven Grumet, "Sunksquaws, Shamans, and Tradeswomen: Middle Atlantic Coastal Algonkian Women during the Seventeenth and Eighteenth Centuries," in Mona Etienne and Eleanor Leacock, eds., *Women and Colonization: Anthropological Perspectives* (New York, 1980), 47–48; John Phillip Reid, *A Law of Blood: The Primitive Law of the Cherokee Nation* (New York, 1970), 30; Gregory Evans Dowd, *A Spirited Resistance: The North American Indian Struggle for Unity, 1745–1815* (Baltimore, 1992), 3–4; Michael K. Foster, "Another Look at the Function of Wampum in Iroquois-White Councils," in Francis Jennings et al., eds., *The History and Culture of Iroquois Diplomacy: An Interdisciplinary Guide to the Treaties of the Six Nations and Their League* (Syracuse, N.Y., 1985), 99–114; Nancy L. Hagedorn, "'A Friend to Go between Them': The Interpreter as Cultural Broker during Anglo-Iroquois Councils, 1740–70," *Ethnohistory,* XXXV (1988), 60–80. Consensus politics should not be confused with modern, sometimes idealized, notions of democracy. Native groups were not always egalitarian. The enslaved and other nonpersons did not participate in decision making. Threats of revenge, retaliation by witchcraft, or public ostracism could be used effectively to create consensus. Euramericans were often frustrated with consensus politics, because it did away with visible signs of hierarchy. Conrad Weiser complained to Richard Peters that there was a large group of Indians following Canassatego down to Philadelphia for treaty negotiations in 1749: "Every one was at liberty to come along or stay at home on such occassions" (Weiser to Peters, Aug. 6, 1749, Pierre Eugene Du Simitiere Papers, Library Company manuscripts housed at HSP).

ment. Still, Euramericans often had to use their own powers of persuasion to create binding legal documents. After agreeing to meet with Teedyuscung and the Delawares, Pennsylvania governor Morris drafted the "Proclamation for a Suspension of Hostilities for Thirty Days" to compel both the provincial army and frontier settlers to suspend hostilities until he completed treaty negotiations. The governor, however, had to persuade Assembly members "to pass a Law to the same Effect" and to enforce the cease-fire in their districts. Only then could he send published copies of his proclamation to Indians on the upper Susquehanna to assure them of his sincerity and their safety.[15]

Although Indians invested ritual speech, oration, and memory with powers to build consensus and whites invested codified legal systems and written words with powers to enforce behavior, on some level each tried to accommodate the other's political forms. During the mid-1750s, when Indians and whites met in a common political arena to negotiate an end to hostilities, each knew enough about the other's methods and technologies to attempt to dominate the spaces of power in which they both operated. In other words, Indians and whites effectively incorporated the other's language—metaphors, ritual speech, and the written word—to assert their demands. When Teedyuscung agreed to meet with the governor of Pennsylvania during the summer of 1756, he combined old and new methods. So that no one would misunderstand his reply, Teedyuscung prepared a written statement to accompany the string of wampum he sent with Augustus and the Iroquois delegates to Philadelphia.[16]

White Pennsylvanians, also concerned with clearly expressing their political needs, often let Indian traditions set the general standards for their meetings. They treated Indians as diplomatic equals and accepted, used, and contributed to the forms and language of native rituals and ceremonies. They did so not because they admired these forms—in fact, they often complained about the length of native political oration, which was so important to consensus formation. Before the first Easton treaty, Governor Morris wrote William Johnson: "The Indians adhere so closely to their Tedious Ceremonies that I am sensible you must have had a most

15. *MPCP*, VII, 142, 147, 175; Foucault, "Truth and Power," in Foucault, *Power/Knowledge*, trans. Gordon et al., 125.

16. "King Teedyuscung's Message to Governor," July 18, 1756, Horsfield Papers, I, APS.

fatiguing time of it." Instead, Euramericans like Morris accommodated native American ritual forms and language to legitimize their own authority in terms that Indians would recognize. Both Indians and whites needed a mutually acceptable diplomatic process, even language, to help balance the delicate tensions between trust and distrust. Each side wanted their demands met and decided that some accommodation would best accomplish their goals.[17]

During the 1740s and 1750s, metaphors and metaphoric language emerged as a potential point of entry to this common understanding. Since the meaning of a metaphor was relative, signifying both what "is like" and what "is not like," the speaker and the listener could read slightly different meanings into their words yet still recognize the resemblance. Metaphors were an important part of discourse between Indians and whites at treaty conferences precisely because they allowed for different meanings within a commonly used diplomatic language. Native Americans often applied metaphoric kinship terms to their political relations to clarify or to delineate their relative position of power with others. When they appealed to their "brothers," "cousins," "uncles," or "grandfathers" during a treaty conference, each of these symbolic kinship designations specified to Indians the role and responsibility of each party and set a hierarchy of authority for the meeting. Within the Iroquois Confederacy, Onondagas, Senecas, and Mohawks were considered the "elder brothers," and Oneidas, Cayugas, and Tuscaroras were the "younger brothers"—the elders having more authority in council. The relationship between Delawares and Shawnees was one of "grandfather" to "grandchildren," which conveyed ceremonial deference but did not oblige obedience. One of the clearest lines of metaphoric obligation lay between the Six Nations and Delawares. In the mid-eighteenth century, Delawares often addressed Iroquois as "uncles" when in council. They were called "nephews" or "cousins" in return. Uncles in Iroquois and Delaware communities, especially mothers' brothers, had greater power over nephews than other male relatives. Despite this clearly marked symbolic kinship relation between the Six Nations and Delawares, Iroquois uncles had great difficulty controlling their Delaware nephews politically, which added to the tensions between the two.[18]

17. Sullivan et al., comps., *Papers of Johnson*, II, 442–443.

18. Paul Ricoeur, *The Rule of Metaphor: Multi-Disciplinary Studies of the Creation of*

When Indians and whites met in treaty conferences to negotiate alliances during the eighteenth century, the ways that kinship, both actual and metaphoric, defined lines of authority created special problems. "Father" was perhaps the most problematic metaphoric relationship that bound Indian and non-Indian communities. The Iroquois addressed the French governor in North America as Onontio, or father, because the Indians regarded the French as allies, trade partners, and intermediaries. Whereas the French regarded their fatherly role as an extension of patriarchal authority, the Iroquois believed that fathers had no real power over their children. The Pennsylvania government, like the French, wanted to believe that their position as father gave them greater power to make decisions for Indians. In the early eighteenth century, the governor assumed that the Conestogas and Delawares looked upon themselves as "Children, Rather to be Directed by this Governmt," their father. The Conestogas had a different view, perhaps based on a new understanding of Euramerican family relations, "for often Parents would be apt to whip their Children too severely, and Brothers sometimes would differ." Instead, the Conestogas wanted to be considered "as the same Flesh and Blood with the Christians," as William Penn supposedly had insisted, "and the same as if one Man's Body was to be divided in two Parts." In his interactions with the

---

Meaning in Language, trans. Robert Czerny, with Kathleen McLaughlin and John Costello, S.J. (Toronto, 1977), 7, 80; "Glossary of Figures of Speech in Iroquois Political Rhetoric," in Francis Jennings et al., eds., *The History and Culture of Iroquois Diplomacy: An Interdisciplinary Guide to the Treaties of the Six Nations and Their League* (Syracuse, N.Y., 1985), 120; Jennings, *The Ambiguous Iroquois Empire: The Covenant Chain Confederation of Indian Tribes with English Colonies from Its Beginnings to the Lancaster Treaty of 1744* (New York, 1984), 44; *MPCP,* V, 476; Sullivan et al., comps., *Papers of Johnson,* XI, 724. Count Nikolaus Ludwig von Zinzendorf noted that the relationship between the elder and younger Iroquois tribes was that of "father" and "sons" (Reichel, ed., *Memorials of the Moravian Church,* I, 21–22). Richard White, *The Middle Ground: Indians, Empires, and Republics in the Great Lakes Region, 1650–1815* (New York, 1991), 36, places "grandfather" on the same metaphoric level as "manitou"; thus, when the French simply became "fathers," "they had taken a step down the generational ladder." Raymond J. DeMaille, "Touching the Pen: Plains Indian Treaty Councils in Ethnohistorical Perspective," in Frederick C. Luebke, ed., *Ethnicity on the Great Plains* (Lincoln, Nebr., 1980), 50, examines the use of metaphors in Plains Indian treaty councils and finds that, though both whites and Indians manipulated relational metaphors for their own advantages, the Indian use of kinship terms was sometimes too subtle for whites to understand.

Pennsylvania governor leading up to the first Easton treaty, Teedyuscung deliberately addressed him as "brother." Although brothers may differ, as the Conestogas suggested, to native Americans brothers also were equals. Whether of "one Man's Body" or brothers, Indians, who vied for parity and recognition of their political autonomy, preferred that relationship to being children to a white man's father.[19]

Indians and whites struggled to delineate their relative positions of authority through the use of kinship metaphors. They also adapted other kinds of metaphors to make their demands understood at political proceedings. Teedyuscung opened the Easton treaty on July 26, 1756, with ritual ceremonies, setting the tone for the conference and trying to appropriate the role of "host," who traditionally controlled the agenda. Key to this ceremony was the symbolic cleansing of the other participants' bodies. To deal with whites in particular, native Americans needed ritual assurances that they would speak clearly and listen carefully. Cleansing the body was necessary, for fear that "an Evil Spirit of great Power and Cunning" might have "blinded you and throwed Dust in your Eyes." At treaties, Indians metaphorically wielded a "fine Feather . . . diped in that pure Oil" to wash out "the inside of your Ears, that you may hear" and "the best Medicines" to cleanse "some Foulness [that] come into your heart through your Throat." Seeing clearly, hearing completely, and speaking candidly were necessary to clear communication and understanding. At Easton, Teedyuscung presented the Pennsylvania governor with four belts of wampum, "one to brush Thorns from the Governors Legs, another to Rub the Dust out of his Eyes, to help him to see clearly, another to open his Ears, to enable him to hear them patiently, and the Fourth to clear his Throat, that he might speak plainly." Teedyuscung symbolically cleansed the governor's eyes, ears, and throat as an act of civility, which promoted honesty and trust, but also demanded that he listen respectfully to the Delawares' concerns.[20]

19. *MPCP,* III, 46; [Charles Thomson], *Causes of the Alienation of the Delaware and Shawanese Indians from the British Interest* (Philadelphia, 1867) (originally published as *An Enquiry into the Causes of the Alienation of the Delaware and Shawanese Indians from the British Interest* . . . [London, 1759]), 9; "King Teedyuscung's Message to Governor," July 18, 1756, Horsfield Papers, I, APS; "Reply of Teedyuscung," July 24, 1756, *PA,* 1st Ser., II, 721; White, *Middle Ground,* 36; Jennings, *Ambiguous Iroquois Empire,* 44.

20. *MPCP,* VIII, 746; "Capt. Newcastle's Report," June 1, 1756, Horsfield Papers, I, APS; S. K. Stevens et al., eds., *The Papers of Henry Bouquet* (Harrisburg, Pa., 1951–),

Ritual cleansing of the body prepared parties to begin negotiations, but more specific ceremonies helped to build new bridges of communication and to ease tensions. For instance, the native American condolence ceremony mitigated the prolonged mistrust between parties and provided compensation for the unexpected or violent loss of lives during the war. When a family member or important chief died, somebody from outside the family or clan performed the ritual, which included wiping away the blood of the victim and the tears of the mourners and presenting gifts to cover the grave. The observance symbolically resurrected the deceased and restored rationality to grieving survivors' souls, after which they could return to their daily activities. The Pennsylvania government found that the condolence ceremony helped to maintain smooth relations with Indian allies by recognizing particular Indian leaders and their influence and continued friendship. In the fall of 1750, Conrad Weiser, the colonial liaison to the Six Nations, learned of the death of the Iroquois leader Canassatego at Onondaga. The Iroquois council was torn between continuing important business and ceasing all activities for a period of mourning. Weiser informed the Pennsylvania government that condolence had to be performed or it would appear "the dead Person was of no Credit or Esteem, and it is a certain affront to the deceased's Friends." The following spring, Weiser returned to Onondaga at the request of the governor "to give them a Small present to Signyfy to them that this Government do condole with them for the loose of Canasako [Canassatego] and others."[21]

During the Seven Years' War, the Pennsylvania government continued to use condolence to placate allies but also to manipulate them. Condolence became standard practice for opening treaty conferences. In early 1757, George Croghan met with 160 Iroquois, Nanticokes, Delawares, and Conestogas at John Harris's on the Susquehanna River to lay the groundwork for a third meeting with Teedyuscung and to gather intelligence

III, 509; *PA*, 1st Ser., II, 725; Michael K. Foster, "On Who Spoke First at Iroquois-White Councils: An Exercise in the Method of Upstreaming," in Foster, Campisi, and Mithun, eds., *Extending the Rafters*, 191.

21. *MPCP*, V, 474, 542; Sullivan et al., comps., *Papers of Johnson*, I, 317; Matthew Dennis, *Cultivating a Landscape of Peace: Iroquois-European Encounters in Seventeenth-Century America* (Ithaca, N.Y., 1993), 81, 101. Dennis notes that the Jesuits first witnessed an Iroquois condolence ceremony in 1645 in which the general purpose was to restore order and peace within the community and to prevent the beginning of a blood feud by the deceased's family (79).

about French movements in the west. Because of "the Death of many . . . Counsellors and Warriors," Croghan symbolically wiped the blood off the council seats and wiped the tears from their eyes before they would even consider further talk. "I with these Strouds," Croghan intoned, "wrap up the Bodies of your deceased Friends and bury them decently, covering their Graves with those Blanketts and half thicks." Indians appreciated that whites used their rituals and responded in kind at treaty conferences. Scarouyady, the Oneida liaison for the Ohio Indians, accepted the presents Croghan offered, thanking him and "our Brother Onas," referring to the proprietor Thomas Penn, who "wisely considered the Antient Custom of our ForeFathers in condoling with us and mixing your Grief with ours." Scarouyady then proceeded to wipe away the blood and tears of the English to "heal your Hearts and free your Minds from trouble that we may meet each other in Council." Rather than giving white negotiators a political advantage over their Indian counterparts, however, accommodating native rituals provided Indians with a sense of diplomatic equality with the English. After condoling with the Pennsylvania agents at John Harris's, Scarouyady announced that the Indians refused to meet with the governor in Philadelphia because they were "affraid of Sickness" that had settled on the city. Instead, they insisted that the governor meet them at Lancaster as soon as Teedyuscung arrived.[22]

The ability to accommodate rituals and share diplomatic forms allowed Indians and whites to negotiate, even if their goals were different. Both used metaphors and rituals to their own purposes. Indeed, the manipulation of language created new power dynamics that affected the outcome of treaties between Indians and whites but also affected the balance of power among Indians, especially between Iroquois and Delawares. During the first half of the eighteenth century, political alliances between the English

22. William Denny to Johnson, Dec. 6, 1756, in Sullivan et al., comps., *Papers of Johnson,* IX, 566 (see also 730, 732–733, 762, 771); *MPCP,* VI, 68; Friendly Association Minutes, Nov. 4, 1756, Cox-Parrish-Wharton Family Papers, box 18, HSP. Upon the death of Conrad Weiser in 1761, Seneca George, who considered Weiser "a great Man, and one-half a Seven Nation Indian, and one-half an Englishman," performed condolences and lamented: "Since his Death we cannot so well understand one another" (*MPCP,* VIII, 631). In August 1736, Delawares came to Philadelphia to extend their condolences after the death of Governor Patrick Gordon (*MPCP,* IV, 53).

and the Indians in New York and Pennsylvania as well as among Indian tribes had been shaped by the provisions of the Covenant Chain. Born of the joint efforts of the English and the Mohawks to suppress New England Algonquians during Metacom's War in the late seventeenth century, the Covenant Chain was a series of alliances among Indians and with the colonial government of New York that gave the Six Nations control over land, resources, and native peoples settled in New York and Pennsylvania. The agreements enabled Iroquois to secure access to trade markets in Pennsylvania and to demand the assistance of the local Indians in their wars with other Indian tribes to the south. The agreements were never perfected or complete in their effect, however. By the late 1740s, the Six Nations lost control over Indians in the Ohio Valley. Within a decade, their power to master Delawares in eastern Pennsylvania was also slipping away.

Still, the Iroquois attempted to reassert political dominance over Delawares by various means—if not by force, then by the force of words. On one hand, the Six Nations acknowledged Teedyuscung's authority to negotiate independently for eastern natives, presumably by making him "king" of the Susquehanna Delawares in 1755. They informed William Johnson in February 1756 that the Delawares no longer concerned them; "We'd always look'd upon the Delawares as the more immediate care of Onas [Pennsylvania's proprietor], that they were within the circle of his arms." The Iroquois pronouncement simultaneously blamed Pennsylvania for failing to prevent war and disassociated the Six Nations from the hostile Delawares. On the other hand, the Six Nations tried to insinuate that Delawares did not deserve that political independence by formulating and spreading rumors, innuendoes, and carefully crafted images. During the 1750s, the Iroquois alternately used representations of Delawares as all-powerful or as subordinates to undermine the Delawares' ability to gain supporters among the English, such as the Moravians or Quakers. Iroquois sometimes projected their own misdeeds on Delawares, making them into a dangerous enemy. But they also employed gendered representations to portray Delawares as weak. Land was the major issue in this rhetorical power struggle. For the English, those who controlled regional Indian politics had the right to sell land to them. Both Iroquois and Delawares knew that access to and control of land was essential to their survival. For Delawares, land provided a permanent home and political autonomy. For Iroquois, claiming the right to sell land gave them leverage over Delawares and legitimized their own authority in the eyes of the English.[23]

In the mid-eighteenth century, the Six Nations claimed that they had conquered the Delawares and Shawnees in battle and conferred on them the metaphoric status of "women." The term originally cast the Delawares as a politically neutral party who adopted the role of mediator between warring tribes. But as the Six Nations and the Pennsylvania proprietors cooperated to control their respective and overlapping frontiers, Iroquois drew on the term to mark Delawares as subordinate to them in all matters concerning the sale of land or political alliances with the British. To confirm their right to sell the parcel of land called the Walking Purchase, Iroquois chief Canassatego admonished the Delawares in July 1742, using the term "women" to shame and embarrass them. "We conquer'd You," he insisted. "We made Women of you, you know you are Women, and can no more sell Land than Women. Nor is it fit you should have the Power of Selling Lands since you would abuse it." Although Indian men sometimes invoked their own ideas of female characteristics and roles in a derogatory manner to shame other males, in this case the Iroquois used a European notion of women to describe their relationship with Delawares. Canassatego was surely aware that the women of his family not only owned longhouses and personal property but were considered the "Truest Owners" of Iroquois land, since they planted the crops and labored in the fields. But the Indian diplomat spoke as much to the English present as to the Delawares. He invoked specific European concepts of the female gender, in which women could not own or sell land, to delineate Delawares' subordinate position in terms that Euramericans would clearly understand.[24]

23. Council at Philadelphia, July 20, 1756, Material Pertaining to Pennsylvania Indian Affairs, Collection of Treaties, deposited by Joseph Parker Norris, APS; *MPCP*, VII, 208; Sullivan et al., comps., *Papers of Johnson*, IX, 368. The English tended to use the term "king" for individual Indian leaders rather than recognizing that Indian communities or nations often had several different kinds of leaders—war chiefs and peace chiefs.

24. *MPCP*, IV, 579–580; Sullivan et al., comps., *Papers of Johnson*, IV, 56, 58; Tooker, "Women in Iroquois Society," in Foster, Campisi, and Mithun, eds., *Extending the Rafters*, 114. For the history of Delawares' being referred to as women, see Jennings, *Ambiguous Iroquois Empire*, 301–302; John Heckewelder, *History, Manners, and Customs of the Indian Nations, Who Once Inhabited Pennsylvania and the Neighboring States*, rev. ed., ed. William C. Reichel (1876; facsimile reprint, Bowie, Md., 1990), 57–58; Jay Miller, "The Delaware as Women: A Symbolic Solution," *American Ethnologist*,

The Pennsylvania colonial government, which had often been impatient with self-proclaimed or dispersed native leaders such as Teedyuscung, welcomed this explanation of Delaware subordination. Relegating Delawares to a female role not only confirmed Pennsylvania's purchase of Delaware land from the Iroquois but helped to assert a patriarchal authority on people whom they thought lacked the gender hierarchies common in Euramerican homes. In Indian communities, with matrilineal clan-based structures of authority and heredity, men had little power to control the actions of women and children. In the eyes of Euramericans, if men did not manage the household and the people within, they were hardly men at all. For Pennsylvanians, the metaphorical subordination of Delawares as women in the context of Indian-white relations reestablished acceptable lines of patriarchal authority. The Six Nations, whose political structure, at least, looked more familiar to Euramericans, acted as the male head of household and cooperated with them to make decisions about "female" dependents.[25]

By the 1750s, gendered representations served Iroquois and Euramericans politically, but the meaning of the political category of "woman" also had the power to redescribe and influence social relations and culture.

I (1974), 507–514. James Smith, a white captive, recalled that, when he had helped some young Wyandot women hoe a cornfield, the men in town laughed at him and said that he "was adopted in the place of a great man, and must not hoe corn like a squaw" (Smith, *An Account of the Remarkable Occurrences in the Life and Travels of Col. James Smith, during His Captivity with the Indians, in the Years 1755, '56, '57, '58, and '59*, ed. William M. Darlington [Cincinnati, Ohio, 1870], 45). Delawares in the Ohio Valley called the English "a parcel of old Women for that they could not travel without loaded Horses and Waggons full of Provisions and a great deal of Baggage that they did not know the Way to their Towns without Pilots and for these they must be obliged to take Indians with them" (Deposition of John Craig of Peters Township, Mar. 30, 1756, no. 78, Penn Papers, Indian Affairs, II, 1754–1756, HSP). Patrick Frazier, *The Mohicans of Stockbridge* (Lincoln, Nebr., 1992), 29, asserts that Indian men "disdained Christian civilization as effeminate."

25. John Bartram, *Travels in Pensilvania and Canada* (Ann Arbor, Mich., 1966) (originally published as *Observations on the Inhabitants, Climate, Soil, Rivers, Productions, Animals, and Other Matters Worthy of Notice* . . . [London, 1751]), 77; W[illia]m M. Beauchamp, ed., *Moravian Journals Relating to Central New York, 1754–66* (Syracuse, N.Y., 1916), 157. See Carole Shammas, "Anglo-American Household Government in Comparative Perspective," and Richard White, "What Chigabe Knew: Indians, Household Government, and the State," both in *William and Mary Quarterly*, 3d Ser., LII (1995), 104–143, 151–156.

After Delawares and Shawnees attacked the Pennsylvania and Virginia frontiers in 1755, the governors of both colonies begged the Six Nations to control the Delawares who were responsible. In January 1756, Robert Dinwiddie of Virginia told the Six Nations: "You looked upon them [the Delawares] as Women, who wore Petticoats; they never dared do anything of Importance without your leave, for they knew if they did you would chastize them." He further taunted the Iroquois by implying that, if the Delawares were not punished, they "will think themselves as good men as you, and you will lose the Name of being their Masters." Anxious about losing control of their subordinates along with the governor's respect, the Six Nations again reminded the Delawares of their position as women in July at Easton, Pennsylvania, using more explicitly sexualized language: "You are our Women; our Fore-Fathers made you so, and put a Petticoat on you, and charged you to be true to us, and lie with no other Man; but of late you have suffered the String that tied your Petticoat to be cut loose by the *French,* and you lay with them, and so became a common Bawd, in which you acted very wrong, and deserve Chastisement." Through language, Euramericans and Iroquois had constructed an alternative cultural category of femaleness that little resembled the real nature of women's authority in native communities. Native women often exercised a public role that reflected their private authority as mothers of men. They attended treaty conferences (seated prominently according to their individual status), advised the men, and even had power to speak indirectly in political forums. They, too, used gendered representations to admonish their kin to *"act like Men,* and true Brothers" during wartime. Despite women's persuasive voice in the community and their presence in public, however, during the 1750s Iroquois and white men turned the concept of native women's authority on its head to shame and exclude men from places of power within the diplomatic arena and to disenfranchise and dispossess Delawares of land.[26]

26. Ricoeur, *The Rule of Metaphor,* trans. Czerny, 7; Robert Dinwiddie to Morris, Jan. 2, 1756, no. 72, Penn Papers, Indian Affairs, II, 1754–1756, HSP; Sullivan et al., comps., *Papers of Johnson,* II, 414–415, IX, 950, 958, X, 849, 947, 959, XI, 41; Van Doren and Boyd, eds., *Indian Treaties,* 148; Grumet, "Sunksquaws, Shamans, and Tradeswomen," in Etienne and Leacock, eds., *Women and Colonization,* 43–62; "Relation von der Treaty in Gnadenhütten am 17. Jul. 1752," *Moravian Records,* reel 35, box 323, folder 1, item 1.

As the repeated use of gendered images within political arenas suggests, the Six Nations were not successful in controlling their "women." Delawares, instead, exploited the same images in order to manipulate Englishmen and Iroquois. They decided where and when they would be women. In September 1755, the Six Nations sent a black belt of wampum to entice Delawares to join them in war against the French. To secure the alliance, they "ordered their Cousins the Delawares to lay aside their petticoats and clap on nothing but a Breech Clout." Two months later, shortly after the first attacks on white settlements along the Pennsylvania frontier, belligerent Delawares and Shawnees told Governor Morris that they were "no longer Women, by which they mean no longer under their [the Six Nations'] Subjection," and instead declared war against the English. Yet, by December, when William Johnson attempted to find out through an intermediary why they had declared war, Delawares again wrapped themselves in their "petticoats." They sent Johnson a message that implied the Iroquois had sent them into battle: "'Tis true, brother, as you say, we are not at our own command, but under the direction of the six nations; we are women, our uncle must say what we must do; he has the hatchet, and we must do as he says." They assured Johnson meekly that they would "stop and repent." In the spring of 1757, however, Delawares and Shawnees in the Ohio Valley reversed their position and once more "looked upon themselves as Men" and were "determined to cut off all the *English.*" They warned that the Six Nations should say no more about it, "lest we cut off your private Parts, and make Women of you, as you have done of us." Delawares deftly used their own status as women to shame Iroquois in front of the Six Nations' most ardent supporters, in particular Johnson. Using the English and their association with the Six Nations, they found just the right moments and ways to manipulate both and to show that they could not be easily controlled by either.[27]

27. *MPCP,* VI, 615; Sullivan et al., comps., *Papers of Johnson,* II, 681–682, IX, 310, 336; Van Doren and Boyd, eds., *Indian Treaties,* 178; *PA,* 1st Ser., III, 193. The use of this powerful cultural metaphor did not easily go away. As late as 1796 there were reports that the Six Nations were once again making men of the Delawares. John Heckewelder recalled Moravian missionary David Zeisberger's account: "With great solemnity, [the Six Nations] had again changed the latter [the Delawares], from the state of Women, to that of Men" (Heckewelder to Peter S. Du Ponceau, Dec. 23, 1816, John Heckewelder Letters, 1816–1822, APS).

Accommodation, exchange, and the sharing of language forms led to mutual understanding as well as mutual manipulation in the political arena. For Delawares, however, the power of language went beyond present diplomatic needs; their future survival also depended on controlling language and how it shaped public opinions and perceptions of the past. Land, as always, lay at the heart of their argument. Teedyuscung and the Delawares thought permanent tenancy on land was the key to their political and social survival. By the 1750s, Delawares had already been moved several times against their will. Most recently, they feared their communities on the Susquehanna in the Wyoming Valley, given to them by the Six Nations in exchange for land at the Forks of the Delaware, would also be taken by white settlers or Iroquois. Just as they wielded native metaphors and gendered representations to vie for political autonomy, Delawares tried to use the written record of treaty proceedings to scrutinize past land purchases and disprove their validity. Teedyuscung, as primary speaker for the Delawares, attempted to use the written word, which constituted political authority for Euramericans, to assert his own power and to assure that the Delaware version of the past became part of the permanent record. To make their case clear to Euramericans in a language that would be most persuasive, however, Delawares had to contend with the Pennsylvania proprietors and the governor who had taken their land away. Paradoxically, the Delawares' primary advocates among white Pennsylvanians, Quakers, had their own ax to grind with the proprietors. Whether they were aware of it or not, Delawares had to negotiate the internal factionalism of white colonial powers to seek their own form of justice.

In July 1756, when Susquehanna Delawares first gathered at Easton to discuss the end to the recent hostilities, both the Six Nations and the Pennsylvania government initially agreed "to acknowledge the Independency of the Delawares, and the Authority of Teedyuscung" over several bands of Delawares and Mahicans "but requested him and his People not to act of themselves, but advise with the Six Nations." The governor had recently given Teedyuscung and Newcastle "Authority to do the public Business together" as agents of the province. Teedyuscung, not surprisingly, refused to consult with the Iroquois. By the second Easton treaty conference in November 1756, which came on the heels of Colonel John Armstrong's attack on the Delaware stronghold at Kittanning, the newly appointed governor, William Denny, also treated Teedyuscung as the chief negotiator for the Susquehanna Delawares as well as speaker for "a Collection of Delawares, Shawonese, Mohiccons, and some of the fugitive Six Nations who were formerly on the Ohio."[28]

Teedyuscung used this initial political legitimacy to his advantage in November when, to everyone's surprise, he stubbornly confronted the Pennsylvania government with the issue of title to Indian lands rather than the recent frontier violence. He demanded assurances that Delawares would be given permanent rights to their current residence in the Wyoming Valley. To make his case, he intended to shame the English into acknowledging their role in previous land frauds. On November 8, 1756, in Easton, Teedyuscung accused the province of illegally taking Delaware lands "lying between Tohiccon Creek and Wioming, on the River Sasquehannah" through the Walking Purchase of 1737. He charged the proprietors, in particular, with "greediness in purchasing Lands" and contended that "*Indians* are not such Fools, as to bear this, in their Minds." "The Proprietaries, who have purchased their Lands from us cheap, have sold them too dear, to poor People, and the *Indians* have suffered for it."[29]

Although Delawares were "not such Fools" to think that the Penns had their best interests in mind, Teedyuscung also had to rely on English advocates who had complex, even self-serving, motives for supporting his claims to land. Quakers sought justice for Delawares, but they also wanted to embarrass the proprietors to further their own political agenda of unseating the proprietary party from power. Quakers hoped they could do both. When Teedyuscung demanded an answer to his charge of land fraud, the proprietors' agents were taken off guard. According to Quaker observers, Conrad Weiser, the provincial interpreter, "endeavour'd to divert the Governor from putting the Question about Frauds and Grievances, pretending it not to be the proper Time for it and that the Indians are not used to give Answers off hand." Richard Peters, the provincial secretary recording the conference, became so agitated that "he was really or affected to appear uncapable of taking Notes of what was said and lay'd down his Pen." Peters, in particular, was incensed about these accusations, insisting that the proprietors had "never been greedy of the Purchase of

28. [Thomson], *Alienation of the Delaware and Shawanese Indians,* 91, 97; Denny to Johnson, Dec. 6, 1756, in Sullivan et al., comps., *Papers of Johnson,* IX, 565.

29. Easton treaty, Nov. 13, 1756, in Van Doren and Boyd, eds., *Indian Treaties,* 157; Friendly Association Minutes, Nov. 15, 1756, Cox-Parrish-Wharton Family Papers, box 18, HSP.

Lands from the Indians." Yet, when Quakers pressed him about the problems over the Walking Purchase, he conceded "that is true, that walk cannot be vindicated." Still, he diverted blame from the proprietors, claiming that the Penns had objected to the "unworthy" actions of the governor at the time. Quakers tried hard to undermine the legitimacy of the proprietors' powers by questioning the efficacy of their past actions.[30]

Whether working together or manipulating each other, Teedyuscung and the Quakers used written records as a means of pressing their respective agendas. The Delawares insisted, and with reluctance Governor Denny agreed, that the province probe further into the complaint about land fraud. Encouraged by the governor's interest, Teedyuscung demanded copies of all deeds and documents pertaining to the questionable land purchase "in order to prevent Misunderstandings." He wished to "have it in my Power to shew to others what has passed between this Government and me: What is committed to Writing, will not easily be lost, and will be of great Use to all, and better regarded." Teedyuscung did not simply want to obtain copies of the questionable deeds to interpret on his own; the Delaware leader also wanted to verify the accuracy of the current treaty conference's written record and the way it was presented in public to make sure the Delawares' story was being told properly. In July 1757, Teedyuscung demanded that the governor let him have his own clerk to take notes of the proceedings, since his land claims were of "the utmost Importance and required to be exactly minuted." The governor, again trying to rein in Teedyuscung's power, denied the request because "no *Indian* Chief before him ever demanded to have a Clerk, and none had ever been appointed for *Indians* in former Treaties." Teedyuscung countered that having a clerk "was the most certain means to searching out the Truth, and of obtaining Justice to the Persons who should prove to be injured." Teedyuscung admitted that writing things down in council might be a new method for the Indians but that he aimed "by having a Clerk of my own, to exceed my Ancestors."[31]

30. Friendly Association Minutes, Nov. 13, 15, 1756, Cox-Parrish-Wharton Family Papers, box 18, HSP; Diautolo, "The Role of Quakers in Indian Affairs," *Quaker History,* LXXVII (1988), 14–19.

31. Easton treaty, Nov. 16, 1756, Aug. 1, 1757, in Van Doren and Boyd, eds., *Indian Treaties,* 163, 200; [Thomson], *Alienation of the Delaware and Shawanese Indians,* 110–111, 112; *MPCP,* VII, 656. Charles Thomson, a Quaker and the author of the treatise cited here, was recruited as Teedyuscung's clerk.

Teedyuscung demanded a clerk to compile an accurate record of the proceedings because, from their first meeting in 1756, the provincial government had so often and so easily subverted the Delaware's power over the language and direction of the treaty negotiations. The Pennsylvania governor successfully manipulated public information about the conferences by controlling the translation of Indian speeches and curtailing any communication or interactions between Delawares and other Euramericans. The governor especially feared that the Delawares would speak freely with the Quakers, who supported and encouraged their demands for reparations. During the first Easton treaty, then-governor Morris, ascertaining that Teedyuscung would not speak with him "unless the Quakers were present," gave orders "that no Person should speak with the Indians, and a guard was set near their lodgings to prevent it." Quakers complained that less-savory characters had plenty of access to Indians: "The lower Class of People are permitted to curse, swear and rail at them and endeavour to incense them against us, within their hearing which appears to be very offensive to them." Even Moravians, the Quakers' spiritual rivals, were "allowed to entertain such Indians as they please and to have the Liberty of freely conversing with them." Others complained that farmers visiting Easton were able to "see the Indians with whom they will either quarrel or if it is possible they will give them Liquor and make them drunk."[32]

In November 1756, when Governor Denny presided over the second Easton treaty council, he, too, ordered that "no Persons be permitted to confer with the Indians" unless on official business. In April 1757, when Delawares met with the provincial Council in Lancaster, the governor ordered that neither Conrad Weiser nor Teedyuscung's interpreter translate anything for the Indians without his explicit permission. Throughout 1757, the governor often and insistently told his agents, Quakers, and Indians that "no Person else [other than his interpreters] should take notes"

32. Friendly Association Minutes, July 1756, Cox-Parrish-Wharton Family Papers, box 18, HSP; William Parsons to the governor, July 1756, Northampton County Papers, Misc. MSS, 1727–1758, HSP. Again, in July 1757, Weiser noted that "the common People behave very ill, in asking the Indians unbecoming Questions, and using ill Language" (Weiser to Denny, July 18, 1757, *PA*, 1st Ser., III, 222). See also David Murray, *Forked Tongues: Speech, Writing, and Representation in North American Indian Texts* (Bloomington, Ind., 1991), 40; Hagedorn, "'A Friend to Go between Them,'" *Ethnohistory*, XXXV (1988), 65–66.

and that no one had the right to treat with Teedyuscung "but myself and Mr. Croghan, the King's Deputy Agent." Although the governor realized that he could hardly control the effects of conversation since "almost all the Delawares speak English, and Teedyuscung We know does, . . . and might converse with whom they pleased," by regulating the public records of the treaties and the public image of Delawares that they conveyed he shaped the ultimate outcome of the final agreement between hostile Indians and the province.[33]

Although Teedyuscung won some of the smaller battles of the peace process, by August 1757 he had essentially lost the war of words. During the late-summer negotiations at Easton, the eastern Delawares and Pennsylvania agreed to end their hostilities. Delawares even agreed to provide military assistance to the British in their continuing struggle against the French in the Ohio. The question of land claims, however, was lost in the internal bickering of white political factions. Teedyuscung finally received his clerk, but his triumph depended as much on Quaker defiance as the Delaware's persistence. In July, Quaker commissioners for Indian affairs Joseph Galloway and William Masters warned the governor that if he "did not allow the Indians a Clerk they [the Quakers] would set off home and take the provincial presents with them and not give a Single shirt to the Indians." Pennsylvania relied on the generosity of wealthy Quakers to provide gifts during diplomatic encounters. The Quakers effectively threatened to remove the incentives that would keep Delawares at the bargaining table. The Quakers and Benjamin Franklin then recommended one of their own, a master at the Friends Philadelphia School, Charles Thomson, as clerk and copyist for Teedyuscung. This gave the Delaware chief the legitimacy he desired and direct assistance from sympathetic whites who would advocate the stabilization of an Indian land base. For Quakers, too, Thomson became a crucial link of influence, tying them closely with the Indian cause and giving them the ability to influence the treaty proceedings. More important, Thomson and his connection to Teedyuscung gave Quakers the means to frustrate and embarrass the proprietors and their appointed governor, perhaps even dominate all Indian affairs.[34]

33. Denny to Weiser, Nov. 3, 1756, Denny to the proprietors, Apr. 9, 1757, *PA*, 1st Ser., III, 18, 107; Lancaster treaty, May 12, 1757, in Sullivan et al., comps., *Papers of Johnson*, IX, 743–744; *MPCP*, VII, 663.

34. Excerpts from the Easton treaty, July 1757, George Chalmers Papers, Indian Af-

Similarly, the Pennsylvania governor and proprietors Thomas and Richard Penn wanted to investigate Teedyuscung's accusations, not to determine their validity, but to unmask Quaker conspirators and to improve their own public reputations. Teedyuscung's claims to land brought into question decades of proprietary purchases and sales of land, the basis of their provincial power. At the end of 1757, Thomas and Richard Penn begged Richard Peters to publish a condemnation of the Delawares' claims, "so our Innocence may appear to the World." They hoped to vindicate themselves from charges of land fraud and, thus, as some claimed, responsibility for the frontier violence of the mid-1750s. After Teedyuscung first presented his claims for the return of land, the governor and his Council hastily convened a committee to look into the charges of fraud. By early 1758, the governor's committee had assembled and reconstructed its own record of land purchases at the Forks of the Delaware and, as the Quakers expected, insisted that Pennsylvania authorities had not perpetrated land fraud against the Delawares. Indeed, "The Report of the Committee of the Council Appointed to Enquire into the Complaints of the Indians at the Treaty at Easton" insinuated that Teedyuscung's "false and groundless Charge" must have come from "some undue Influence"—a thinly veiled reference to the Quakers—"or to the Difficulty he was under to invent any other plausible Excuse for the cruel Murders and horrid Devastations committed by them on our back Inhabitants."[35]

Quakers, in turn, were more interested in attacking the proprietors' abilities to manage their colony than in assisting the Delawares. With the information that Charles Thomson gathered, Quakers compiled a record of the Delawares' "alienation" from the English during the war. The

---

fairs, 1750–1775, microfilm, APS; Jennings, *Empire of Fortune,* 346–347; Boyd Stanley Schlenther, "Training for Resistance: Charles Thomson and Indian Affairs in Pennsylvania," *Pennsylvania History,* L (1983), 191–198.

35. Thomas and Richard Penn to Peters, Dec. 8, 1757, Richard Peters Papers, 1697–1845, V, pt. 1, HSP; *MPCP,* VIII, 246–259; Jennings, *Empire of Fortune,* 328. For the many investigations of land purchases, see The Walking Deed Purchase investigation, nos. 18–32, Penn Papers, Indian Affairs, IV, 1733–1801, Indian Walk, HSP (see also nos. 39, 40, I, 1687–1753). The copies of the 1730s deeds, recreated in 1757 and 1758 by the commissioners investigating Teedyuscung's charges of fraud, were themselves incomplete; dotted lines and dashes marked the pages where "the Writing in the original is eat away by Mice or Insects." Ironically, the 1757–1758 copies are today stained and disintegrating and may soon add another layer of confusion to the historical record.

Friendly Association and the Quaker commissioners for Indian affairs, greatly concerned with the outcome of the government's inquiry, also rushed to get copies of "any Minutes of the Governor and Council of this Province relative to Indian Affairs" to find out the "true State of the Indian Claims on the Lands in this Province." A barrage of land deeds and treaty records in hand, Quakers presented the evidence directly to the king, asking that he investigate the matter and make a final decision about the land-fraud issue. Benjamin Franklin, in London on the Assembly's business and being no friend of the Penns, agreed to bring the petition to the king's Privy Council for investigation.[36]

The king's investigation languished for years. William Johnson, the royally appointed superintendent of Indian affairs, however, acted immediately, adding another layer of colonial intervention to the frontier situation. Angry that Quakers had appropriated his diplomatic role, Johnson actively denounced them to the king. To assure his own primacy in Indian affairs, he maintained that the Iroquois, his principal allies, controlled all decisions for Pennsylvania Indians. Johnson blocked the Delaware land claims but also helped to reconstruct Teedyuscung as an impotent leader with no business in politics. Two years earlier, the English had accepted Teedyuscung as the lead negotiator for the Delaware peace process, yet by July 1758 Johnson declared to the governor that "he is not the consequential person he hath pretended to be in your Indian proceedings, and that he is . . . a Tool made use of by some in your Province." The Six Nations, also willing to forgo past promises to maintain their own position of power vis-à-vis the English, took their cue from Johnson. They, too, disclaimed Teedyuscung's authority. In the fall of 1758, they denied having any political connection with him, alleging that "he was a Stranger to them." By the early 1760s, most Indians in Pennsylvania viewed Teedyuscung with pity rather than respect, and, "being desirous of living in peace and Friendship with our Brothers the Proprietaries, and the good People of Pennsylvania," Teedyuscung reluctantly agreed to "bury under Ground all Controversies about Land" and "Sign a Release for all the Lands in Dispute."[37]

36. Friendly Association Minutes, January 1757, Cox-Parrish-Wharton Family Papers, box 18, HSP; Jennings, *Empire of Fortune,* 333.

37. Johnson to Denny, July 21, 1758, Manuscript Papers on the Indian and Military Affairs of the Province of Pennsylvania, 1737–1775, APS; Benjamin Chew Journal,

In essence, the battle for dominance in North America took place as much in treaty conferences as on the field. There the war of words and images shaped the history and future of Indian-white relations. Although words could not destroy life as guns or disease could, as Euramerican and native American leaders manipulated the language of diplomacy and the treaty record words determined the political boundaries and balance of power in Pennsylvania. Teedyuscung lost his crucial battle partly because white colonial leaders were less interested in creating or placating Indian allies than in using the proceedings to promote their own political agendas and to enhance their own reputations. Quakers and their proprietary antagonists accused each other of inciting the catastrophes of war, especially the surprising and damaging attacks on frontier settlements in 1755 and 1756. Such violent conflicts were not supposed to happen in Pennsylvania, where careful negotiations throughout the first half of the eighteenth century had brought relative peace to the colony and its diverse communities. Quakers in the Assembly and proprietors and their agents had neglected to keep these complex alliances in balance and increasingly blamed the marginalized frontier inhabitants for their own failures. Ultimately, this political war of words, along with the trope of the demon Delaware, would contribute to the growing rhetorical arsenal that solidified racial boundaries between Indians and whites in the 1760s.

Oct. 15, 1758, Easton treaty, Indian Papers, HSP; *MPCP*, VIII, 190, 194, 740; Sullivan et al., comps., *Papers of Johnson*, III, 786.

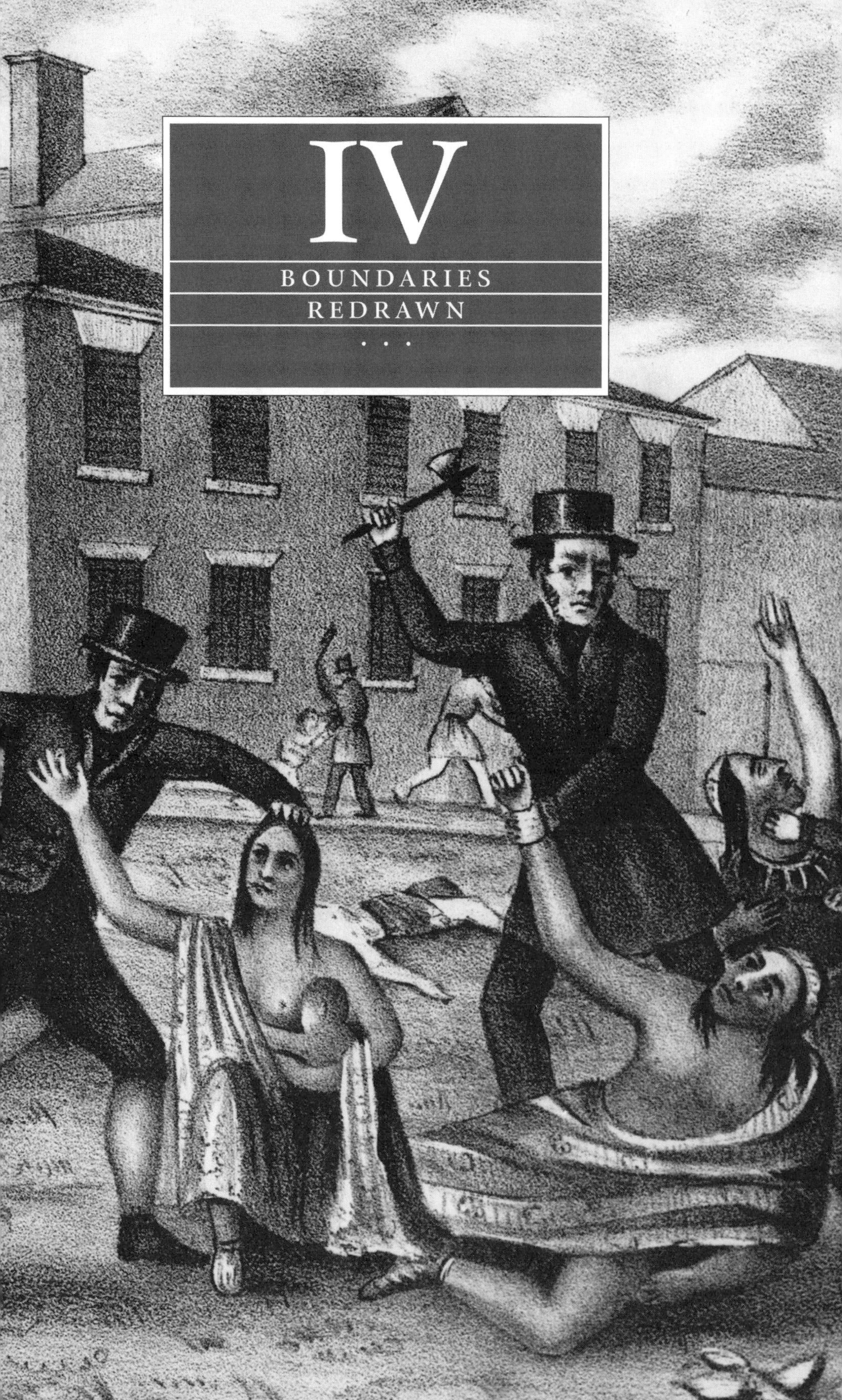

IV

BOUNDARIES REDRAWN

. . .

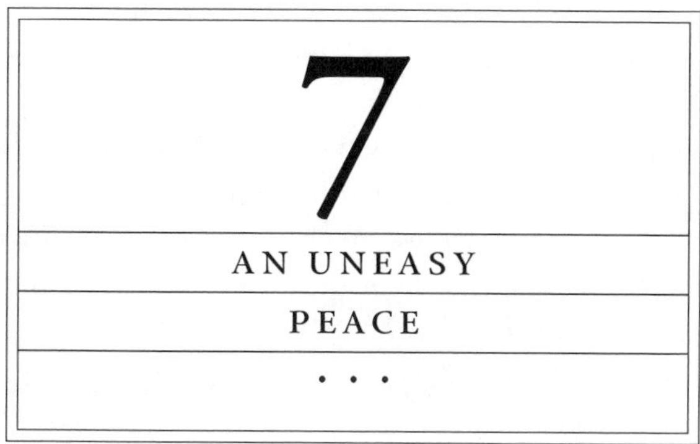

7

AN UNEASY PEACE

By the end of 1758, although the Seven Years' War raged on elsewhere, the Indian war in eastern Pennsylvania and the Ohio Valley had effectively come to an end. Until the summer of 1763, however, the peace was an uneasy one. Despite factionalism among whites, the English eventually obstructed efforts to determine the genealogy of Pennsylvania land claims and acquisitions, leaving the Delawares without a historic claim to territory and, thus, without an indisputably permanent place for community. By collaboration, the Iroquois and Pennsylvania proprietors had denied the Delawares' past of political independence and autonomy. Yet, through these diplomatic struggles, neither the Iroquois nor the English had completely dominated or completely dictated the actions and political life of Pennsylvania Indians.

Although Teedyuscung began to lose his power as a leader by the end of 1758 and the Delawares once more assumed tributary status to the Iroquois, remnant Indian groups established new political alliances with other refugees, even creating small confederations to keep their bearings in a sea of change. Instead of ethnic alliances, region became more important to political ties. Ohio Indians, including some Iroquois, acted independently of their eastern kin, and, by the early 1760s on the upper Susquehanna River, Wyalusing Indians, including Nanticokes, Conoys, Mahicans, Munsees, and Tuscaroras, spoke separately from their western brethren but with "one Mouth" and "as one Man." Within the eastern alliances, Indians who had left the Moravian mission towns before or during the war as part of the Christian diaspora emerged as leaders in refugee communities. When Delaware and Mahican leaders on the Susquehanna River, about fourteen or fifteen miles from Wyoming, met with Teedyuscung in June 1758 to discuss the next step in fulfilling the treaty settlement of the previous fall, several Indians baptized by the Moravians had prominent roles at the council. Those present included the Delawares "Memenwoot, or Capt. Augustus," "Mampoohalind, or David," "Alamerochum, or Jonathan," "Nalananguenund, or Paulus," and Mahican "Welawamick, or Moses." Christian affiliation carried less weight than it once had, at least in Indian circles. Now identified by their native names first, these leaders would help determine the new face of Indian politics and identity in the years to come.[1]

The Seven Years' War and the subsequent struggle to control the peace process in Pennsylvania had also rearranged political alliances within the white community. Quakers, although key to diplomacy during the 1750s, found themselves reviled publicly by the proprietors' agents and the general public, since they had taken the unpopular position of supporting Delaware land claims. The Quaker leadership of the Friendly Association aroused strong personal animosity among political opponents that verged on violence. Benjamin Chew, a proprietary lawyer, privately admitted in October 1758 after running into Quaker Israel Pemberton on the streets of Easton that he "only wanted a fair Opportunity to hit him a slap in the Chops." The struggle for power over Indian policy did not stop at the Pennsylvania borders. William Johnson, the British superintendent of Indian affairs stationed in New York, continued to argue with the proprietors, the Pennsylvania governor, Assembly members, and the Friendly Association over their respective roles in Indian affairs.[2]

As Indians and whites charted an awkward diplomatic course between Delaware complaints, Quaker ideals, Iroquois demands, and proprietary powers, Shingas's vision of reconciliation that would bring skilled Euramerican craftsmen and traders to Indian-controlled communities seemed unworkable. Although most Indians had retreated far from white frontier settlements to the upper reaches of the Susquehanna River or west to the Ohio, points of contact and potential conflict remained. Trade

1. *MPCP,* VIII, 132–133, IX, 46. In early 1761, Jo Peepy acted as speaker for "the Three Nations of Indians"—Nanticokes, Conoys, and Oneidas—north of Wyoming (VIII, esp. 566).

2. Benjamin Chew Journal, Oct. 17, 1758, Easton treaty, Indian Papers, HSP. Francis Jennings, *Empire of Fortune: Crowns, Colonies, and Tribes in the Seven Years War in America* (New York, 1988), 344–345, contends that Chew's own ambitions to become provincial chief justice led him to fabricate inflammatory information about Quakers, Pemberton in particular.

and diplomacy brought Indians and whites together at frontier forts on the Susquehanna and in the Ohio Valley. Even remnant Christian mission communities near Bethlehem continued to have social and economic ties to nearby whites. Many white settlers, however, like those arriving from Connecticut in the late 1750s, believed that Indians had lost their rights to share common ground in Pennsylvania, since some had taken up arms against the English. Temporary misunderstandings, which in earlier decades could be mitigated through kinship rituals or local diplomacy, took on greater significance in the postwar period. The passionate struggles for power in treaty councils during the war had generated a rhetoric of difference that articulated divergent ideas of both the past and future. If the tentative peace of 1758 was to become a lasting one, Indians and whites would need to negotiate a mode of interacting that could bridge these discrepancies without conflict. More and more, Pennsylvanians looked for permanent means of marking political boundaries to separate Indians physically from non-Indians, although they disagreed about how to create these boundaries and what they meant.[3]

For Great Britain and Pennsylvania, creating a boundary on the frontier meant enforcing policies that protected and controlled white settlers while maintaining economic ties with Indians. Provincial armies and colonial militias thus increasingly dictated the terms for Indian travel, migration, and contact with whites. The Pennsylvania government laid the foundations for regulating the frontier during the early years of conflict. Upon the request of the proprietors in late 1755, the Assembly commissioned a militia and built a series of forts to protect white settlements. By 1758, these forts acted as gateways for diplomacy and trade, where delimited interactions between Indians and whites could take place. Settings such as Fort Allen, constructed on the ruins of the Moravian mission town at Gnadenhütten, or Fort Augusta, built near the now-abandoned Indian town of Shamokin, became the places "where the Susquahannah Indians

3. Peter C. Mancall, *Valley of Opportunity: Economic Culture along the Upper Susquehanna, 1700–1800* (Ithaca, N.Y., 1991), 72, asserts that boundaries between peoples came in the late 1760s, when "tribal sachems and provincial officials alike realized that only a firm boundary between their peoples would allow them both to maintain their own economies and live in peace, a goal they thought could be attained." "By 1768," he continues, "stability demanded segregation." Yet, throughout the late 1750s and early 1760s, both Indian and white leaders demanded some form of separation.

are by Treaty obliged first to come to, when they arrive on Our Frontiers." The military, as the only visible authority on the Pennsylvania frontier, took charge of Indian policy at these remote locations after the war. Fort commanders, such as James Burd, Joseph Shippen, and Samuel Hunter, were gatekeepers, leaders of a police force that oversaw the activities of Indians and whites alike. The new protocol attempted to make Indian-white relations predictable, orderly, and profitable.[4]

Fort Augusta, in particular, became a major point of contact between Indians and whites on the frontier by the late 1750s. When construction first began in the summer of 1756, Governor Robert Hunter Morris thought that the fort's location at Shamokin would help sway the course of treaty negotiations with Teedyuscung and be a "means of securing the Sasquahana Indians to our Interest." Morris's successor, William Denny, further hoped that the fortified post could protect white settlements against Indian attack from the west and also serve as a center for the Indian trade in the east. Denny considered Fort Augusta the initial step to a lasting peace, a trading post that would entice once-hostile Delawares and Shawnees to return from the Ohio, thus creating a human buffer of allied Indians at the Susquehanna. As incentives, he set aside goods and land for their use. After meeting with Susquehanna Delawares in the spring of 1757, Denny appointed Indian trader Thomas McKee to oversee the future resettlement of Indians around Fort Augusta. McKee's personal experience with the trade and the contacts he had through his Shawnee wife made him an ideal candidate for reestablishing economic alliances with Indians. The governor, confident in McKee's diplomatic and managerial skills, instructed him to put aside "several Spots of Land near Fort Augusta, already cleared and fit for planting." "I woud have you purchase a proper Quantity of Indian Corn," he wrote, "and see that it be planted as soon as you get there." Still, Denny wanted to keep Indians at arm's length and had little money to spend on their welfare. He told McKee "to be as frugal

4. Jennings, *Empire of Fortune*, 255; Sally Schwartz, *"A Mixed Multitude": The Struggle for Toleration in Colonial Pennsylvania* (New York, 1987), 210; General Council of Cumberland County, Oct. 23, 1755, Lamberton Scotch-Irish Collection, I, 23, HSP; Petition, Robert Erwin to Robert Hunter Morris, Aug. 21, 1756, *PA*, 1st Ser., II, 757; William Denny to James Ambercromby, Apr. 7, 1758, in James Sullivan et al., comps., *The Papers of Sir William Johnson*, 14 vols. (Albany, N.Y., 1921–1965), II, 814; Michael N. McConnell, *A Country Between: The Upper Ohio Valley and Its Peoples, 1724–1774* (Lincoln, Nebr., 1992), 147.

as possible." "The more the Indians hunt, the more it will conduce to their Health. When their Demands are reasonable, and for Things absolutely necessary, they are to be granted, but not otherwise."[5]

Despite their desire to reestablish economic ties and provide a place for Indian settlement after the war, the governor and his gatekeepers felt great ambivalence about those who gravitated to Fort Augusta in 1757. By June, nearly one hundred Indians had arrived at the old site of Shamokin, though most did not come as permanent residents, as the governor had hoped. Instead, many needed only food. "They were a Starving up this River and were coming to Fort Augusta for Flour, and that agreeable to the Promise of the Governor and Commissrs. to them; They Expected to find large Store of Indian Goods here where they wou'd be allways supplyed." Colonel James Burd, the commander in charge of completing Fort Augusta, simply called them "Devilish Sods of Indians that every now and then Interrups me." He and Thomas McKee noted that even those who had been allies or friends harbored anger and resentment from the war. Thomas King, an Oneida leader among the refugees at Fort Augusta during the summer of 1757, "did not prove so free or familiar" as McKee had expected. When asked "which of his People he wou'd leave here" to help build the new Indian community, King obliquely "replied that he wou'd leave none but what died here." Indians, too, had emerged from war much more unsettled and suspicious, reluctant to discuss openly their future plans.[6]

By 1758, however, after the final capitulation of eastern Delawares, encounters at Fort Augusta became less tense. Delawares en route to Philadelphia made sure to pay their respects to the commander at Fort Augusta, stopping to smoke a calumet (a ceremonial pipe) as "an expressive Em-

5. Robert Hunter Morris, September 1756, Simon Gratz Collection, French and Indian War, 1756, box 18, case 15, HSP; "Instructions from William Denny to Thomas McKee," May 24, 1757, Shippen Family Papers, II, HSP; *MPCP,* VII, 550. For a thorough study of the evolution of Shamokin and Fort Augusta, see James H. Merrell, "Shamokin, 'the very seat of the Prince of darkness': Unsettling the Early American Frontier," in Andrew R. L. Cayton and Fredrika J. Teute, eds., *Contact Points: American Frontiers from the Mohawk Valley to the Mississippi, 1750–1830* (Chapel Hill, N.C., 1998), 16–59.

6. Col. James Burd to Denny, June 16, 1757, Shippen Family Papers, Letter Book of Col. James Burd, 1756–1758, HSP; Burd to Edward Shippen, July 25, 1757, Shippen Family Papers, III, HSP; *MPCP,* VII, 597.

blem of Friendship." Indian families could once more come and go as they pleased—to hunting cabins for seasonal trapping, to Nescopeck for family visits, to Bethlehem for spiritual needs, or to Easton and Philadelphia for diplomatic missions. Within the span of two weeks at Fort Augusta in early 1758, "three Mingo Hunters" arrived to sell their skins; King Nutimus and his family, including "his Sons Joseph and Pontus, his Grand-Daughter, and 4 Children, a Negro-Man and 2 Negro Women," came down by canoe from Nescopeck; a "Young Indian Man and 2 Women" made the trip upstream from Conestoga; and "Job Chillaway a Delaware and his Wife with a few Skins, from the Munsey Country at Heads of the Cayuga Branch above Diahoga" came to trade. Some, such as Job Chillaway, who was "determined to live among his Brethren the English wth whom he has always enjoyed peace and Friendship," sought refuge from still-hostile Indians to the north and west.[7]

Whether to trade skins or to seek asylum, native Americans arrived at the frontier post after 1757 hoping to create and manipulate the same kind of alliances they had before the war, to negotiate relations of mutual self-interest with whites. Like his father before him, John Shickellamy acted as go-between for the Six Nations, carrying messages from Conrad Weiser, agent for the Pennsylvania government, to the Iroquois by way of Fort Augusta. Once a powerful leader at Shamokin, Shickellamy retained a certain amount of leverage over white activities along the Susquehanna River. The Pennsylvania government sought his advice and endorsement when planning improvements to the fort or its vicinity. When the army began building a road from Tulpehocken to Fort Augusta in 1760, they asked Shickellamy for "the Consent of the Indians." The fort commander sought similar approval to extend some "fences as far upon the Plain as we Please that his People will have no objection to our making any improvements necessary for the garrison." Shickellamy did not object. For Indians, the road at Augusta meant access to cheaper English goods, and the garrison provided protection. After several years of war and hardship, Indians were eager for the return of trade.[8]

7. "Journal of Capt. Jos: Shippen at Fort Augusta, Shamokin," Jan. 4, 9, 10, 18, Feb. 15, 1758, Shippen Family Papers, HSP; Joseph Shippen to Burd, Jan. 20, 1758, Shippen Family Papers, 1701–1856, Military Letter Books of Joseph Shippen, 1756–1758, HSP.

8. Hugh Mercer to [Burd?], Apr. 23, 1760, Shippen Family Papers, V, HSP; Fort Augusta Diary, Feb. 17, 1760, June 11, 1763, Burd-Shippen Papers, 1708–1792, APS;

Economic exchange also remained a key component of Indian policy for the English. Quakers, in particular, hoped to use the trade to recapture a small amount of control over Indian affairs. By 1758, William Johnson had wrested Indian diplomacy from the hands of the Quakers, forcing Teedyuscung and the Delawares to deal directly with him as an agent of the British crown. Ironically, Quakers found themselves cooperating to a certain extent with the Pennsylvania governor and Assembly to keep control of one aspect of Indian affairs, the trade. As publicly appointed commissioners of Indian affairs and members of the privately organized Friendly Association for Regaining and Preserving Peace with the Indians by Pacific Measures, Quakers established and operated trading posts at Fort Augusta and the later-liberated Fort Pitt. In the summer of 1758, the commissioners for Indian affairs hired Quaker merchant Nathaniel Holland to negotiate and manage the Indian trade at Fort Augusta. Quakers were less concerned about profit than with maintaining goodwill between Pennsylvania and the Susquehanna Indians, which would keep economic exchange open and the Friendly Association's role in these political alliances secure. They heavily subsidized the trade from private donations and appropriation of public funds through the commissioners of Indian affairs. The number of furs and skins exported from Pennsylvania had dropped precipitously during the war, with a meager £876 worth in 1758. Although trade increased as frontier hostilities subsided, the Quakers had to make up for substantial losses. Between May 1, 1758, and November 3, 1760, for instance, the trade at Fort Augusta cost the commissioners more than £7,582, and it only produced £5,376 and 14s. in revenue. Still, trade brought Indians back to the region, which pleased the governor. According to James Burd, by 1760 the refugee Indian population at Fort Augusta was "seldom less then 100 Indians here and often 200 and upwards."[9]

Meeting between Capt. Francis Johnson, Commissioner Peter Bard, and John Shickellamy, Aug. 7, 1760, no. 58, Logan Family Papers, 1664–1871, XI, Indian Affairs, HSP.

9. Friendly Association Minutes, June 21, 1758, Cox-Parrish-Wharton Family Papers, box 18, HSP; Miscellaneous business file of John Reynell Papers, July 1758, Gratz Collection, 1343–1928, Commissioners of Indian Affairs, Letters, 1759–1765, box 10, case 14, HSP; Ledger, 1758–1765, Trade at Fort Augusta, Records of the Proprietary Government, Commissioners of Indian Trade Accounts, 1758–1766, RG-21, microfilm 0597, roll no. 1, Pennsylvania State Archives, Harrisburg; Burd to Henry Bouquet, Mar. 1, 1760, in S. K. Stevens et al., eds., *The Papers of Henry Bouquet* (Harrisburg, Pa., 1951–), IV, 475. For each of their general accountings between May 1758 and 1765, the

Trade revenue might have flagged, but Quakers profited politically. During this period of uneasy peace, their store at Fort Augusta was considered a neutral meeting ground, an informal arena for diplomacy when conflict arose between Indians and whites. And, even though the war had ended for Susquehanna Delawares, discord still lay close to the surface. For instance, in February 1760, west of the Susquehanna River, Delaware Indian Doctor John and his son were "found dead and scalped, his Cabbin plundered, and his goods taken away, and there is reason to believe that a Woman and child, the other part of his Family, are likewise killed, as they are missing and hitherto cannot be found." The governor, apprehensive about the potential for renewed frontier violence, offered a reward of one hundred pounds for the capture of those responsible. In addition, he wanted to meet with native leaders along the Susquehanna to reassure them that he would act swiftly to "discover the authors" of this "most cruel murder" and, according to Indian custom, would perform "any Ceremonies it were proper and usual on this Occasion." At Fort Augusta, Commander James Burd asked Quaker merchant Nathaniel Holland "to Acquaint all the Cheeffs of the Indians that I had a message to deliver them from the Governor" and suggested that they meet at Burd's house "to day or tomorrow at any hour." The Indians, however, refused to "come into the Fort," fearing Burd would "cut them all off." Instead, they agreed to meet at the Quaker store, where Burd assured them that the governor would do all he could to capture the murderers.[10]

James Hamilton, who succeeded William Denny as governor in 1760, had good reason to fear reprisal. Despite the truce, Indians and whites mistrusted each other, even as they resumed economic activities. White

---

commissioners lost money on the trade. Only on Sept. 16, 1765, did their books balance out because of a large donation from "the New Commissioners." See also "The Province of Pennsylvania with the Commissioners for the Indian Trade, Appointed by an Act of Assembly Passed in the Third Year of King George the Third," Frank M. Etting Collection, Pemberton Papers, 1654–1806, II, shelf 3, book 29, HSP. For export figures, see Stephen H. Cutcliffe, "Colonial Indian Policy as a Measure of Rising Imperialism: New York and Pennsylvania, 1700–1755," *Western Pennsylvania Historical Magazine*, LXIV (1981), 242. Eric Hinderaker, *Elusive Empires: Constructing Colonialism in the Ohio Valley, 1673–1800* (New York, 1997), 33–34, further explores the use of trade as a tool of empire building in western Pennsylvania.

10. Gov. James Hamilton to Burd, Feb. 22, 1760, Shippen Family Papers, V, 15, HSP; *MPCP*, VIII, 455; Fort Augusta Diary, Feb. 26, 27, 1760, APS.

settlers, who had returned to their frontier farms, and Delawares on the Susquehanna acted on threats and rumors; mere suspicions became the motive for revenge. In May 1760, under pressure from the Pennsylvania government, several Scots-Irish men from Paxton and Lancaster County confessed to the murder of Doctor John. They had heard that the Delaware boasted of killing sixty white people and capturing six more during the war. Angry about the death of his own kinsman during the September 1756 raid on Kittanning, Doctor John had recently threatened to "kill and Scalp" another white prisoner should war break out again. Confessions notwithstanding, the province moved slowly to bring the white men to trial. The case was still open two years later when three of Doctor John's relations arrived in Philadelphia and demanded news from the governor. The Friendly Association once more intervened, offering presents to the visiting Delawares and promising to expedite the legal process. But Quakers themselves walked a fine line between mediating mistrust and generating further conflict. Although Quakers acted as go-betweens and contributed diplomatic gifts, white settlers more often suspected that the Quaker trade simply gave Indians a greater capacity for revenge. Indians traded skins for powder and lead, since it was essential to their ability to hunt and survive, but whites suspected these arms would just as easily be used against them. James Irvine, the store clerk at Fort Augusta in 1763, felt caught in the middle and "at a loss." Whereas frontier settlers resented the sale of "ever so trifling a quantity of Powder" to Indians, native hunters accused him of forcing "them to take part against us by depriving them of the Means of Subsisting among us." Either way, a bad situation on the Susquehanna River could only become worse.[11]

Although eastern Delawares had agreed to end hostilities by 1758 and nominally accepted Fort Augusta as a major site for trade and diplomacy, western Delawares and other Indian groups in the Ohio had not participated but watched the outcome of diplomatic encounters with interest. The provincial government, fearing that Ohio Indians would assist

11. Deposition of Richard Davis, Mar. 7, 1760, Deposition of John Loughry, May 6, 1760, *PA,* 1st Ser., III, 706, 731; *MPCP,* VIII, 709–712; Minutes of the Friendly Association, May 6, 1762, Cox-Parrish-Wharton Family Papers, box 18, HSP; James Irvine to the commissioners, June 30, 1763, Reynell Papers, Gratz Collection, 1343–1928, Commissioners of Indian Affairs, Letters, 1759–1765, box 10, case 14, HSP.

the French, hoped to regain their allegiance. The government's three-part policy included diplomatic overtures, conducted by Moravian missionary Christian Frederick Post, to restore good relations with Ohio Delawares and Shawnees; a military campaign, led by Brigadier General John Forbes, to defeat the French and recapture Fort DuQuesne; and, finally, economic opportunities, overseen by Quaker merchants, to maintain the fur trade with Indian tribes in the west. Ohio Indians, tired of the war and disillusioned with the French, also initiated peace talks. Ideally, the treaty conferences would yield agreement about territorial boundaries and economic interactions. In reality, the uneasy peace of 1758 created a new set of problems predicated on an emerging sense of nationalism among Indians and laid the foundation for renewed conflict in the west.[12]

The Pennsylvania government and William Johnson, the British superintendent of Indian affairs, hoped that diplomacy in the west would help to subdue Ohio Indians to the same extent that it had subdued Indians east of the Alleghenies. In the spring of 1758, with the cooperation and encouragement of the Six Nations, who also hoped to subjugate western Iroquois and Delawares, Governor Denny called on several mediators to initiate contact with Ohio Indians. Although Denny had been frustrated by Teedyuscung's persistent claims to land, he asked the Delaware and his family to act first as military agents and then as diplomatic go-betweens. Teedyuscung provided kinship networks and community ties that would open roads to western diplomacy. Many Ohio warriors had lived at the Forks of the Delaware in the early eighteenth century, and some even came from Teedyuscung's Unalachtigo Delaware band. From Fort Augusta in April, Teedyuscung's sons, Johann Jacob (also known as Captain Bull) and Amos, and his nephew and his wife's brother traveled to the Ohio Valley. They presented "three large Belts" to Delaware leaders Shingas and Tamaqua (the Beaver), who had emerged as an advocate of peace. The two brothers agreed to make contact with the Pennsylvania governor. In June 1758, Teedyuscung met with the Ohio Indian delegates at his home on the Susquehanna River, accepted the calumet and wampum that those representatives carried, and escorted Pisquetomen, the third and elder Delaware brother, to Philadelphia to meet the governor. Although kinship ties

12. Richard White, *The Middle Ground: Indians, Empires, and Republics in the Great Lakes Region, 1650–1815* (New York, 1991), 249–255; McConnell, *A Country Between*, 113–141.

made Teedyuscung and his sons reliable messengers for the English and astute diplomats for western Indians, he was dismissed as a go-between once he introduced the Ohio delegates to Governor Denny. To Denny, Teedyuscung had completed his task as liaison for two more powerful allies, the English and Iroquois. The governor then focused on dominating the Ohio Indians.[13]

In the summer of 1758, the governor hired Moravian missionary and colonial agent Christian Frederick Post, who also had Delaware kinship connections, to gather more direct information about the inclinations of Ohio Indians and to finalize peace initiatives in the west. Post first traveled to the Wyoming Valley to confer with Teedyuscung and meet delegates from Ohio. Post reminded them all that he "had been twice married" to Indian women and assured them that he could be trusted, for he "had a great Love towards their Nation, and would speak very free with them." Pisquetomen, sent by his brother Tamaqua to mediate between the Ohio Delawares and the Pennsylvania government, agreed to escort Post west later in the summer. Post, in turn, whose second wife had been a Delaware—from Teedyuscung's clan, no less—had "much conversation" with Pisquetomen to hammer out an acceptable proposal for peace. Still, that kinship tie did not ameliorate the bitter political rivalry between the Delaware leader and Post. Teedyuscung, jealous about losing his position as diplomatic liaison, tried to dissuade Post from his mission. According to Post, in July Teedyuscung attempted to lay "many obstacles in my way," warning Post that he would be killed in Ohio and that he should only go as far as the Susquehanna River, lest he put his life in danger.[14]

After arriving in the Ohio Valley in August 1758, Post cautiously said

13. Burd to Denny, May 3, 1758, Shippen Family Papers, Letter Book of Burd, 1756–1758, HSP; *MPCP,* VIII, 84, 96; "Journal of Capt. Jos: Shippen at Fort Augusta, Shamokin," Mar. 9, 10, 16, 1758, HSP; William Patterson to Burd, Jan. 21, 1759, Shippen Family Papers, IV, HSP; Jennings, *Empire of Fortune,* 387; McConnell, *A Country Between,* 126–127. Johann Jacob and Amos were cousins of Killbuck, a Delaware warrior with Shingas and Tamaqua. See James Kenny, "A Journal to the Westward," June 1, 1759, HSP; "Christian Frederick Post Journal to the Ohio," in Reuben Gold Thwaites, ed., *Early Western Travels, 1748–1846* (Cleveland, Ohio, 1904), I, 211 n. 45.

14. *MPCP,* VIII, 144; Michael N. McConnell, "Pisquetomen and Tamaqua: Mediating Peace in the Ohio Valley," in Robert S. Grumet, ed., *Northeastern Indian Lives, 1632–1816* (Amherst, Mass., 1996), 285–287; "Christian Frederick Post Journal to the Ohio," Aug. 4, 1758, in Thwaites, ed., *Early Western Travels,* 187, 190.

little about his kinfolk, knowing that Ohio Delawares under Tamaqua harbored suspicions about eastern Delawares' renewed status as props of the Longhouse. Indeed, although there were close bonds between their communities, Tamaqua distrusted Teedyuscung because of the Pennsylvania Delaware's close association with the Six Nations and their English allies. They feared Teedyuscung might step beyond his role as a neutral intermediary and help the Iroquois establish dominance in the west. Ohio Indians had not taken part in the peace negotiations with Susquehanna Delawares in 1756 and 1757 because of these suspicions. Instead, western Delawares and Shawnees created a separate confederacy and refused to accept the Six Nations as overlords. After watching Teedyuscung transformed from a critic of the English and Iroquois to an agent of both, Ohio Indians preferred to take their own course, using Post as intermediary. During August, Post and Pisquetomen made their way to Kuskuski, a collection of four Delaware towns northwest of Fort Duquesne, to speak with Pisquetomen's brothers, Tamaqua and Shingas. They then proceeded to Logg's Town to present a larger group of Delawares and Shawnees with Pennsylvania's invitation to a treaty conference.[15]

Despite their willingness to meet with Post in late August and early September 1758, the Delawares distrusted Euramerican motives and were unwilling to declare their allegiance to the English. The war had proved to be one fought for only British or French interests, leaving the Indians in a dangerous position between the two powers. Not everyone welcomed Post at Logg's Town. Some young warriors menacingly drew their knives. Even the older and more prudent leaders remained skeptical. An Onondaga chief rose during one session and, using a derogatory term for "white man," addressed the assembly: "I do not know this *Swannock;* it may be that you know him. I, the *Shawanese,* and our father [the French] do not know him." Tamaqua assured Post that "all our young men, women and children are glad to see you" as they sat down for a three-day feast to mark the reopening of diplomatic relations with Pennsylvania, but he expressed

15. "Christian Frederick Post Journal to the Ohio," July 21, Aug. 15, 1758, in Thwaites, ed., *Early Western Travels,* 187, 195; Jennings, *Empire of Fortune,* 394; "Report of Charles Thomson and Christian Frederick Post to the Governor," June 1758, nos. 49, 50, 51, "Journal of Christian Frederick Post Journey from Philadelphia to Wayomick, June 20, 1758," no. 52, Penn Papers, Indian Affairs, III, 1757–1772, HSP; McConnell, "Pisquetomen and Tamaqua," in Grumet, ed., *Northeastern Indian Lives,* 286–287.

more skepticism in his formal remarks. Speaking for his brothers and village, Tamaqua informed Post that "we have great reason to believe you intend to drive us away, and settle the country; or else, why do you come to fight in the land that God has given us?" One of Tamaqua's compatriots, Shamokin Daniel, put it less delicately: "D[am]n you, why do not you and the *French* fight on the sea? You come here only to cheat the poor *Indians*, and take their land from them." Other Delawares worried that the provincial government would retaliate for their wartime activities: "When we lived among you, as sometimes it would happen, that our young men stole a horse, kill'd a hog, or did some other mischief, you resented it very highly, we were Imprisoned etc. Now, we have kill'd and taken so many of your people, will you heartily forgive us and take no revenge on us." Still, despite their criticisms and concerns, the Ohio Delawares agreed to send word by Post that "all Indians from the sunrise to the sunset should join the peace" with the English, if the English, in turn, agreed to leave the Ohio Valley.[16]

Western Indians had good reason to be wary, since diplomatic efforts by the provincial government came at the same time that the British military presence in the west steadily grew. Whereas Governor Denny used Indian kin networks to help open metaphoric roads that would lead to the treaty table, the British army wanted to extend physical roads across Pennsylvania that would link military posts and aid in communication between English fighting units. In 1758, Brigadier General John Forbes, with the assistance of Colonel Henry Bouquet, had already begun to build the road that would bear his name across Pennsylvania in an attempt to recapture Fort Duquesne from the French. He stationed troops along an extended military line between Fort Augusta and their intended target. Forbes also depended on native neutrality, if not military assistance, to succeed in his goal. He supported the diplomatic mission of Christian Frederick Post and made his own overtures to potential native allies, but he often had little luck managing those alliances once negotiated. Even his most trusted military allies eventually became elusive. In April 1758, nearly one thousand Cherokees joined the British before they marched through Pennsyl-

16. "Christian Frederick Post Journal to the Ohio," Aug. 23, 24, 28, Sept. 1, 1758, in Thwaites, ed., *Early Western Travels*, 201, 212, 213; Speech of Ackowanothio, September 1758, *PA*, 1st Ser., III, 548–549; "The Speech of Ackowanothio," Penn Papers, no. 63, Indian Affairs, III, 1757–1772, HSP. See McConnell, *A Country Between*, esp. 113, for the rise of Tamaqua as king of the western Delawares from 1758 to 1760.

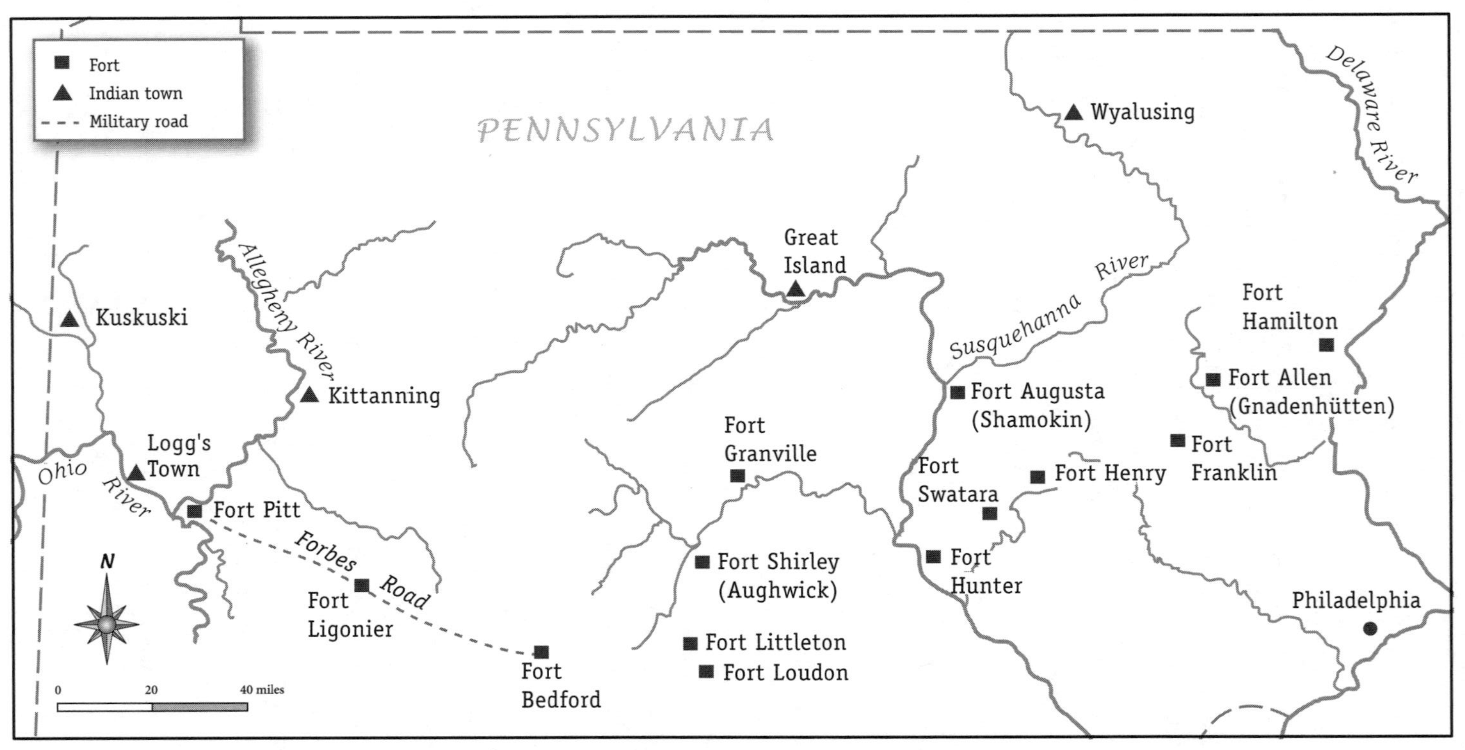

MAP 6. System of Colonial Forts by 1758. *Drawn by Gerry Krieg*

vania. Forbes preferred them to the Delawares, who, "when all collected together, would not make a breakfast to the Cherokees." "So," he wrote, "I am very clear of giving those last the preference in everything." By August, however, the company chaplain complained that a group of Cherokees, who "had receiv'd the best of Treatment, besides very valuable Presents—basely deserted us, without acquainting any Person with their Design." Forbes did not help matters by vocalizing his growing irritation with most of the Indian allies. Besides Cherokees, Catawbas, Ottowas, and Tuscaroras also incurred Forbes's anger. By the time his troops reached Rays Camp in October 1758, he had run out of patience with "the most imposing Rogues that I have ever had to deal with." He thought Indian allies cost Britain "incredible sums of money, and except about 14 Catawbas who have behaved well at major Grants affair, no one other tribe has done any one piece of service."[17]

Wary of English intentions, Indian allies had their reasons for initially accepting gifts and promising to fulfill alliances but ultimately withdrawing their military assistance. Nearly seven hundred warriors, many from the south, slowly left Forbes's service during the summer and fall of 1758. They complained that Forbes plodded slowly across Pennsylvania, leaving them too easily exposed to enemy attack. The Cherokees feared the English would prove duplicitous, perhaps mobilizing Iroquois and Delaware warriors against them. Even the Ohio Delawares, to whom Forbes finally offered more favorable treaty arrangements, distanced themselves from the fighting. They assured Post that they would participate in the council at Easton and would not help the French but declined Forbes's subsequent invitation to move back to the Susquehanna and into the provincial sphere of influence.[18]

17. Burd to Joseph Shippen, Dec. 29, 1759, box 2, "Return of the First Battalion," July 10, 1760, box 3, Burd-Shippen Papers, Letters, APS; Bouquet to John Forbes, June 3, 1758, in Stevens et al., eds., *Papers of Bouquet,* II, 15; Forbes to Major General James Abercromby, Apr. 24, Oct. 8, 1758, in Alfred Procter James, ed., *Writings of General John Forbes Relating to His Service in North America* (Menasha, Wis., 1938), 72, 226; Rev. Thomas Barton, "Journal of an Expedition to the Ohio Commanded by His Excellency Brigadier-General Forbes," Aug. 8, 1758, HSP; George Croghan to William Johnson, Jan. 30, 1759, in Sullivan et al., comps., *Papers of Johnson,* X, 91.

18. Jennings, *Empire of Fortune,* 376; "Christian Frederick Post Journal to the Ohio," Aug. 28, 1758, in Thwaites, ed., *Early Western Travels,* 214; Forbes to Bouquet, June 27, July 17, 1758, in Stevens et al., eds., *Papers of Bouquet,* II, 135, 224.

The treaty conference at Easton in October 1758 was a pivotal moment for Indian-white relations in Pennsylvania and, consequently, the Seven Years' War. Besides the crucial question of military support for Forbes in the west, the conference helped to consolidate new political alliances among Indian groups, although it also exacerbated some familiar rivalries. Larger and more fractious than earlier meetings, the council drew representatives from many conflicting Euramerican parties. Antiproprietary members of the provincial Assembly faced off with proprietary agents, and William Johnson's deputy George Croghan clashed with Quaker Israel Pemberton. Indians jockeyed for position as well. The small, but crucial, contingent of western Delawares led by Pisquetomen bristled at the numerous Iroquois from the Six Nations, who envisioned the conference as key to affirming their power over all Pennsylvania Indians. Like previous years, Teedyuscung attended as the leader of a loose assortment of Susquehanna Indians, but he stood as one voice among many, effectively isolated by Iroquois leaders.[19]

The western Delawares assured the Pennsylvania governor that they wanted to reestablish the past "Peace and Friendship," which had been destroyed during the war, but, like Teedyuscung and the eastern Delawares, they also wanted to use diplomacy to redefine their relationship with the Six Nations and to force the removal of English settlers from land they claimed in the west. Pisquetomen pointedly told delegates that the Iroquois had undermined their initial participation in the negotiations by delaying the delivery of a peace belt in early 1758, as Forbes's army marched west. He insisted that the Six Nations had no power over Delawares, nor could they speak for any Ohio Indians at the conference. Teedyuscung, however, subverted Delaware autonomy when, after years of resisting, he formally capitulated eastern Indian political power to the Iroquois ten days into the conference. The Six Nations found other ways to put pressure on the Ohio Indians, whom they still thought of as subordinate. They entreated William Johnson to force Thomas Penn to give them back portions of the Albany Purchase on which Delawares and Shawnees now lived. During the conference, Conrad Weiser, as agent to the Penn family, restored all the land "Westward of the Allegheny or Appalaccin

19. Fred Anderson, *Crucible of War: The Seven Years' War and the Fate of Empire in British North America, 1754–1766* (New York, 2000), 274–279; *MPCP,* VIII, 192.

Hills" to the Six Nations as part of his and the governor's pledge to keep white settlers from the west.[20]

Although the Easton treaty settlement ostensibly made landlords of the Iroquois, their tenants, the Ohio Indians, were not displeased. Despite the Six Nations' power over future land sales and the future of native habitation, Indian control of the west allowed Delawares to demand a territorial boundary line to separate themselves from the English. And only when assured of political independence from the Six Nations did Pisquetomen agree to cease hostilities and sign the treaty. More difficult for the relatively new confederation of Delawares and Shawnees in the west would be holding the English to their part of the bargain, which, as they understood it, included returning the Ohio Valley to its native inhabitants. When Pisquetomen and Post returned to Ohio in November 1758 (this time on the heels of General Forbes's repossession of Fort DuQuesne from the French), Delawares and Shawnees converged on the newly named Fort Pitt to hear Governor Denny's message from Easton. Tamaqua and his brother, happy that the army would prevent white settlers from moving west but still wary of the English military presence, insisted that, like the French, British troops should also withdraw from their territory. Ketiuskund, a Delaware headman who had accompanied Pisquetomen to the Susquehanna that summer, gave Post an ultimatum: "If the *English* would draw back over the mountain, they would get all the other [Indian] nations into their interest; but if they staid and settled there, all the nations would be against them; and he was afraid it would be a great war, and never come to a peace again." Foreshadowing the Proclamation Line five years later, Indians wanted clear boundaries drawn between themselves and whites to indicate diverging national interests and to protect their access to land.[21]

20. *MPCP,* VIII, 187–188, 204; Jennings, *Empire of Fortune,* 402–403; Anderson, *Crucible of War,* 277–278.

21. "Christian Frederick Post Journal to the Ohio," Nov. 29, 1758, in Thwaites, ed., *Early Western Travels,* 278. Early the next year, Colonel Bouquet wrote General Forbes about subsequent negotiations with Ohio Delawares. Far less sympathetic than Post was, Bouquet said, "The Delawares say that you or I have promised them to withdraw the troops from the Ohio as soon as the French for their part have evacuated their forts and the country on this side of the lakes" (Bouquet to Forbes, Jan. 15, 1759, in Stevens et al., eds., *Papers of Bouquet,* III, 52). See also McConnell, *A Country Between,* 132.

Yet boundaries between nations were often more ambiguous or permeable than either Indians or whites described them. They did not, for instance, preclude the presence of English traders in the Ohio. The Easton agreement made Fort Pitt a gateway for trade and diplomacy between Indians and whites, much like Fort Augusta at Shamokin. But the post also became a point of contention for control over that trade and Indian affairs in the west. General Forbes wanted a trading post at Fort Pitt to reinforce Indian dependence on the English. Indians, too, desired English goods once the French abandoned the trade in the vicinity. Commerce did not assure peaceful relations, however. Distrust between Indian hunters, English traders, and army officers lingered, and, as at Fort Augusta, British agents and Quakers battled to regulate prices, trading, and each other at Fort Pitt. In April 1758, William Johnson appointed George Croghan as his representative, and by early 1759 the Pennsylvania governor agreed to send him to Fort Pitt to oversee the Indian trade. Croghan insisted that "he had Authority for to Regulate the Trade and to see that the Indians are not wronged." In particular, Croghan competed with Quaker merchants who arrived in the Ohio around the same time. His animosity toward Quakers had begun years prior, when he sided with Johnson against the Friendly Association and their eastern Delaware associates. At the Easton treaty conference in October 1758, he had helped to weaken the Quakers' diplomatic role. Once in the Ohio, Croghan accused the commissioners of Indian affairs of cheating Indians by not paying enough for the furs and skins that Indian hunters exchanged. Quakers leveled similar charges against Croghan. The commissioners had hired Quaker James Kenny to open a store at Fort Pitt in early 1759. Kenny thought that Croghan and the military commander provided too much alcohol to the Indians living nearby or visiting Fort Pitt. Croghan did his share of drinking and fighting with Indian hunters, but Kenny also accused Croghan of undermining the Quaker trading enterprise by stealing his provisions. In August 1759, before Kenny could retrieve a bundle of wampum he had expected in a general shipment from Philadelphia, "Geo. Croghan saw it and kept it," promising to pay Kenny back sometime in the future.[22]

22. George Allen to commissioners, July 2, 1759, Simon Gratz Collection, 1343–1928, Commissioners of Indian Affairs, Letters, 1759–1765, box 10, case 14, HSP; John W. Jordan, ed., "James Kenny's 'Journal to the Westward,' 1758–59," *Pennsylvania Magazine of History and Biography*, XXXVII (1913), 425, 437–439.

Whether trading with Croghan or Kenny, Ohio Indians complained that in the post-treaty period they received much "less than what the Traders formerly gave" for skins and furs. After the disruptions of war, Ohio Indians were in dire straits; extreme poverty plagued their communities. Many of the warriors that joined the English troops at Fort Pitt arrived "entirely naked except the Moccasons Shirts and Leggings they have received," and most relied on some form of assistance to survive. Low fur prices made them further dependent on trade and the English at Fort Pitt. Angry at the British stranglehold on trade and their stingy gift giving during diplomatic meetings, Delawares and Shawnees resorted to other means of getting things they needed. Killbuck, a Delaware warrior who had signed the Ohio agreement to renew English alliances at Easton, turned to "Villiany," according to Colonel Hugh Mercer at Fort Bedford. In August 1759, Killbuck took sixteen horses from the army "and scalped the driver who reclaimed them." Beyond economic necessity, the motivations driving Killbuck and other Indians to commit "Insults upon The Road" point to their resentment of low trade prices and the continued British military presence.[23]

After 1758, the British army leadership attempted to monitor and control the consequences of renewed encounters along "the Road" that had been opened between the east and western Pennsylvania. This road brought Indians and whites together again. It led Croghan and Kenny to Fort Pitt to trade with Delaware and Shawnee hunters and provided Indian warriors with an avenue for political resistance and retaliation. But for Colonel Henry Bouquet, the commander at Fort Pitt, the road represented the hard-earned advancement of British colonial authority. He now planned to teach Indians the proper protocol for their behavior in a British world. When Ohio Indians complained about trading practices and turned to petty theft, Bouquet simply increased trade regulations. He made Fort Pitt into a fortress, denying Indians entry, further alienating them from English interests. He prohibited the white inhabitants of Pittsburgh, especially unauthorized traders, from selling liquor to Indians "under penalty of the offenders having their Houses Pulled down,

23. *MPCP*, VIII, 385; Col. Hugh Mercer to Brig. Gen. John Stanwix, Aug. 12, 1759, Bouquet to Mercer, Aug. 16, 1759, in Stevens et al., eds., *Papers of Bouquet*, III, 545, 571, 591. Horses seemed to be a favorite target for Indians near Fort Pitt. See also Bouquet to Robert Monckton, May 15, 1761, ibid. V, 482.

their Stores plundered and being themselves Banished this place." Bouquet sometimes punished particular Indian groups for their actions. In May 1761, after a rash of horse stealing, Bouquet dispensed a standing order "to forbid all Traders And other [of] his Majestys Subjects at this Place to Trade with Any Indian of the Shawanese nation, without first obtaining the Commanding officers leave for that purpose."[24]

As the English presence became more permanent and military control more prohibitive, Ohio Indians increasingly found themselves pressured by the colonial demands of the British and the Six Nations. They created intertribal alliances to counter these political pressures and to help secure resources for their economic survival. They demanded territorial boundaries to hold back the potential tide of Euramerican settlement on their lands. In defining new strategies for survival, Ohio Indians began to act less as individual clans or communities, and they more often spoke of themselves and their situation in terms of region or national identity. They even began to call upon a relatively new cosmology of separate creation to justify the need for boundaries between Indians and whites. At the Easton treaty in the fall of 1758, the Ohio Delawares drew color lines as they articulated national differences between themselves and the English. According to Pisquetomen, all Euramerican colonists were "of one Nation, and one Colour" and sought to make peace with "the Nations of my Colour." In 1760, Shawnees, emphasizing that Indians were literally oceans apart from the English, told George Croghan that "God who made all things gave us this Country and brought us through this Ground, he gave you a Country beyond the Great Water." Together they could forge "a Silver Chain of friendship," but, just as the Nanticoke dreamer had suggested nearly a decade earlier, the creator sanctioned physical separation. Although Ohio Indians publicly stated that separate creation and the difference of "Colour" between nations justified territorial boundaries, native American concepts of group identity were still predicated on kinship rather than race. By demanding and constructing claims to land, however, Pennsylvanians of all colors edged closer to defining more rigid concepts of who belonged on one side or the other of those boundaries.[25]

24. Bouquet to Mercer, July 13, 1759, "Orders concerning Pittsburgh Inhabitants," Oct. 8, 1760, "Order Limiting Trade with Shawnees," May 13, 1761, all in Stevens et al., eds., *Papers of Bouquet*, III, 410, V, 470, 477, 482.

25. Easton treaty, Oct. 13, 1758, in Carl Van Doren and Julian P. Boyd, eds., *Indian Treaties Printed by Benjamin Franklin, 1736–1762* (Philadelphia, 1938), 223–224; Treaty

Like Ohio Indians, many natives on the Susquehanna, although willing to trade with the English, also believed that some sort of physical boundary should be drawn to separate Indians and whites. They, too, wanted a buffer to protect their access to land and resources. Yet, like the Ohio Indians, defining these demarcations proved difficult. As early as 1757, Teedyuscung announced his intentions to settle a group of Delawares at the Wyoming Valley and insisted that the governor "have certain Boundaries fixed, between you and us; and a certain Tract of Land, fixed, which, it shall not be lawful, for us, or our Children, ever to sell, nor for you, or any of your Children, ever to buy." Still, Teedyuscung planned to adapt certain useful aspects of an English way of life. He requested that Pennsylvania help the Delawares build "different houses from what we have done heretofore, such as may last not only for a little time, but for our Children after us." He believed that frontier posts, such as Fort Augusta, would provide protection as well as "a fair Trade" for his permanent Indian settlement. By 1758, the Pennsylvania governor had appointed several commissioners "for constructing a Stockade Fort and buildg a Number of Houses for the Accommodation of the Indians at Wyoming," after which the Friendly Association sent carpenters to complete the construction in the spring of 1758 and "to encourage the Indians to plant and settle there this Spring." With Quaker support, Teedyuscung further requested "two Ministers to teach me, that my soul may be instructed, and Saved at Last" and "two Schoolmasters, for there are a great many Indian Children who want Schoolmasters. One, therefore, is not sufficient to teach them all." Just as Teedyuscung found it necessary to use English methods of writing to seek political advantage at treaty conferences during wartime, he recognized that Indians at peace also had to find ways to understand and negotiate with their increasingly dominant white neighbors.[26]

---

conference at Fort Pitt, Apr. 7, 1760, Indian conference at Fort Johnson, Sept. 10, 1762, in Sullivan et al., comps., *Papers of Johnson*, III, 211, X, 506; Gregory Evans Dowd, *A Spirited Resistance: The North American Indian Struggle for Unity, 1745–1815* (Baltimore, 1992), 30; Nancy Shoemaker, "How Indians Got to Be Red," *American Historical Review*, CII (1997), 629–633.

26. [Charles Thomson], *Causes of the Alienation of the Delaware and Shawanese Indians from the British Interest* (Philadelphia, 1867) (originally published as *An Enquiry into the Causes of the Alienation of the Delaware and Shawanese Indians from the British Interest* . . . [London, 1759]), 115; Easton treaty conference, July 28, 1757, in Van Doren

Not all Indians agreed about the role that English culture and politics would play in their communities. More specifically, many Indians distrusted Teedyuscung and resented his ties to the English. Some thought he had adopted the wrong kind of white behavior and had begun to act too much like an agent for English interests. According to Will Sock, a Conestoga Indian who occasionally worked as a messenger for George Croghan, by 1758 the Susquehanna Indians "would not be Commanded by Teedyuscung who is reported as one that wants to make English Men of the Indians and bring them under English Government, and reign over them as his Vassals." They complained of Teedyuscung's personal behavior in public, especially his increasing use of alcohol, which became a problem at the October 1758 Easton treaty conference. In August 1760 at Pittsburgh, Teedyuscung showed up at another council meeting to receive "an equal share of the presents," although he did not participate, "being either too Drunk, or not permitted by the other Indians, who seem'd to be all ashamed of him and treated him with great contempt."[27]

Indians did not necessarily reject the culture or financial assistance that the English offered. Even Will Sock assured the Pennsylvania governor that, despite their disgust with Teedyuscung, the Indians on the upper Susquehanna "are well affected to the English, and no danger of Breaking with them again." But Teedyuscung's invitation to Quaker carpenters, ministers, and schoolmasters opened up the possibility of further white settlement and revived old territorial issues between the Iroquois and their reluctant subordinates. Quaker Isaac Zane, commissioned by the Friendly Association to help complete the Delaware houses at Wyoming, found that some Iroquois "were Dissatisfied with the building on this land for the Delawers without having the consent of 6 nation Indians to whome this land belongs." The Six Nations also claimed title to nearby land on which Shawnees lived, causing tension among Indians in the region. Some Indians took out their frustration on those whites who professed to help them. On May 27, 1758, as the Quaker delegation completed the ten houses for Teedyuscung, a group of "Enemy Indians" "kill'd and Scalped" one of

---

and Boyd, eds., *Indian Treaties*, 197–198; Croghan to Denny, *PA*, 1st Ser., III, 248–249; *MPCP*, VII, 730, VIII, 47; Joseph Shippen to Burd, Oct. 23, 1757, Shippen Family Papers, III, 1–169, HSP; Friendly Association Minutes, Apr. 11, 1758, Cox-Parrish-Wharton Family Papers, box 18, HSP.

27. *MPCP*, VIII, 120–121; Monckton to Richard Peters, Aug. 15, 1760, no. 92, Penn Papers, Indian Affairs, III, 1757–1772, HSP.

the masons. Over the succeeding years, resentment of the English persisted. On the way home from a long trip to the Ohio Valley in June 1760, Christian Frederick Post and his companion John Hays ran into one of the Shawnees who had "Kill'd Mr. Kroker at Waiomick" two years earlier. Angry and, according to Post, "half Drunk," the Shawnee picked up a large stick and "struck Mr. Hays across his Back that the Blood gush'd out, and then rid away full gallop."[28]

The Shawnee's visceral reaction yielded immediate satisfaction, but it masked a deeper sense of impotence in the face of white encroachment. Delawares, Shawnees, and Iroquois might have haggled over which tribe ultimately owned the upper Susquehanna River, but, like the Ohio Valley Indians, by the early 1760s natives in the east found that outside intruders proved the more persistent competitors for land. From the early 1750s, New Englanders had been interested in the Wyoming Valley as a potential site for expansion. Connecticut and Pennsylvania both claimed rights to the land, and in 1753 a group of Connecticut investors had created the Susquehanna Company, which began petitioning their colonial Assembly for permission to establish a settlement at Wyoming. The company had supposedly secured a deed to land from members of the Six Nations at the Albany Conference in July 1754 for 1,705 Spanish dollars. The Iroquois rightfully complained that they had been persuaded to sell the valley under false pretenses. A minister, Gideon Hawley, had lived among them, promising "to instruct the Indians in the Principles of the Christian Religion, and to settle a Mission there under a Scotch Society." But, instead, Hawley and his compatriot Timothy Woodbridge persuaded the Iroquois to sell the Wyoming Valley to a representative of the Susquehanna Company, John Henry Lydius, who negotiated the land deed with a few Iroquois in Albany outside open council, leaving the details hidden from colonial officials and the leadership of the Six Nations. Whether disingenuous in their indignation or in fact deceived, those Iroquois who had signed Lydius's deed complained that he took "Indians slyly by the Blanket one at a time," got them drunk, gave them some money, and "perswades

28. *MPCP,* VIII, 120–121, 134; Joseph H. Coates, ed., "Journal of Isaac Zane to Wyoming, 1758," *PMHB,* XXX (1906), 421, 424; Christian Frederick Post, Journal, June 17, 1760, HSP. The Shawnee, Pashechqua, had been retained as a member of their escort back to Wyoming and Easton. Post learned that the entire escort was hostile to them: "Exceedingly disagreeable to us, they were all from that Town which had threaten'd to Roast us" (ibid., June 19, 1760).

them to sign deeds for our lands upon the Susquehanna which we will not ratify nor suffer to be settled by any means."[29]

Despite the accusations of fraud, in the summer of 1760 the first group of Connecticut settlers under the auspices of the Susquehanna Company moved west to Pennsylvania. Initially, they built a town at Cushietunk on the Delaware River, with a deed of purchase from Delaware Indians in hand. They also brought with them certain assumptions about Indian relations, predicated on their own experience with New England Indians, who had been defeated and subdued nearly a century before during King Philip's War. They did not recognize the Indian policies developed under the proprietorship of William Penn and ignored the authority of the current governor of Pennsylvania, James Hamilton, and the superintendent of Indian affairs, William Johnson. The Cushietunk settlers ultimately planned to take Susquehanna land they claimed under the Lydius deed and warned that "if the Indians who lived there should hinder their Settlement they would fight it out with them, and the strongest should hold the Land." By 1761, the group began to assert their claims to the Wyoming Valley more forcefully, first by sending Timothy Woodbridge to "prepare the minds of the Indians" for the arrival of the New Englanders, if not to intimidate them to leave. By September 1762, nearly one hundred armed men had finished cutting a road from the Delaware River settlement at Cushietunk to the Susquehanna, insisting that their deed from the Six Nations was still valid.[30]

The Delawares in Wyoming, exasperated with both the Connecticut interlopers and their Iroquois landlords, asked the Pennsylvania government to intervene. At a treaty conference in Easton in August 1761, Teedyuscung, who still spoke for his small band, reprimanded the Six Nations, pointing out that his "Uncles" had "took me by the Hairs of my Head and shook me," forcing the Delawares to live at Wyoming in the first place.

29. Deed signed between July 11, 1754, and Mar. 4, 1755, Report of John Penn to Richard Peters, and "Extract from the Journal of Ezra Stiles, Containing the Journal of Stephen Gardner on the Susquehanna, June 4–July 1, 1755," all in Julian P. Boyd, ed., *The Susquehannah Company Papers,* 10 vols. (Ithaca, N.Y., 1962–1971), I, 101–121, 124, 284; Edmund B. O'Callaghan and Bethold Fernow, eds., *Documents Relative to the Colonial History of the State of New-York,* 15 vols. (Albany, N.Y., 1856–1887), VI, 984; Jennings, *Empire of Fortune,* 107.

30. Meeting of the Pennsylvania Council, Apr. 6, 1761, in Boyd, ed., *Susquehannah Company Papers,* II, xxiv, 70–71.

Slipping in a caustic reference to the Walking Purchase, Teedyuscung reminded them that "the Reason why I complied with your first Request was, Because I thought you would give me the Lands at *Wyoming* in the Room of Some of Our Lands you had Sold the English." "Now again you desire me to move off from thence and would place me some where Else." Other Indian nations settled in the Wyoming Valley agreed with Teedyuscung on this point. Conoys, Mahicans, Nanticokes, Senecas, and Cayugas also hoped to create permanent communities of their own. They, too, had often been invited by the Six Nations to settle on new territory, just to have the land sold out from under them. As an alternative, the Wyoming Indians asked colonial administrators to create a permanent homeland for them. After Teedyuscung censured the Six Nations at Easton, another delegation of Indian leaders arrived in Philadelphia to ask the governor and his Council to draw up a deed for Wyoming land in the name of "Jo Peepy and Isaac Stille, not for themselves, but for the Delawares, that they may take it and get it signed by the Six Nations; for we are afraid these Lands may be taken from us." With legally recognized title to land and a legal boundary between themselves and outsiders, Indians could keep white settlers at a distance and cut their ties to the Six Nations.[31]

Although Governor Hamilton agreed that land had been reserved for Delaware use by the Six Nations in the 1740s, an arrangement specifically acknowledged by the English at the treaty of Easton in 1757, he refused to provide Indians with deeds or legal title to the land. Hamilton instead washed his hands of the matter and lay responsibility for the situation in Wyoming at the feet of the Iroquois. He contended that "these Lands were not purchased from the Six Nations, and that therefore he could not meddle with them at all, nor Draw any Deed about them, because the six Nations might take offence at it." The Iroquois, on the other hand, insisted that they had not been responsible for selling land at Wyoming to Lydius or the Susquehanna Company and believed that, since it was an English colonial matter, Pennsylvania should evict the Connecticut settlers. Hamilton, however, was reluctant to press the case against the New En-

31. Minutes of Easton treaty, Aug. 11, 1761, in Boyd, ed., *Susquehannah Company Papers,* II, 112; *MPCP,* VIII, 660. Teedyuscung also asked for a deed to land in Wyoming so his "Children and Grandchildren would live there as long as the World lasts" (Conference at Easton, Aug. 5, 1761, in Van Doren and Boyd, eds., *Indian Treaties,* 251).

glanders, even though the presence of whites in Wyoming created a delicate situation that might lead to renewed war with the Indians. He initially petitioned his counterpart in Connecticut, Thomas Fitch, asking him to prevent his people from settling in Pennsylvania. The Connecticut government, much like Pennsylvania, disavowed any control over the private investment company. In other words, neither Pennsylvania nor the Six Nations nor Connecticut wanted to take responsibility for the situation, and Delawares and other Susquehanna Indians found themselves caught in the middle.[32]

With no legal impediment to their settlement, nearly 150 white men arrived at Wyoming in the summer of 1762 to establish their community. Indian women and children hastily fled to the woods, frightened by "the Approach of such a Number of Armed men into their Country." Native men, concerned with their families' safety, but more incensed at trespassers on their land, confronted the Connecticut settlers "with their Guns and Tomahawks, (which was afterwards confirmed by the Indians themselves) and demanded to know their Business." Augustus, now a leader among the Christian Delaware diaspora, along with several other Susquehanna chiefs "ordered the Connecticut people to go away, and quit the Land," threatening to kill them if they did not comply. Through the concerted efforts of the Indians at Wyoming, the Connecticut settlers left, but they returned the following spring, ready once more to begin construction.[33]

Mutual threats and increasing tensions between Indians and whites in the Wyoming Valley finally forced the Pennsylvania government to take action in the spring of 1763. Yet, by that time, their response on behalf of aggrieved Indian nations was too little and too late to prevent renewed violence. In mid-April 1763, Teedyuscung was found burned to death in his cabin. Although the Delaware leader had many enemies, both Indian and white, and the responsible party never was discovered, most inhabi-

32. *MPCP,* VIII, 600, 660–661; Peters to Johnson, May 18, 1761, in Boyd, ed., *Susquehannah Company Papers,* II, 97.

33. Narrative of Daniel Brodhead's journey to Wyoming, Sept. 27, 1762, in Boyd, ed., *Susquehannah Company Papers,* II, 167, 169; *MPCP,* IX, 7. In November 1762, the Ohio Indians under Tamaqua sent a belt of wampum to Teedyuscung, inviting the Delawares and Mahicans settled at Wyoming to remove to the Allegheny as a temporary measure. The Delawares, who had been removed several times before, rejected the offer (*MPCP,* IX, 8).

tants along the Susquehanna assumed that some of the New Englanders had killed him. Teedyuscung's death and the threat of Indian retaliation prompted the British government to intervene. The Board of Trade and the king pressured Connecticut to remove their settlers immediately, and William Johnson, in his capacity as superintendent of Indian affairs, urged Thomas Penn to consider "the fatal consequences wh[ich] would infallibly attend such a Settlement." In June 1763, "having received fresh Complaints from the Indians at Wyoming," Governor Hamilton finally issued a proclamation "requiring those Intruders forthwith to remove from the said Lands." He then commissioned James Burd and Thomas McKee as justices of the peace to remove the white settlers from Wyoming and take their leaders to jail at Lancaster. The governor's actions momentarily calmed some Indians' fears. Telenimut, a Six Nations representative, with Delaware interpreter Job Chillaway, visited James Burd at Fort Augusta to voice their approval: "This Gladness I feel at my Heart; and Nutimus, Tepascowan and Wawpaway do the same, and if anything happens, we will lett you know as two Brothers ought to do." But others thought that the provincial government had accomplished little or nothing. By the end of June, Teedyuscung's son, Captain Bull, disgusted by the governor's reluctance to act quickly on their behalf and tired of the changing whims of Iroquois landlords, packed up his household and moved to the West Branch of the Susquehanna River, "to the Long Island, the New England People being in Possession of their Lands." There he would bide his time and seek retribution in his own way.[34]

The Seven Years' War and its aftermath created both the motive and the means for a new wave of migration across the mid-Atlantic that once more

34. Johnson to Thomas Penn, May 18, 1763, "Order of the King in Council," June 15, 1763, and "Instructions from the Privy Council to Thomas Fitch," June 15, 1763, all in Boyd, ed., *Susquehannah Company Papers*, II, 218, 244–246, 255, 256; *MPCP*, IX, 27; Speech sent by Col. Burd and Thomas McKee, June 10, 1763, "Answer to the Message Sent from James Burd and Thomas McKee," both in Shippen Family Papers, VI, 17, 25, HSP; James Irvine to the commissioners, June 26, 1763, Reynell Papers, Gratz Collection, 1343–1928, Commissioners of Indian Affairs, Letters, 1759–1765, box 10, case 14, HSP; Anthony F. C. Wallace, *King of the Delawares: Teedyuscung, 1700–1763* (1949; reprint, Syracuse, N.Y., 1990), 258. From 1756 on, various whites and Indians threatened to kill Teedyuscung. See, for instance, "Journal of Charles Thomson and Christian Frederick Post," June 16, 1758, *PA*, 1st Ser., III, 421.

destabilized frontier communities. Faced with potential violence and limited resources, many inhabitants abandoned their towns to search for new land farther west or refuge in more settled regions. Once again, roads, both metaphoric and real, provided people with ways to negotiate uncertainty. By the early 1760s, treaty agreements and a system of military roads and forts brought Indians and whites together for trade and diplomacy. Mobility, however, caused new tensions and conflicts. Indians and whites on the margins of empire again competed for access to land, where commanders at military forts and trading posts both invited their presence and cursed the consequences of their actions. Familiar power dynamics between colonial authorities and their dependents also muddied the course of Indian-white relations. The Six Nations attempted to dominate Indian groups of the Susquehanna and Ohio River valleys, but, since they also used those communities and their land for political leverage with English colonial authorities in New York and Pennsylvania, they unwittingly opened the region to white settlement, such as the immigrants from New England. Pennsylvania proprietors, Quakers, and British agents still battled for dominance over Indian affairs. Each tried to control trade as a tool of empire building or local power while placating Iroquois allies to avoid a renewed Indian war. Caught in the middle, Delawares and Shawnees attempted to negotiate a path for themselves, clear of colonial machinations. After attempting various social means to secure territory, whether by alliances of kinship, ethnicity, or religious affiliations, they turned to new political alliances and confederations to set themselves off as distinctive nations and to demand permanent separation from white settlers.[35]

In the fall of 1763, Shingas, Tamaqua, and Teedyuscung got their boundary line after a fashion. Influenced in part by the confrontations between Indian and white settlers in the Wyoming Valley, King George's proclamation for peace with France on October 7, 1763, included provisions for a dividing line "to reserve under Our Sovereignty, Protection, and Dominion, for the Use of the said *Indians,* all the Lands and Territories . . . lying to

35. William Johnson speech, May 5, 1765, *PA,* 1st Ser., IV, 327; Croghan to Benjamin Franklin, Oct. 2, 1767, in Howard H. Peckham, ed., *George Croghan's Journal of His Trip to Detroit in 1767 . . .* (Ann Arbor, Mich., 1939), 23. Again, in 1768 at Fort Stanwix, the Iroquois and the English attempted, but failed, to define a permanent boundary. See White, *Middle Ground,* 351.

the Westward of the Sources of the Rivers which fall into the Sea from the West and North West." The Proclamation Line placed power over western expansion firmly in the hands of British authorities. For the time being, most of Iroquoia and the West Branch of the Susquehanna River remained under Indian control. The proclamation, however, did not suggest, at least to the British crown, Indian political independence. The king gave native Americans one thing they wanted, a secure dividing line between Indians and whites that helped define new national identities. He strictly forbade "on Pain of Our Displeasure, all Our loving Subjects from making any Purchases or Settlements whatever, or taking Possession of any of the Lands above reserved, without Our especial Leave and Licence for that Purpose first obtained." But the king, like William Penn a generation before, still saw Indians as "our good Subjects"—under his protection and, thus, also under his authority. Native Americans and Euramerican colonists, however, did not agree on what constituted a "good Subject" of empire.[36]

36. Sullivan et al., comps., *Papers of Johnson,* X, 982–983; *MPCP,* IX, 60; McConnell, *A Country Between,* 249.

8

INDIAN NATIONS AND EMPIRE

• • •

By the early 1760s, lingering resentments about the atrocities of war fueled demands for national boundaries between native Americans and Euramericans. Formal lines between cultures, such as the Proclamation Line of 1763, however, did not keep people apart. Indians still lived, worked, and traded with whites after the war, and the legacy of shared spaces and common practices continued to bring Indians and whites together. Drawn by more readily available land, white settlers once more moved to the Pennsylvania frontier. These new settlers relied less on Indians for survival or as trade partners, and Indians found it more difficult to incorporate white settlers into their communities. Many non-Christian Indians from the Susquehanna had moved to the Ohio Valley during the war; still, at the end of 1763, William Johnson, the British superintendent of Indian affairs, noted that at least two hundred Nanticoke, Conoy, Tutelo, and Saponi warriors and nearly three hundred Oneidas and Tuscaroras still resided along the Susquehanna River. Although the bustling mission towns at Gnadenhütten and Meniolagomekah had been long abandoned, several hundred Christian Delawares and Mahicans and their kin lived in and around Bethlehem, Nain, and Wechquetank under the auspices of the Moravians. Fort Augusta remained a lively point of political and economic exchange for these people. If boundaries existed, they remained porous, inducing Indians and whites to renegotiate their relationship to the frontier, each other, and colonial leaders.[1]

1. James Sullivan et al., comps., *The Papers of Sir William Johnson,* 14 vols. (Albany, N.Y., 1921–1965), IV, 242; [Richard Smith and Richard Wells], "Notes of a Tour to the Head of Susquehannah in the Year 1769," folder 1, Pierre Eugene Du Simitiere Papers, Library Company of Philadelphia; Memorabilia, 1759, *Moravian Records,* reel 7, box

Not only had attempts at physical separation been ineffectual by 1763; cultural boundaries between Indians and whites had also become undeniably blurred. Because their communities had overlapped for decades, the appearance of Indian and white settlers—at least selective markers of clothing, language forms, and behavior—now reflected those encounters. This was a world where military men sent speeches and belts of wampum to Indians along the Susquehanna, asking them to "be strong and dont Herken to the French to take up the Hatchet against the English," and Indian warriors shook hands with whites and "had no Wampum and on that accound did not know what to do, but as is usual among the English" made "use of writings." And it was a world where religious white men adopted native metaphors and ritual language when preaching to Indians. Soon after the November 1755 murder of white missionaries at Gnadenhütten, the Moravians addressed a group of Nanticokes: "We have a dear and faithful Friend, that is our Creator, who is also our Brother, for He is become a man like us, and this Friend has comforted us abundantly, so that when you came, to wipe off our Tears and to clear our Eyes, He our Lord had done it long before and had already cleaned our inward Parts and open'd our Ears." Similarly, Indians incorporated Christian expressions in treaty speeches. In June 1758, a visiting Allegheny Indian at Wyoming addressed Christian Frederick Post by "Lifting up his Hands to Heaven, wished that God would have Mercy upon them and help them and bring them and the English together again, and establish an everlasting Ground and Foundation for Peace between them. He wished further that God would move the Governor and People's Hearts towards them in Love, Peace and Union."[2]

As cultural similarities increased, however, Indians and whites struggled to reestablish their differences. Native Americans reacted to the in-

---

125, folder 2. Johnson estimated that there were some "10,000 Indian Hunters" in the "Northern Department" in 1764 and encouraged the British to plan the Indian trade accordingly (Sullivan et al., comps., *Papers of Johnson,* IV, 558). See also Peter C. Mancall, *Valley of Opportunity: Economic Culture along the Upper Susquehanna, 1700–1800* (Ithaca, N.Y., 1991), 86.

2. Samuel Hunter to James Burd, June 14, 1763, Shippen Family Papers, VI, 21, HSP; Report of Newcastle's journey to Onondaga, Oct. 24, 1756, no. 104, Penn Papers, Indian Affairs, II, 1754–1756, HSP; "Nanticoke Indians in Bethlehem," no. 12, [post-1755], Penn Papers, Indian Affairs, IV, 1733–1801, Indian Walk, HSP; *MPCP,* VIII, 144–145.

tensified, or maturing, frontier, with its growing population and competition for resources, by attempting to reposition the balance of power in their favor. Pennsylvania Indians drew away from their associations with whites, such as the Moravians or individual English traders, and instead built larger confederations of Indian communities from which they could deal directly with the British Empire. To protect their land from the consequences of expanding white settlement, they created new political alliances based on region and nation, not simply clan or tribe. Delawares, Nanticokes, Mahicans, Conoys, and other small tribes in Pennsylvania approached diplomacy in the 1760s as the "United Nations of Indians," the "Three Nations of Indians," or various groupings of the "Ohio Indians." More and more, native Americans defined their political identity collectively. In essence, as Pisquetomen intimated in 1758, they began to see themselves as "Nations of my Colour," with both national and racial affiliations.[3]

White Pennsylvanians also felt uneasy with blurred boundaries, and they often tried to recreate distinctions to maintain cultural distance from Indians. Drawing boundary lines on a map was one way to define difference, or at least to maintain physical distance, between cultural groups. Yet whites also became adept at formulating metaphysical differences, especially through racial descriptors. The concepts of the noble savage/good Indian and the ignoble savage/bad Indian had existed since the first encounters between Europeans and native Americans. But the resurgence of violent confrontations along the Pennsylvania frontier in the early 1760s galvanized these images as no prior period had. Iroquois, Delawares, Germans, and English invented ideal representations of each other with their attendant histories of essential and preferred cultural behaviors to critique the problems of the immediate postwar period. Just as there were good Indians, there were good whites. During the first half of the eighteenth century, each had created and manipulated representations of noble savages and peaceful William Penns to reestablish and enforce definite and understandable rules of engagement. By appealing to these ideal images

3. *MPCP*, VIII, 566, 660; Chiefs of the Senecas, Cayugas, Nanticokes, Conoys, Mahicans, Delawares, and Opres to the Pennsylvania goveror and Council, Aug. 27, 1761, in Julian P. Boyd, ed., *The Susquehannah Company Papers*, 10 vols. (Ithaca, N.Y., 1962–1971), II, 113; Easton treaty, Oct. 13, 1758, in Carl Van Doren and Boyd, eds., *Indian Treaties Printed by Benjamin Franklin, 1736–1762* (Philadelphia, 1938), 11–12.

during the treaty negotiations of the 1740s and 1750s, for instance, Indians and whites thought they might compel the other to uphold peace for the common good. However, the diplomatic impasse reached in the late 1750s over landownership and political independence changed the nature and use of these representations. The ideal images of tolerant, caring whites and noble savages gave way to the opposite, a world inhabited by heartless white men and cruel savages. The bad Indian took on the worst traits and vices of white men. Conversely, the bad white seemed to act uncannily like a "savage."[4]

Paradoxically, these merging antitypes worked to polarize frontier communities who otherwise had much in common as they struggled to maintain their autonomy from colonial powers. For colonial leaders, frustrated by their inability to control frontier populations, these common typologies served to justify violent oppression or military action against savages of any color. White frontier inhabitants—often non-English, religious dissenters—and Christian Indians, on the other hand, were forced to define themselves in relation to the savage, to clarify the differences between themselves and those outside civilized society. Scots-Irish had competed with native Americans for land and resources for decades. They found colonial leaders unsympathetic—suspicious of their motives, condescending toward their way of life, quick to ignore them when in need and to remove them when unwanted. Yet, even as they reviled British authority, these settlers demanded participation in the English colonial world. To restore their position and privileges as subjects of the empire, they reconstructed Indians as outsiders. As they remembered and recorded the violent outcome of their encounters with Indians in the 1750s and 1760s, white settlers drew on a language of "savagism" to describe and circumscribe Indians, to differentiate themselves from their frontier rivals. Christian Indians still living among whites faced the more difficult task of defusing stereotypes. Christian Indians had adapted the markings

4. For the standard work on the noble and ignoble savage, see Robert F. Berkhofer, Jr., *The White Man's Indian: Images of the American Indian from Columbus to the Present* (New York, 1978). See also Bernard W. Sheehan, *Savagism and Civility: Indians and Englishmen in Colonial Virginia* (New York, 1980); Cornelius J. Jaenen, "'Les Sauvages Ameriquains': Persistence into the Eighteenth Century of Traditional French Concepts and Constructs for Comprehending Amerindians," *Ethnohistory*, XXIX (1982), 43–56.

of English civility. Yet their visibility within or at the margins of white communities also made them vulnerable. They, like their white counterparts, redefined themselves to clarify the boundaries between civility and savagery, between themselves and those Indians capable of violence. In doing so, they contributed to the increasingly rigid racial boundaries that separated Indians and whites by the late eighteenth century. The creation and use of these categories of behavior that drew on the supposed essential nature of Indians informed the course of events on the Pennsylvania frontier in the 1760s. Racial rhetoric displaced the nuances of the negotiated interactions that had previously characterized relations between white settlers and native Americans. The more antagonistic the relationship between frontier inhabitants, the more they turned to colonial leaders for protection, empowering the British imperial forces now occupying their land and forfeiting the independence that they had fought so hard to preserve.

As Indians in Pennsylvania tried to make sense of the incongruent actions of their white neighbors in war and in peace, they constructed a golden past in which William Penn represented the ideal model of white behavior. In 1760, the Conestogas recalled that "old William Penn" might have loved all Indians, but "there was a singular love between him and the people who came with him, and the Conestogo Indians." Teedyuscung remembered that Penn had been "adopted and received into [the Delawares'] Family as a Child." "Further that it had been formerly agreed to by all the Nations that the Delaware Country shod never be incommoded with War, but always enjoy an undisturb'd peace and Tranquility." The myth of William Penn and the vision of a Golden Age even lingered in the Ohio Valley as Indians began treaty negotiations with Penn's successors. In the fall of 1758, Ohio Delawares addressed the Pennsylvania governor through Christian Frederick Post: "Father, thy children remember the many good counsels we held with our grandfather William Penn when we first come in this country and with what great love You received us as your own children your own family and what peace and love we enjoyed with our grandfather." They had constructed the ideal white man—tolerant, loving, and compliant—and had given William Penn a revered status, adopting him as their own "grandfather." Yet Indians had not revived a mythic Penn to honor white Pennsylvanians and their seventeenth-century past. Rather, they used that past to shame the English for their recent unacceptable behavior.[5]

In the Euramerican version of the golden past, every Indian was the noble savage, the Lenni Lenape of the first meeting at Shackamaxon—his language eloquent, "lofty," and filled with "words of more sweetness or greatness" than any European tongue. Every Indian was supposed to adhere to the oral traditions of his forefathers. In October 1745, after a Mohawk interrupted the New York governor at Albany, Conrad Weiser took the wampum belts and reprimanded him: "I am Ashamed for our sakes and no doubt some of you are too, we ought to use one another well and not behave as Drunkards. I desire you will hear the Governor first and go to your Lodgings and agree upon an answer unanimously according to your old and good ways." Indians' "old and good ways" did not include angry interruptions, nor did they include writing. Or so David Zeisberger thought when he refused to write a letter for some Onondagas in July 1753, saying "that if they had any message to send to Weiser, they should do it by means of a [wampum] belt, which was a much better and surer way than by letter." Indeed, to the governor of Pennsylvania, writing for Indians was "quite a new Method, and was never practised before," as he reminded Teedyuscung many times in treaty conferences of the late 1750s. The governor preferred an ideal Indian, who acted naively within set guidelines of behavior. If only Indians were more malleable—like "Indians" and less like the English—he could understand and calculate their response, thus manipulating the political process.[6]

5. *MPCP,* VIII, 457; Christian Frederick Post, Journal, May 13, 1760, HSP. As seen by the quotation below, Post's English was nearly incomprehensible. After meeting with the Ohio Indians in late summer and fall 1758, he stopped at Fort Augusta and had several soldiers copy his notes into a readable journal form (Peter Bard to Burd, Sept. 26, 1758, Shippen Family Papers, III, 207, HSP). See C. F. Post, notes of his first journey to Ohio, July 15–Sept. 21, 1758, *Moravian Records,* reel 28, box 219, folder 3, item 1 ("Fader Dey schildern remember de menny gud counsels wi held wit auer gran fader wiliam pen wen wi first com in Dies contri en wit wat grot loff ju resieft us as jur on schyldern jur on femeli en wat pies en lof wi in schlid widauer grandfaders"). Thomas J. Sugrue, "The Peopling and Depeopling of Early Pennsylvania: Indians and Colonists, 1680–1720," *Pennsylvania Magazine of History and Biography,* CXVI (1992), 3–4, reminds us that white people also maintained myths of Penn's peaceable kingdom well into the twentieth century.

6. William Penn, "Letter to the Free Society of Traders" (1683), in Jean R. Soder-

White Christians also created ideal Indians for whom they had a variety of uses. Some held up noble savages as models of true faith to criticize their own backsliders or other whites living on the margins of colonial society. Quakers had always sanctified native Americans on some level. Quaker trader James Kenny wondered why Indians would ever want to become Christian, "Whilst they see frequently better and honester Men amongst themselves then Most English People going by that Name amongst them." In 1761, during a treaty conference at Easton, one Quaker woman admonished a group of "thoughtless, stupid" Germans to look to "those they called Heathen, [who] demonstrated by their conduct that they were nearer the Kingdom, than many of those called Christians." Even white Christians who had lived and worked closely with Indians constructed and used idealized representations. Just before and during the war, Moravians had experienced a crisis of faith when many Christian Indians left the mission communities. They described some as "impudent and hostile" and others as "sinister." After Delawares, including some who had been baptized by the missionaries, attacked settlers' plantations in 1755, the Moravians drew on the power of forgiveness to reconcile Indian violence with a sense of failure in their role as Christ's vicar among the "Heathen." August Gottlieb (Joseph) Spangenberg, surprised to see some baptized Indians, such as Teedyuscung, among the attackers, reminded the white congregations at Nazareth and Bethlehem, "Love your enemies," for the Indians "have only been slaves of Satan." He called for the Brethren to rid themselves "of all the thoughts and prejudice, which are not according to the mind of Jesus Christ," and accept Indians again in their communities.[7]

---

lund, ed., *William Penn and the Founding of Pennsylvania, 1680–1684: A Documentary History* (Philadelphia, 1983), 312–313; Treaty of Albany, Oct. 8, 1745, Penn Papers, Indian Affairs, I, 1687–1753, HSP; W[illia]m M. Beauchamp, ed., *Moravian Journals Relating to Central New York, 1745–66* (Syracuse, N.Y., 1916), 179; *MPCP,* VII, 689, IX, 8. In March 1754, Conrad Weiser complained to Richard Peters that the Onondagas had become "apostates as to their Old Natural Principle of Honesty, and become Drunkards, Rogues, Thieves, and Liars" (Weiser to Peters, Mar. 15, 1754, in Boyd, ed., *Susquehannah Company Papers,* I, 66).

7. John W. Jordan, ed., "Journal of James Kenny, 1761–1763," *PMHB,* XXXVII (1913), 182; Quaker Journal (attributed to Susanna Lightfoot), Aug. 9, 1761, Easton, Pa., 7, William L. Clements Library, University of Michigan, Ann Arbor; Johann Jacob Schmick to Br. Mattheus, *Moravian Records,* Nov. 5, 1754, reel 5, box 118, folder 5,

By the 1760s, Moravians had welcomed many Christian Indians back but expected contrition and remorse. They asked returning Indians to confess their sins and beg forgiveness from the congregation at Bethlehem. The confessions of ideal Indians provided spiritual lessons for both their white and native congregations. In addition, whites could more easily come to terms with saintly Indians and reincorporate them as neighbors and allies after the hostilities of war. Once Indians repented, however, Moravians preferred that they somehow fade into the background of a larger white world, or even die. For instance, the Delaware chief Augustus, who moved late in the war to Wyoming with Teedyuscung's urging, had been on bad terms with the Moravians for several years. In late 1762, word reached the Moravians that Augustus lay dying on the Susquehanna, torn with remorse by his departure from the mission community. He asked the Brethren, "Have pity on me and to forgive all my sins." He had presumably turned to Christ during his illness, advising his followers, "Think no more on my previous life and follow not my evil example, but think of the Savior and follow him and the Brethren." Augustus died within a week, his life and dying words recorded, translated into English and German, and circulated for years among Moravian congregations in both Europe and the American colonies.[8]

---

item 3; Diary of Nazareth, Dec. 26, 1755, English translation, Moravian Historical Society, Nazareth, Pa.

8. *Moravian Records*, Apr. 22, May 16, 1758, reel 7, box 125, folder 1, Oct. 15, 1762, reel 7, box 125, folder 3 ("die Brr. haben sich meiner erbarmet, u. mir alle meine Sunden vergeben." "Nun ist mein armes u. furchsames Herze zufrieden gestellt, u. ich werde bald zum Hld gehen. Darum denket nicht mehr an mein voriges leben, u. folgt nicht meinen böser Example, sondern denkt an den Hld, u. folgt ihnen u. der Brrn."). The Moravians also used the confessions and death of Mahican elder, Abraham, in a similar manner. *Moravian Records,* Nov. 10, Dec. 2, 1762, reel 7, box 125, folder 3, Feb. 12, 1763, reel 7, box 125, folder 3, June 13, 1763, reel 6, box 124, folder 4. For other examples of the returned, repentant, yet dying Christian Indian, see Diary of Nazareth, July 18, 1758, English translation, Moravian Historical Society; Bethlehem Register, Jan. 15, Apr. 1, 1757, July 24, Nov. 18, 1758, "Bethlehemisches Kirchen=Buch," II, from November 1756, 216–217, 233–234, 238, Moravian Archives, Bethlehem, Pa. Teedyuscung himself returned to Bethlehem several times to gain support from the Moravians, at which time he confessed that he was "now bad and his heart wretched," though he promised that "it would be better with him and he would keep with no one except the Brethren." ("Spangenberg Conversation between Moravians and King Teedyuscung, August 27, 1757," *Moravian Records,* reel 30, box

Whereas ideal Indians returned to the fold, repented, and blessedly expired, actual Indians and their continued presence in white settlements and towns represented a challenge even to Moravians. They had to be housed, clothed, protected, and integrated into white society. After the Gnadenhütten murders in November 1755, baptized and unbaptized Indians fled to the protection of Nazareth, Bethlehem, and the nearby Indian village of Nain. By January 1757, "public service[s] began to be performed in Bethlehem in the Indian language," and several hundred Indians lived either in town or camped nearby along the Lehigh River. In the early 1760s, many of these Indians moved to a new mission at Wechquetank, about forty miles north of Bethlehem. Here the Moravians contended with the problems of a mixed community of both Christian and non-Christian Indians, not to mention the resentment of white neighbors. Moravians could draw on the tenets of their Christian mission to help rehabilitate the idea of Indians as allies. Other Euramericans on the Pennsylvania frontier, however, had more difficulty fitting individual Indians into ideal categories of behavior or into their current lives. From the first attacks on white settlements in the fall of 1755, Scots-Irish and German immigrants at the Forks of the Delaware and west of Philadelphia in Lancaster County ranted about the Pennsylvania Assembly's inaction toward their Indian problem. They demanded, and finally received, government funding for forts to protect their homes. After the war, they saw something far more sinister lurking behind the repentant, saintly Indian.[9]

In 1763, the settlers' fears took form. The year before, Indian refugee communities in the Great Lakes and Ohio Valley had suffered a series of social and economic crises, including famine, epidemics, crop failures, curtailed trade, and lack of British assistance. In May 1763, the Ottawa leader, Pontiac, under the spiritual guidance of Delaware prophet Neolin and with the support of many Indian nations in the west, successfully led a coordinated attack on British posts throughout the Great Lakes region. Inspired by his resistance, Indians in western Pennsylvania initiated offensives against frontier posts at Fort Pitt, Venango, Ligonier, and Bedford. By summer, rumors spread that settlements east of the Susquehanna

223, folder 10, item 1). He managed the same demeanor with the Quakers as well; see Friendly Association Minutes, Nov. 17, 1756, Cox-Parrish-Wharton Family Papers, box 18, HSP.

9. George Henry Loskiel, *History of the Mission of the United Brethren among the Indians in North America,* trans. Christian Ignatius La Trobe, pt. 2, 182, 189.

River would soon be under attack as well. In early June, Samuel Hunter, the commander at Fort Augusta, told his superior, James Burd, that the "Indians is all gone off from about the Fort and all that was below us on the River gon upwards which is a bad omen and I believe there will come very few here to trade as there is not powder in the Province Store which has been the first article they have wanted to buy."[10]

Pontiac's uprising and rumors of renewed Indian war prompted several eastern Pennsylvania counties to organize their own militias. Governor James Hamilton, although criticized later for his delay, eventually appropriated money for seven hundred men "for the defence and protection of our Frontiers, against the Incursions of our cruel and barbarous Enemies the Indians." In Northampton County, Timothy Horsfield, a local justice of the peace in Bethlehem, was commissioned to raise troops to defend the Forks of the Delaware. German and Scots-Irish men quickly enlisted. Despite their commitment to fighting Indians, many were sometimes less than courageous in confronting their enemy. In August 1763, for example, Captain Patterson "with a party of 114 men" arrived at Fort Augusta "on their way to destroy some Indian Towns about Sixty miles up the West Branch from here." Two days later, they returned, "Disapointed of their Scheme," after running away from a Delaware war party that fired upon them. Taking an easier tack, a group of twenty-six soldiers instead waylaid "three Indians comeing from Bethlehem after dealing their peltry [and] took them prisoners." One account indicates that the three Indians "begged the Captain not to fire upon them," but the soldiers "let fly and killed them on the spot and took off their scalps." They confiscated the trade goods, including three horses, three rifles, knives, matchcoats, strouds, linen, and thread. By late summer, the militia had regular confrontations, though not always violent, with non-Christian Indians who frequently traveled to Bethlehem or Easton to trade furs.[11]

10. Richard White, *The Middle Ground: Indians, Empires, and Republics in the Great Lakes Region, 1650–1815* (New York, 1991), 271–277; Michael N. McConnell, *A Country Between: The Upper Ohio Valley and Its Peoples, 1724–1774* (Lincoln, Nebr., 1992), 182; Samuel Hunter to Burd, June 7, 1763, Shippen Family Papers, VI, 13, HSP; Fort Augusta Diary, Samuel Hunter, commander, June–December 1763, APS.

11. *MPCP*, IX, 42; Horsfield commission, July 11, 1763, Timothy Horsfield Papers, II, APS; Fort Augusta Diary, Aug. 25, 27, 1763, Samuel Hunter, commander, June–December 1763, APS; Edward Shippen to Governor James Hamilton, Sept. 1, 1763, Burd-Shippen Papers, Letters, APS; Capt. Nicholas Wetterholt's journal, Northamp-

Indians closer to home—those whom they once considered friends—now loomed as a greater threat to these reluctant militiamen. In particular, they watched with deep suspicion Christian Indians at the Moravian mission community of Wechquetank. Captain Jacob Wetterholt, a German American officer stationed at Fort Allen, often complained to the local magistrate that the Moravian Indians were allowed to travel freely and suspected that they helped enemy Indians track the militia's movements. They feared Christian Indians might themselves "fall upon the white People," and, by September 1763, the captain warned Moravian missionaries that, if he found any Indian "in the Woods far or near, I'll kill him." In late September, a group of Scots-Irish volunteers came into the mission town and vowed to do the same. To these men, golden pasts had little resemblance to the postwar present, in which the children or families of once-hostile Indians still lurked among them. For white frontier settlers, no Indian had lived up to the ideal once promoted by William Penn, despite Moravian attempts to rehabilitate their Christian converts. Instead, by 1763 they feared all Indians had the capacity to act the opposite: willfully independent, proud, enigmatic, perhaps even savage.[12]

As suspicions about Indians' loyalties coalesced in the minds of settlers, native Americans, too, had to deal with the tangible consequences of white fear and anger. Some calculated that confession to and forgiveness from Moravians or the Pennsylvania governor might protect them from random threats and bodily harm after the war. But the rise of the "bad Indian" as a prevalent negative representation in the 1760s also pushed Indians once connected to white communities by kinship, religion, or trade to react with malevolence, in essence, embracing savagery in defiance of subservient civility. Such was the response of Teedyuscung's oldest son. At age twenty, he was baptized as Johann Jacob by the Moravians, and he adopted the Christian faith, confessing "the unrest [he felt] in his heart, which he had created himself, since he had not been obedient to the Lord and the Brethren." Committed to life as a Christian, Johann Jacob married a baptized Delaware woman a few years his junior, and together they briefly

---

ton County Papers, Miscellaneous Manuscripts, 1758–1768, HSP. For scalps, see Lt. Jonathan Dodge to Timothy Horsfield, Aug. 4, 1763, Northampton County Papers, Misc. MSS, 1758–1768, HSP.

12. Jacob Wetterholt to Horsfield, Aug. 18, 1763, Northampton County Papers, Misc. MSS, 1758–1768, HSP; Wechquetank diary, Sept. 5, 1763, in English, *Moravian Records*, reel 6, box 124, folder 4, item 4, Sept. 20, 1763, reel 6, box 124, folder 4, item 4.

lived at Meniolagomekah. In 1754, however, they moved to the Susquehanna to live at Nescopeck among his relatives, and once more the context of his life shifted. Among predominantly hostile Delawares, Johann Jacob, now preferring the name Captain Bull, took part in several attacks on white settlements with his father in 1755 and 1756. At the end of 1756, he traveled to the Easton peace conference, again with Teedyuscung, and agreed to cease fighting. By the end of the decade, Captain Bull fulfilled yet another role; he began to frequent Fort Augusta on the Susquehanna, selling venison and deer pelts and offering his services as a guide and messenger for the Pennsylvania government and provincial army.[13]

Habits, choices, material circumstances, and family pressures all had a part in shaping the actions of this young Delaware as a Christian, head of household, dutiful son, angry warrior, and repentant ally. In 1763, however, the racially charged actions of white settlers against supposedly savage Indians would prompt Captain Bull to refashion himself once more. First, in April, his father Teedyuscung, who had adamantly opposed white settlement in the Wyoming Valley, was burned to death in his home on the Susquehanna, most likely by Connecticut immigrants. Then, in late summer, Captain Bull's cousin, Zacharias, a baptized Delaware, also met a violent end. Fearful of aggression by white people at the Forks of the Delaware, Zacharias had left the Moravians to live with others of the Christian diaspora at the Great Island on the West Branch of the Susquehanna River above Shamokin. When returning home in August from a visit to family members at Wechquetank, Zacharias, his wife and child, and another woman stopped briefly at Nicholas Kern's house to purchase two blankets and some cloth. Unfortunately, Captain Wetterholt and several members of the Northampton militia had stopped at Kern's the same afternoon to drink. Frustrated by rumors of hostilities and chance sightings of Indians on the frontier and certain that all Indians acted in common against them, the inebriated captain and two others followed the

13. "Der Unruhe seines Herzens, die er sich selber gemacht hätte, weil er dem Hld u. denen Brüdern nicht wäre gehorsam gewesen"; see *Moravian Records*, Feb. 2, 1754, reel 5, box 118, folder 1; Joseph Shippen to Edward Shippen, Dec. 12, 1757, Military Letter Books of Joseph Shippen, 1756–1758, Shippen Family Papers, 1701–1856, HSP; "Journal by Capt: Jos: Shippen at Fort Augusta, Shamokin," Mar. 9, 11, 1758, Shippen Family Papers, HSP; Fort Augusta Diary, June 24, 1763, Samuel Hunter, commander, June–December 1763, APS; Conference at Fort Augusta, June 25, 1763, Shippen Family Papers, VI, HSP.

three Indians to a nearby field. As Zacharias tried to "Defend him Selves with his knif," Moses Beers shot him "by Capit. Wetterhold order." The violent scene ended when Wetterholt and two of his men "kildt the Indian Woman and her boy."[14]

For Captain Bull and other Indians at the Forks of the Delaware and on the Susquehanna, this senseless murder revealed a savagery of its own kind. When Moravian missionary Bernhard Grube told Delawares at Wechquetank of the incident, Zacharias's mother, "the old Justina," cried. His brother Christian and cousin Jamy tried to recover two horses stolen from Zacharias, with little luck. When Indian hunters returned from the white settlements to Nescopeck or other native towns on the Susquehanna with word of Zacharias's death and the other "insults and robberies for which they could obtain no redress," they plotted their own responses. By early October 1763, native allies warned the commander of Fort Augusta that the Susquehanna Indians were once more preparing to attack the Pennsylvania frontier.[15]

The climate of suspicion, hostility, and fear did not bode well for Wetterholt and the small group of militiamen who decided to stop for the night at John Stenton's tavern between Bethlehem and Fort Allen on October 7, 1763. Stenton and those frequenting his establishment were known for their contempt and intolerance of Indians. The summer before, a group of Indians had stayed there after trading furs in Bethlehem. According to the Moravians, Mrs. Stenton had encouraged her white clients to rob the Indians of their goods during the night, saying "that she would freely give a gallon of rum to any one of them that would kill one of these black devils." The Indians "lodged their complaint with a justice of the peace" at Bethlehem but were unable to receive satisfaction for their stolen goods.

14. Bernhard Grube to Petrus, Aug. 1, 1763, *Moravian Records,* reel 26, box 211, folder 16, item 8; Henry Geiger to Horsefield, n.d., Geiger to Jacob Wolle, Sept. 5, 1763, Letter, Oct. 7, 1763, all in Northampton County Papers, Bethlehem and vicinity, Misc. MSS, 1741–1886, HSP; Loskiel, *History of the Mission,* trans. La Trobe, pt. 2, 208–209.

15. Grube to Nathanael Seidel, Sept. 9, 1763, *Moravian Records,* reel 26, box 211, folder 16, item 12, Deposition of Lawrence McGuire, Oct. 15, 1763, reel 6, box 124, folder 6, item 3; "Heckewelder's Account of the Indian Nations," in *Report of the Commission to Locate the Site of the Frontier Forts of Pennsylvania,* 2 vols. (Harrisburg, Pa., 1896), I, 164–165; Fort Augusta Diary, Oct. 5, 1763, Samuel Hunter, commander, June–December 1763, APS.

Certainly, after returning to the Susquehanna River, they apprised other Indians of the situation. Captain Wetterholt and company could not have provided a more appropriate target for revenge—they were responsible for the recent death of Zacharias and a multitude of threats against the local native population, and they were lodged at a place of which many Indians had complained.[16]

And what better person to confront the militia than a once-noble Indian turned savage? In the early morning of October 8, 1763, Captain Bull led fifteen or twenty Indians in an attack on Stenton's tavern. One sergeant inside remembered hearing a lone voice shouting in English, "Come out you cowardly Dogs, come out you cowardly Sons of Bitches, what Way of fighting is this? come out and fight fair," before the band of Delawares shot Wetterholt and several soldiers, mortally wounding John Stenton. They set fire to the tavern and rode on to destroy several other plantations in nearby White Hall and Allen Townships. Lieutenant Jonathan Dodge, trapped in the tavern, frantically scribbled a message to local justice Timothy Horsfield, "Prey send me help for all my men are killed But one and Capt. Wetterholt is almost Dead he is shot threw the Body for god sake send me help." After their attacks at the Forks of the Delaware, Captain Bull and his warriors swept through the Wyoming Valley. Further avenging the death of Captain Bull's father, they burned the settlement of whites from Connecticut. During the October raids, the Delaware warriors killed fifty-four white people in Northampton County and ten at Wyoming, and they captured another twenty.[17]

Despite every indication that a Delaware war party from the Susquehanna was responsible for the attack, most of the white community in Northampton County felt that Indians close at hand were just as guilty and should pay for the death of the local tavern owner and the well-loved officer. Pressured by their demands, on October 29, 1763, George Klein,

16. "Heckewelder's Account of the Indian Nations," in *Report of the Commission,* I, 164–165.

17. Deposition of Lawrence McGuire, Oct. 15, 1763, *Moravian Records,* reel 6, box 124, folder 6, item 3; Note from Lt. Jonathan Dodge, Oct. 8, 1763, Northampton County Papers, Bethlehem and vicinity, Misc. MSS, 1741–1886, HSP; Joseph J. Mickley, *Brief Account of Murders by the Indians, and the Cause Thereof, in Northampton County, Penn'a, October 8th, 1763* (Philadelphia, 1875), 19, 21; *Pennsylvania Gazette,* Oct. 27, 1763; Fort Augusta Diary, Oct. 17, 20, 1763, Samuel Hunter, commander, June–December 1763, APS; Boyd, ed., *Susquehannah Company Papers,* II, 282.

the deputy sheriff, arrested Renatus, a Christian Mahican living at Bethlehem, for the murder of John Stenton. Although Renatus did not embody the savage Indian—like Captain Bull—he and other Christian natives also contended with the representation and its implications. The personal betrayal implicit in the Delaware attacks of 1755–1756 was still fresh in the minds of white settlers, and the fear of a renewed and bloody frontier war helped to coalesce their anger into generalized images of an Indian enemy. Familiar natives—the Moravian converts, in particular—became the target of their hatred. Using the court system to express their rage, white residents, with little evidence except the words of a grieving widow, demanded a swift trial and conviction of the Mahican. Christian Indians, on the other hand, faced with the growing hatred of white inhabitants with whom they had been neighbors for many decades, struggled to redefine themselves in relation to these images and to present themselves as worthy of equal justice in court. Renatus, imprisoned in Philadelphia, would be a test case.[18]

To champion Renatus, Lewis Weiss, his attorney, built a defense that reflected the complicated state of Indian affairs in the 1760s. Weiss recognized that, on some level, Renatus's arrest came as an extension of the Seven Years' War. Since the British crown considered Indian affairs an imperial concern, Weiss felt justice might be better served through diplomacy. First, he presented a petition to the Pennsylvania Assembly concerning his client, who still lingered in jail in December 1763. It contained unusual language for a legal document, but it had the common cadence and body metaphors used at treaty conferences: Renatus "saith that he is a blind Man and can not see what is the Danger that surrounds him, and that he hath no Tongue to speak to all People of his Innocency, and he hath desired your Petitioner [Weiss] to be his Eyes and his Tongue." Weiss, taking on the role of mediator, demanded that the case be dropped for lack of evidence. He argued further that, if a trial did proceed, it should be held in Philadelphia, since the inhabitants of Northampton County were "full of Resentment against that [the Indian] Nation in general." Weiss read the situation well. He knew that general animosity impeded his client's ability

18. "Statement of Rebecca Langley," Oct. 24, 1763, *Moravian Records,* reel 6, box 124, folder 6, item 5, "Statement of Conrad Reiff," Nov. 1, 1763, reel 6, box 124, folder 6, item 12; Earl P. Olmstead, *Blackcoats among the Delaware: David Zeisberger on the Ohio Frontier* (Kent, Ohio, 1991), 119.

to get an impartial jury and, thus, a fair trial. Diplomacy, however, did not work. The Assembly, instead, remanded the case to the Northampton County court for trial.[19]

Weiss next changed his strategy to address the prevailing rumors circulating about Renatus. From Lancaster to Easton, white settlers had heard stories about the events at Stenton's tavern, and many assumed that Renatus was guilty, since those Indians who lived at Wechquetank and Bethlehem supposedly "carried on a correspondence with our Enemies" and were naturally "unfaithful and perfidious." Weiss, in turn, collected testimony from character witnesses—both white and Indian—that portrayed the defendant as "good natured and religious," incapable of committing what was essentially a war crime. He described Renatus in the holiest of terms, emphasizing his Christian upbringing; he had been baptized in 1749 when he was twelve years old, which, at least to the Moravians, indicated that "he has never been a Savage or has imbibed those Principles of cruel Savages but he has been educated by Christian parents under a strict Discipline in respect to his Morals." Admittedly, in the past four years he had "been drunk several times," but "in his drunken fits hurted nobody else but himself and after he got sober again always repented with many Tears." Above all, "his Christian patience in these great Trials" provided the most compelling evidence of his integrity and obedience. In defending Renatus, Weiss went beyond the question of individual innocence. He, in essence, deconstructed the increasingly prevalent stereotypes that equated "Indianness" with cruel savagery. Instead of refuting or dismissing these stereotypes, however, on some level Weiss reconfirmed their power by helping to articulate the markers that set Christian Indians apart from savages.[20]

19. *Moravian Records,* reel 6, box 124, folder 6, item 16; Olmstead, *Blackcoats among the Delaware,* 130.

20. "The Apology of the Paxton Volunteers," 1764, HSP. Although "The Apology" was written in 1764, after the murder of the Conestoga Indians, the authors referred specifically to Stenton and the arrest of Renatus. See *Moravian Records,* reel 6, box 124, folder 6, item 20. During his time in jail, Renatus had suffered a series of family tragedies. His father, wife, and several children died of smallpox when held in protective custody at the Philadelphia barracks. Interestingly, in describing Mrs. Stenton's character and actions, Weiss implied that she knowingly brought false accusations against Renatus, in addition to being a bad mother who "behaved with great Freedom, and even left her Child . . . whilst she went to the Morning Preaching" (*Moravian Records,* 1764, reel 6, box 124, folder 6, item 17).

Many Pennsylvania Indians repeatedly tried to distance themselves from the implications or potential consequences of savagism. Those who were English allies worried that white neighbors no longer cared to distinguish between friend and foe, between civilized and savage behavior, but judged them on their exterior appearance alone. In November 1763, before the trial, Renatus's father, Jacob, addressed the governor on his son's behalf but also for the community at large: "I am sent in the Name of all the Indian Men Women and Children who . . . sit there with Concern and dare not stirr from home since the bad Indians have begun to murther. We are not of that kind but we love peace, we also love the white people and look upon them as our Friends. We have no Share in what these Indians have done, nor will we have a Share in it." More specifically, Jacob described the outward markings of Christian Indians, with which whites could differentiate them from their "wild" counterparts: "Wild Indians generally go only in a Shirt whereas [Christian Indians] are always cloathed with something. A wild Indian is generally painted and weareth a Feather, or some other Indian ornament, these are never painted and wear no feather, but they wear Hats or Caps. The wild Indians get their Heads shaved but these let the Hair grow naturally."[21]

By late 1763, many Indians, whether voluntarily or under pressure, went to great lengths to strip themselves of the remnants of savagism, to take on the external markings of good Indians that would distinguish them from hostile warriors. Even old enemies made a point to renew and redefine their alliances with the English. Nutimus, once the most powerful Delaware chief on the Susquehanna River, decided in July that he had become "Old and the World in a bad Condition." He arrived at Fort Augusta with a representative from the Six Nations and offered to "wash and brighten" the chain of friendship between themselves and the British. Although he addressed Colonel James Burd as "Brother," Nutimus described his Delawares as "but children and poor People," dependent on the favors of Pennsylvania. In November and December, the Indians at Nazareth and Bethlehem as well as some neutral communities in Wyalusing on the upper Susquehanna River also subordinated themselves to colonial authorities. They agreed to move to an army barracks in Philadel-

21. *Moravian Records,* Nov. 8, 1763, reel 6, box 124, folder 6, item 13, "Characteristics of Peaceable Indians," 1763, reel 6, box, 124, folder 7, item 4 (also in Horsfield Papers, II, APS).

phia by order of the governor, ostensibly for protection from angry white settlers. Before leaving Nazareth, the local sheriff confiscated "guns and tomahawks" from one group, which, according to the Moravians, "they all in childlike manner and submission consented to do." Some white intermediaries remarked on how the excision of savage symbols, whether raiment or weapons, somehow had rendered Indians legitimate or, in other words, tamed. Thomas McKee assured William Johnson that the Indians, now under surveillance in Philadelphia, "in a Manner were become white People, and expected the same Protection from us." McKee, like the governor, thought that native frontier dwellers and their white counterparts should submit to British authority to become full members of civilized English society.[22]

Still, conceding dependence on English protection and giving up the outward trappings of Indianness did not guarantee that native Americans would be widely accepted as "white People." Instead, it made whites even more certain that Indians somehow masked their inner nature by superficially dressing themselves as friends. Although justice prevailed in Northampton and the white male jury eventually acquitted Renatus of murder, Weiss knew, as he earlier feared, that many settlers, "common soldiers" in particular, would ignore the well-publicized markings that distinguished "wild" Indians and those under provincial protection. The verdict could have come from a clear lack of evidence against Renatus, but, more likely, the jury, along with other frontier inhabitants and the governor, feared retaliation and a renewed Indian war that would have erupted with a guilty verdict. After the trial, settlers told the governor they still thought the Mahican had murdered Stenton, and friends of his widow planned to appeal the case. The governor and his Council proposed a new bounty on Indian scalps and prisoners, even as the governor decided to wash his hands of Renatus; according to Weiss, the governor did not want Renatus in Philadelphia. "He will never put his hand to any thing that concerns Indians Lett his ffriends take him and bring him where they please." In the end, the case of Renatus, rather than easing tensions between Indians and whites, helped generate a racial discourse that would limit the options for Indians throughout Pennsylvania. Since many whites thought a natural

22. Conference at Fort Augusta, July 19, 1763, Shippen Family Papers, VI, 43, HSP; Diary of Nazareth, Nov. 7, 1763, English translation, Moravian Historical Society; *MPCP,* IX, 94; Sullivan et al., comps., *Papers of Johnson,* XI, 56–57.

savagery lay hidden beneath external signs of "whiteness," they considered Indians guilty until proven innocent. As Pennsylvanians attempted to clarify what characterized goodness and badness in Indian behavior, the interplay of actions, reactions, reprisals, and denials engendered a set of qualities forever attached to Indians.[23]

Rhetoric about the essential qualities of Indianness crystallized in the early 1760s, forcing Indians to redefine themselves in relation to that discourse. Some native Americans, like Captain Bull, angry over white encroachment and unfulfilled treaty promises, embraced savagism as a sign of resistance. Others refashioned themselves to blend in with white society and to avoid the potentially violent consequences of appearing savage. Yet stereotypes of Indians also influenced the actions of Euramericans. Images of the "bad Indian," in particular, provided language to describe and criticize uncivil settlers. Even if some white settlers saw great cultural distinctions between Indian and white communities, other colonists saw them as uncomfortably alike. Elites of Philadelphia feared the unpredictable behavior of all frontier inhabitants, who seemed to act in inappropriate ways. The ruling classes had always negatively characterized the "lower sorts." Non-English immigrants, in particular, were "loose and ungovernable," "idle," "worthless," had "uncultivated Tempers," and were "perpetually crowding in upon us." But, by the early 1760s, Pennsylvania proprietors, governors, and colonial agents more often applied the language of savagism to white settlers as an expression of frustration and a negative measure of behavior. Just as they had attempted to reduce Indians to a state of civilized submission, colonial leaders hoped to reduce white frontier inhabitants. But many white settlers resented colonial authority as much as they hated Indians. Indeed, they marshaled the rhetoric of sav-

23. Lewis Weiss to Horsfield, Aug. 1, 1763, Northampton County Papers, Misc. MSS, 1758–1768, HSP; Capt. Lewis Ourry to Col. Henry Bouquet, June 9, 1763, in Sylvester K. Stevens and Donald H. Kent, eds., *The Papers of Col. Henry Bouquet,* XIX (series 21649), pt. 1 (Harrisburg, Pa., 1942), 138–140; Weiss to Frederick Marshall, June 28, 1764, *Moravian Records,* reel 6, box 124, folder 6, item 23; *MPCP,* IX, 189. Timothy J. Shannon, "Dressing for Success on the Mohawk Frontier: Hendrick, William Johnson, and the Indian Fashion," *William and Mary Quarterly,* 3d Ser., LIII (1996), 18–19, examines the importance of external refashioning, clothing in particular, to political influence within Iroquois-English diplomacy before 1755.

agism against Indians to reassert their own autonomy and demand fuller participation as subjects of the British Empire, even as they proved their critics right with brutal actions.[24]

In many respects, whether they agreed or not, Indian and white frontier inhabitants shared similar traits and circumstances. Scots-Irish and German settlers often arrived in Pennsylvania poor and illegally occupied Indian or proprietary lands on the margins of provincial boundaries. They could not or would not pay quitrents, and they eked out a meager living by using the natural resources at hand. Similarly, Pennsylvania Indians at war's end struggled to make ends meet. The Conestoga Indians of Lancaster County, for example, had done away with most external signs that might mark them as Indian. They wore English clothing and commonly went by their English names—George, Harry, Sally, Betty, Molly, Bill, John Smith, Peggy, Little John, Little Peter, and Jacob. They lived and worked on a reserve of land during the first half of the eighteenth century and barely supported themselves by gardening and selling small manufactured brooms and bowls to whites nearby. Although poor and living on the edges of white society, Conestoga Indians, like Moravian converts, carefully distinguished themselves from the savage Indian, if not from their unruly white neighbors. They purposefully collected and preserved legal documentation of their alliances with colonial leaders, clinging to these prized possessions like totems. The sheriff, John Hay, who recorded a detailed inventory of the Conestogas' goods, noted an original "Article of Agreement" between William Penn and "the King of the Indians" from April 1701; another treaty of "Peace and Amity" between the governor of Maryland and the Conestogas of the same year; letters from James Logan and Governor William Keith to the Conestogas' leader Civility signed some fifteen years later; and "Two Belts of Wampum." Despite the wampum, one of the few symbols of their Indian past, Conestogas thought written documents more important to their survival as a community. These

24. James Logan to John, Thomas, and Richard Penn, Apr. 24, 1729, Peters to proprietors, July 5, 1749, Michael Schlatter to the proprietors, June 12, 1750, Penn Papers, Official Correspondence, II, 53, IV, 219, V, 17, HSP; Samuel Blunston to Thomas Penn, Mar. 3, 1737/8, Lancaster County Papers, 1724–1816, HSP. For using the "other" as critique of one's "own kind," see John Comaroff and Jean Comaroff, *Ethnography and the Historical Imagination* (Boulder, Colo., 1992), 293; Michael Taussig, *Mimesis and Alterity: A Particular History of the Senses* (New York, 1993), 142.

papers provided safe passage in a world increasingly dominated by the English.[25]

Unlike white settlers, however, the Conestogas had a unique relationship with the Pennsylvania proprietors, as did other native groups, and enjoyed the assistance and protection of the governor and Assembly. They maintained that they had been the first Indians to greet William Penn upon his arrival and, thus, had the right to welcome the proprietors and all newly appointed governors when they came to Pennsylvania. When John Penn arrived as lieutenant governor in November 1763, the Conestogas assured him that they had "always lived in Peace and Quietness with our Brethren and Neighbours round us during the last and present Indian Wars." Since they could no longer hunt to support themselves, they asked Penn to "consider our distressed Situation, and grant our Women and Children some Cloathing to cover them this Winter." The Conestogas often asked the governor for gifts of leather or clothing as continued recognition of their special affiliation with the proprietors and their appointed officials. The Conestogas, as poor and dependent as they were, hardly resembled any of the prevalent representations of an Indian—they were neither noble hunters nor fierce warriors.[26]

Whereas the proprietors and the governor saw Pennsylvania Indians, such as the Conestogas and Moravian converts, as tamed and now malleable, their white neighbors thought them unduly coddled and protected. Although many Delawares had taken up arms against the English, they were allowed to stay on their lands on the Susquehanna River immediately after the war. The governor even forcibly removed some white settlers from frontier regions in favor of Indian inhabitants, as he had with the controversial Connecticut settlement in Wyoming. In October 1763, the governor promised these same Indians—the Delawares, Nanticokes, and Munsees in the Wyoming Valley—some protection against "those enraged, ungovernable people, in their attempts to revenge the blood of their Fathers, Brothers, and Children." Most of all, white settlers resented the freedom with which Indians now traversed the frontier, moving openly across boundaries to hunt and trade—a freedom that they could not en-

25. *MPCP*, IX, 102, 103–104. See Chapter 1 for details of white immigration, settlement, and conflict.

26. *MPCP*, IX, 89. Throughout the 1750s, Conestogas petitioned the governor for assistance. See *MPCP*, VII, 768–769, VIII, 113.

joy for fear of Indian attack. Jonas Seely of Reading noted that "our people have become almost infuriated to madness" by this liberty. The Indians traveled "in companies from five to twenty, visiting Wyalusing, Wichetunk, Nain, Big Island and Conestogue, under the mark of friendly Indians." Treaties with William Penn meant little sixty years later to Scots-Irish in Lancaster, who insisted that Indians only "pretend themselves friends."[27]

Like Northampton's militia, Lancaster County Scots-Irish had long feared that Indians living and trading on the margins of English society conspired against them. From the late 1750s, they insisted that "strange Indian messengers" came and went with "frequent Dispatches . . . relating to the Motions of the Army of this Province." And, also like Northampton's militia, the Scots-Irish suspected that outward marks of identity did not signify inner loyalties. All Indians, no matter their professed intentions or way of life, were thought "deadly enemies" and "willing to take up the Hatchet against the English when the French requested them." For example, an armed group of men from Paxton township in Lancaster County, angry that they did not receive protection during Pontiac's recent uprising in the west and anxious about the renewed frontier violence in Northampton County, marched on Conestoga Manor early in the morning of December 14, 1763. They killed and scalped six Indians, burning their houses and effects. Most of the Conestogas escaped death because they had "gone towards Smith's Iron Works to sell brooms," baskets, and bowls that day. When the remaining Indians returned, they were placed in the workhouse at Lancaster for their own protection. Yet even sympathetic whites who felt compelled to shelter the survivors from vengeful settlers could not always look beyond racial stereotypes. Edward Shippen, a merchant in Lancaster, on one hand wished to keep the Indians from harm's way, but also he thought:

27. William Johnson to Thomas Penn, May 18, 1763, Hamilton to Burd, June 2, 1763, "Order of the King in Council," June 15, 1763, "Instructions from the Privy Council to Thomas Fitch," June 15, 1763, Hamilton to Burd and Thomas McKee, July 2, 1763, all in Boyd, ed., *Susquehanna Company Papers,* II, 218, 244, 246, 255, 256; *MPCP,* IX, 27, 68; Speech sent by Col. Burd and Thomas McKee, Oct. 22, 1763, Shippen Family Papers, VI, 17, HSP; Jonas Seely, Sept. 17, 1763, quoted in Daniel I. Rupp, *History of the Counties of Berks and Lebanon* (1844; reprint, Spartanburg, S.C., 1984), 77–78; *The Declaration of the Frontier Inhabitants of Pensilvania and a Brief Sketch of Grievances,* Feb. 1, 1764, Cox-Parrish-Wharton Family Papers, Friendly Association, box 18, HSP.

> Had it not been for the great Snow which fell here the day the Indians were killed at the Conestogo Town, harmless as they might have been before, it would not have been in our Power to have put them under any Confinement, but they would immediately have sought revenge as their Custom is (on such occasions) killed then next some of their neighbours, and then made off in the best way they could in Order to join their blood thirsty brothers the Delawares, and Shawanese, our most inveterate, and implacable Enemys.

In Shippen's mind, placing the remaining Conestogas in the Lancaster jail prevented revenge killings by naturally "blood thirsty" Indians as well as protected them from the anger of their white neighbors.[28]

Under these circumstances, the Lancaster workhouse proved unsafe for the survivors. Thirteen days after the original attack, fifty or sixty men on horseback armed with rifles, tomahawks, and scalping knives surrounded the jail at two in the morning. Though the sheriff, John Hay, and the coroner assured the governor that they had attempted to stop the attack, the mob brutally killed the fourteen Indians. One wonders whether the angry men deliberately acted out an elaborate ritual of revenge for a decade of frontier violence or whether they had simply absorbed some cultural lessons of their own. The description of the scene could have been Penn's Creek or Gnadenhütten in the fall of 1755. After the mob rode away, the residents of Lancaster found William Sack and his wife with "two children, of about the age of three years, whose heads were split with the tomahawk, and their scalps taken off." Another man's "legs were chopped with the tomahawk, his hands cut off, and finally a rifle ball discharged

28. Depositions of Anne Marie Le Roy, Feb. 25, 1764, and Thomas Moore, Feb. 27, 1764, "The Apology of the Paxton Volunteers," in John R. Dunbar, ed., *The Paxton Papers* (The Hague, 1957), 196–197; *MPCP,* IX, 89; Coroners inquisition on Conestoga Indians, 1763, *PA,* 1st Ser., IV, 147–148; Edward Shippen to Joseph Shippen, Dec. 19, 1763, Edward and Joseph Shippen Papers, Correspondence, 1750–1778, APS. Karen Ordahl Kupperman, "Presentment of Civility: English Reading of American Self-Presentation in the Early Years of Colonization," *WMQ,* 3d Ser., LIV (1997), asserts that, in the sixteenth and seventeenth centuries, the English thought that presentations of the body—clothing, gait, posture, etc.—"reflected the reality of the inner self" (198). They applied these assessments to Indians as well. By the eighteenth century, however, the association of outward accoutrements with inner selves came under serious reconsideration because of the cultural encounters between Euramericans and native Americans.

in his mouth. . . . In this manner lay the whole of them, men, women and children spread about the prison yard; shot, scalped, hacked and cut to pieces."[29]

The brutal actions of the Paxton Boys, as they later became known, revealed the power dynamics at work between white frontier settlers and colonial leaders, rather than simply a hatred of Indians. To the Pennsylvania elite, both uncontrollable Scots-Irish and beggarly Indians had the capacity to act as dangerous elements to frontier social order. Militiamen, such as those who eventually joined the Paxtons, were a particularly nasty bunch. They drank too much, they fought with each other, and they terrorized the local women. On one hand, the provincial government had encouraged, even depended upon, the fierceness of frontier inhabitants to protect its borders. The proprietor had prompted the governor to ask his militia to "attack the Indians in their Towns on the East Branch of [the] Sasquehannah and Delaware" in late 1763, with the exemption of those "that are our Friends." But, when white settlers acted on their own against the Conestogas, they had stepped outside the bounds of colonial authority and, thus, outside civilized society. After the massacre, John Penn condemned what he called the "lawless party of Rioters" from Paxton. He told his military commander Colonel John Armstrong to apprehend the leaders of the group—not to serve justice for the victims of the violence, but to discourage and suppress "all such Lawless Insurrections among the People." James Burd at Fort Augusta was also concerned about the murders at Conestoga and Lancaster, "not so much upon Accot. of the Indians, as the Thorough contempt show'd the Government" by the Paxton Boys. Their actions represented "a Vyolent Encroachment upon the Laws of the Land," and he wondered what the consequences would be "in a Country where there is no standing Army to inforce its Laws and Support the Government." In general, the colonial elite thought, as Benjamin Franklin suggested in a January 1764 pamphlet on the "late massacres," that the Paxtons were "CHRISTIAN WHITE SAVAGES," not because they had killed some Indians, but because they had challenged colonial authority.[30]

29. *MPCP*, IX, 103; Dunbar, ed., *Paxton Papers,* 29; J. I. Mombert, *An Authentic History of Lancaster County: In the State of Pennsylvania* (Lancaster, 1869), 185.

30. Mancall, *Valley of Opportunity,* 84; Complaint of William Lawrence against Lt. Dodge, Aug. 27, 1763, Jacob Wetterholt to Horsfield, Oct. 7, 1763, Northampton County Papers, Misc. MSS, 1758–1768, HSP; *Frontier Forts of Pennsylvania,* 168; Thomas Penn to Hamilton, in Boyd, ed., *Susquehannah Company Papers,* II, 284; John

Similarly, the Paxtons saw the Pennsylvania government as a greater threat to their community. Scots-Irish settlers, largely Presbyterians, reviled and defied the Anglicans and Quakers who wielded power in the colony. By early February 1764, the Paxton Boys had gathered some 250 men and began to march on Philadelphia. They initially intended to kill the Moravian Indians held at the army barracks in the city, as they had the Conestogas, but their real grievances lay with the governor, the Assembly, and, most of all, Quakers. Although a violent confrontation was avoided when a volunteer force headed by Benjamin Franklin stopped the group in Germantown, a pamphlet war ensued. In *A Declaration and Remonstrance of the Distressed and Bleeding Frontier Inhabitants of the Province of Pennsylvania,* Matthew Smith and James Gibson complained about the lack of political representation in the west. The five frontier counties had only ten seats in the Assembly, compared to twenty-six seats for Philadelphia and the eastern counties. According to the "Paxton Volunteers," as the marchers called themselves, the colonial leadership had abandoned them during their time of crisis. Quakers, in particular, refused to help them during the war with funds for a militia and forts, then they failed to help the families of white refugees after the war. The Friends had supposedly "made light of [their] sufferings" when the settlers applied for relief, whereas they used public money and private donations to assist Indians. The Paxtons puzzled why "men in Power refused to relieve the sufferings of their fellow subjects." Faced with disenfranchisement and dislocation, these white settlers transferred their frustration and anger at colonial elites who controlled their fate onto poor neighboring Indians who had no power to resist.[31]

Penn to Rev. John Elder, Dec. 29, 1763, John Penn to John Armstrong, Dec. 29, 1763, *PA,* 1st Ser., IV, 153; Burd to Joseph Shippen, Jan. 19, 1764, Shippen Family Papers, VI, HSP; Alden T. Vaughan, "Frontier Banditti and the Indians: The Paxton Boys' Legacy, 1763–1775," *Pennsylvania History,* LI (1984), 1–29; [Benjamin Franklin], "A Narrative of the Late Massacres, in Lancaster County, of a Number of Indians, Friends of This Province, by Persons Unknown," Charles Read to John Ladd, 1764, both in Dunbar, ed., *Paxton Papers,* 72, 79; McKee to Johnson, Feb. 15, 1764, in Sullivan et al., comps., *Papers of Johnson,* XI, 56.

31. Alison Olson, "The Pamphlet War over the Paxton Boys," *PMHB,* CXXIII (1999), 31–55; Vaughan, "Frontier Banditti and the Indians," *Pa. Hist.,* LI (1984), 3; "The Apology of the Paxton Volunteers," 1764, HSP; *A Declaration and Remonstrance of the Distressed and Bleeding Frontier Inhabitants of the Province of Pennsylvania . . . ,"* Feb. 13, 1764, in Dunbar, ed., *Paxton Papers,* 103, 107.

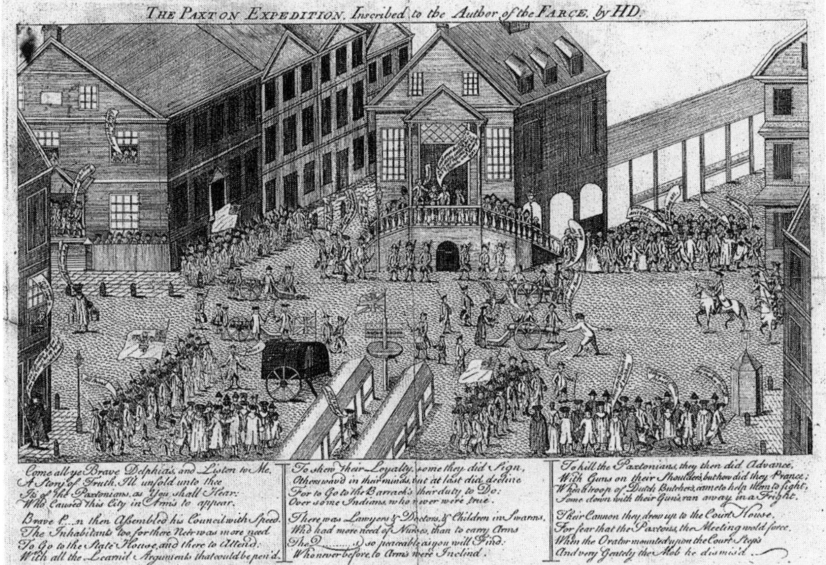

FIGURE 13. *The Paxton Expedition.* By Henry Dawkins. 1763.
Courtesy, American Philosophical Society, Philadelphia.
During the crisis of 1763–1764, the popular sentiment seemed to weigh in favor of the Paxtons (who actively used satire to condemn their rivals). Both the Paxtons and their detractors focused on restoring order—whether by eliciting the assistance of the colony to protect frontiers or to subdue an unruly mob who usurped authority—rather than the crime against the Conestogas. In the engraving, Henry Dawkins lambastes the colony's attempt to mount an armed response to the Paxton Boys march on Philadelphia.

For Scots-Irish settlers, the previous five decades, rife with competition for land and a war that pitted frontier inhabitants against each other, had raised questions of citizenship: Who belonged to the colonial British Empire, and who should benefit from it? The more the settlers were lumped together with Indians as savages, the harder they struggled to change their status as outsiders. The Paxtons, in particular, attempted to rehabilitate themselves as the real subjects and supporters of English interests by describing Indians as separate and disloyal nations. British military leaders had often questioned white settlers' own loyalties. They complained that the same men who screamed the loudest about the Indian threat had rarely come forward to volunteer or provide support to the army during the war; they were, in fact, cowards. "Will not People Say that they have found it easier to kill Indians in a Goal," lamented Colonel Henry Bouquet in 1764, "than to fight them fairly in the Woods?" To the Paxtons, however,

FIGURE 14. *Massacre of the Indians at Lancaster by the Paxton Boys in 1763.* From James Wimer, *Events in Indian History . . .* (Lancaster, Pa., 1841). Courtesy, The Library Company of Philadelphia.
Historians of the nineteenth century openly placed blame for "the horrible butchery" of Conestoga Indians on Scots-Irish. In this lithograph from 1841, men in top hats are shown tomahawking women and children, once again portraying Scots-Irish as savages and outsiders, whereas Indians are viewed as sympathetic victims.

Indians were untrustworthy, and, by implication, the Quakers and provincial Assembly who protected them also demonstrated duplicity. They concluded that Indians, like their colonial defenders, should have no claim to the rights and privilege of empire. The Paxtons pointed out that Indians belonged to "independent Nations" and "never came under our Laws, nor acknowledged subjection to our King and Government; but they always governed themselves by their own Customs, and exercised the Power of Life and Death over their own People." Because of their autonomy and protected status, they had been able to operate in concert as one nation against colonists. "In what nation under the Sun," the Paxtons asked rhetorically, "was it ever the custom that when a neighboring Nation took up Arms, not an individual should be touched but only the Persons that offered Hostilities?" "Who ever proclaimed War with a part of a Nation, and not with the Whole?" The Paxtons implied that Indians, as members of separate nations, had particular political loyalties and that whites, too, as British subjects, were part of one nation and merited equal participation and representation within the empire.[32]

For the Paxtons, there was not a great leap from portraying Indians as a separate nation to portraying them as a separate race. By the late eighteenth century, categories of difference had changed, moving away from cultural distinctions, such as clan affiliation or religion, to more scientific measures favored by natural history, such as the body. Many Euramericans believed that national affiliation, based on place of origin, also encompassed a particular "temperament" or "national complexion," often tied to the climate. Prolonged exposure to harsh environs over successive generations could lead to the darkening of skin. If they saw Indians' physical nature and bad character stemming from the American environment, however, they could not ignore that they, too, came from or now lived on

32. Bouquet to Burd, June 8, 1759, box 2, Burd-Shippen Papers, Letters, APS; Bouquet to John Harris, July 19, 1764, in Stevens and Kent, eds., *Bouquet Papers,* XX (series 21650), pt. 2 (Harrisburg, Pa., 1943), 32; "The Apology of the Paxton Volunteers," 1764, HSP; *MPCP,* IV, 49, VIII, 344, IX, 140.

I use the terms "nation," "nationality," and "citizen" in a similar manner to David McCrone and Richard Kiely, in "Nationalism and Citizenship," *Sociology,* XXXIV (2000), 23, who distinguish "nationness" as a cultural identification and "citizenship" as a political affiliation. They examine how these two concepts interact in modern Britain, where the Welsh and Scottish, for instance, think of themselves as citizens of the British Empire, but their national identity is that of Wales and Scotland (19–20). Historically, then, the concept of British citizenship helped the empire expand, since subjecthood could encompass a variety of nationalities and absorb them under imperial control (26). Yet Benedict Anderson, *Imagined Communities: Reflections on the Origin and Spread of Nationalism,* rev. ed. (New York, 1991), points out that nation can also have political connotations (6). The America colonies, as a "creole community," developed a sense of nationhood perhaps even before European nations. Common language was the root of these national communities, but language was also a tool of nationalism, bestirring patriotic feelings that were sometimes expressed through racist actions (145–154). The Paxton Boys certainly played on a sense of national patriotism when trying to garner support for their violence against Indians. Eric Hinderaker, *Elusive Empires: Constructing Colonialism in the Ohio Valley, 1673–1800* (New York, 1977), 260–262, discusses more specifically citizenship and race in post-Revolution America. Definitions of U.S. citizenship emphatically excluded people of color but offered Indians a way to become "white" if they gave up their tribal membership.

that soil. Since they could not change the climate, nor did they want to move from the region, they, instead, changed the ways they depicted Indians. Creating an enemy other was not new to the 1760s. During the early years of the war with France, white settlers had blamed Delawares and other Indians collectively for precipitating frontier attacks. They cursed native allies and refugee families for commanding resources and sympathies while settlers had, supposedly, been forbidden to kill Indians, "be they friends or enemies." But, by 1763, whites more readily and more publicly drew on dehumanizing racial descriptions of native savage behavior to distinguish and demonstrate their own national loyalties to the British Empire. On one hand, the Paxtons vilified their Euramerican rivals. They "Unmask'd" the supposed hypocrisy of Quakers with satire and "Plain Truth," questioning their worldly ambitions, masculinity, and commitment to pacifism, but they saved serious invective for Indians. The Paxtons exaggerated the past narrative of recent events, which they insisted lay "in the memories of thousands in the Province." According to them, Indians, including the Conestogas, had behaved with abnormal cruelty; "Many Children were either spitted alive and roasted or covered under the Ashes of a large Fire, before their helpless Parents Eyes. The Hearts of some taken out and eaten reeking hot, while they were yet beating between their Teeth and others, where Time and Opportunity would admit of it were skinned, boiled and eaten." By making cannibals of Indians, the Paxtons, in essence, combined the concept of a separate native national temperament with the physicality of native bodies to refine the language of savagism and a racial discourse about Indians.[33]

33. Joyce E. Chaplin, "Natural Philosophy and an Early Racial Idiom in North America: Comparing English and Indian Bodies," *WMQ*, 3d Ser., LIV (1997), 236. See also Chaplin, *Subject Matter: Technology, the Body, and Science on the Anglo-American Frontier, 1500–1676* (Cambridge, Mass., 2001), which explores the influence of science and technology on Indian-white relations and Euramerican notions of racial superiority. Roxann Wheeler, *The Complexion of Race: Categories of Difference in Eighteenth-Century British Culture* (Philadelphia, 2000), picks apart the shift from categorizing by culture to categorizing by body type. See Bernard W. Sheehan, *Seeds of Extinction: Jeffersonian Philanthropy and the American Indian* (Chapel Hill, N.C., 1973), 35–42; David B. Brunner, *The Indians of Berks County, Pa., Being a Summary of All the Tangible Records of the Aborigines of Berks County, with Cuts and Descriptions of the Varieties of Relics Found within the County,* 2d ed., rev. (Reading, Pa., 1897), 56, 67; Weiser to Gov. Robert Hunter Morris, Nov. 19, 1755, in *Frontier Forts of Pennsylvania,* I, 73–74; [David James Dove], *The Quaker Unmask'd; or, Plain Truth . . .*, 2d ed. (Philadelphia,

FIGURE 15. *Benjamin Franklin and the Quakers.* Attributed to David James Dove. 1764. Courtesy, The Historical Society of Pennsylvania [Bc 612 Q24]. *This anonymous engraving depicts the growing political and cultural conflicts between Presbyterians and Quakers in the wake of the Paxton Boys massacre of Conestoga Indians. The engraver (possibly Presbyterian) especially criticized the close relationship between Quakers and Indians. On the right, a native woman and Quaker man engage in mutual seduction. On the left, Israel Pemberton distributes tomahawks to Indian warriors while saying: "Exercise those on the Scotch Irish and Dutch and I'll support you while I am Abel." Scots-Irish used these satiric images to justify violence against Quaker allied Indians.*

Through this discourse and their own violent actions on a nationally and now racially bounded other, the largely Scots-Irish contingent from Paxton voiced apprehension about its place within the British Empire. Like the Iroquois trying to redirect suspicions about their disloyal activities during the Seven Years' War onto conveniently hostile Delawares, the Scots-Irish projected their inner anxieties onto Indians as a whole. By conflating separate Indian nations—whether Delawares, Iroquois, Mahicans, or Conestogas, whether Christians or non-Christians—as a unified enemy other and by casting doubt on the authority and actions of the colonial elite, the Scots-Irish obfuscated their own past as outsiders in the

---

1764), reprinted in Dunbar, ed., *Paxton Papers,* 205–215; Olson, "The Pamphlet War over the Paxton Boys," *PMHB,* CXXIII (1999), 32, 40–44; "The Apology of the Paxton Volunteers," 1764, HSP; "The Apology of the Paxton Volunteers to the Candid and Impartial World," in Dunbar, ed., *Paxton Papers,* 185.

English colonial world. Rhetorically, they differentiated themselves from their savage Indian neighbors and demanded the autonomy and privileges that they thought native inhabitants commanded, especially the rights to frontier land and protection. As the Paxton Boys massacre is meant to illustrate, some forms of racism have their roots in the internal struggles over resources and power as well as nascent nationalism. The Paxtons generated a sense of group solidarity by recalling a common past of settler persecution by both colonial authorities and Indians. They tied national and racial differences together to create an essentialized Indian enemy whose blood descendants could and would be disinherited from their claims to a "native" American past and, thereby, the land they possessed.[34]

Although white settlers in the 1760s more often attached descent to national and, thus, cultural identity, national and racial boundaries, like proclamation lines on a map, remained porous, complicated by more than a half-century of interactions on the Pennsylvania frontier. For Indians, kinship rather than skin color still determined who belonged on which side of a national divide. The repatriation of white captives after the war presented the most difficult test of these different measures of identity. An officer of the provincial army, patrolling into Indian territory after the French abandoned the Ohio Valley, noted a country "Thickly Settled by Delaware Indians, who have amongst them, a Prodigious number of En-

34. Immanuel Wallerstein, "The Construction of Peoplehood: Racism, Nationalism, Ethnicity," in Etienne Balibar and Wallerstein, *Race, Nation, Class: Ambiguous Identities,* trans. Chris Turner (New York, 1991), 77–79; Daniel K. Richter, *Facing East from Indian Country: A Native History of Early America* (Cambridge, Mass., 2001), chap. 6; Mechal Sobel, "The Revolution in Selves: Black and White Inner Aliens," in Ronald Hoffman, Sobel, and Fredrika J. Teute, eds., *Through a Glass Darkly: Reflections on Personal Identity in Early America* (Chapel Hill, N.C., 1997), 171–172. The projection of self on an alien other involved "complex love-hate relationships with their enemy figures" (ibid., 172). Chaplin, "Natural Philosophy," *WMQ*, 3d Ser., LIV (1997), 230–232, suggests that Puritans similarly used "natural philosophy" about bodies to sanctify their dispossession of Indians. That Indians were dying from disease and Puritans were not was proof of God's providence and approval of colonization as well as a sign of their "natural" constitutional superiority. Indian hating was prevalent in the British army as well by 1763. Colonel Bouquet discussed the possibility of infecting enemy tribes with smallpox, and William Trent and others actually sent blankets from the smallpox hospital to a few native groups, a tactic that would never have been considered against French troops in Quebec (McConnell, *A Country Between,* 194–195).

glish Women and Children." Many had been taken during the most ferocious years of war (1755 and 1756), but, by early 1759, Colonel Bouquet demanded that all white captives held by western tribes be returned to their families or other white communities in Pennsylvania as part of the peace settlement. He specified that the English would not "purchase our People" of the Indians but would "offer them Peace, on the Condition of every one of the Captives being brought home and delivered up early in the Spring." Like the English, Indians also thought captives an integral part of postwar diplomacy. But returning white captives to the English involved more deliberation, since Indians had adopted many as family members, creating close community ties. Indeed, Indians often thought that to return these captives would do more harm than good to the uneasy peace between Indians and whites.[35]

By 1762, under the threat of military retribution, Ohio and Susquehanna Indians brought hundreds of white captives to Pennsylvania government officials. Thomas King, an Oneida chief who accompanied a group to Easton, reiterated the emotional and social ties that captivity had created between Indians and whites and the threat to those kin bonds that repatriation represented. He lamented: "I have brought an English Prisoner, who I love as my own Wife: I have a young Child by her. You know it is very hard for a Man to part with his Wife. I have delivered her, therefore take Care of her, and keep her safe." King especially feared that his wife might simply end up another kind of captive among whites. If the white families of returning young captives had been killed during the war, the Pennsylvania government would just as likely indenture the captives to a strange master. King reprimanded the governor: "No wonder why they [the captives] are so loath to come, when you make Servants of them."[36]

35. Gregory Evans Dowd, *A Spirited Resistance: The North American Indian Struggle for Unity, 1745–1815* (Baltimore, 1992), 30; Captain Lee's journal, Oct. 1, 1759, in Sylvester K. Stevens and Donald H. Kent, eds., *Wilderness Chronicles of Northwestern Pennsylvania* (Harrisburg, Pa., 1941), 173; Bouquet's meeting with Ohio Delawares, Nov. 25–Dec. 4, 1758, Mercer to Bouquet, Feb. 7, 1759, in S. K. Stevens et al., eds., *The Papers of Henry Bouquet* (Harrisburg, Pa., 1951–), II, 621–624, III, 107–108.

36. Lancaster treaty conference, Aug. 19, 1762, in Van Doren and Boyd, eds., *Indian Treaties*, 279; *MPCP*, VIII, 744; Address of Shingas, King Beaver, Delaware George, and Pisquetomen to Christian Frederick Post at Kuskuski, in Reuben Gold Thwaites, ed., *Early Western Travels, 1748–1846*, I (Cleveland, Ohio, 1904), 214. Colonel Bouquet cru-

White captives were often as "loath" to return to English society as Indians were reluctant to part with them, especially if they had been adopted into native households as children and had come to see the Indians as family. On July 14, 1758, a young girl brought to Philadelphia refused to "tell her name nor Speak a Word, and made a great resistance to her being delivered up." Some restored captives became so intractable that white relatives had to use restraints. John McCullough remembers that he "wept biterly" on his return, and his white father had to tie him on a horse to take him home. He soon escaped back to his adoptive brother and hunting companions. At Easton in August 1761, a sixteen-year-old girl, unwilling to leave her native family, "hid herself among the bushes" until an Indian man reluctantly brought her in, whereupon "the Squaw she belongs to came with her and both she and the girl cryed exceedingly, they were so afraid of being parted." The incorporation of white captives into Indian communities during the war had complicated group identity and the ability to neatly separate English from Indians or to clearly distinguish their respective national loyalties.[37]

Whereas Indians, through tears, offered up their family members as bitter tokens of their commitment to peace, the English saw these captives in a different light. White colonists in Pennsylvania, whether allied, kin, or captive to Indian communities, were British subjects first and foremost. An individual's affiliation rested, not on a personal relationship to a family, but on a nation of origin. Pennsylvania officials did not recognize the desire of captives to remain with their adoptive families. Governor James Hamilton addressed Iroquois and Delawares in the summer of 1762 at Lancaster: "We do not well understand your meaning, when you say some of the Prisoners chuse to live with you. If you intend it as a reason for not delivering them up, till they consent to come, we must inform you that we cannot admit of it. They were born Subjects of our Great King, and as

---

saded for six years to repatriate more than two hundred captives but also to "prevent their Escape" back to "their Savage Masters" (*MPCP,* IX, 207).

37. *MPCP,* VIII, 148; John McCullough, "Preliminary Draft of Captivity Narrative," in *A Selection . . . of Outrages Committed by the Indians* (Carlisle, Pa., 1808), n.p., mircrofilm, Pennsylvania State Archives, Harrisburg; Quaker Journal, Easton, Pa., 1761, 7–8, Clements Library. For more tales of the reluctance of "Prisoners" to return, see Aug. 27, 1762, in Van Doren and Boyd, eds., *Indian Treaties,* 296–297; Deposition of Mathias Warren, Mar. 30, 1764, in Stevens and Kent, eds., *Papers of Bouquet,* XX (series 21650), pt. 1, 81.

such he has a right to demand them." Yet English demands for repatriation of captives went beyond the belief that the king had dominion over his subjects. Despite the reluctance of many white captives to return, colonial leaders, like white settlers, clearly associated race with national loyalty. In August 1761, Governor Hamilton, in conference with the Six Nations and Ohio Indians at Easton, lamented, "I have frequently sent Messages into the *Indian* Country, to put them in Mind of their Promise to return to us our Flesh and Blood, who are Prisoners among them, and to press them to fulfil that Promise." In November 1764, Thomas McKee, under the orders of Colonel Bouquet, also demanded that the Susquehanna Indians deliver "up immediately any of our Flesh and Blood, that you may have amongst you." Yet blood relations, too, were susceptible to new family associations. Whites often feared that captives would forget the ties of "Blood" and become Indian, especially if the races had intermingled. Indeed, many feared that those of mixed race were even more likely to forget "their Ancestry on one side" and, according to William Johnson, "are found to be the most Inveterate" traitors to their English heritage. Bouquet agreed fully. During the early 1760s, he insisted that Indians return not just white captives who were "Flesh and Blood" but even Indians' "own Children born from white women." Apparently, if caught young enough, these children could be taught where their racial loyalties belonged.[38]

The fear of blurred cultural boundaries and racial merging resulted not just in the mob actions of disenfranchised Scots-Irish on the frontier or the demand for the return of captives by British military leaders. The escalation of Indian hating after 1763 also came from a most unlikely place, from those who had intimate ties to natives in Pennsylvania.

38. *MPCP,* VIII, 732–733, IX, 207; Treaty conference at Easton, Aug. 7, 1761, in Van Doren and Boyd, eds., *Indian Treaties,* 253; Conference between Thomas McKee and the Indians at Fort Augusta, Nov. 10, 11, 1764, Johnson to Bouquet, Dec. 17, 1764, in Sullivan et al., comps., *Papers of Johnson,* IV, 579, 620; Bouquet to John Penn, Nov. 15, 1764, in Stevens and Kent, eds., *Wilderness Chronicles,* 289. Hamilton complained that Pennsylvania was the only colony actively seeking the return of white captives, "at an Enormous expence" (Hamilton to Bouquet, Nov. 11, 1762, in Stevens and Kent, eds, *Papers of Bouquet,* XVIII [series 21648], pt. 2, 144–145). In August 1762, captive Peter Weese, then an adult, privately told the governor of "his Inclination to stay among the *Indians.*" The provincial government, skeptical of his ability to make a free choice, allowed him to remain but insisted that he meet the governor again the following spring to reconsider his decision (Treaty conference at Lancaster, Aug. 27, 1762, in Van Doren and Boyd, eds., *Indian Treaties,* 296–297).

FIGURE 16. *The Indians Delivering Up the English Captives to Colonel Bouquet. . . .* By Benjamin West. From William Smith, *An Historical Account of the Expedition against the Ohio Indians, in the Year 1764 . . .* (Philadelphia, 1765). Courtesy, The Library Company of Philadelphia.
The Euramerican engraver captured the ambivalence that came with the repatriation of English after the war. The blond child cringes from Colonel Henry Bouquet's outstretched hand, while his Indian father attempts gently to turn him back. In the background, other children cry over the prospect of their own return. Indians, who had adopted most of the surviving captives into their own families, reluctantly gave them up and accused the English of exploiting them.

Many times the most fervent Indian-hater had once been an Indian-lover, living with Indian neighbors as trade partner, family member, employer, or spouse. For nearly five years, David Owens had lived among Indians on the Susquehanna River, having deserted from an independent militia company near Sherman's Valley. He married a Delaware woman, Maria, who was Teedyuscung's sister-in-law and a one-time Moravian convert. He did well, knowing both Delaware and Shawnee languages, "His Father having been long a Trader amongst them." In the spring of 1764, however, while out hunting with his wife, children, and other kinfolk, he decided to kill them all—"three men, two women and two Children"—as they slept, "but only Scalpt five." Some speculated that Owens feared for his own safety. Others thought he killed his Indian family "rather to make his peace with the English, than from any dislike either to them [Indians] or their Principles." Indeed, a few months after the murders he hired out his services as interpreter to Colonel Bouquet, reconfirming his English allegiance, while using his acquired skills as go-between. James Smith, taken captive by Indians as a young man in 1755, also wrestled with cultural loyalties. In the early 1760s, when Smith returned to his frontier home in Pennsylvania after nearly five years in an adoptive native household, he reminisced fondly of his Indian family and their love for him. But soon after returning from captivity, he became the captain of a company of rangers that fought Indians near Pittsburgh, obsessively seeking revenge against a nation for whom he had lost love, even as he trained his men in tactics of Indian warfare. For Owens and Smith, their dramatic change of heart revealed some inner demons of identity with which they both struggled. They were torn between their attachment to individual Indians, which they had acquired through years of recurring, intimate interactions, and the hatred and fear of an abstract "Indian," which permeated their world and threatened to engulf them. By murdering wife and kin, by hunting down people once family, they not only redeemed themselves as loyal British subjects; they killed the Indian-lover inside and emphatically marked the line between self and savage Indian other.[39]

39. *MPCP*, IX, 190, 215–220; John Penn to Johnson, June 9, 1764, in Sullivan et al., comps., *Papers of Johnson*, XI, 225; Colin G. Calloway, "Neither White nor Red: White Renegades on the American Indian Frontier," *Western Historical Quarterly*, XVII (1986), 61; James Smith, *An Account of the Remarkable Occurences in the Life and Travels of Col. James Smith, during His Captivity with the Indians, in the Years 1755, '56, '57, '58, and '59*, ed. William M. Darlington (1799; reprint, Cincinnati, Ohio, 1870), 106–107.

In 1723, Whiwhinjac, the leader of a group of Conoys living along the Susquehanna River, recalled that William Penn had promised a new relationship between Indians and whites that would essentially dissolve all boundaries. They would not be merely "Brethren by joining Hands" but instead "must all be one half Indian and the other half English, being as one Flesh and one Blood under one Head." In a sense, Pennsylvania natives took this advice. They adapted many Euramerican cultural practices, combining the traditions of the past to create a new way of being Indian. Yet, forty years later, Penn's successors rejected the possibility of such an intimate merging of cultures. Colonel Henry Bouquet, after fighting a frontier war against these "Brethren," only hoped to "clear the roads of that Bloody race." What had occurred in the intervening years? Why could Bouquet and his compatriots not envision "being as one Flesh and one Blood" with Indians?[40]

By the mid-eighteenth century, the balance of powers that governed life and survival on the mid-Atlantic frontier had shifted, and native Americans, in particular, contended with the consequences. As neighbors, frontier inhabitants—both Indian and white—had been interdependent, intimately coexisting, borrowing from each other culturally, and finding a common enemy in the colonial authorities who professed to control them. As the white population increased, however, the competition for land and resources on the frontier intensified, engendering distrust, fear, anger, and violence among settlers and Indians who shared common space on the margins of English society. Attempting to mitigate the violence, Indians and whites mustered memories of a golden past. Each blamed the other for failing to live up to their constructed ideals of civilized behavior—whether as noble natives or moral white Christians. At the same time,

---

For an explanation of "Indian hating," see White, *Middle Ground,* 368–377. Richard Drinnon, *Facing West: The Metaphysics of Indian-Hating and Empire-Building* (1980; reprint, New York, 1990), uses literature to trace the evolution of Indian hating from Puritans in the seventeenth century to the nineteenth century, although his real target is American imperialism and racism in Vietnam. Interestingly, he ignores the eighteenth century, perhaps for good reason. Encounters during this late-colonial period do not fit neatly into his model of repressive, racist colonizers and their Indian victims.

40. *MPCP,* III, 217; Bouquet to Lt. Archibald Blane, July 4, 1763, in Stevens and Kent, eds., *Papers of Bouquet,* XIX (series 21649), pt. 1, 196.

frontier populations realigned themselves behind the collective power of national allegiances. Indians began to make decisions about their political and economic survival, not as communities, but as larger allied tribes and confederations. Once part of clan-based ethnic groups, Indians now acted as "one nation" and, by implication, one race. Sporting their own brand of nationalism, white settlers used the Seven Years' War as justification for scapegoating their Indian neighbors—be they allied or hostile. Stereotypes of savages excluded Indians from partaking in the privileges of colonial society and made the next step of dispossession that much easier for the Euramerican majority.[41]

Paradoxically, because contentious frontier factions insisted that the British Empire acknowledge and protect their claims to separate national identities, Indians and whites helped the crown consolidate its control over the American colonial world in the second half of the eighteenth century. What they thought would bring them separation and autonomy instead empowered British imperial forces. The Proclamation Line was a symbol of that power, carving up territories without colonial consent, keeping white settlers from expanding to the west, and preventing large Indian groups from remaining in the east. By the early 1760s, British officials wrested control of some administrative decisions from local colonial leadership and increased British military presence in North America. Indian affairs, in particular, became key to British control of the colonies, since native inhabitants represented both potential subjects and an obstacle to expansion. Sir Jeffrey Amherst, commander in chief of the British army and architect of the crown's conquest policy, appointed Colonel Bouquet to repel hostile Indians from Fort Pitt and secure the possession of the Ohio Valley. In the summer of 1764, Bouquet criticized the liberal terms of peace that his colleague Colonel John Bradstreet had initially negotiated with the Great Lakes and Ohio tribes. Instead of forcing Indians

41. Fred Anderson, *A People's Army: Massachusetts Soldiers and Society in the Seven Years' War* (New York, 1984), suggests that an American nationalist sentiment developed among Massachusetts soldiers during the Seven Years' War because of their bad experiences with the British army. I see a different dynamic between white frontier settlers in the mid-Atlantic and the British. Although there was tension between troops and the civilian frontier population, settlers in Pennsylvania thought that British imperial forces would at least protect their interests, since the colonial elite had not. Thus, their national identity emerged in opposition to colonial leaders, such as the Quakers, and native Americans, not the British.

to capitulate to British demands through battle, Bradstreet had invited them to sign treaties that promised them political autonomy, equal justice, the continuance of trade, and the sanctity of their tribal territory if they returned white captives and allowed the British to maintain military posts. Infuriated, Bouquet took "no notice of that pretended Peace" and led troops against the Delawares and Shawnees in the Ohio. To Bouquet, Indians were a conquered people and had to be contained. He cared little about the give-and-take of negotiated interactions. He ignored the rituals and shared legal forms that had once characterized frontier diplomacy. In November 1764, after a Seneca warrior killed one of Bouquet's soldiers, a Seneca representative attempted to "wipe the tears from your Eyes, and remove from your heart the resentment which this murder has raised against us." Bouquet, on the other hand, simply demanded that "the murderer be delivered up to be punished Capitally."[42]

In general, the new policy called for greater control of Indians and greater interference in Indian politics. Through men like Bouquet and William Johnson, Great Britain appointed and used Indian agents, interpreters, even missionaries and blacksmiths for its own purposes. More important, the empire claimed the power to choose war captains, tribal chiefs, or regional representatives, even to "confer such honors and rewards on the Indians as shall be necessary." Bouquet took particular pleasure in that duty. On November 11, 1764, he deposed the Delaware chief of the Turtle Tribe, being "dissatisfied with his Conduct." Bouquet insisted that he alone would confirm the election of any subsequent tribal chief. By the end of 1764, Bouquet had resorted to threats, refusing to trade with any Indians at Fort Pitt until they had complied with his treaty conditions. He warned the Shawnees that the British *"tread heavy,* and can Crush them under our feet, if they make us angry." General Thomas Gage was pleased to say that "Colonel Bouquet had reduced the Shawanese and Delawares etc. to the most Humiliating Terms of Peace."[43]

42. *MPCP,* IX, 195–196, 197, esp. 208, 224, 225; Jennings, *Empire of Fortune,* 450; McConnell, *A Country Between,* 199–200; Fred Anderson, *Crucible of War: The Seven Years' War and the Fate of Empire in British North America, 1754–1766* (New York, 2000), 568–570, 620–632.

43. "Plan for the Future Management of Indian Affairs, 1764," *PA,* 1st Ser., IV, 184–185; *MPCP,* IX, 229, 253; Bouquet to Custaloga, King Beaver, and King Samuel, chiefs of the Delawares, Dec. 3, 1764, Gage to Johnson, Dec. 6, 1764, in Sullivan et al., comps., *Papers of Johnson,* XI, 484, 496.

Great Britain also sought to consolidate its control of more powerful Indian allies, such as the Iroquois Confederacy. The Six Nations, though generally supportive of the British military and its frontier policy, found themselves in a weakened position. Instead of dealing directly with colonial governors in New York or Pennsylvania, even manipulating colonies or empires for their advantage, they, too, were pressured by the encroachment of white settlements and the decline of their role in the fur trade. After the massacre of the Conestoga Indians, Governor John Penn, concerned about Iroquois reaction, asked William Johnson to placate the Six Nations: "Take the properest method of acquainting them with the Truth of this Transaction, and of removing any disadvantageous Impressions they may have received from an imperfect account of the matter." In early 1764, Johnson delivered several belts of wampum and covered "the Graves of the deceased." In return, the Iroquois "expressed some satisfaction" but pointed out to Johnson that the English often "upbraided them for not keeping their people in order, which they were sorry to see, was too much our own case."[44]

Their reprimand notwithstanding, the Six Nations took pains to remain valuable partners of the British. For instance, in early March 1764, a group of Iroquois, whom the British referred to as "our Friendly Indians," took military action in concert with the British army to capture their mutual nemesis, Captain Bull, and subdue the few remaining hostile Delawares in eastern Pennsylvania. The Iroquois warriors surprised and captured forty-one Delawares at the Great Island on the West Branch of the Susquehanna River and brought them to William Johnson in Albany, New York. They placed Captain Bull in "the Heavyest Irons that cou'd be got and all the rest are likewise in Irons and Confined in one of the Cellars under the Hospital, where with the Sentry's that are over them I think will make all Attempts they may make to Escape impossible." Although rewarded for their loyalty by Johnson, who gave them Delaware prisoners to "replace some of their Friends deceased," the Iroquois were, in essence, reduced to the role of retainer, playing henchmen for British colonial aspirations. They helped to regulate the frontier, keeping the remnant native communities in line, but they had lost their previous ability to command respect from Indians and whites alike. By mid-1765, according to the gov-

44. *MPCP,* IX, 106; Johnson to John Penn, Feb. 9, 1764, in Sullivan et al., comps., *Papers of Johnson,* IV, 323.

ernor of New York, Johnson had checked the ambition of the Iroquois who had long "assumed too much to themselves in directing affairs with all the other Nations." With the French expelled from North America, Indians could no longer use the competition between nations to extract favorable terms from treaties. Forced to fight or negotiate with the British alone, Indians gave up the flexibility and accommodation formerly possible on a loosely structured and ungoverned frontier.[45]

Although the Six Nations turned their attention away from their southern border to consolidate their own power in New York and to protect their immediate homeland, which was now threatened, there were still intermediaries who spoke on behalf of Pennsylvania Indians. Papunhank, the Munsee spiritual leader at Wyalusing on the upper Susquehanna, acted as critic of the colony's white leadership and a key diplomatic figure in the 1760s. He had witnessed and experienced a lifetime of change during a critical period for Pennsylvania Indians and tried to understand the nature of Indian-white relations, the attendant misunderstandings, and the future possibilities. He had adapted to the presence of Euramericans, accommodated their culture to a certain extent, yet still retained core values that placed Indian needs first. Papunhank used the rhetoric of Christian virtue to compel whites to act by the precepts of Christian morality in their economic and political dealings with Indians. By 1760, he had established a strong connection with Quakers in Philadelphia, and, since he had kin among the Moravians, he decided to be baptized by them in the summer of 1763. Among both Quakers and Moravians, Papunhank portrayed himself as a religious man with special capacities for love and forgiveness. "From the time God first shewed himself to my Mind," he told some Quakers in 1760, "and put his Goodness in my Heart, tho' the Flesh had been whipped off me with Horsewhips, yet I thought I could have endured it with out being angry at them that did it."[46]

45. *MPCP,* IX, 170–171; Gage to John Penn, Mar. 9, 1764, General Thomas Gage Papers, American Series, XV, Clements Library; Johnson to Gage, Mar. 16, 1764, Robert Eliot to Johnson, Mar. 19, 1764, Witham Marshe to Johnson, Apr. 2, 1764, Gov. Cadwallader Colden to Johnson, June 13, 1765, all in Sullivan et al., comps., *Papers of Johnson,* IV, 368–369, XI, 105, 120, 786.

46. "Some Remarks Made by a Person Who Accompanied Papunahoal and the Other Indians from Philadelphia," [1760], folder 5, Historical Society Collection, Miscellaneous Manuscripts, 1661–1931, Indian Affairs, box 11c, HSP. Papunhank tried

As he began to deal more frequently with Pennsylvania political agents in the early 1760s, Papunhank built on his image as compassionate peacemaker. He often assured the governor that he was "a great lover of peace I have never been concern'd in War affairs." He even invoked the loving memory of William Penn and promised to stay true to the "old friendship which subsisted between the Indians and your forefathers." Papunhank went out of his way to act as mediator and to pacify warring native factions on the Susquehanna. When Pennsylvania requested the return of white captives from Indian villages in the postwar period, Papunhank negotiated their release. He appeared at Easton in August 1761 with about eighty Delawares from his town to participate in a conference. After the treaty council, when the kinfolk of a murdered Delaware Indian set out to exact revenge on a nearby white settlement, Papunhank and his people "joined in a Collection of Wampum and delivered it to them to pacify them, on which they returned home."[47]

The year 1763 brought further opportunity for political conciliation and bridge building. In the fall of 1763, as Captain Bull burned farms in Northampton County and the Paxton Boys rampaged across Lancaster County, Papunhank sent word to the governor, assuring him: "We cannot see that there is the least Reason that there should be any Difference between our Brethren, the English and ourselves, the Wighalousin Indians. . . . We do not concern ourselves with any thing but the Worship of God." When the Conestoga murders threatened to renew war between the English and the Six Nations, Papunhank offered to act as mediator to assure the Iroquois and other Indian groups on the Susquehanna River that the murders had been committed by a few disgruntled white settlers and not by order of the Pennsylvania government. Moravian missionary Johann Jacob Schmick assured the Council that Papunhank "thinks he has some Influence with the Indians, and that they will believe what he says; That he will recommend to them the tenderness of the Governor and the great men of

---

hard to control his reputation; he was concerned, for instance, that Quakers might hear rumors about his ill behavior during a fight with another Indian, "which he said was lies" ("Some Account of a Visit Divers Friends Made to the Indians at the Time of Treaty at Easton," Quaker Journal, Easton, Pa., Aug. 8, 1761, 14, Clements Library).

47. "An Account of a Visite and Conference of Some Indians (of Penselvania) Mostly of the Minisink Tribe," [1760], Historical Society Collection, Misc. MSS, 1661–1931, Indian Affairs, HSP; *MPCP,* VIII, 634–635, IX, 45; Minutes of the Friendly Association, Aug. 7, 1760, Cox-Parrish-Wharton Family Papers, box 18, HSP.

this Province towards the poor Indians, in respect to their maintenance and Protection, etc." Despite his own "Young Men, who lie dead on the Susquehanna" at the hands of the English and despite the increasing appetite for Indian land and resources, Papunhank assured his "Brother" the governor that he would use his "endeavours to preserve our Friendship."[48]

Papunhank might have been a champion of Indian communities, a critic of Pennsylvania colonial leadership, and a vocal advocate of peace, but, in many ways, his story, like many native stories, became as much a product of white memory as Indian history. We know about him primarily because in 1760 and 1761 Quakers carefully constructed, recorded, and published his biography in the form of "conversations," trying to recapture their once-vital role in Indian diplomacy. They had been drawn to his professed pacifism and used this pious, even noble, Indian voice to critique the unchristian behavior of white colonists and the avarice of their political opponents. This fact does not bring into question the truth of his tale; Papunhank did relate his life story to the Quakers, he did act as mediator for hostile Delawares and indignant Iroquois, and he did criticize the economic deceptions and religious hypocrisy of whites. Still, by co-opting Indian stories as well as Indian land, Quakers, white frontier settlers, Moravians, and later immigrants unwittingly altered a native American past to chronicle their own emergence as Americans. Through Indian voices, Quakers and Moravians could be peace-loving advocates of the poor and persecuted; white settlers could be hardy but embattled yeomen who conquered savagism to make way for American civility; and nineteenth-century newcomers could create a kind of "nativity," made legitimate by the invitation of a long-dead, but still eloquent, "Indian squaw."[49]

48. *MPCP,* IX, 45, 78, 136, 170–171. See also John Penn to Johnson, Dec. 31, 1763, in Sullivan et al., comps., *Papers of Johnson,* IV, 284–285; Johnson to John Penn, Feb. 9, 1764, *PA,* 1st Ser., IV, 162.

49. The many recorded and published records of Papunhank (Papunahoal, Papoonan, Papounan, Papunchay, Papunehang, and so forth) were written anonymously, prior to and during the treaty conference at Easton in August 1761. After being shut out of diplomacy in October 1758, the Quakers attempted to reclaim their role as advocates for Pennsylvania Indians. See "Some Remarks Made by a Person Who Accompanied Papunahoal," [1760], folder 5, Historical Society Collection, Misc. MSS, 1661–1931, Indian Affairs, box 11c, HSP; "Account of a Visite and Conference of Some

No matter how civilized the Delawares, Munsees, or Mahicans had become, by the late eighteenth century there was no longer a place for them in Pennsylvania except in a memorialized colonial past. Actual Indians continued to struggle to keep hold of their land, but Euramericans, whether noble or savage, were quickly displacing them. Once the threat of a further Paxton Boys riot subsided in 1765, Papunhank and a group of native families, under the auspices of the Moravians, left the Philadelphia army barracks and moved back to Papunhank's old village of Wyalusing on the upper Susquehanna River. The Pennsylvania governor, assuming that any Indians remaining in the east were dependent on provincial protection and should be considered subjects of Great Britain, if not its implacable enemy, demanded quitrents from them, while whites seeking new land settled on their borders. In 1769, Papunhank petitioned the governor, insisting that Indians were exempt from land fees because they had settled at Wyalusing many decades before with the express permission of the Six Nations. Since then, according to Papunhank, the Indians had "become in some degree civilized, using agriculture and other domestic business, have built at the place aforesaid 25 great strong Loghouses, an elegant church or Meeting house, . . . in full expectation that they and their posterity should enjoy the fruits of their Labor on a small [piece] of their native Country." Within a few years, Papunhank and the Mahican leader, Josua, gave power of attorney to Moravian missionary John Ettwein to sell their land and improvements "for the best price." Like Sassoonan at Tulpehocken in the 1720s, like Teedyuscung at the Forks of the Delaware a generation later, Papunhank conceded to the pressures of white encroachment. With some financial assistance from the Quakers, the Indians at Wyalusing pulled up roots on the Susquehanna River and moved west of the Alleghenies.

Indians," [1760], Historical Society Collection, Misc. MSS, 1661–1931, Indian Affairs, HSP; "Some Account of a Visit Divers Friends Made to the Indians," Quaker Journal, Easton, Pa., 1761, Clements Library; *An Account of a Visit Lately Made to the People Called Quakers in Philadelphia, by Papoonahoal . . .* (London, 1761). See Laura Jane Murray, "Going Native, Becoming American: Colonialism, Identity, and American Writing, 1760–1820" (Ph.D. diss., Cornell University, 1993), 5–6, 23; Carolyn Eastman, "The Indian Censures the White Man: 'Indian Eloquence' and American Reading Audiences in the Early Republic" (paper presented at the McNeil Center for Early American Studies, Philadelphia, Apr. 30, 1999); Philip J. Deloria, *Playing Indian* (New Haven, Conn., 1998), 1–9.

Whereas Indians and whites might have wanted to keep metaphoric roads "clear and open, free from all Stops or incumbrances" in the 1730s, after more than half a century of easing travel between cultural communities, Kanickhungo's road was finally closed.[50]

50. Petition of John Papunhan and Josua the Mahican to the governor, Feb. 2, 1769, "Transcriptions, etc.," June 22, 1772, power of attorney, both in Northampton County Papers, 1682–1887, Bethlehem and vicinity, Misc. MSS, HSP; Treatise from Israel Pemberton to "Papunehang," Aug. 8, 1772, II, Collectanea by Jonah Thompson [Jonah Thompson Collection], 1683–1854, HSP; Colin G. Calloway, *The American Revolution in Indian Country: Crisis and Diversity in Native American Communities* (New York, 1995), 51, 126–128; Mancall, *Valley of Opportunity,* chap. 6.

APPENDIX A
Moravian Indian Lebenslauf (Life Stories)

1. **Salomo,** Delaware. Chief Tammekappei / Keposch, a leader at the Forks of the Delaware, who, in his seventies, asked to be baptized by the Moravians.

January 1749. "An honored old man from the Delaware, and designated a chief of his nation by the Delaware King at the Forks [probably referring to Nutimus or Teedyuscung]. Was born around 1672 in the Jerseys at the Rocky Hill near Cranbery, lived with his father and mother in Penny town, but most of the time he dwelt at the Forks of the Delaware or on the Raritan River. At his baptism, Br. Johannes, Joseph Cammerhoff and Nathanael laid their hands on him and then Br. Johannes baptized him under an indescribable out pouring of the blood, . . . and two days afterwards he went to communion and appeared to be right blessed by the loving side wounds. In his youth he was called by the Delaware Keposch, however when he became a man, he received the name Tammekappei, i.e. stand off to the side, and, it happened by the following happy chance. It is said that our Br. Salomo took the wife from another chief of the Delawares and made her his own. This annoyed the old chief and he bewitched Tammekappei so that he died after a long illness. Afterwards, they gave notice [of his death] to the Indian chiefs and kin after four days passed they gathered together. Early on the 4th day, about the time of his burial, he received some life back in his hand and pulled away the burial covering which his wife, mother, and aunt had placed over his mouth and face. They sat just above his head and when they saw the face uncovered, they covered him again and laid his hand in the previous position on his breast. But, he moved it away again. Upon which they became disquieted and examined him. He could not really speak, but he could open his eyes, and when they noticed some life in him, they gave him some water in his mouth. That revived him, and as they were still more startled that he was not dead, they made him water gruel and thus he came to life gradually. During the time he was dead, he thought he saw a man in a bright white robe floating in the air, who called to him and said: you shall not die, but live, and be called after my name, Tammekappei. It seemed to him, he was lifted up to the white man in the air, and saw the world below him as a small ball in a large child's playground, in which there were white, brown, and black people. And the man, who spoke with him, showed him how evil the people of the world acted and how gruesome were the sins they committed, beating each other to death and spilling one another's blood. And he admonished Tammekappei, that he should not do that, but be a good influence and not fall into the wickedness of the world, and therefore he should not die prematurely, but live until his proper time would come."

"Ein alter ehrwürdiger greiß aus den Delaware, und ein Chief seiner Nation ins gemeine auf der Delawar Konig in den Forks genannt. Ist gebohren ao. 1672 in den Jerseys at the Rocky Hill gegen Cranbery zu sein Vater und Mutter haben in Penny town gewohnet, u. aber hat sich meistens in den Forks of Delaware oder auch an der Raritan aufgehalten. Von seinem Tauffe legten ihre Br. Johannes, Joseph Cammerhoff u. Nathanael die Hande auf, und denn tauffte ihn Br. Johannes unter eine unbeschreibl. Ergießung des Bluts wohins aus den Pleben daß es reichl[ich] von ihm tauffte, und er ging 2 Tagen darauf mit zum Abendmahl und sahe als ein recht seel. [selig] Seitenhölhens herzel[ich] aus. In seine Jugend wurde Er von den Delaware Keposch genannt, als Er aber ein Mann worden war so bekam er den Nahmen Tammekappei i.e. teilt auf die Seite, stand off, und zwar bey folgender erfreudigen Gelegenheit. Es hieß ein zweiter Chief der Delaware seine Frau von sich und diese nahm unser Br. Salomo vor seine Frau an, das verdroß den alten Chief und bezuberte ihm daß Er nach eine langen Krankheit gar starb, Sie beweisen darauf als Indianl. Chiefs und Freunde, und es verlaufen 4 Tagen ehe sie zusammen kammen. Am 4tn Tage fruh um das Hohnen Geschay krigte er wieder etwas leben in seine Hand und zog die decke damit sie ihne den Mund und Gesicht bedecket zum begrabniß von seinen Munde weg, seine Frau, seine Mutter und Aunt saßen zu seinen Haupten, und als sie das Gesicht entblößet sahen, deckten sie ihn wieder zu, und legten seine Hand wieder in die vorige Position auf die Brust. Er zog sie aber wieder hinweg. Darauf wurden sie bedenkl[ich] und besehen ihn, er konnte zwar nicht reden, aber seiner Augen konnte er aufthun, und da sie etwas leben in ihm merkten gaben sie ihnen etwas waßer in den Mund, das erzuckte ihm, und da sie noch mehr erschrek wurden daß er nicht todt sey, machten sie ihm Water gruel und so kam er nach und nach zum leben. Die Zeit aber da er todt gewesen, dachte ihm er sahe eine Mann in einen weißen hellen Kleide in der Lufft schweben, der ruffte ihm zu und sagte: du solst nicht sterben sondern leben, und nach meinen Nahmen Tammekappei genannt werden. Es kam ihm vor, er wurde auch zu dem weißen Mann in die Lufft erhoben, und sahe die Welt unter sich wie ein kleiner Kugel ums Kindes Hoffs groß darauf weiße, braune und schwarze Menschen gewesen. Und der Mann der mit ihm redte zeigte ihm, wie übel die Menschen auf der Welt handelten, und wie grauliche Sunden sie ausübten einander todtschlagen und blut vergoßen und ermahnte ihn, er sollte das nicht thun. Sondern sich des guten befleißigen und nicht mit der Welt in ihre boßheiten verfallen; und darum sollte er nicht vor der Zeit sterben sondern leben, bis seine rechte Zeit kommen werde." (Bethlehem Register, I, "Tauf Register der Erwachsenen," Jan. 13/24, 1749, Moravian Archives, Bethlehem, Pa.)

2. **A Delaware family from the Jerseys.**

January 1749. "At New Year an Indian family was in Bethlehem, who lived for some time in Nazareth and recently, by their request, came to Bethlehem and they were unceremoniously included in the baptism, they were baptized with each other in the side wounds and bound in the covenant of predestination. Together there were 5 of them, namely the mother, one son, 2 daughters, and her son-in-law. 1. The mother was named **Elizabeth** and baptized by Br. Cammerhoff. She was otherwise called by her Indian name, Awialschashuak, i.e. always in joy, [she] was born in Southampton in the South East part of Long Island in Richmond County and, in her 18th year, married a Long Island Indian named Abraham, who was a famous Doctor and died around the 1st of March 1738 in Burlingtown in the West Jerseys. She lived in marriage with him some 20 years and had 10 children by him, of whom 7 died and the 3 who were baptized with her are still living. After that, she also married her second husband and with him had a small boy, Nathy, who was born around 1744 during strawberry time. However, this man abandoned her again and now lives in the Jerseys. She formerly lived in Cranbery among Brainerd's Indians; however, she confessed to them that the baptized Indians there drank themselves so full and beat each other and for that reason, her daughter's husband, who was then still single, told her something of the Brethren in Bethlehem, what good people they were and that one finds none of the same corruption among them. At first she resolved [with her future son-in-law] to give her daughter to him in marriage and that they also would move with her to the Forks of the Delaware. And thus in May 1748 she delivered to Indian Thomas her application for permission to live in Nazareth. Further, they came to Nazareth and by the end of the year, they came to Bethlehem. 2. Her daughter, **Dorothea,** who in Indian is called Awachschauschqua or Aursaungochqua, which in German means *on the other side,* and in English she was called Hittebel after her mother's sister. She was born in the springtime 1727 in the Jerseys at the sea side, in a place called good Luck. She had a husband whose name was Will, whom she abandoned, however, when she became pregnant by him, she stays at present in Cranbery. She bore a small girl, who came into the world in 1746 two weeks before Christmas. 1747, at New Years day, she married her second husband, namely, 3. **Heinrich,** in Indian, Nolematwenat, i.e. one can't hold great Mountains, in English, Jacob, a Delaware Indian, who at the time when the Indian corn was first piled, was 22 years old. He [Heinrich] was born in the Indian town on the Delaware several miles above Hunters Settlement, opposite the Jerseys. His father Charles, who was many times in Bethlehem, visited his sister Schaschamochquehs 2 years ago in Waabhallobank and when drunk there, he drowned in the Susquehanna. She, however, still lives and has no husband. His [Heinrich's] mother died 3 years ago. His grandmother Ogehemochqua was buried in our graveyard in Nazareth on Dec. 6/17 at her last request, after she passed away during her 80th year under the blessing of the Brethren there. His step grandfather, Tammekappei, otherwise called Keposch, is still in Nazareth, but [is] sickly and has a great longing to come to Bethlehem when he is well. His Uncle and Aunt live in the Shawnees Town at Wyoming. He still has 2 brothers, who are younger than he; one of them is James, but the youngest is called Dagohs, both live in Nazareth at present. His 2 sisters—one is Elioechqua, the other named Quetitis—are also still in Nazareth, and attend to their grandfather in his illness, both have a great longing to come to Bethlehem. This Indian [Heinrich] came here with Indian Isaac when he traveled to Bethlehem from Shekomeko 5 years ago and heard many words about the Savior from Indian Br. Isaac, the same from Indian Thomas and especially Benjamin, one of the single Indians who went to the Lord in Bethlehem. However, at the time he [Heinrich] did not believe in his heart what they said, but he also could not be free of it, but always retained an inclination for the Brethren in Bethlehem, until finally with his mother's brother Thomas and his wife's kin moved to Nazareth in May of 1748. He was baptized by Br. Johannes and named Heinrich, his wife was baptized by Br. Nathanael and named Dorothea. 4. **Matthaeus,** Dorothea's brother, who, in Indian, was called Nahnquei, i.e. growling dog, after his grandfather (Tammekappei or Keposch is his step-grandfather), was born in little Egg Harbour in the Jerseys and is now about 16 years old. He came last summer to Bethlehem, however two months passed and his mother, now [named] Elisabeth, took him again with her, which caused him much suffering and tears. The mother had been made fearful by our neighbors around Nazareth, that we would make a slave of him, and if she demanded to have him back, would take him to another country. She regrets it now, but at the time she had no better understanding of it. Day and night, this boy was concerned with Bethlehem in his soul, he had much love for the boys and spoke of and with them many times in his sleep. He also begged his mother continually to let him come back to Bethlehem. With the burial of the 80 year old Indian woman, Ogehemochqua [Heinrich's grandmother, Salomo's wife] in Nazareth, his [Matthaeus's] mother was newly assured of the particular love that the Brethren had for the poor Indian people, and consoled her son about this, that he should have patience, they all wanted to go together to Bethlehem, which then finally happened last year. The boy was very happy about it, and because of his heart-felt longing, was baptized along with his mother and 2 sisters on the appointed day in Bethlehem by Br. Pyrlaus and named Matthaeus. 5. His younger sister, who has no Indian name, but is called **Sara** in English, was born in Salem in the Jerseys, to where her father was called to one of the sick wealthy English women [crossed out is: who wanted to get rid of her pregnancy]. [Her father,] as reported above, has a good understanding of herbs, roots, and the like medications. She [Sara] is 14 and a half years old, and was baptized at the same time by Br. Joseph Spangenberg and received the name Hanna."

"Zum neun Jahre in Bethlehem wurde eine Indianische Familie die seit einiger Zeit in Nazareth gewohnet und kurzl[ich] auf ihr Verlangen nach Bethlehem gekommen war und daselbst recht schlicht um die Tauffe enthalten hatte mit einander aus dem Seitenholhen getaufft und ins bundlein der Gnadenwahl angebunden. Ihrer waren zusammen 5 nehmlich die Mutter, 1 Sohn, 2 Tocher, und ihr Schwieger Sohn. 1. die Mutter wurde genannt *Elisabeth* und getaufft durch Br. Cammerhoff. Sie hieß sonst mit ihren Indianischen Nahmen Awialschashuak i.e. always in joy, ist in Southampton in the South East part of Long Island in Richmond County gebohren und hat in ihren 18th Jahr einen Long Island Indianer Nahmens Abraham geheirthet, welcher ein beruhmter Doctor war und ao 1738 den 1st Mart. bey Burlingtown in den West Jerseys gestorbt ist. Mit denselben hat sie etliche 20 Jahre in der Ehe gelebt und 10 Kinder von ihm gehabt denen 7 gestorben und die 3 die mit ihr getaufft worden noch ubrigen leben sind. Sie hat darauf auch ihren 2ten Mann geheirathet und mit ihnen einen Knaben Nathy gehabt der ao. 1744 zur Zeit der Erdbeeren gebohren worden, diese Mann aber hat sie wieder verlaßen u. wohnt jezo in den Jerseys. Sie hat sonst ein Littany in Cranbery unter Brainards Indianern gewohnet hat sich aber denen gestehen daß die dortigen getaufften Indianer sich so voll gesaffen und einander schlagen und hat daher den ihr Tochter Mann der damals noch ledig war ihr von den Brudern in Bethlehem gesagt was das von gute Leute waren und daß man keine dergleichen [Unverdungen or Unverdorben?] unter ihnen finde, sich zuerst 2 resolvirt ihnen ihre Tochter zur Ehe zu geben und auch mit ihre im die Forks of Delaware zu ziehen. Und so ist sie denn in May o. 1748 den dem Thomas Ind. auf seine Anfrage Erlaubniß, gegeben worden in Nazareth zu wohnen, weit nach Nazareth gekommen, u. von den zu Ende des Jahres nach Bethlehem gekommen. 2. Ihre Tochter Dorothea, welche auf Indianisch Awachschauschqua oder Aursaungochqua heist, welches auf teutsch bedeutet, *auf der andern Seite,* und auf Enlgisch wurde sie, nach ihren Mutter Schwester, Hittebel genannt; Sie ist 1727 im Frühling in denen Jerseys an der See Seite gebohren, der Ort heist good Luck. Sie hatten einen Mann Nahmens Will, welches sie aber, alß sie von ihm schwanger war, verlies, und hält sich p.t. [present time] in Cranbery auf. Sie gebahr ein Mädgen, welches 1746, zwey Wochen vor Weinachten zur Welt kam. 1747, just am Neu Jahre Tage heyrathete sie ihren 2ten Mann nahmlich, 3. Heinrich, auf Indianisch Nolematwenat i.e. one can't hold great Mountains, auf Englisch Jacob, ein Delaware-Indianer, welcher zur Zeit, wenn man das Welschkorn zum erstenmal häufelt 22 Jahr gewesen ist. Er ist der Indian Town an der Delaware, etliche Meilen über Hunters Settlement, gegen über in Jerseys gebohren. Sein Vater Charles, welcher vielmal in Bethlehem gewesen besuchte seine Schwester Schaschamochquehs vor 2 Jahren in Waabhallobank und ersoff im Trunk in der Susquehanna daselbst. Sie lebt aber noch, und hat keinen Mann. Seine Mutter starb vor 3 Jahren. Seine GroßMutter Ogehemochqua wurde, nachdem sie unter dem Seegen der Brüder in ihren 80 Jahr zu Nazareth heimgegangen war den 6/17 Dec. a.c. auf ihr leztes Bitten auf unsern dortigen Hutbery begraben. Seine Stief-Groß-Vater Tammekappei, sonst Keposch genannt, ist noch in Nazareth, aber kränkl[ich] und hat ein groß Verlangen auch nach Bethlehem zu kommen, wenn er gesund ist worden; Sein Uncle und Aunt wohnen in Wayomik in der Schawanos Town. Er hat noch 2 Brüder, die junger sind als er, davon einer James, der jüngste aber Dagohs heist, wohnen beyde in Nazareth p.t. [present time] Seine 2 Schwestern davon eine Elioechqua, die andere Quetitis heißet, sind auch noch in Nazareth, und warten ihren GroßVater in s[eine] Krankheit, haben beyde ein groß Verlangen nach Bethlehem zu kommen. Dieser Indianer kam mit Isaac Ind. als er von Checomeko nach Bethlehem reiste vor 5 Jahren mit hieher und hörte manches Wörtigen vom Heiland von diesen unsern Br. Isaac, Ind., des gleichen von Thomas Ind. und sonderlich Benjamin, einen ledigen Indianer, der in Bethlehem zum Heiland gegangen. Er glaubte aber zu der Zeit nicht in seinen Herzen, was sie sagten, konte es aber auch nicht wieder loswerden, sondern behielt immer einen Hang zu den Brüdern in Bethlehem, bißer endlich mit seiner Mutter Bruder dem Thomas Ind., und seiner Frau anverwandten nach Nazareth gezogen im Majo 1748. Er wurde durch Br. Johannes getaufft und Heinrich, seine Frau aber durch Br. Nathanael getaufft u. Dorothea genennt. 4. Matthaeus, der Dorothea Bruder, welcher auf Indianisch Nahnquei i.e. Knurrender Hunde, nach seinen GroßVater (denn Tammekappei od Keposch ist sein Stief-GroßVater) genennet worden, ist gebohren in little Egg Harbour in den Jerseys und ist nun ungefähr 16 Jahre alt. Er kam vorigen Sommer nach Bethlehem, kriegte 2 Monathen aber kam seine Mutter die jetzige Elisabeth und nahm ihn wieder mit sich, welches ihm viel Schmerzen und Thränen verursachte, die Mutter war von unsern Nachbarn hinter Nazareth in die furcht gesetzet worden, wir würden ihn zum Sclaven machen, und ihn, wenn sie ihn wiederhaben wolte, in ein ander Land bringen. Sie bedauret es aber iezo, sie habe es aber damalhs nicht beßer verstanden. Dieser Knabe hatte Tag und Nacht in seinem Gemüthe mit Bethlehem zu thun, er hatte die Knaben sehr lieb und redete vielmahl im Schlaf von und mit ihnen, bat auch seine Mutter continuirlich, daß sie ihn wieder nach Bethlehem solte kommen laßen. Bey dem Begräbniß der 80 jährigen Indianerin Ogehemochqua in Nazareth wurde seine Mutter von neuen versichert von der besondern liebe der Brüder zu dem armen Indianer Volck, und sprach diesene ihren Sohn zu, er solte sich gedulden, sie wolten alle miteinandern nach Bethlehem gehen, welches denn zu Ende voriges Jahres geschah, darüber freute sich der Knabe sehr, und wurde auf sein herzl[ich] Verlangen nebst seiner Mutter und 2 Schwestern an obbemelden Tage in Bethlehem durch Br. Pyrlaus getaufft und Matthaeus genannt. 5. Seine jüngere Schwester, welche keinen Indianischen Nahmen hatte, aber auf Engl[ish] Sara hieß, ist gebohren bey Salem in denen Jerseys, als wohin ihre Vater, der wie oben gemeldet guten Verstand in Kräutern, Wurzeln und dergl[eichen] Medicamenten hatte, zu einer kranken vornehmen Engl[ish] Frau gehohlet worden war, [crossed out is: die . . . auch ihre Geburth wegzu schaffen] Sie ist 14 1/2 Jahr alt, und wurde zu gleicher Zeit durch Br. Joseph Spbg [Spangenberg] getaufft und bekam den Nahmen Hanna." (Bethlehem Register, I, "Tauf Register der Erwachsenen," Jan. 1/12, 1749, Moravian Archives, Bethlehem, Pa.)

3. **Christian Renatus,** a Delaware.

November 1748. "(In Indian, Depaakhossi, i.e. a necklace of wampum, that is wide enough) among white people called Joseph Growden after a lawyer who through service to these Indians succeeded in the defense of a woman condemned to death, a chief of the Delawares who was born around 1689 during the wheat harvest at Christina Bridge in New Castle county and had particularly distinguished himself in the war against the Flatheads, and some years ago first heard about the Lord from our blessed Indian Br. Thomas. After he lived in Conestoga, Oley, on the Delaware, and the last 4 years in Meniolagomekah, he arrived in Gnadenhütten several months ago anxious to hear the word of the Lamb and his flowing blood, was touched in the heart and on the same day mentioned, in his 59th year, in the blessed presence of our dear Altesten [probably Nikolaus Ludwig von Zinzendorf or August Gottlieb (Joseph) Spangenberg] was absolved and baptized in the sideholes of the Lamb with blood and water by Br. Cammerhoff. His 3 brothers, Quetäigun and Wunsehilaechin and David; as well as his 2 dear sisters Wuntschimachquè and Leschelintschachqua; and his older sister's sons Philip and Daniel all still live in Shamokin. He had 2 wives. From the first, who died in Shamokin, he had a daughter, Nahalehmhigan, who with her husband also lived in Shamokin; the second wife died 2 years ago in Meniolagomekah."

"(auf Indianisch Depaakhossi d.i. ein halßband von Seewand, das breit genug ist) untern weißen Leuten genannt Joseph Growden nach einen Lawyer, der durch den dienst dieses Indianer in der Defension einer zum Tode verurtheilten Weibs Person reusoiret [from the French reussir] ein Chief der Delaware Indianer welcher ao 1689 in der Weizen Ernde bey Christina Bridge in New Castle County gebohren worden, und sich in Krieg gegen die Flatheads besonders signalisirt hat, und vor etlichen Jahren von unsern seel. [selig] Br. Thomas Ind., zuerst vom Heiland gehöret, nach dem er in Canstogoe, Oley, an der Delaware und die lezten 4 Jahren in Melolagamegak gewohnet hatte, kam er vor etlichen Monathen nach Gnadenhütten hörte das Wort vom Lämmlein und seinen Blut vergießen begierig an, wurde in Herzen angefaßt und an oben erwehnten Tage daselbst durch Br. Cammerhoff in seinem 59 Jahre unter einer besondern Gnaden Gegenwart unsers lieben Altesten absolviert und aus dem Seiten Hohlgen des Lammes mit Blut u. Waßer getaufft. Seine 3 Brüder Quetäigun u. Wunsehilaechin & David; des gleichen seine 2 leibl[ich] Schwestern Wuntschimachquè u. Leschelintschachqua; u. seiner ältern Schwester Söhne Philip u. Daniel wohnen alle noch iezo in Schamoko. Er hat 2 Weiber gehabt, von der ersten, welche in Schamoko gestorben hat er eine Tochter Nahalehmhigan, die mit ihren Mann auch in Shamoko wohnt; die zweyte ist vor 2 Jahren in Melolagamegak gestorben." (Bethlehem Register, I, "Tauf Register der Erwachsenen," Nov. 15/26, 1748, Moravian Archives, Bethlehem, Pa.)

4. **Johannes Papunhank,** a Munsee religious leader on the Susquehanna River who joined the Moravians in the 1760s.

May 1775. "Divers brothers and sisters came from Gnadenhütten to visit our sick Brother Johannes, who the Lord received in his own peace on the 15th in his united resting place. He was buried on the 16th with numerous people in attendance, for which many brothers and sisters came here from Gnadenhütten. He was baptized June 26, 1760 during David Zeisberger's second visit in Wyalusing where he had preached a short time. Since an Indian war broke out at that time and Brother David again went back to Bethlehem, he [Papunhank] stayed there, but in time made arrangements with the Six Nations, that the Brethren could live with them to preach to them in their language, just as he had been commissioned. He also came soon afterwards to Bethlehem and brought the Brethren the news and advised them that they now had liberty to come to them and to live there, but he allowed them to do as they thought proper. Because that could not happen, on account of the Indian war, they came to that place the same winter that our Indians were in Philadelphia. The Quakers there, who were acquainted with him and made a great deal of him, kept him to themselves and provided for him and his people. He nonetheless, could not rest contentedly until he was with the Brethren, even though he could have had it and did have it much better than with us. He came after that in May 1765 with the Indian congregation to Wyalusing, which was afterwards called Friedenshütten, on the Susquehanna and was himself a participant in the first communion held there. He served the congregation and the Brethren faithfully to his ability, came in Aug. 1772 with the same [congregation] to Langendoutenünk on the Ohio and soon thereafter [he came] here. On the trip, he had said several times (which the brothers and sisters now recall) that after he arrived at the destination and the Indian community was established anew, he readily wanted to rest his body. This and still more the Lord let him live to see. At the beginning it did not entirely please him here, it took him a little while to become acquainted with the place and he was not used to hearing so many lies, [and] lewd and abusive words about us from the wild Indians. However, since he returned again from Bethlehem last autumn, he liked it here better than all the other places and was always here. On his [return trip from Bethlehem], he was already sickly, but has since then completely recovered; however, he was glad that he had seen Bethlehem once more. His heart clung firmly to the Savior and congregation, thereby he had easily passed more than enough trials. But, among the Indians he had many enemies, who accused him of much evil, especially that he was believed to possess poison, about which so much fuss was made among the Indians, who made it very difficult for him. He adhered all the stronger to the Lord and let nothing disturb or much less alienate him and for his sake, we oftentimes were more concerned about it than he was, but for some time he has resolved [the problems] and we have heard nothing more of it. For a time here, he was especially blessed and cheerful, performed his business with great liveliness and accuracy, because he had overcome caring for worldly things. For about 12 days he got side stitches and coughs, which weakened him terribly. In his illness he spoke incessantly about how much he wanted to go home [die] and did not long to get well again, yet [he] asked to greet all the brothers and sisters in Bethlehem and said he had love for them all and held nothing against anyone and thus he passed away with the blessing of the community elders, approximately 70 years."

"Von Gnadenhütten kamen verschiedene Geschw[ister] unser kranken Br. Johannes zu besuchen, welchen d. Hld [Heiland] d. 15th in seine einige[?] Ruhe einnahm [seine Hütte wurde] d. 16, unter einem Zahlreichen Gefolge, wozu auch viele Geschw[ister] von Gnadenhütten her kommen waren, beerdiget. Er war den. 26th Jun. 1760 bey Br. Dav. Zeisb[erger] 2tens Besuch in Wihilusing wo er eine kurze Zeit geprediget hatte, getauft. Weil aber damals ein Indianer Krieg ausbrach u. Br. David wieder nach Bethl. zurück kehrte, so blieb er noch da, macht aber in der Zeit mit den 6 Nationen aus, daß Brr. bey ihnen wohnen dürften [dürfen], die ihnen das Lang. predigten, wie ihm war auf tragen worden. Er kam auch balde darauf nach Bethl. u.

brachte den Brrn. die Nachricht u. meldete ihnen, daß sie nun Freiheit hätten zu ihnen zu kommen u. da zu wohnen, überließ es ihnen aber zu thun wie sies vor gut fänden. Weil das aber wegen des Ind. Krieges nicht geschehen konte, sie kam der selbigen Winter da unser Ind. in Philadelphia waren, auch dahin. Die Quaker daselbst welche Bekantschaft mit ihm hatten u. viel aus ihm machten, behielten ihm bey sich u. versorgten ihn mit seiner Leuten, er kente [konte?] sich aber doch nicht zufrieden geben bis er bey den Brrn. war, obschon ers viel besser hätte haben können u. gehabt hatte als bey uns. Er kam darauf ao. 1765 in May mit der Ind. Gem[eine] an die Susquehanna nach Wihilusing welches hernach Fridenshütten genennt wurde u. war beym ersten AMhl. [Abendmahl] daselbst ein Mittgenoß derselbe, diente der Gemeine u. den Brrn. treul[ich] nach seinem vermögen, kam in Aug. 1772 mit derselben nach Langendoutenünk [Langredontenünk] an der Ohio u. bald darauf hinher. Er hatte auf der Reise einige mal gesagt, woran sich die Geschw. jezo erinnerten, daß wenn er würde an Ort u. Stelle gekommen u. die Ind. Gem[eine] wieder häbsch [hübsch?] eingerichtet seyn, so wolte er seine Gebeine gerne zur Ruhe legen. Dieses u. noch mehr hat ihn dHld [der Heiland] auch noch sehen lassen. Im Anfange gefiel es ihm wol nicht so ganz hier, es ging ihm ein bisgen zu kent[?] her u. es kein ihm ungewohnt ver so viele Lügen, Lüsterungen u. Scheltworte über uns zu hören von den Wilden; seitdem er aber vorigen Herbst von Bethl zurück gekommen, so gefiel es ihm hier doch vor allen andern Orten am besten u. war ganz da. Er war auf selbiger Reise schon kränklich hat sich auch seitdem ein wieder ganz erholt, er freute sich aber daß er Bethl. nach einmal gesehen hatte. Sein Herz hing feste am Hld [Heiland] u. der Gemeine, davon hat er genugsame Proben abgelegt. Er hatte aber unter den Indianern viele feinde, die ihn viel übles beschuldigten, insonderheit daß er das Gifft wovon unter den Ind. so viel Wesens ist, solle gehabt haben, welches ihm manche schwere Stunde machte; er hielt sich aber desto fester an den Hld [Heiland] u. ließ sich nichts stören vielweniger abwendig machen u. wir waren seinetwegen oftmals darüber mehr bekümmert als er selber, doch seit einiger Zeit hat sich das auch gelegt u. wir haben nichts mehr davon gehört. Er war eine Zeit her besonders selig u. vergnügt, that seine Geschichte mit grosser Munterkeit u. Treue, denn er hatte [die Besorgung des Aussern] [?] über sich. Vor etwa 12 Tagen aber krigte er Seitenstechel u. Husten, welches ihn sehr angrif. Er redete auch in seiner Krankheit nur immer davon, wie gerne er heimginge u. verlange nicht wieder gesund zu werde, bat noch alle

Geshw[ister] in Bethl. zu grüssen u. sagte, er habe alles lieb u. habe nichts gegen jemand u. so verschied er mit dem Segen der Gemine Seines Alters etwa 70 Jahr." (*Moravian Records,* May 14, 1775, reel 8, box 141, folder 6.)

5. **Judith,** a Mahican who died while being held at the Philadelphia barracks during the Paxton Boys crisis.

June 1764. "In the night our dear Judith, Bathseba's sister, passed on, blessed and cheerful in her husband's arms. She was baptized in 1743 in Shekomeko by the blessed Brother Büttner and when the Indians from the same region were expelled, she came with her kin to Gnadenhütten and lived there; she had the grace to take communion and took a peaceful and blessed course in life; [she] was 20 years a widow. During the difficult circumstances that we have found ourselves in for the past ½ year, she was of good cheer and kept herself in the Lord. When her Brother Johannes died three weeks ago, she said to her choir sisters: I am right joyful that my brother was saved of all the congregation and I wish that the Lord might soon also take me to him, which then happened on the 5th day of her illness."

"In der Nacht, ging unsere l[iebe] Judith Bathseba Schw[ester] seel. [selig] und vergnügt in ihres Mannes Arme über. Sie war get. [getauft] ao. 43 in Checomeco durch den seel. [selig] Br. Büttner und als die Indianern aus selbigen Gegend vertrieben würden, kam sie mit ihren Freunden nach Gnadenhütten und wohnte daselbst, hatte die Gnade mit zum AbendMahl zu gehen und ging einen stillen und seel. Gang, war 20 Jahr eine Wittwe. In den schweren Umständen seit wir uns 1/2 Jahr befinden, war sie getrost u. hielt sich am Heiland. Als ihr Bruder Johannes vor 3 Wochen heimging, sagte sie zu ihren bande Schwestern: Ich bin recht froh, daß mein Bruder aus aller Geschw.? errettet ist, um wunsche ich, daß mich der Heiland auch bald zu sich nehmen möge, welches denn auch geschehe an 5 Tage ihrer Krankhiet." (*Moravian Records,* June 5, 1764, reel 7, box 127, folder 2.)

6. **Sara,** a Mahican. The wife of Abraham. Became part of the Christian Indian diaspora in the Wyoming Valley during the mid-1750s.

June 1764. "Before this noon our dear old Sara, Abraham's widow, the first among the blessed sisters went to the Savior. She was baptized in 1742 by blessed Brother Christian Heinrich in Shekomeko when the blessed Jünger [Nikolaus Ludwig von Zinzendorf] himself was there and arranged a Conference; thus she was appointed as elder around 1749. She came with her family to live in Gnadenhütten, had several times been the disciple of goodwill. But when her husband was made the Captain of the Stockbridge Indians and the Nanticokes and Shawnees had made an alliance with the Brethren, he was lured away from Gnadenhütten and [persuaded] to live in Wyoming, [a decision with] which our dear Sara did not agree; however she had to follow her husband, and thereby came to bad circumstances. But, she was happy whenever she saw one of the Brethren from the congregation, and longed all the time to hear something of the Savior. The trust of old Abraham, ere he died, was with her: As soon as I die, you go again to the congregation and ask the Brethren if they will take you in again and forgive you, which she also did and came last year with her daughter and youngest son to Nain and received permission to live in Wechquetank, about which she was very happy and for which she thanked the Lord. However, she still had no real peace, and she was often in tears [wishing for] absolution, which grace also allotted to her, she was also soon readmitted to Communion, which humbled her and made her ashamed. She was sinful and insignificant and in our difficult circumstances she, in fact, kept herself childlike and confident in the Lord. In her illness she said: I go willingly to the Savior and that will happen on the coming Sunday, which then also happened and we were heartily thankful to the Lord, that he found this first one again and through his wounds made [her] blessed."

"Dieser Vormittag ging unsere l[iebe] alte Sara Abrahams Wittwe der Erstling unter den Schww seel. [selig] zum Hld. [Heiland] Sie wurde ao. 42 vom seel. [selig] Br. Christian Henrich in Checomeco getauft, als der seel. [selig] Jünger daselbst war und eine Conf[erence] einrichtete, so wurde sie zur Ältester ernannt ao 49. Kam sie mit ihrer Familie nach Gnadenhütten zu wohnen, hatte einigemal die Gnade Jüngerin zu seÿn. Als aber ihr Mann zum Capt. von den Indianern in Stockbridge gemacht wurde, und die Nanticoks u. Schawanoos mit den Brüdern Bund machten, wurde er dadurch verleitet von Gnadenhütten weg u. nach Wajomick zu ziehen, welches unsern l[iebe] Sara wohl nicht einerleÿ war, doch muste sie ihren Mann folgen, und kam dadurch in schlechte Umstände. Freuete sich aber doch allemal wenn sie einen Bruder von der Gemein sahe, und verlangte allezeit was vom Heiland zuhören. Der Verlaß des alten Abrahams ehe er heimgang, war mit ihr: du gehst so bald ich gestorben bin, wieder zur Gemeine und bitte die Brr. daß sie dich wieder annehmen und vergeben, welches sie auch that und kam vorm Jahr mit ihrer Tochter u. jüngsten Sohn nach Nain, und kriegte

Erlaubniß in Wecquetank zu wohnen, worüber sie sich sehr freuete und dem Heiland davor dankte. Sie hatte aber doch kein rechte Ruhe, und sie oft mit thränen um absolution, welche Gnade ihr auch zutheil wurde, sie wurde auch bald wieder zum AbendM[ahl] readmittirt welches sie sehr beugte und beschämte. Sie war sünderhaft und Klein, und in uns[er] schweren Umständen hielt sie sich zwar Kindl[ich] u. zu versicht[lichkeit] vom [zum?] Heiland. In ihrer Krankheit sagte sie, ich gehe gerne zum Heiland, und das wird aufen künftigen Sonntag geschehen, welches denn auch eintroft, und wir waren dem Heiland herzl[ich] dankbar, daß Er diesen Erstling wieder gefunden, und durch seine Wunden seel. [selig] gemacht hat." (*Moravian Records*, June 10, 1764, reel 7, box 127, folder 2.)

7. **Esther,** a Mahican. The second wife of Delaware chief Memenowal/Augustus. Lived in Meniolagomekah.

March 5, 1754. "Tonight around 2 o'clock Brother and Sister Mack were called to the sick Esther. She was faint of heart, understood us all the same and was happy that we visited her. Augustus was there, as well as the Indian sisters Sarah, Bathseba, Rahel, Esther, who, for 3 nights watched and attended to her. Since Esther was in her 4th month of pregnancy, they assumed, she would deliver, which happened in a half hour after that. The child soon began to cry, the mother asked how soon it could be baptized, after all, it might not live long. Brother Josua also came to us, Augustus said: yes what my dear Esther said about the baptism of my child, that I also ask. It was small, but truly perfect and cute, looking around at all. Brother Martin baptized it "Esther" in the death of Jesus. The sisters who were present consecrated it. Sister Sarah told Esther that now her child was baptized, she said: I thank you, dear Savior. Soon after she pulled Sarah to her and said: Soon, soon, I will die and kiss the wounds, which immediately came to pass."

March 6, 1754. "At mid-day was the burial of our Sister Esther. She appeared truly respectable. All the brothers and sisters were surprised by her kindness, as she also had her child in arm, which passed away this morning. Brother Augustus had bought her a white linen cloth, with which Anna had made a burial dress. Several of the unbaptized, whose eyes filled with tears, also paid a visit to the body."

"Diese Nacht um 2 Uhr wurde Geschw[ister] Macks wieder zu der kranke Esther geruffen. Sie war von Herzen matt, kante uns aber gleich, u. freute sich, daß wir sie besuchten. Der Augustus war da, als auch die Ind. Schww.

[Schwestern] Sarah, Bathseba, Rahel, Esther, die schon 3 Nächte beÿ ihr wachten u. sie bedienten. Weil die Esther in 4th Monat schwanger war, vermutheten sie, sie wurde niederkommen, welches auch in einer halben Stunde drauf geschahe. Das Kindgen fing bald an zu weinen, die Mutter bat noch wenn es balde konte getauft werden, es würde doch nicht lange leben; Br. Josua kam auch zu uns; der Augustus sagte: Ja was meine l[iebe] Esther gesagt, wegen der Taufe meines Kindgens, das bitte ich auch; Es war ḳlein, aber wirkl[ich] vollig u. niedl[ich], sahe sich auch um. Br. Martin taufte es in dem Tod Jesu, Esther. Die Schww. [Schwestern], die zugegen waren segneten es ein. Die Schw. Sarah sagte es der Esther, daß nun ihr Kindgen getauft wären, sie sagte: Ich danke dir, l[iebe] Hld. [Heiland] bald darauf nahm sie die Sarah um den Hals, u. sagte: bald, bald, wede ich heimgehen, u. die Wunden küssen, welches auch sogl[eich] geschahe." (*Moravian Records,* Mar. 5, 1754, reel 5, box 118, folder 1.)

"Zu Mittag war die Beerdigung der Hütte unsrer Schw[ester] Esther; sie sahe wirkl[ich] respectable aus. Alle Geschw[ister] wundersten sich über ihre freundlichkeit, in dem sie auch ihr Kindgen in Arm hatte, welches den Morgen verschied. Br. Augustus hatte ihr weisse leinwand gekauft, daraus ihr die Ana ein Sterbe Kleid gemacht hat. Einige Ungetaufte besachen sich die Leiche auch, denen gingen die Augen über." (*Moravian Records,* Mar. 6, 1754, reel 5, box 118, folder 1.)

APPENDIX B
Native American Family Genealogies

1. Teedyuscung and Kin

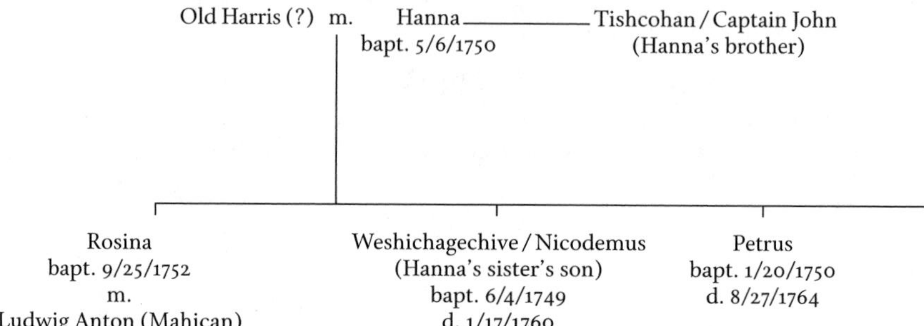

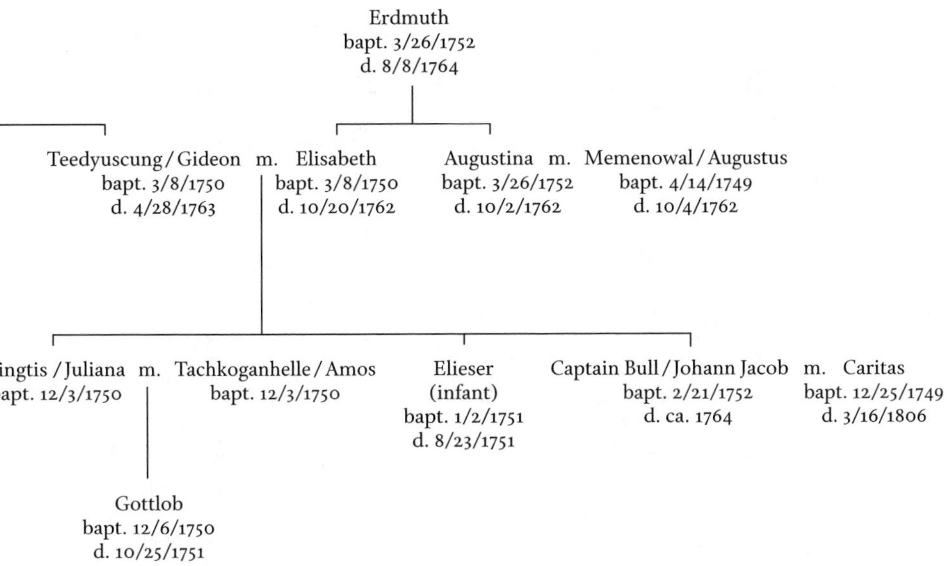
Erdmuth
bapt. 3/26/1752
d. 8/8/1764
Teedyuscung / Gideon
bapt. 3/8/1750
d. 4/28/1763
m.
Elisabeth
bapt. 3/8/1750
d. 10/20/1762
Augustina
bapt. 3/26/1752
d. 10/2/1762
m.
Memenowal / Augustus
bapt. 4/14/1749
d. 10/4/1762
Pingtis / Juliana
bapt. 12/3/1750
m.
Tachkoganhelle / Amos
bapt. 12/3/1750
Elieser
(infant)
bapt. 1/2/1751
d. 8/23/1751
Captain Bull / Johann Jacob
bapt. 2/21/1752
d. ca. 1764
m.
Caritas
bapt. 12/25/1749
d. 3/16/1806
Gottlob
bapt. 12/6/1750
d. 10/25/1751

2. First Mahican Family to Be Baptized

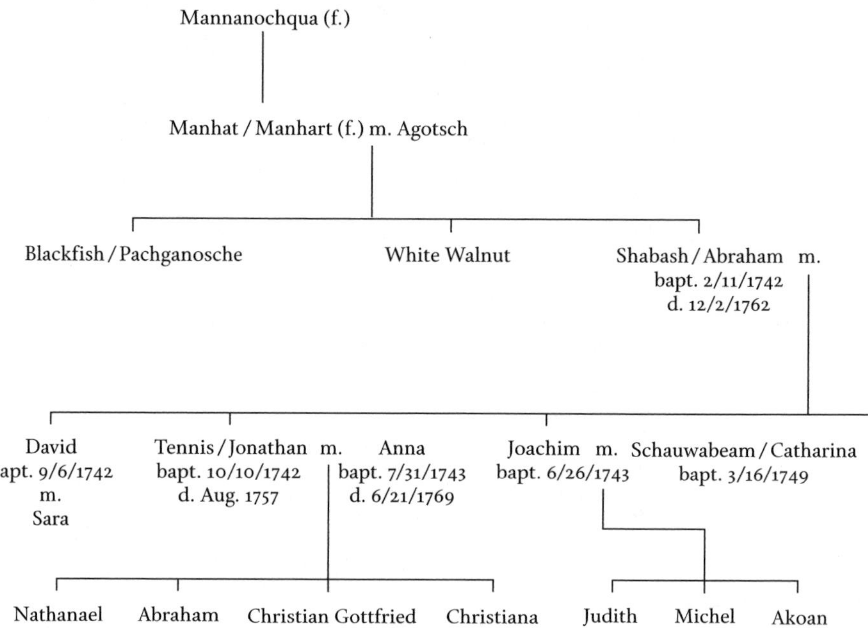

Sara
bapt. 8/11/1742
d. 6/10/1764

Isaac	Friedrich	Tobias	Sara
bapt. 5/8/1747	bapt. 8/5/1749	bapt. 9/17/1749	bapt. 9/17/1749
d. 7/24/1764		d. 1/22/1750	m.
			Punkschees

3. Delawares at Meniolagomekah

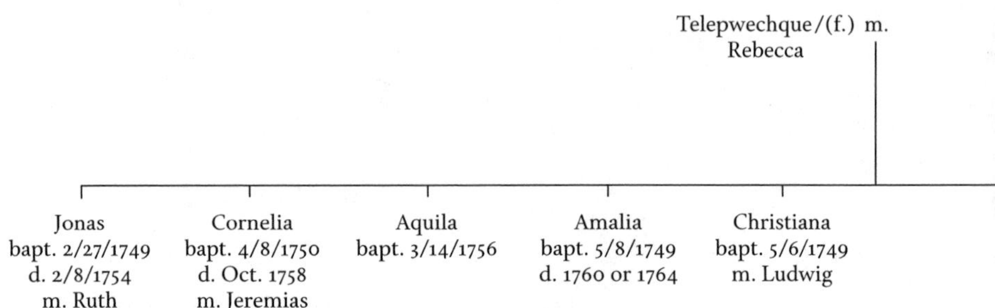

Hanna
bapt. 4/12/1752
d. 7/30/1753

Joseph
"Wayward Joseph"

Wiwunikamek / Simeon
(stepfather, medicine man)
bapt. 1/6/1756
d. 10/17/1756

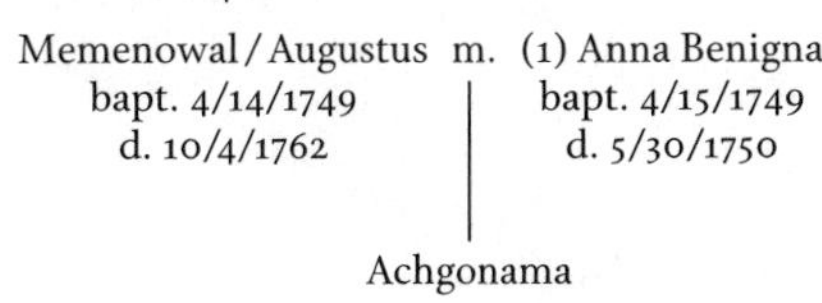

Memenowal / Augustus m. (1) Anna Benigna
bapt. 4/14/1749 bapt. 4/15/1749
d. 10/4/1762 d. 5/30/1750

Achgonama

m. (2) Esther
(Mahican)
bapt. 5/14/1744
d. 3/5/1754

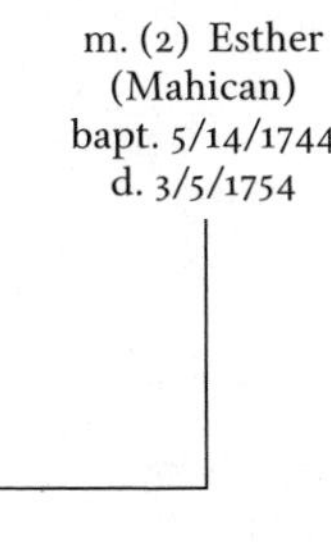

Esther

m. (3) Augustina
bapt. 3/26/1752
d. 10/2/1762

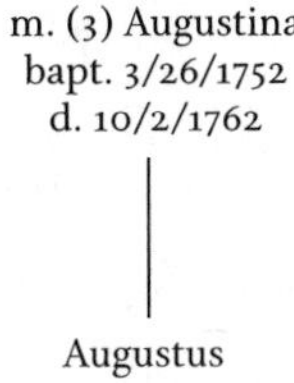

Augustus

INDEX